Gender in the Legal Profession

Law and Society Series
General Editor: W. Wesley Pue

Gender in the Legal Profession inaugurates this new series. It will grow to
include works in legal culture, critical social theory and law, law and gov-
ernance, law and economics, law and the environment, First Nations legal
issues, feminist legal studies, legality in plural societies, political science
and law, post-colonialism, critical race theory, the consequences of global-
ization for legal order, and critical legal history.

LAW AND
SOCIETY

Joan Brockman

Gender in the Legal Profession:
Fitting or Breaking the Mould

UBC Press · Vancouver · Toronto

Printed in Canada on acid-free paper ∞

ISBN 0-7748-0834-9 (hardcover)
ISBN 0-7748-0835-7 (paperback)
ISSN 1496-4953 (Law and Society)

National Library of Canada Cataloguing in Publication Data

Brockman, Joan.
    Gender in the legal profession

    (Law and society series, ISSN 1496-4953)
    Includes bibliographical references and index.
    ISBN 0-7748-0834-9 (bound)
    ISBN 0-7748-0835-7 (pbk.)

    1. Women lawyers – Canada. 2. Sex discrimination against women – Canada. 3. Sex discrimination in employment – Canada. I. Title. II. Series: Law and society series (Vancouver, B.C.)
KE332.W6B76 2001   331.4'133'0971   C2001-910150-3
KF299.W6B76 2001

This book has been published with the help of a grant from the Humanities and Social Sciences Federation of Canada, using funds provided by the Social Sciences and Humanities Research Council of Canada.

UBC Press acknowledges the financial support of the Government of Canada through the Book Publishing Industry Development Program (BPIDP) for our publishing activities.
Canadä

We also gratefully acknowledge the support of the Canada Council for the Arts for our publishing program, as well as the support of the British Columbia Arts Council.

Set in Stone by Brenda and Neil West, BN Typographics West
Printed and bound in Canada by Friesens
Copy editor: Ann-Marie Metten
Proofreader: Patryce Kidd

UBC Press
The University of British Columbia
2029 West Mall, Vancouver, BC V6T 1Z2
(604) 822-5959
Fax: (604) 822-6083
E-mail: info@ubcpress.ca
www.ubcpress.ca

To my parents
Velma and Edward,
with love and thanks

Contents

Preface

As a child, I grew up in a warm supportive environment with nine brothers and a sister. Our parents never dissuaded us from the notion that we could do anything we wanted to as long as we worked hard enough to accomplish it. It never would have crossed my mind that this applied only to my brothers. I was a true believer in formal equality in the paid workforce. However, I also held the view that women should have a choice as to whether they ventured out into the paid workforce or whether they married and stayed at home to work. I don't recall thinking that men had this same choice.

As an articling student and lawyer called to the bar in British Columbia and Alberta, I never personally experienced discrimination until I worked for the federal Department of Justice in Vancouver in 1983. Members of the Canadian Bar Association Task Force on Gender Equality in the Legal Profession tittered at the unintentional irony of my statement to them in January 1993, ten years after my experience at the Department of Justice. I was no Perry Mason in court, but as an articling student with the Department of Justice I had heard by the grapevine that a Provincial Court Judge in Vancouver had commented that I had "good courtroom presence." Two years previous, while articling in Calgary, I conducted a trial against a lawyer who had been called to the bar for seven years. He demanded to know where else I was called and was loath to believe this was the first trial of my short career as a lawyer.

I was blatantly discriminated against at the Department of Justice when I applied for a position in the Criminal Section to follow my call to the bar in British Columbia. I was up against a man who had told men lawyers in the office that he would "never hire a woman as a prosecutor, because women aren't any good in court." To my face he was much nicer. He told me that I had an impressive résumé and good reports from other lawyers on my work as an articling student. However, he did want someone to start immediately in May, and I would not be called in British Columbia until July. In past years, men (who were not called in another province as I was) had bypassed the remainder of their articles to move into their choice position. Immediately after I left his office and flattering comments, he approached one of my colleagues who was scheduled to be called in May. My colleague had no interest in joining the Criminal Section, but was prepared to join it in order to make his move to his first-choice section when such a position became available. The act of discrimination was so overt and recognizable by my colleague that before accepting the offer he asked me whether I would appeal his appointment. I said, "No," and he took the position on the condition that he could first take a holiday, as opposed to starting immediately. He then moved to another section at the first opportunity.

Practising law was my second choice as a career, so the discrimination I experienced was not as devastating as it might have been. It was not that I disliked the practice of law, it was more that I had other goals in mind when I went to law school. My first experience with law school was during a doctoral program in sociology at the University of Alberta in the mid-1970s. As a doctoral student, I wanted to study plea bargaining. I was intimidated by the legal profession and had the impression that it would be nearly impossible to get lawyers to talk to me about plea bargaining, since the official party line was that plea bargaining did not exist in Canada. I decided I needed to know more about criminal law and procedure before I could study plea bargaining. After gaining the approval of the Dean of Arts and the Dean of Law at the University of Alberta, I enrolled in a course on criminal law and procedure at the law school. I was told that as a non-law student I would not receive a grade higher than seven (on a scale in which nine would be the highest grade possible for everyone else); I was "Joan," whereas all of the other students in the class were called by their surnames. The experience did not result in any greater confidence that I could study plea bargaining, as I was still very much an outsider. This was reinforced by the orientation session I attended for first-year students who were all told they were the "cream of the crop." So, I decided to attend law school at the University of Calgary, which had recently opened and claimed to have a "different" approach to the study of law. When, in response to a question about my career path, I relayed this history to Malcolm Feeley, a professor of law from the University of California at Berkeley, on one of his visits to Vancouver, he responded, "Well, of course we all know that plea bargaining takes place over urinals." In retrospect, I have concluded that either he had not kept up with the meagre "progress" women were making into the world of prosecuting, or that women prosecutors had learned how to do it standing up.

After law school at the University of Calgary, I articled with a small shopping centre firm and was called to the Alberta bar in 1981. The following day, I moved to Vancouver to commence graduate work in law at the University of British Columbia. I did not experience discrimination during articles in Calgary. I had a job offer before I left. When I told my principal I was moving to Vancouver, he offered me more money to stay with his firm. Clients asked specifically for me to do work for them before I left, and one of the secretaries said she was waiting for me to go out on my own so she could join me. I was not driven from the profession, but rather attracted out of it.

I obtained a master of laws in 1982 from the University of British Columbia, articled with the Department of Justice, and was called to the bar in British Columbia in 1983. After six years bouncing back and forth between Simon Fraser University and the Department of Justice on short-term contracts, I was appointed to a tenure-track position at the School of Criminology in 1989, which was retroactive to an early contract in 1987.

I did not go to law school to practise law, but rather because I wanted to teach law to criminology students. So my first choice for a career was the academic world – hardly a pinnacle of equality. Still a bastion of male privilege, women were excluded from consideration by some members of hiring committees at universities because they had a spouse in the same department, men were given higher salaries because they had current or former spouses and children to support, and women did not need the going salaries because they had spouses to support them. Numerous chilly climate reports from universities across Canada confirmed that my observations were not unique to Simon Fraser University.

My interest in studying gender bias in the legal profession was triggered, in 1988, by one of my field practice students at Simon Fraser University who, after only thirteen weeks of working in the legal profession, commented, "I always thought that if I were to find equality anywhere it would be in the legal profession. Men [lawyers] have all the advantages. Oh, how I wish I were a man; if I could just snap my fingers, just like that, I'd be a man. Men have it so much better than women in the practice of law."

When I approached the Law Society of British Columbia about studying gender bias in the legal profession, I was told to speak to Kate Young, chair of the Subcommittee on Women in the Legal Profession, who was interested in having such a study conducted. In 1989-90, I conducted two mail-out surveys for the Law Society, one of members and one of former members. I then conducted similar surveys for the Law Society of Alberta in 1991. Fiona Kay and John Hagan were conducting similar studies in Ontario, and soon other law societies were doing the same. In 1991, Dorothy Chunn and I organized a Research Consultation on How to Study

Gender Bias in the Law, the Courts, and the Legal Profession through the Feminist Institute for Studies on Law and Society at Simon Fraser University. Social scientists and legal academics focused on how to conceptualize and conduct research on issues of gender bias, and to develop strategies to eliminate it. In 1993, Madame Justice Bertha Wilson conducted a major study of gender bias in the legal profession in Canada for the Canadian Bar Association. Her report summarized much of the work that had been conducted in Canada on the issue. For the most part, these studies used mail-out surveys. None conducted in-depth interviews of a random sample of lawyers, as was done for this research project.

Throughout my academic career I have struggled to integrate the disciplines of law and sociology. This has been a much more difficult task than I had first anticipated. I just assumed that if I became a lawyer and understood what lawyers did, I could use my knowledge of sociology to conduct studies on lawyers' activities. However, I soon discovered that promotion in the academic world meant that I had to be a lawyer (evaluated by lawyers) or a sociologist (evaluated by sociologists). Since I had abandoned my doctorate in favour of a master of laws, I had to be a lawyer for the purposes of promotion. When it came to conducting the research for this book, I once again attempted to integrate my two disciplines. It was clear to me that when this manuscript was sent out to three reviewers, the two reviewers who provided the most useful and detailed suggestions and criticisms were a social scientist (asking that I do social science type things to the manuscript such as embed my analysis in more of the literature) and a legal academic (asking that I expose my argument in Chapter 1 and elaborate more on my own views and assessments in Chapter 7). What is the difference between the two? Mary Jane Mossman (1993 at 157), borrowing from Guth, describes legal research as "searching" and social science research as "researching." To some extent, "lawyers are trained to look for that which is relevant to their case or issue, and to ignore the rest as irrelevant" (Brockman and Chunn, 1993 at 13). To social scientists, findings are never irrelevant. That which does not support your case or might be viewed as irrelevant by some is as important as findings that support your hypotheses. I have tried, for the most part, to wear my social scientist's garb for this research project. However, there are times when the gown comes out and I cannot resist making an argument that might extend beyond the data. This is not entirely incompatible with a social science approach, as such research often ends with suggestions for other avenues of research.

This book first reviews the historical exclusion of women, Aboriginal peoples, and racialized groups from the legal profession in Canada, and more specifically British Columbia, and then examines a small segment of the legal workforce, young lawyers in British Columbia. Drawing on interviews I conducted with a random sample of 100 lawyers, from throughout British Columbia and called to the bar for between three and seven years, this book examines why they went to law school, their hopes and aspirations, what they think of the adversarial system, and their experiences with discrimination and sexual harassment in the profession. It also looks at how they are managing their personal lives in conjunction with a career that is demanding more and more of their time, and what they think they might be doing in the future.

The purpose in writing this book is to generate discussion about the legal profession, both inside it and out, on some of the issues both women and men face in the broader paid and the unpaid workforce, and some they face differently. At a time when work gurus are telling us that *Working Harder Isn't Working* (O'Hara), and that maybe *Shooting the Hippo* (McQuaig) is not the way to deal with the so-called deficit, it is important to examine how women and men are coping in a world of the expanding, rather than shrinking, workweek. In the late 1950s in the United States, experts predicted that by the early 1990s workers would have "a twenty-two hour week, a six-month work year, or a standard retirement age of thirty-eight."[1] Similar predictions were made in Canada in the late 1960s and early 1970s. Clearly, these predictions have not been borne out.

The young lawyers in this book have something to say to the thousands of students who write the LSAT every year and who are thinking about law school, to the women and men in law school, and to those who are presently practising law. They also have something to say to the general public about the legal profession, as well as to other professionals and workers in the paid and unpaid workforce today.

Acknowledgments

This research was funded by a research grant from the Social Sciences and Humanities Research Council for a project entitled "Women Lawyers at Work: Fitting in or Altering the Mould," and SSHRC's support is gratefully acknowledged. I am thankful to the Law Society of British Columbia for their contributions as a partner in this SSHRC project. Bryan Ralph, Q.C. (then Secretary of the Law Society, and now a judge of the British Columbia Supreme Court), his secretary Helen Barclay, Peter Beblo, and Lisa Fisher were of invaluable assistance in selecting the sample, and making the initial and follow-up contacts with the lawyers I interviewed. They, of course, are not responsible for what the lawyers said, nor for the contents of this book. I am especially grateful to the 100 lawyers throughout British Columbia who took time from their busy schedules to meet with me and respond to my questions. Without their thoughtful responses, this study would have been impossible.

Throughout the years that it took to transcribe interviews and write this book, I have had the assistance of a number of research assistants and transcribers from Simon Fraser University. Thanks go to Dana Christensen, Shelly Cooke, Denise Evans, Jan Gates, Kristi Hines, Carla Hotel, Rita Karajaoja, Lydia Loizides, Dorothy Lott, Nicole Mahussier, Angela McEachern, and Kristoffer Ruitenbeek. I am also grateful to my colleagues Dorothy E. Chunn, Margaret Jackson, and Bill Glackman for their assistance. Detailed comments and helpful suggestions by Susan B. Boyd and anonymous reviewers are very much appreciated. Last, but not least, I would like to thank V. Gordon Rose for his editorial comments and support throughout this project. The staff at UBC Press were excellent to work with. Many thanks to Jean Wilson, Ann-Marie Metten, and Ann Macklem for their hard work and encouraging comments.

1
Introduction

Historical Exclusion from the Legal Profession

The history of the legal profession in Canada, as elsewhere, is one of the exclusion of women, Aboriginal peoples, ethnic and racialized[1] groups, and those from the less privileged classes. The beneficiaries of these exclusionary tactics were usually upper- or middle-class English men. In fact, many experts on the history of professions describe the creation of professions as strategies to gain a monopoly over the provision of services, and the use of barriers to entry and other systematic actions to exclude or reduce competition from both outside and inside the profession.[2] Professions, then, are occupations that have been "fortunate enough to obtain and keep the title of profession."[3] In addition, the concept of profession is a "gendered" one. According to Anne Witz, this is because "it takes what are in fact the successful professional projects of class-privileged male actors ... to be the paradigmatic case of profession."[4] More recently, the literature on the professions has recognized more explicitly that these exclusionary strategies were aimed, not only at women, but also at other groups.[5] Even today, those who depart from the normative "man of law"[6] remain "fringe dwellers"[7] of the legal profession.

Those who were excluded from the professions were not passive recipients of their designated fate. The professions' exclusionary strategies were met by two general inclusionary strategies: 1) credentialistic tactics (that is, efforts to meet the standards [or barriers] raised by the profession), and 2) legalistic tactics through the lobbying of government to remove barriers, when meeting the criteria was insufficient to allow entry.[8] A brief examination of the struggles of the first women to be called to the bars in the provinces in Canada clearly illustrates how external, political pressure was necessary in order for women, and later racialized groups, to gain entry into the legal profession. Simply meeting the educational requirements was insufficient. One of the themes that runs through the concerns expressed by the male legal profession (including the judiciary) is the effect that women might have on competition, which was jealously guarded by men through their monopoly on legal services.[9] This monopoly on legal services, together with the power to decide who would be called to the bar and be allowed to practise law, gave the law societies in Canada incredible power to exclude women and racialized groups from the legal profession. Historically, the entirely male judiciary assisted the legal profession in its exclusionary tactics.

In 1891, Clara Brett Martin applied to the Law Society of Upper Canada (now Ontario) for admission as a student-at-law. A Committee of the Law Society decided that the Law Society was permitted to admit only "persons," and while the *Interpretation Act* stated that "words importing ... the masculine gender ... shall include ... females as well as males," the fact that women were not admitted in Canada or Great Britain, and were not allowed to vote, was sufficient for the Committee to conclude that if women were to be admitted to the legal profession, the legislature would have to change the legislation. In 1892, the Ontario legislature introduced an act that would permit the Law Society to allow women to be admitted as solicitors, a compromise to full admission. It still took the intervention of the attorney general of Ontario (as an ex officio Bencher) to ensure that the Law Society would exercise their discretion in favour of Martin's entrance. Many of the Benchers and other members of the legal profession were strongly opposed to the admission of women.

In 1895, Clara Brett Martin won another battle when the Ontario legislature passed an Act permitting the Law Society to admit women as barristers. She again had to lobby, and the attorney general intervened, to ensure that the Benchers would exercise their discretion in favour of her admission. In 1895, she became the first woman called to a bar in Canada. The opposition by men lawyers to the admission of Clara Brett Martin resulted in her being subjected to sexist and mean-spirited comments, as well as disparaging comments by the press.[10] The legal profession was also concerned about the possible competition that would result from opening the doors of the legal profession, at a time when they still did not have control of and a monopoly on legal services.[11]

When Mabel Penery French applied to the Barristers' Society of New Brunswick for admission in 1905, the Society referred the matter to the Supreme Court, which decided that French was not a person under the legislation and the Society's rules. Chief Justice Tucker wrote, "If I dare to express my own views I would say that I have no sympathy with the opinion that women should in all branches of life come in competition with men. Better let them attend to their own legitimate business."[12] Mr. Justice Barker quoted from the infamous *Bradwell* case from Illinois, in which Mrs. Bradwell was refused admission to the bar: "The paramount destiny and mission of women are to fulfil the noble and benign offices of wife and mother. This is the law of the Creator. And the rules of civil society must be adapted to the general constitution of things, and cannot be based on exceptional cases."[13] In 1906, the Legislature passed *An Act to remove the Disability of Women so far as it relates to the Study and Practice of Law* and French was called to the bar in New Brunswick in 1907.[14] Following the finding that she was not a person, French stopped paying her bills for six months. In defence of a lawsuit to recover money owed by her, French argued (unsuccessfully) that since she was not a person, she could not be sued. She was ordered to pay her bills and the costs of the legal action.[15]

Similar efforts to exclude women from the legal profession were used in British Columbia. When Eva Powley first inquired about admission to the bar in 1908,[16] the Secretary of the Law Society responded that "the fair sex have not yet threatened to invade the legal profession in British Columbia."[17] While two other women inquired about entry in 1910, the first real challenge to the Law Society's position came in 1911 from Mabel Penery French, the first woman admitted to the bar in New Brunswick. French simply announced that she intended to present herself for the examinations in June, and asked the Law Society to confirm that her application was in order.[18] The Secretary stated that he would submit her papers to the Benchers for their meeting in July, although the Rules "contemplate the admission of men only."[19] A flurry of letters and telegrams ensued, as French attempted to force the Law Society to accept her application to write the examinations. She was unsuccessful. Her application went to the Benchers' meeting on 3 July 1911, and they decided that they did not have the authority to admit "lady applicants."

Having been unsuccessful in her attempts to convince the Law Society to admit her, French applied to the British Columbia Supreme Court for an order requiring the Law Society to admit her, under the legislation that stated the Benchers could call and admit "any person." The British Columbia *Interpretation Act* stated that words referring to the masculine gender only included females as well as males. On 23 October 1911, the judge dismissed French's application on the basis that the legislature had not contemplated women when it referred to "persons." French appealed her case to the British Columbia Court of Appeal, but lost again. She then turned to the political arena, where the Conservative attorney general, William J. Bowser, who was "openly opposed to the expansion of women's rights,"[20] had to deal with a persistent advocate, Evlyn Farris, the founder of the Vancouver University Women's Club, and with widespread media support for French's position. When the Court of Appeal rejected French's appeal, the *Victoria Daily Times* reprinted a comment from an unidentified advocate of political equality, which included the following comment:

Men are suffering from a whole mass of misconceptions. It is one of their pet delusions that women were created for the sole purpose of mother-hood. If they were, then it is equally logical to assert that they were cre-ated for the sole purpose of fatherhood, although to the contrary, they arrogate to themselves such a wide range of functions that it is a wonder that they have not long since ousted women from that one small depart-ment which they consider distinctly hers.[21]

While women could not vote until 1917 in British Columbia, the attor-ney general was concerned that they might have some influence in the upcoming election. The attorney general caved in, and introduced *An Act to remove the Disability of Women so far as it relates to the Study and Practice of Law* on 24 February 1912. The Bill received Royal Assent on 27 February 1912, and French was called to the bar on 1 April 1912. A second woman, Edith Louise Paterson, was called to the bar in British Columbia in 1916, and a third woman, Gladys Kitchen, was called in 1918.[22]

Melrose Sissons, of Manitoba, also had to take her case for admission to the Law Society to the provincial legislature, which amended the legisla-tion in 1912. In 1915, Sissons and Winnifred Wilton were the first women called to the bar in Manitoba.[23] The first woman called in Alberta, in con-trast to those in Ontario, New Brunswick, British Columbia, and Manitoba, met no public resistance by the Law Society. Ruby Clements was called in Alberta in 1915. Neither was there resistance to the first woman who arti-cled in what was then the Northwest Territories. Erella Alexander, of Calgary, was admitted to the Law Society as a student-at-law in 1899; how-ever, she did not complete her articles or seek admission to the bar.[24]

Quebec was the last province to admit women to the practice of law, and it did not pass enabling legislation until 1941, one year after women were given the right to vote in provincial elections in Quebec.[25] Annie Langstaff was the first woman to attempt to enter the legal profession in Quebec, in 1914. She had worked for a law firm, and with its support and approval was the first woman to attend law school in Montreal. She graduated fourth in her class, while bringing up an eight-year-old daughter on her own. She petitioned the Quebec Superior Court for a writ of mandamus, to order the Quebec bar to admit her to the examination, which was required before she could become a student at law. When the court asked Annie Langstaff whether she had consulted her husband about studying law, she responded, "No, I did not. I did not know his address."[26] She had been sep-arated as to property from her husband since 1906, which meant she could administer but not sell her property, and was not entitled to carry on busi-ness without her husband's permission. Divorce was not open to her.[27]

The judge held the view that it was "within the range of possibilities though by no means a commendable one" to allow women to become solicitors, but that to admit women as barristers, to allow them to plead cases "*in open court and in the presence of the public,* would be nothing short of a direct infringement upon public order and a manifest violation of the law of good morals and public decency."[28] The judge went on to say that "no woman possessing the least sense of decency could possibly [defend or prosecute a rape case] without throwing a blur upon her own dignity and without bringing into utter contempt the honour and respect due to her sex."[29] At the end of the judgment he wrote, "The proof filed in the record I have before me shows that the petitioner in the present case is a young woman of good morals and that she is possessed of considerable ability. After what I have said above, she will no doubt understand that her ambition in life should be directed towards the seeking of a field of labor more suitable to the sex and more likely to ensure for her the success in life to which her irreproachable conduct and remarkable talents give her the right to aspire."[30]

He dismissed her petition. Annie Langstaff lost again at the Court of Appeal. She returned to the law firm with which she was previously employed, worked there until she retired in 1965 at the age of seventy-eight, and died in 1975.[31] Women were finally allowed admission to the bar in Quebec by an amendment to the *Bar Act* in 1941, which passed with "what was in some instances almost violent opposition on the part of the members of the Bar."[32] In 1942, Elizabeth Monk was the first woman called to the bar in Quebec.

Unlike Caucasian women, members of racialized groups in British Columbia were less successful in being admitted into the legal profession. Although there is some evidence that two Black men from the United States practised law for a short period of time in Victoria in 1858,[33] the legal profession in British Columbia had managed to remain an all-white profession. In 1918, the Law Society of British Columbia introduced a requirement that members be entitled to vote provincially, in response to a request by the Vancouver Law Students' Society that the Benchers of the Law Society "request the Provincial Legislature to amend the Legal Professions Act, and Amending Acts, being Chapter 136 of the Revised Statutes of British Columbia, 1911, so that Japanese, Chinese or East Indians, or any such persons of Asiatic origin, whether of British Birth or otherwise, be prohibited from being enrolled as Articled Clerks and Students-at-Law, or being admitted as Solicitors or called to the Bar of British Columbia." The students also requested that the amendments apply retroactively.

The request by the law students, and consequent amendment to the Rules by the Benchers, took place around the time that Gordon Won Cumyow was corresponding with the Law Society concerning his January 1918 application for enrolment as a student.[34] Cumyow was the son of

Won Alexander Cumyow, the first Chinese person to be born in British Columbia, who later was a court interpreter for both Chinese and Aboriginals, between 1888 and 1936. The Benchers rejected Cumyow's application on the basis of their new rule, and took the position that they had the "uncontrollable discretion" to admit or reject any applicants.[35] This was in sharp contrast to the position that they took to exclude women, in which they decided they had no authority to admit them. The rule was used to exclude Asian applicants from the practice of law until the British Columbia legislature removed the barriers to their voting in the late 1940s.[36]

The *Indian Act* of 1867 stated that any Aboriginal person who was admitted to a university, or "who may be admitted in any province of the Dominion to practice law" became enfranchised and lost their status under the *Indian Act*.[37] This provision was not removed from the legislation until 1951. The first Aboriginal lawyer in British Columbia, Alfred Scow, was called to the bar in 1962.[38] In 1973, it was estimated that there were four Aboriginal lawyers in Canada. In 1993, there were approximately 290. The Law Society of British Columbia estimated that if Aboriginal people were proportionately represented in the legal profession then there would have been 1,500 in 1993.[39] Starting in 1993, a number of studies have recommended ways to improve the position of Aboriginal peoples in law school and the legal profession.[40]

Along with the expanded franchise, which opened the door of the legal profession to all racialized groups, the British Columbia Law Society increased its educational requirements. In 1949, the Law Society required students to have a bachelor of laws before the one-year articling period[41] and, in 1950, articled students were required to serve a continuous year of articles, rather than three four-month periods over three years.[42] While this might indicate that the Benchers were interested in the competence of lawyers, it seems somewhat questionable, because the educational requirements were relaxed for men returning from the Second World War who had part of their articles waived in recognition of their war service.[43] One can well imagine the response if women, who took maternity leave, requested that the Law Society waive part of their articles in recognition of their child-bearing service.

Few women followed the trailblazers into the legal profession in Canada. By 1931, women made up only 1% of the legal profession. Two decades later they made up only 3% of the profession and, by 1971, they represented only 5% of lawyers in Canada.[44] Although women lawyers who wrote about law in the 1970s described explicit sexism by law professors and in the legal profession, many of the women lawyers did not think there was discrimination in the legal profession. Linda Silver Dranoff, a graduate of Osgoode Hall Law School in 1972, conducted a survey of women lawyers in Toronto in the early 1970s, and only 26% of the women thought they were discriminated against in the legal profession. Some of the women who said that there was no discrimination stated that women just had to "work hard" to succeed in the profession, and allegations of "prejudice" were "used as an excuse by those who are not prepared to make the sacrifices or do not have the ability to succeed in law." Dranoff found this interesting, in light of another survey in which 40% of Ontario law firms admitted to discriminating against women in their hiring practices.[45] In 1972, Lynn Smith and her colleagues sampled women and men who ranked in the top quarter of their law class during their second year and found that 72.4% of the men, compared with only 53.8% of the women, articled with the firm that was their first choice.[46] In 1974, Jennifer Bankier, another graduate from Osgoode Hall Law School, gave a speech about the treatment of women law students and lawyers. She described some of the sexist attitudes and behaviours of law students, law professors, and members of the legal profession. Specifically, "the male representative on the Osgoode student council ... refused to assign his criminal trial cases from Parkdale Community Legal Services to a female representative on that same council who was succeeding him on the grounds that judges, Crown attorneys, and criminal lawyers are male, and that accordingly he assigned his criminal trials 'to the transferee who had the better statistical chance of impersonating a criminal lawyer.'"[47] One woman was denied a position at the Crown attorney's office because "she would be a disruptive influence in the office." Bankier also described a survey of women articling students, which "reported a wide range of stereotyped and insulting remarks dealing with women's competence, motivation, personal life, or the mere fact of their being a woman."[48]

It was not until 1973 that women started to make up more than 20% of those enrolled in the bachelor of law programs in Canada, and not until 1983 that they started to represent more than 40% of such students.[49] In British Columbia, women represented one-third of law school admissions in the late 1970s. In the 1980s, women made up 43.3% of law school admissions at the University of British Columbia, and 41.5% of law school admissions at the University of Victoria.[50] The sharp rise in the number of women attending law schools in the 1970s resulted in the percentage of women in the legal profession in Canada rising to 15% in 1981, and to 22% by 1986.[51] At this point, women were reaching a critical mass as law professors[52] and lawyers.

A number of events at the law schools challenged the traditional male-dominated model of law schools in the mid-1980s. In 1986, Professor Sheila McIntyre wrote a memo to herself on her experiences teaching at the Law School at Queen's University in Kingston, mentioning the hostile reaction from male students when she used gender-neutral and gender-inclusive language in her class, and the mutiny when they were required to analyze a case discussing fist fights in the bar in terms of whether the legal reasoning by the judge applied to men or people. The memo was later circulated to her colleagues at the Law School, and the hostility intensified. McIntyre describes the events, and her reactions to them, in a *Journal* article.[53] In 1987, after Mary Jane Mossman did *not* receive the appointment as Dean of Osgoode Hall Law School, 121 lawyers, law students, and legal academics filed a complaint with the Human Rights Commission about the decision.[54]

Between 1990 and 1997, the percentage of women admitted to the Law School at the University of British Columbia varied from 45% to 50% from year to year, and women represented 47.8% of the total admissions during this period. During the same period, the percentage of women admitted to the Law School at the University of Victoria varied from 36% to 53% from year to year. Women represented 45.7% of the total admissions during this period[55] and, by 1991, they made up 29% of the legal profession in Canada. By 1996, women made up 31% of the profession.[56] Throughout the 1990s, law societies in Canada sponsored surveys of their members and former members, on issues of bias and discrimination in the legal profession.[57]

The history of women entering the legal profession is not complete without a discussion about them leaving the profession.[58] A study of lawyers in British Columbia showed that in January 1990, the average yearly attrition rate for women called to the bar between 1974 and 1988 was 23%, whereas it was only 13% for men. The total attrition rate for the fifteen-year period was 22% for women and 13% for men. However, the absolute number of men (523) who left during that period was higher than the number of women (322).[59] A similar study in Alberta in 1991 showed that the attrition rate for those called between 1976 and 1990 was higher for women (33%) than for men (28%). Again, in absolute numbers, a greater number of men (1,012) than women (443) had ceased to be active members by 1991.[60] In a study of Ontario lawyers, Fiona Kay found that women left the profession "60% more quickly than men."[61]

Women and men leave the profession for a variety of reasons. Before the introduction of non-practising status, members of the Law Society of British Columbia abandoned their membership most commonly because of fees. In a survey of former members, 70% of the women and men indicated this was why they had not renewed their membership.[62] Approximately half of the former members indicated that the "nature of the work" was a factor, as were stress, hostility and lack of courtesy from other lawyers, no personal satisfaction, social stigma attached to being a lawyer, and so on.[63] The hours the practice demanded were a factor in leaving the profession for 35% of the women and 23% of the men, and low pay was a factor for 33% of the women and 41% of the men. Child-care commitments were a concern for 30% of the women and 9% of the men. A better position out-side of law drew 45% of the men, compared with only 27% of the women, out of the profession. Other reasons included loss of employment, lack of opportunity for advancement, and spouse's career.[64] In a similar Alberta survey, hours demanded by practice was the most common reason for women lawyers to leave the practice of law, whereas the most common rea-son for men was they "wanted to use different skills."[65]

Fiona Kay, using life course and event history analyses on questionnaire responses from a random sample of Ontario lawyers, examined what effect "affective characteristics (i.e., job satisfaction and organizational commit-ment), structural changes in the profession (i.e., number of lawyers and economic climate), [and] transitions across the life course (i.e., marriage and children)" had on gender differences in departures from law.[66] Her findings show, for example, that lawyers who encounter discrimination leave the profession 81% more quickly than their colleagues, and that "taking a parental leave actually reduces the risk that women will leave law practice by 74%, demystifying the assumption that women are leaving law to care for their children."[67] Her data also support the "ghettoization perspective rather than the genuine integration of women" in the legal profession.[68]

Today, the early discrimination against women and racialized groups by the legal profession seems so blatant and unfair. Can we shake our heads at such historical discrimination and say that we have left it behind? The results of my research indicate that discrimination on the basis of gender in the legal profession is still prevalent. The nature of the discrimination has moved from keeping women out of the profession to discouraging or preventing their full participation within the profession. In Thornton's words, women remain "fringe dwellers" of the legal profession. Are there any lessons to be learned from this unsavoury history of the exclusion of women and racialized groups from the profession? Historically, women had to seek solutions to discrimination by the legal profession from out-side the profession. While much necessary work has been done by law societies and the Canadian Bar Association to address discrimination, the ultimate solution (as I suggest in Chapter 7) might still lie in additional changes outside the legal profession, as it was found to be by the early pioneer women who first gained access to the profession.

Studying Gender in the Legal Profession

Shortly after my field practice student expressed her disappointment with women's lot in the legal profession (see Preface), I began to think about how to study gender bias in the legal profession. Sandra Harding's work on feminism and science provided an initial framework of research methods and methodology.[69] The attraction to Harding's work was that she asked interesting questions, and she accepted a multitude of feminist approaches.

Harding recognizes that how one conceptualizes a problem and asks questions will, to a large extent, determine the solution: "People who identify and define scientific problems leave their social fingerprints on the problems and their favoured solutions to them."[70] Or, in other words, "conceptualizing is part of ruling."[71] Questions which imply that women ought to adjust to male structures, or that structures ought to be adjusted so that women can continue their unfair share of child care, housework, home management, and emotional labour, were not questions designed for women, but rather for men and the status quo. The questions that remain unasked are often more important than the ones that are asked.

Harding examined the social construction of gender in her search for the subordination of women. In virtually all cultures, male characteristics and activities are more highly valued than female characteristics and activities. If women move into a prestigious male-dominated occupation and men move out, the occupation loses its status, prestige, and financial reward. It does not matter if women are as good as, or better than, men in providing the occupational service. Harding suggests that the social production or creation of gender takes place at three levels: 1) through symbolic dichotomies that value socially assigned male traits (for example, reason) over socially assigned female traits (for example, emotion), 2) through gender structure in which women are assigned unpaid emotional labour in the private sphere (for example, housework, child care) while men are assigned paid work in the public sphere, and 3) at the individual level, through the public and media images of what it means to be a woman or a man. The implications for such an approach are that we should examine the social construction of not only the public paid workforce, but also the so-called private unpaid work of women and men, and the socially constructed images of what it means to be a man or a woman. In addition, sexual harassment and gender bias and harassment in the workplace, as forms of social control, are important aspects of a study that takes women's perspectives into account.[72]

Between 1989 and 1992, I conducted four mail-out surveys of lawyers – two for the Law Society of British Columbia (one of former members and one of members)[73] and two for the Law Society of Alberta (one of active members and one of inactive members).[74] The questionnaires covered general demographic characteristics of respondents, and their attitudes and experiences in the legal profession on a wider variety of issues, including sexual harassment, gender bias, job satisfaction, and maternity/paternity benefits.

The results of the surveys indicated that barriers to women's participation in the legal profession followed their entrance into it. In the survey of active members of the Law Society of Alberta, 97% of the women and 78% of the men were of the view that there was some bias or discrimination against women in the legal profession. In the survey of members of the Law Society of British Columbia, 97.5% of the women and 83% of the men thought there was some bias or discrimination against women in the legal profession. "Career advancement" was mentioned most frequently by women and men in both surveys as an area in which women are discriminated against – by 82% of the women and 42% of the men in the Alberta survey, and by 75.5% of the women and 44% of the men in the British Columbia survey. Similar studies were carried out in Ontario by Fiona Kay and John Hagan,[75] and in other parts of Canada,[76] with similar results.

Barriers to women's participation in the legal profession, both visible and invisible,[77] continue to exist today. Studies from a number of jurisdictions show that women are over-represented among unemployed lawyers and, if employed, they are more likely than their male colleagues to work in marginal positions and to earn less money. If women are in private practice, they work longer than men before becoming partners. Many women lawyers face gender discrimination, including sexist behaviour, sexual harassment, demeaning comments, patronizing behaviour, and a negative courtroom environment. Women lawyers are less likely than their male colleagues to be married, although this is changing for the younger generation. Women lawyers are less likely to have children; however, if they do they shoulder a disproportionate amount of the child-care and household responsibilities.

In August 1993, shortly after I commenced the interviews of 100 lawyers for this study, Madame Justice Bertha Wilson's report for the Canadian Bar Association, *Touchstones for Change: Equality, Diversity, and Accountability,* was released. In addition to her 290-page report, there were fourteen appendices, which included an action plan, model policies, summaries of what provincial working groups were doing, a synthesis of provincial law society reports, a conference and consultation report, a special report on corporate counsel and one on federal government lawyers, reports on *Women of Colour in the Legal Profession, Aboriginal Women in the Legal Profession, Sex Discrimination in Employment,* and *The Structure Dynamics of the Law Firm,* as well as an *Annotated Bibliography on Gender Equality in the Legal Profession.* Madame Justice Wilson had also conducted a confidential survey of women judges. Earlier surveys in British Columbia, Alberta, Saskatchewan, Ontario, and Quebec showed that many women and men lawyers believed that bias against women exists in the legal profession.[78] Wilson listed what she referred to as a "somewhat numbing" list of barriers to women in the legal profession: "sexual harassment; salary differentials; difficulties in obtaining articles; difficulties in securing good files and problems with work allocation; problems in career advancement in terms of promotion and access to partnership; the lack of women in management and leadership positions; segregation into certain areas of practice; and an

unwillingness to accommodate female parents who have family responsibilities."[79] In reference to the barriers to women lawyers who are mothers,
in Chapter 6 of this book I question whether the problem is simply lack of
accommodation for mothers, or whether it is more fundamental to the way
that we, as a society, look at gender roles when it comes to parenthood and
home management.

A number of respondents in my surveys of British Columbia and Alberta
lawyers commented that women would find their place in the legal profession – it was just a matter of time, whereas others thought this was not the
case. Such comments raise a number of interesting questions. Are younger
women lawyers fitting into the established legal profession, or are they
altering the old mould in which lawyers have traditionally been formed, or
at least having some impact on it? One might also ask whether young men
are fitting into the legal profession or altering the way law is practised.
These questions are difficult to answer, as we do not have a measure or an
accurate description of the old mould. However, if things were improving
for young lawyers, then perhaps the influx of women into the legal profession (or the workforce) was having some impact on the legal establishment. If not, perhaps in-depth interviews could shed some light on what
was happening.

Up until 1993, my research on lawyers involved mail-out questionnaires.
A need for a more detailed approach to the issues, that would allow for context and explanation, was identified by a number of respondents through
their comments on the questionnaires.[80] While self-response questionnaires
have advantages (more coverage for less cost and time, and anonymity),
face-to-face interviews allow for a more in-depth study, as suggested by
the respondents to the surveys. In 1993, I received a grant from the Social
Sciences and Humanities Research Council to interview women and men
lawyers. The interviews were designed to examine the experiences of young
women and men lawyers, the impact that the increasing numbers of
women were having on the practice of law, and how the changing role
of women was affecting the practice of law for both women and men
lawyers. Four areas of interest, identified through the earlier surveys, were
canvassed:

1 career advancement
2 the conciliatory-adversarial continuum in the practice of law
3 gender bias, discrimination, and sexual harassment
4 the balancing of careers, children, and chores

Interviews with 100 British Columbian Lawyers
According to the literature and the earlier surveys, between three and
seven years after they are called to the bar, lawyers face major choices in

their lives about career advancement, leaving the legal profession, child-bearing, and child-rearing, and so this group was the focus of this study. The population from which I drew my sample included all women and men called to the bar in British Columbia between 1986 and 1990, and who were still members on 25 June 1993. Those who were inactive or former members, who worked in legal education or at the Law Society, or who were suspended from practice were eliminated from the population so that only those practising law in government, a private firm, or in industry remained in the frame sampled.[81] Those who lived outside of British Columbia, or who were called to the bar in another province, were also eliminated from the population, in order to study a more uniform group. At the time the sample was drawn, the attrition rate for the women called between 1986 and 1990 was 31.4%, and 25.6% for men.

A stratified random sample of fifty women and fifty men was drawn from the list of members remaining. Within the strata of women and men, a proportional random sample was drawn from each of the five years of call (that is, from three to seven years at the bar).[82] Between the time the sample was drawn and the time of the interviews, four women in the sample were no longer practising law, but were retained in the sample.[83] With the exception of one lawyer, who was on an indefinite leave and could not be contacted, and for whom a substitute was randomly selected, the response rate was 100%.

I interviewed the 100 lawyers, at locations throughout British Columbia, between 8 July 1993 and 19 January 1994. Most of the interviews were conducted in the lawyers' offices; however, some were conducted at their homes, at their request. The interviews ranged from twenty to 110 minutes in duration, and averaged forty-eight minutes. The interview schedule had a variety of questions. Many were open-ended, allowing the respondents to answer in whatever way they saw fit – for example, questions about why they went to law school, their likes and dislikes about the law, factors that might interfere with their career goals, why they would or would not be interested in becoming a judge, and the ways women were discriminated against in the legal profession (if they thought there was such discrimination). When asked whether they were ever discriminated against in the legal profession on the basis of the characteristics listed in the Law Society's Rules of Professional Conduct, the respondents were shown a copy of the rule. Some questions asked respondents to place themselves on a scale ranging from one to seven in terms of their approach to the practice of law (conciliatory to adversarial) and their satisfaction with various aspects of the practice of law (very satisfied to very dissatisfied). Even with these scales, respondents were allowed to elaborate on why they chose the range they chose or why they varied between one and seven. Such an open-ended approach makes it much easier for respondents to express themselves, but it also makes the data much more difficult to code. Given that I had already used a more structured, self-response questionnaire, I favoured allowing the respondents the opportunity to express themselves in their own words.

The respondents had between three and seven years of experience in the legal profession. The women ranged in age from twenty-eight to fifty-nine, with a median age of thirty-five, and 20% were over the age of forty. The men ranged in age from twenty-eight to fifty-eight, with a median age of thirty-four, and 10% were over forty years of age. Ten percent of the women and 6% of the men were under thirty years of age. Pseudonyms are used in this book,[84] and quotations have been edited, both to ensure that respondents cannot be identified, and to make their comments more readable. For some of the more sensitive topics discussed, including discrimination and sexual harassment, pseudonyms are abandoned in favour of references to the respondents' gender, to further ensure anonymity. These were the only areas in which some respondents expressed concern about not being identified.

While conducting 100 interviews throughout British Columbia seems a large number, in practice, it is not nearly a sufficient number of interviews to also study the effects of discrimination against lawyers on the basis of race, ethnicity, sexual orientation, and disability. Such studies would require a much more focused stratified sample. It would also be impossible to take such a sample. While the Law Society could provide me with a list of lawyers by gender and year of call, they could not provide me with such a list of lawyers based on these other characteristics. Such studies would have to rely on snowball samples or perhaps total populations of those lawyers who were prepared to identify themselves. Law societies across Canada and the Canadian Bar Association have recently begun to conduct such studies.[85] It is because of the small numbers in my study, not because of lack of importance, that race, ethnicity, sexual orientation, and disability fall by the wayside in this book.[86] Respondents were not asked about these characteristics. However, when I asked respondents about discrimination on the basis of these characteristics, I noted any reference they made to their own situation. According to these notes, 10% of the women respondents and 2% of the men belong to a racialized group, one respondent is Aboriginal, 6% of the women are lesbians, and 2% of the men are gay. I observed that one of the respondents has a physical disability; however, a number of other respondents talked about disabilities that were not visible. Because of the sample size, this book cannot properly address discrimination on the basis of these other characteristics. As pointed out by one of the reviewers of an earlier version of this book, I also do not have any indication of the social class of my respondents. While social class is a difficult concept to measure, I regret not having some indication of it, as law is very much a class-based profession, and the "man of law" is "a middle-class man of the market."[87]

Outline of the Book

Chapter 2 examines the reasons the respondents went to law school and what they like and dislike about the practice of law. Some respondents had advice for people considering law as a career. Chapter 3 looks at the educational background of the respondents, their work histories, why they work where they do, and their career aspirations, including whether they would like to be a judge at some time in the future. Chapter 4 discusses their experiences with and perceptions of discrimination and sexual harassment. Chapter 5 sets out how the respondents see themselves and other lawyers on a scale ranging from very adversarial to very conciliatory and their perception of the effectiveness of the adversarial system. Chapter 6 examines how the respondents combine, or do not combine, their careers with co-habitors, children, and chores. Finally, Chapter 7 addresses the question of whether these young lawyers are fitting or breaking the mould, and some of the changes that might be necessary for true equality in the legal profession.

2
Law's Attractions and Detractions

A 1965 study of lawyers in the United States refuted the stereotype that women go into law to become social workers and men go into law to make money. White found no statistically significant difference between the percentage of women (59%) and the percentage of men (53%) who indicated that a "desire to help society" was an "important" or "very important" motivation to attend law school. However, the women (70%) were more likely than the men (60%) to state that "good remuneration" was important or very important to them.[1] Twenty-five years later, another study in the United States found that women (48%) were more likely than men (38%) to identify an interest in social service or helping others in their top three reasons for going to law school, and men (78%) were more likely than women (60%) to identify financial opportunity.[2] While some of these differences may be explained by the wording of the question in the two studies and their samples, it might also indicate changes over the twenty-five-year period. Helping others seems less important to both women and men over time, and the importance of financial reward increased for men and decreased for women. It could be that the increase in women entering the profession in the later period resulted in greater diversification in their motives.

Lentz and Laband compared a 1990 survey by the American Bar Association with a similar survey it had conducted in 1984, and concluded that there was a consistent pattern in that "men are driven more than women by financial considerations when choosing a career, whereas women's career choices are determined more by the desire to help others than are men's career choices." According to Lentz and Laband, this carried over into the respondents' initial choice of jobs, and the jobs in which they were currently working; however, they could not offer any "compelling insights into why or how such sex-based differences develop initially."[3]

I asked my respondents a series of questions, all of which were open-ended and did not provide them with a "grocery list" to pick from: Why did you go to law school? Do you think that you will still be practising law five years from now?[4] If you could "do it over again," would you become a lawyer? Why or why not? (Respondents were probed on their likes and dislikes about the practice of law.) Are you satisfied with "the practice of law overall"?[5] As an afterthought, I also asked some of them what advice they would have for anyone who was contemplating a career in law. This chapter examines their responses to these questions.

Reasons for Going to Law School
Many people think that women and men must have a keen interest in law to spend three years at law school (after three or four years as an undergraduate) and then another year articling for a low wage. As with any other career, there are numerous reasons for going to law school and pursuing law as a career.[6] While approximately one-third of the respondents (38% of the women and 32% of the men) were keen to go to law school, an equal number of women and men (34%) did it for lack of anything better to do. They went to law school by default.

The Keeners
A little more than one-third of the women respondents and one-third of the men respondents said that they had a keen interest in law, or that law was something they always wanted to do. Elizabeth, now in her late thirties, fell in love with Erle Stanley Gardner (the author of Perry Mason novels) when she was seven years old; she watched every television show that had a lawyer in it, and read every book about lawyers that she could get her hands on. She is very happy with her criminal and family law practice, and would definitely choose to become a lawyer if she had to do it again. Barbara, a corporate-commercial solicitor in her late twenties, was on her way to becoming a concert pianist when an accident prevented her from pursuing her first passion. Becoming a lawyer had always been in the back of her mind when she was doing her undergraduate degree at university. After the accident, realizing that she couldn't "have the whole enchilada" with a career as a pianist, she did not want it at all. So Elizabeth went to law school, and would do it again. She is not sure where she will be in five years. If she has a child, she would like to spend more time at home, or work part time. Either of these options would be a major change for a woman who works sixty-hour weeks at the office.

For Pamela, a woman in her early thirties who practises administrative law, it was watching her lawyer-father at his office that drew her attention to law. She decided at a young age that she wanted to be a lawyer. Happy with practice overall, Pamela would do it over again and will likely be practising in five years, unless she is on maternity leave. She would like to work at a firm with five other women who all practise law and to balance her personal life and career work.

Rosa was exposed to law through the lawyer her parents used for their business. Now, doing a mixture of family law and civil litigation (and still in her early thirties), Rosa is somewhat dissatisfied with the practice of law. She expects to be practising in five years, unless she wins a lottery. However, Rosa would choose to go into law again, even though she is extremely unhappy with her income of $36,000 a year; after four years of practice, "the money definitely is not there."

Some women delayed going into law school for financial reasons, or because they were discouraged from going early in their lives. Flora, who is in her early forties, had always wanted to go to law school, but she had to support herself, and the student counsellor suggested that she go into nursing, teaching, or dental hygiene. The counsellor told her that "a woman would be very unhappy in law, because women just don't go into law." Flora, who practises family law and civil litigation, is very dissatisfied with the practice of law, tired of the conflicts, and tired of "cleaning up the mess"; however, she will likely still be practising in five years.

In her late fifties, Sandra, a family law and civil law litigator, explained that since she had no elderly relatives to take care of and her youngest child was in school, she could go to law school, something that had always been in the back of her mind. Similarly, Yvonne, a general solicitor in her mid-forties, had wanted to be a lawyer since she was fourteen. But she ended up in a bad marriage and did not go to law school until later. She had always been attracted to legal matters, and she thought that practising law would provide intellectual stimulation, which it did, but she finds the practice of law very dissatisfactory. She hopes not to be practising in five years, and would not become a lawyer if she had to do it over again. She explains, "There are more satisfying ways to earn a living and to contribute to society. Law is much more time-demanding and less financially rewarding than I had initially thought it would be."

Lois, a civil litigator in her mid-thirties, had always been fascinated by law, but was in another career. When she injured herself, she studied for the LSAT to keep sane, and later went to law school. She is very happy with the practice of law, and plans to continue to practise for the foreseeable future.

Iris, a real estate lawyer in her mid-thirties, was inspired to enter law school through a law course in high school. Although she had entertained other possibilities, Iris thought she was too stable for social work (the people taking the courses had a lot of problems), teaching did not suit her, and digging up a few things over a long period of time (archaeology) was not her idea of fun. She will "definitely" be practising law in five years.

Paula's classmates in high school always knew she was going to be a lawyer. She was not that sure herself, but it was a profession that she thought would be interesting. Now in her early thirties, she works as a prosecutor, and would probably become a lawyer if she had to do it over again. However, she is ambivalent about her satisfaction with law, and whether she will still be practising in five years. She has entertained alternative careers that have a legal edge to them. About her future, she commented, "I have no idea what I'll be doing five years from now. I have no idea what I'm doing month to month."

The men were more likely than the women to say that they had always wanted to be a lawyer, or had known it from a young age, or from the time they were in high school. For the most part, these men did not attribute their calling to any role models, although Vincent ascribed his interest to magazines (*Ramparts*), books (a biography of Clarence Darrow, the United States lawyer), and plays (Jerome Lawrence and Robert E. Lee's *Inherit the Wind*) he read as a schoolboy. He is very satisfied with his work as a Crown prosecutor, and would become a lawyer if he had the opportunity to do it again.

Murray's mother said he had wanted to be a lawyer since he was six (although he does not recall this, he deferred to his mother). It was something he always planned to do. Now in his early thirties, Murray is also satisfied with his work as a corporate and securities solicitor, and would become a lawyer if he had to do it again.

Jeff had exhausted another career and had nursed an interest in the law for several years. It was either law or a doctorate. The doctorate would have complicated his family situation, so he chose law. His friends in law seemed to enjoy it. Jeff likes the tradition of law, and all the "trappings" of the profession – the sense of historical continuity, institutions, and the challenges. Now in his early forties, Jeff is satisfied working as a commercial civil litigator.

Law School by Default

Perhaps surprisingly to some people, 34% of the women and 34% of the men said that their entry into law school was unplanned or by chance, that they were unemployed or looking for something to do, and so they went to law school by default.[7] Angela's parents sat her down at the age of sixteen, and over a series of nights harassed her about what she was going to be when she grew up. Doing a doctorate, so that she could teach at a university, was too long a haul. She added, "You know, that book they give you at the beginning of law school that says going to law school because you don't know what else to do is not a good reason to go to law school? Well, I did." She is ambivalent about her work in the business arena: "I think I'd be more satisfied if I were doing something more aligned with my personal views. I don't perceive that there are as many opportunities to do things that are more closely aligned with my personal values (women's rights, human rights, and so on) as there are things to do that are not so aligned." She is also ambivalent about whether she would do it again, although she does like the financial security of her work.

For Betty, it was the comparative wage survey that her father showed her. He said, "Look how much doctors make." Betty responded, "Oh, god, the sciences. I could never go into medicine." Her father countered, "Lawyers are second on the list ... I always wanted a Cadillac." According to Betty, she went to law school because her father wanted a Cadillac. Law was the "catch-all for bright people who didn't know what else to do." Law was for those who were not artistically gifted enough to go into architecture, or who did not have the stomach for medicine. She had also considered doing a doctorate, but was worried that she might end up with a big student loan and no job. Betty is dissatisfied with her work as a civil litigator, and knowing what she knows now (the low pay – a little more than $50,000 after five years, the financial uncertainty, the whims of the partners, and financial disasters), she would have pursued a more academic career.

Deborah, a solicitor in her early thirties, had a degree in criminology and did not know what to do with it. Georgina, a solicitor in her late twenties, was in education and hated it. She wanted to salvage the years she had completed, so she switched to law. She commented that going into law because there is nothing else to do is the worst reason. Similarly, Jillian (also in her late twenties) in her fourth year of university did not want to do a thesis, or to look for a job in her alternative fields. Laura, a barrister in her late thirties, examined the MCAT and the LSAT, and decided on law over medicine, because it looked easier and took less time. Sybil, a solicitor in her late thirties, went to law school because her husband sent in her application and drove her off to write the LSAT. She allowed him to apply on the basis that she would have her life sorted out before September. Not having sorted it out, she went to law school by default.

Alex, a barrister and solicitor in his early thirties, flipped a coin. Law school won. Bruce, a barrister in his late twenties, went to law school to postpone the decision of what he wanted to do. Leon, a solicitor in his mid-thirties, went to law school as a whim, without a plan. Neil, a solicitor in his late thirties, was passed over for a promotion, and went to law school to get out of a dead-end job. Patrick, a barrister in his late fifties, fell into law after he decided he needed a change in career. Nicholas, a barrister in his mid-thirties, went to law school because there were no real jobs in political science, and he was not good at the sciences.

Frank would have preferred veterinary medicine, but he was not accepted. For this barrister in his mid-thirties, law school was something he could get into, but it was not his first choice. Stewart, a barrister in his late thirties, would have gone into education, but the Social Credit government was cutting back, and there did not appear to be any future in teaching. Law school was something he could get into, and he "basically just needed a job."

Jack's wife had a major influence on his decision to go to law school. She was insistent, because she wanted to live in the city where she wanted him to apply. She also thought Jack would be good at it, but he initially resisted because he did not want to follow in his father's footsteps, and he wanted to be a teacher. However, he realized that teaching might be a burnout career after ten years, so he went to law school with the intention of maybe teaching, and then going back to law. After law school, he realized that it was difficult to break up a law career. It was something you had to stay in. Now a barrister in his mid-thirties, he teaches part time and enjoys giving talks.

Vernon, a barrister in his mid-forties, was working himself to death at a job when his marriage broke up. He considered taking a year off and going to Europe, but instead he used the money he had saved to go to law school. He still kicks himself for not taking a year off: "Anally retentive, I wasn't comfortable doing that, so I went to law school."

Douglas was looking for a new career. He was tired of being a teacher, "tired of telling children to sit down and be quiet, teaching them stupid stuff, and wasting their time and our tax money." He tried manual labour, but his back started to give out, so he needed something else to do. People told him to become a lawyer and so he did. As a barrister in his late forties, he is very satisfied with the practice of law, and would do it again.

Commitment to People and to Society

Sixteen percent of the women and 10% of the men went to law school in order to improve society or help people.[8] Amy went to law school because she wanted to "change the world, promote feminist values, and advocate on behalf of women." Similarly, Emily had worked on a number of different women's issues before going to law school and thought she could further the cause through legal education. Megan, now a barrister doing mostly immigration and criminal law (but not sexual assault cases), thought she would work in a rape crisis centre after obtaining her law degree. Other women expressed a more general interest in helping people.

Simon had always wanted to work with Aboriginal people, and chose law school over a master's degree in social work. Riley was interested in social change and felt that law was one way of training for that, "even though practising law might not be the way to do it." Tony went to law school to become a criminal lawyer, a "defender of the poor and oppressed"; however, that changed in his first year of law school when he got the impression he would be defending criminals, not the innocent, and discovered that civil practice would be more lucrative.

Law as a Challenging Career

Fourteen percent of the women and 6% of the men went to law school because they wanted a challenging career or intellectual stimulation.[9] Carissa compared English (a subject she was familiar with) with law, which was the unknown and a greater challenge. She loved law school, the Socratic teaching method, the "tightly knit collegiality, almost cliquishness." It made her feel special, one of the "chosen ones." Carissa also saw law, unlike the sciences, as something that was constantly evolving: "People say law is a conservative, traditional profession, and it is. But laws change rapidly; they change with government, they change with judges. You see the Supreme Court of Canada coming down with amazing decisions today, which five years back, when I went to law school, I would never have dreamed of. I find that fascinating, intrinsically interesting." However, law is not for everyone, according to this solicitor in her mid-thirties: "If you're in it just for the money and you think that it compensates for all the other things, then you'll be disappointed and you'll hate it. And there's no point in doing it unless you find it intrinsically interesting, and you get some internal satisfaction from [it]." Donna, a barrister in her mid-forties, and Zoe, also in her mid-forties, found law more intellectually challenging than education, their former careers. Tina was also attracted to law because she thought it would be intellectually challenging.

Things came easily to Kevin. He found that he would learn things quickly, and then lose interest. He knew nothing about law, and did not even know a lawyer. Law appeared as a daunting task, and so Kevin decided to take up the challenge of law. As a barrister in his early thirties, he finds that there is always someone scrutinizing his work – partners, associates, friends, clients, lawyers and clients on the other side, judges, and so on. Kevin finds law "a real motivator." Asked whether he gets a "buzz" out of practising law, he responded, "It's not that I get a buzz out of it ... I can't figure out what it is ... As soon as I've figured it out I'll probably quit."

Money and Financial Security

Ten percent of the women and 18% of the men went to law school to earn money or achieve financial security. For Sally, law was a pragmatic decision and she thought she could earn a reasonable living. However, she finds the so-called economic security behind law a "phantom security." The work is hard, and the stress is great. William went to law school to achieve more versatility in his professional career path; then he added, "I guess I'd be lying if I didn't say it wasn't also money, seeing as it was also a route to a better salary." Conrad was led on by one of his wife's rich girlfriends, who said, "Hey, why not become a lawyer and become really rich?" He continued, "I was naive enough to think that's what was going to happen. I thought I'd make a lot of money. No one in my family but me has ever been to university and I really did believe that lawyers all drove Mercedes Benzes and made megabucks. I was cured of that rapidly in first year; there wasn't much out there at the time."

Other Reasons for Going to Law School

Ten percent of the women and 24% of the men went to law school to broaden their education, and to have more control over their lives. For these lawyers, law offers more variety in learning, work, and job options. It provides them with a broader perspective on society, and on how things work. Some see law as providing a more independent and flexible career. It opens up more doors if they decide to go into politics, business, or some other career. Tim's philosophy on education is "to learn as much as possible in life, whether useful or not." He objects to education systems that cater to specific industries and job training: "It's incomprehensible to me that people should be focused on wasting precious high school and university time in framing somebody to a specific task." He added, "Really out of touch with reality in that regard, aren't I?"

Twelve percent of the women and 4% of the men mentioned pressure and expectations from family.[10] Some of these women are the same ones who went into law by default, as it was often family expectations that forced them to decide what to do with their lives. Law was a "fallback" to meet these expectations. For example, Betty (whose father wanted a Cadillac) and Angela (who was harassed by her parents at the age of sixteen to decide what she was going to do when she grew up) felt pressure to go to law school. Nicole, who has left the practice of law, described the pressure from her family: "I had a lot of pressure from my family. In fact, when I discussed the possibility of going into education, I was strongly discouraged. I didn't take a year off or years off to travel or work, and I was probably too young to be making major career decisions. I was easily influenced by my parents, so I got into it. Also, I probably had a poor notion of what practising law was all about." Opal, who is in her early fifties, and Sybil, who is in her late thirties, were talked into going to law school by their husbands. Viola and Harvey, both in their early thirties, came from families of professionals, and there was pressure to enter one of the professions. For Lucas, who came from a traditional ethnic family, it was the only occupation that interested him, that was also acceptable to his family: "It was a matter of choosing among a limited list of acceptable things, and law had an element of creativeness to it."

Eight percent of the women and 10% of the men went to law school because someone recommended it to them. Some lawyers could not remember who recommended it; for others, there was a high school history teacher, their spouse, or friends. Dorothy's friend told her she would make a good lawyer. He added, "If anyone was meant to be a lawyer, it's you."

Women mention other reasons for going to law school. Elizabeth, a barrister in her late thirties, went to law school because she was told "girls don't go to law school." She explained, "I was young (thirteen or fourteen), and someone made the mistake of telling me that little girls don't become lawyers." That was her main reason for going to law school, "because I was told little girls didn't do it. That's the honest truth, I swear." Olive, a barrister in her mid-thirties, went to law school because someone told her she would never pass the LSAT. Jessica went to law school to "redeem herself." Heather, a solicitor in her mid-thirties, explained it this way:

> Candidly, when I was younger the prestige appealed to me – not the prestige in terms of income or anything like that, but in terms of being a woman and being a lawyer. It was important to me to be something [practise a profession] so that people acknowledged I was smart. I don't say this every day to people, but I grew up in the seventies, and I had a subscription to *Ms. Magazine* when I was about thirteen years old. I wanted to be something non-traditional. I didn't want to be a teacher; I didn't want to be a nurse like my mother and my grandmother. I wanted to do something that women didn't usually do. Of course, in my law class it was half women by the time I got there, which is great.

Three women went to law school because they equated knowledge with power, although none of the men mentioned similar reasons. Kristine, a barrister in her mid-thirties, said she wanted to know the answers, and did not want to be "taken advantage of by people." Melanie, in her late twenties, remembered being a student, and having landlord problems and getting pushed around. She did not like that, and wanted to know more about the system. Theresa, a barrister in her early forties, explained, "Knowledge is power. I was working in a unionized environment and I was holding positions on the union executive going to grievances and arbitrations ... I thought that I could be a more effective advocate if I had some more knowledge."

Attractions to Practising Law

In the entire sample of 100 lawyers, 50% of the women and 62% of the men were satisfied with the practice of law overall, and 68% of the women and 78% of the men thought they would be practising law five years from the time of the interview. However, only 60% of the women and 70% of the men said they would go to law school, if they could "do it over again." Given that 31.4% of the women and 25.6% of the men who were called to the bar in British Columbia at the same time as these respondents had already left the practice of law, what is it about the practice of law that the remaining lawyers like and dislike? Following on the question, "If you could 'do it over again,' would you become a lawyer?," respondents were asked what they liked and disliked about being a lawyer. There were some common likes and dislikes by both the women and the men, and there were some unique responses.

Challenge and Satisfaction

The most frequent aspect of law that both the women (34%) and men (38%) liked is the fact that law is challenging, interesting, or satisfying. Carissa, who is in her mid-thirties, finds law fascinating and intrinsically interesting:

> You're dealing with a variety of people every day, and you're dealing with a variety of files every day. As long as your area of practice is relatively broad, it provides you with variety. And it's an exciting life – going to court, preparing for a case, interviewing witnesses, interviewing clients, putting together a deal, travelling to different places to complete the transaction – it's an exciting lifestyle. If you've done well at law school and you're prepared to make sacrifices (that's a different story), you can have a fairly nice lifestyle. How many people at university think (I certainly never did) that they might end up in a downtown office such as this where I have twenty-four-hour secretaries if I want them or were so inclined, showers in the building, and couches in the offices? We're at a different level than most of society. Lawyers forget that the real world out there is not what they see in here. It's not *L.A. Law*, but it has its moments, and if you like law it's wonderful, but it's not for everyone.

Carissa always wanted to be Clarence Darrow or Perry Mason, because "that's all you see on television, and so I had my heart set on doing litigation." However, the job opportunity that she took was doing corporate-commercial work in a large firm. She had the advantage of speaking Chinese, and had worked for a corporate-commercial firm. Carissa loves the law. Since large law firms expect you to choose between being a barrister or a solicitor in a large firm, being a solicitor suited her just fine: "This job opportunity came up. I thought that since I had to choose anyway, and I love both, I'd just go for it. I like the firm and the people and the work." Carissa is good at what she does. She is good at organizing and keeping track of the paperwork involved in a corporate-commercial practice: "I like things to be in their place." She also thinks that being a woman is to her advantage: "Our negotiating style is not generally as aggressive. We don't have the need to win over the other side every time. I think that's useful in solicitor's work because you have to keep in mind, as a lawyer in a business deal, that your goal is to bring the two parties together as opposed to trying to win. The perfect deal is one in which both sides walk away thinking they got what they wanted. This quality I have, as a woman, is helpful to the practice."

Gail, a barrister in her early thirties, finds that she is learning new things all the time. Her job is never stagnant, there are different areas, different people. It is intellectually and physically challenging. She finds the stress of practice challenging and rewarding, as does Iris, a solicitor in her mid-thirties. Likewise, Melanie appreciates the challenge in learning about a case and getting a snapshot of her client's situation or business. Nancy, a solicitor in her mid-thirties, enjoys putting deals together and helping complete the deals. Her job allows her to be creative, "and it's a challenging career because every new deal is something different. I like that." Wendy, who is no longer practising because of a family crisis, thrived on the stress of practice:

> I liked the interaction. I liked winning. I'm an arguer, and nothing made me feel more omnipotent than getting up in chambers and making an argument. My very first week of practising law, I was in a new firm and got sent to the Court of Appeal. I was scared to death. But I won and I won big and I was just omnipotent – no one could tell me I was wrong about anything. That feeling is something that most lawyers probably thrive on: winning is good, losing is bad. I don't like losing, and I don't take it well. I'm not a good loser, and I'm also one of those types who thrive on stress. I guess they call me a Type A [personality] or something? Until recently I couldn't imagine a day going by when I didn't have to be doing something all the time. So, the job was perfect for that.

Similarly, Wanda, a barrister in her mid-thirties, enjoys the challenge of going to court, in that it keeps her on her toes all the time. Leon, a solicitor in his mid-thirties, found law a constant challenge: "The intellectual challenge is great. I don't know whether there are any other jobs out there where you always have to be on your toes, and keep up on stuff. There's a downside to that because it can be tedious; but, in the long term, I think that's one of the great things about law." Oscar, a solicitor in his early thirties, enjoys the challenge of putting big deals together:

> I get access to the most senior people in a corporation. I'm forced to write a story about how their business works in a prospectus. This means I have to understand their business. How does this company work? What makes it tick? Those are the kinds of questions I have had to get into, and every deal I do is with a different company. Because you're dealing with the most senior people and you're asking them big-picture questions, it's fascinating.

The other thing we do – if there's a contested takeover bid or you're acting for the bidder or the target – the types of transactions that make the headlines in the paper (it's not the fact that they're in the headlines [that I like them] but because they're big, interesting) – these complicated deals challenge you. I guess a lot of it is the challenge – to be able to make these big transactions work. You have to bring all your skills to bear and you juggle a lot of balls. There's a lot of scope to be creative, surprising scope to be creative. It's like the *Tax Act*. I view the *Tax Act* as a big game. There's a set of rules, you have to trudge your way through them, and if you can find a loophole your client will make millions. It's not the same, but there's some of the same flavour in securities – there's a whole bunch of rules in the *Securities Act* and a whole bunch of rules in the *Company Act*, and a whole bunch of business considerations, and you have to think about how can you design or structure a transaction that will work. So it's intellectually challenging, and it's a lot of fun – probably warped – but it is.

Similarly, Rob, a solicitor in his early thirties, enjoys the big deals:

I enjoy it. I enjoy getting caught up in the big deals. I get to make decisions and get caught up in things that I could never be caught up in if I weren't in this capacity, because I'll never have the money to be involved, as principal, in the deals that I work on. They're exciting; there's a rush that comes with that. Not to say that magnitude alone makes something exciting, because you could be doing a billion dollar deal and, if it's a cookie-cutter deal, it's not going to be that exciting – it just has more zeros in it. But this stuff [land development] is leading edge – we're changing the rules as we go – or rather the city is changing the rules, it depends on how you look at it. But it's exciting to sit there and be dealing with things that have never been done before, having to work them out from scratch, having to think forward and not say, "Well, I have a precedent for this," having to say what's going to matter ten years from now on this point, having to think it through. I find that challenging. I guess that's what it amounts to. I guess I find being a lawyer challenging, and I find achieving things rewarding and satisfying. Challenge and achievement are the two things that I'm looking for and definitely getting.

Interaction with People
Approximately one-quarter of the women (28%) and men (24%) like the interaction with people, clients, and other lawyers they encounter in the practice of law. Paula, a barrister in her early thirties, finds that work is never boring. Every day is different, and she meets a lot of people on the job – witnesses, police officers. In addition, she never knows what the day

has in store for her. What appears to be a normal trial can result in something different happening, whether it is a legal issue or just something funny.

Leon, a solicitor in his mid-thirties, likes being able to develop long-term
relationships with his clients. Their appreciation for a job well done, in
which he helps them organize their affairs, is rewarding. He likes "being
part of the service industry." Above all else, Lucas, a solicitor in his early
thirties, likes his clients: "I thoroughly enjoy the fact that I get to meet so
many people who come from so many different walks of life, and to do
something that may make a difference." Ray, a barrister in his mid-thirties,
likes the exposure to different types of people and situations: "You have
the honour of people confiding in you and relying on your advice."
William, an in-house counsel in his mid-thirties, enjoys the social aspect
of law, in that it brings him into contact with a lot of different clients and
different people. In addition, he believes that if you get the right practice,
the camaraderie is great. Having left private practice, it was what he miss-
es the most about his previous job: "Here, it's more of a job. You come in
in the morning and go home at night. There's not as much camaraderie."

Knowledge and Intellectual Stimulation
Approximately one-quarter of the women (26%) and men (26%) like being
a lawyer because it provides them with knowledge, a good education, and
intellectual stimulation. For example, Donna, who is in her mid-forties,
likes litigation because there is always an opportunity to learn new things:

> Each case probably involves something that you're unfamiliar with, either
> a medical condition or some engineering concept. I do some aviation
> work, and so I've had an opportunity to learn about flight, or how a par-
> ticular component of an airplane works. I'm inquisitive, I'm curious, and
> I like to learn. There's always, always something to learn. If you have a
> case about a defective piece of machinery or something, you've got to
> find out all about that.

Similarly, William likes the mental stimulation law provides. However, he
has found that as time passes, he is moving away from the law and more to
"just juggling files and relying on your wits to get through, rather than
relying on your intellect." Emily, a solicitor in her late forties, appreciates
the opportunity to be constantly learning, and feels that she can use her
knowledge to make a difference. However, she would like more balance in
her life so that she can "put the law to work in a volunteer way."

Flexibility and Control Over One's Life
For 22% of the women and 16% of the men, law provides them with flexibility and control over their lives. Some of the women find that law offers

them more control over their lives than the institutionalized work of their previous professions (dental hygienist, teacher, nurse), as did a man who had been a social worker. Law provides Lois, a barrister in her mid-thirties, with control over her life:

I'm the one who decides that I get up and start work at five in the morning because I didn't feel like doing it at some other time. Because I'm partner here, if I want a three-hour lunch or I want a day off in the middle of the week, then I take it as long as things are covered. So, my hours are flexible, bearing in mind we've got bills to pay every month and salaries to meet. So I can't abuse it, but I like the hours, I like the freedom especially, being partner. I leave at three every Friday afternoon. I like the control [law] has given my life. I'm single, I make more money than most people I date, I have my house, I have my dogs. I have control over my life, which is something that's always been important to me. I've never been one to be dependent on anyone, even back before becoming a lawyer. I've always believed in being self-supporting.

Fred, a solicitor in his late twenties, likes the flexibility of his workday: "Sure, it's long, but if I have to go and get a car repaired or something, I just take off and do it. I may work a little longer that day. You just make sure you get your work done. Even friends who work at multinational firms don't have that ability. They are generally in an office all day and, if a personal problem comes up, they've got to work around it."

Earlier in the interviews, when they were asked whether they were satisfied with the control they had over their work, 68% of the women and 84% of the men said that they were.[11] Many of the environments that lawyers work in provide them with control over their work. Amy, who is in her mid-thirties, likes the autonomy of her work, in terms of projects and the directions that she can take in her administrative law job; however the overall organization "is such that everything is required to go through a tiny funnel at the top, and that can cause frustration." Donna, a barrister in her mid-forties, was very dissatisfied with the control she had over her work, until she moved out on her own. Olive has as much control as she can expect for her type of practice:

The control – I have fairly good control. But obviously the other side of that is that you can't tell your clients, despite whatever you might actually say to them about it, "Don't get into trouble for two weeks, I'm taking a holiday." They don't believe that you're entitled to a holiday. They get arrested at four in the morning. You don't have any control over that. They're going to get in trouble, and if that means that you're at [Provincial Court] at nine o'clock to do a show cause for somebody when you've got to be at Supreme Court at ten, well, that's what you've got to do to keep the business. They don't understand about holidays.

Helping Others

Although touted as a helping profession, only 18% of the women and 14% of the men said they liked law because it gave them an opportunity to help people. Laura, a barrister in her late thirties, likes to deal with people on a personal level: "I enjoy it when clients come in and we set up a good rapport, and I enjoy being able to help them. It's a great feeling of satisfaction when somebody comes to you with a problem and you're able to solve it, and they can set their lives straight again." Holly, a barrister in her early forties, also likes being able to help:

> For many people, it's frightening to be faced with the court system. They don't know what they're doing in it, and there's a mystique about it. I like to be able to educate and to unravel that mystique so that people understand. I try to make the habit of saying, "This is the process" and then explaining every time what has happened so that people become more at ease with it [the court system]. That's the educating part, and I like to help. I think that's why I like family law, because you do get to help right away. It's not the same as doing a commercial thing, fighting over the value of a sign, you know. It's very satisfying.

Heather, a solicitor in her mid-thirties, finds helping ordinary people buy houses, negotiate leases or bank terms, set up companies, or get their divorce very satisfying, and that it provides her an opportunity to be creative. She adds, "I don't come from a real business family at all ... Business was never something I thought I'd enjoy. My family was distrustful of business people, actually. But I find, to my surprise and my father's horror, that it's satisfying because you're making jobs for people, and we provide a really good service for our clients."

Kristine, a barrister in her mid-thirties, also likes helping people: "I like knowing the answers. I like having people come in with problems, and being able to calm them down and sort the problems out – break them down into pieces and start solving them." Lois, a barrister in her mid-thirties, talks about the power that comes with her job, and how it assists her in helping people: "You've got some client who comes in, and they're having a terrible, terrible problem, and you can just pick up a phone with them sitting in your office and say, 'Well, Mrs. X is in my office, and she says this is happening, and what she wants is this. I don't want to get involved, and so on. Can we do something?' And it's dealt with in a phone call. And, being able to do that for people is really, really nice." Dorothy, a barrister in her mid-thirties, does a lot of *pro bono* work, and also works at a substantial discount: "I have a little old lady who's never given us a retainer, and the senior partner doesn't understand what I'm doing. But she needed some good legal advice, and she came to me, and I stuck with her. I bill her next to nothing for my time. There's also a lot of *pro bono* work I've done for friends, and I find that gratifying." Owen, a barrister in his late thirties, finds that helping people makes him a better person: "It makes me more responsible to others and consequently to myself." Zeke, a barrister in his mid-thirties, finds it rewarding to assist "someone who runs up against a dead end, for example, a bureaucracy that is unyielding. To be able to assist in that way is rewarding and intellectually stimulating."

Prestige, Status, and More Weighty Opinion
Sixteen percent of the women and 14% of the men appreciate law's prestige and status, and the weightier opinion that it gives them. Amy, who is in her mid-thirties, would consider law if she had to do it again, because of the financial aspects and the status: "A law degree and a practice certificate allows one the status to make comments and offer opinions that carry weight. As a feminist, as a lesbian, and as a social justice advocate, it has been a real asset to have that status and credibility and that authority. The views I have now are simply more evolved views than the ones I had before I went to law school, yet the credibility I'm afforded now is exponentially greater than it was prior to my going to law school." For Flora, a barrister in her early forties, being a lawyer means people take her seriously. She is not "just a housewife." Viola (in her early thirties) likes the recognition that it gives her: "I mean, I think people, if they know you're a lawyer, they know that you've some sort of brain and will give you, whether it's deserving or not, the benefit of the doubt to start with." Likewise, Adams, who is in his mid-thirties, believes, "Fairly or not, if people know you're a lawyer, they accord your opinion weight they wouldn't accord the same opinion of a non-lawyer." Stewart, a barrister in his late thirties, thinks that people are "impressed when you tell them [you're a lawyer]. That may be because they've been watching too many *L.A. Law* shows." There are limits to the status, but he notices that people judge him differently now than when he worked at a camp washing dishes.

Financial Rewards
Twelve percent of the women and 16% of the men mentioned the financial rewards as one of the aspects they liked about being a lawyer. Earlier, when they were asked whether they were satisfied with their income, only 48% of the women but 70% of the men said they were.[12] Differences in income between the women and men are discussed in Chapter 3.

Amy had to switch law jobs to find a satisfactory income: "My income, when I worked for a non-profit organization, was a disgrace. I have registered this concern with the non-profit and the funding body. It was exploitative." Now, in private practice doing administrative law, she is confident that she could earn more money, just by working more hours. Elizabeth's move from working for the Crown to private practice was profitable: "In the first three months, I made what I made with the Crown last year." Lois, a barrister in her mid-thirties, is happy with her income, although she works long hours and thinks she deserves everything she earns.

Other Attractions

Eight percent of the women and 2% of the men said they liked going to court. This is a rather low percentage, since 44% of the women and 54% of the men identified themselves primarily as barristers. However, it should be kept in mind that the respondents were not asked whether they liked going to court, only what they liked about the practice of law. The issue of going to court is dealt with again in Chapter 5, in a discussion of the adversarial system.

Nicole was surprised at the number of likeable people she has met in the practice of law, "because I think, from my experience, not many people do enjoy us." Law also helped her "grow as a person" and gain "a lot more self-confidence working in a professional atmosphere." Viola appreciates the fact that law taught her "to think in an organized way," and to articulate her "thoughts in a half decent way." It also gave her writing skills, "a powerful tool."

Detractions of Law

Stress and Responsibility

Some lawyers thrive on stress, others dislike it intensely. For many lawyers, law is a double-edged sword. What they like about it may also be what they dislike about it. Both Gail and Simon illustrate this. Gail likes the challenge and stress of law. When I asked her what she dislikes about law, she said, "Same coin, other side – demands, stress, responsibility. Sometimes it can be too much." Simon likes, among other things, the challenge of law. When asked what he dislikes, he responded, "Some of the same things you have on the other side of the coin. There are the demands of the practice, having to constantly make sure that you don't do anything wrong. There's a lot of pressure not to screw up."

Thirty-eight percent of the women and 40% of the men disliked the stress, responsibility, and decision making that go with the practice of law. Some lawyers do not like being responsible for other people's problems. Holly finds that "having other people's lives in your hands ... weighs very heavily" on her, and is stressful. Frank explains, "There's a lot of stress. People pay us to take over their problems, and they're usually not small problems, they're big. Each one of those people has one big problem, lawyers have many." This is one of the reasons he thinks he might like to move to doing solicitor's work. Ray finds it stressful "being involved in making critical decisions on a daily basis. And usually the decisions you're making are some of the most important decisions in your clients' lives, even though they're not in yours."

For some, the stress of law means lack of sleep from worrying about files, or waking up in the middle of the night worrying about clients and files. For example, Zeke elaborated:

The job does pay well, but it doesn't pay well enough for the stress you carry with you – waking up in the middle of the night, worrying about what you're doing on a certain file, not being able to leave the job at work, taking it home with you. In a sense it never goes away. When I go on holidays, it's not like working at the mill where somebody else deals with your lumber. You come back here, and there's a big pile of stuff that's been waiting for you for the past three weeks. You work like mad to be able to go away, and you come back and work even harder to catch up.

Riley left private practice because of the stress:

I found the stresses of private practice to be severe. The hours certainly were difficult. The hours on the job weren't all that bad – it was all the time off the job that I spent thinking about all the things I had and hadn't done. Like a lot of lawyers starting out, I got very little sleep. I developed a sleep pattern in which I would wake up at three in the morning thinking about cases, and I would be unable to get back to sleep again. I just don't have the physical stamina to deal with that sort of thing. I recognize that that's something that often wears off, that as you practise you become more comfortable and you don't spend all night worrying. But I don't have much interest in seeing how long it would take to get to that point. I found that stressful. I came to law late and I think, because of my physical disability, I also have less stamina. I just felt there were more important things in life than worrying about cases that meant nothing to me personally, that I was only worried about because I wanted to do a good job for the clients. So it was the stress – the stress of always having to do what was best for the client even if that was sometimes distasteful. I found that difficult.

Melanie also finds that it is impossible "to take off for two months of the year. It's difficult to take off for more than two weeks, and when you do, you work twice as hard to get away and twice as hard when you come back, and you're phoning in while you're away."

For Vera, the stress comes from "always covering your ass, and that's the term used all the time. You're covering your ass with clients, with other people you work with, the lawyers, everybody is out to get you. That's a reality, and I don't think that's a paranoid comment." She attributes this partly to the fact that lawyers are less likely than other professionals to be supportive of one another: "Very few lawyers remark about the capability of other lawyers. They're more willing to say, 'That's not a good lawyer,' whereas in other professions they're more supportive of one another. I think that that's being recognized, and that may change over time, but I don't see that in the medical fields or accounting fields or engineers."

Neil dislikes "the stress – always having to be right, and having the threat of being sued if you are wrong." Similarly, Conrad finds the threat of lawsuits stressful: "Every file you've got is a time bomb waiting for you to make a mistake, so you can be sued for professional negligence. I can whine about that, but I guess any profession is the same. Every time a doctor takes a look at someone for a head cold, he knows that he might be missing a telltale sign of cancer or something. So I guess every professional has to deal with that. Stress is a blanket that covers everything." Stewart finds that there is "a lot of pressure, in terms of time and not making mistakes. There's always the pressure of worrying about whether you have done the right thing or not, and whether you are about to be sued for negligence, and whether you have missed the limitation period. It's almost like the Law Society is Big Brother keeping an eye out on everyone, and I don't like that – the pressure that comes from the rules and regulations you have to conform to."

Tony wonders whether the stress has a sufficient payoff:

If I were to focus on one complaint with the practice of law, I guess it flows from the financial concern. Given the economic climate, the number of people entering the profession, the business of it (becoming less of a profession more of a business) I don't think the return (when you look at it from what the law asks you to give and the economic payback) – I don't think it's worth it any more. I think we get paid very well, but you look at it thinking you're putting a hell of an investment into what you're doing, and it's the kind of thing that gives a lot of stress to your life. You probably have all the stresses, concerns, and difficulties you have in running your own business. But when you run your own business you're building up a capital asset – something that has a value, and something you can look at in ten years and say, "I accomplished something. I built something where nothing was before." Second, you can say, "Not only that, but I have something that is worth x. This is my retirement that I'm building up." I think with the law you can't say you've created anything except your personal capabilities. So you don't have something to look at and show for what you've done, and you don't have the possibility of the higher financial returns that I think you could get by running your own business other than law. I think that's the principal concern I have. The toil and the stress and the costs in terms of your own personal life that the profession takes – the return isn't worth it.

Likewise, Vernon asks himself whether the payoff is worth the stress:

The amount of stress and emotional demand, the level of responsibility versus any return on that – when I was articling (at a major firm) people who had been lawyers for a long time said that they are now working three times as hard for one-third of the pay. And I don't see that changing. I also see it here in my own little shop. The overhead continues to increase and the billing. If it's your own hours you hit a peak, but the secretaries still want raises every year and everything still keeps going up. It's a lot of work to keep it going. Because I take it all very seriously, it's emotionally demanding, draining, and stressful. You're dealing constantly with people who are unhappy, and in family law you can't be happy about the outcome of the process. You can't make a client happy. They can't get it all. They can't get their family back, they can't be reunited, and they can't get a result that's going to get them everything. They're losing something no matter what happens, and often their lawyer takes the blame, even though the lawyer may have done beyond the best possible. And I have felt on occasion, from what I know could have happened, that the outcome is wonderful, but the client is still dissatisfied. I used to find it hard disassociating myself emotionally from some of the files. That's probably one of the biggest challenges I see, and what I like about other professions. I don't know what my dentist does, but I suspect that when he goes home he doesn't worry about my teeth; and, I can't say that for me.

Long Hours and Pressure to Bill
The hours demanded by the practice of law are often associated with the stresses of practising law. Twenty-four percent of the women and 24% of the men disliked the hours demanded, or the pressure to bill. For some, the pressure to market their services was also the target of their disfavour. Although Nancy enjoys the practice of law, because it is a challenging career and allows her to be creative, she dislikes billing:

One thing I hate about law (this is actually the biggest thing and everyone would admit it), it's the only profession I know of where you have to keep track of every minute of the day, of what you do, and be accountable, and feel like a failure if you haven't billed seven-and-a-half hours in that day. To legitimately bill seven-and-a-half hours, you have to work at least twelve hours, otherwise you're padding or bumping up time. I think that's the biggest pitfall, and one of the main reasons I want to go in-house as counsel. That would be the main reason I don't want to do private practice, because I think it's so hard to be judged every day by how many hours you bill a client. That's the worst thing about law.

Edward sees his contemporaries who went into real estate doing a lot better financially than he is. Given the amount of effort that it took to get his practice going, and the number of hours he works (fifty to sixty a week – fewer than some lawyers), he could have been better off financially, and had time for recreation, had he done something else. He adds, "I can't take a vacation for more than two weeks." Likewise, Fred mused about the path not chosen:

If I could do it over again with the knowledge [I have] now, I would take a closer look at some other options. I may still have chosen law. My experience hasn't been bad enough that I would say "No," but I'm careful about people who come up to me and talk to me about my law school [experience]. My perceptions, I think, were more realistic than many of my classmates, but I was still off base. There's a lot about the practice that isn't known. The remuneration is reasonable but, if you look at the hours people work, and the stress they're under, and the chances of real advancement, given that there's no pension at the end of the road, it's all or nothing. I think the remuneration is reasonable. I think a lot of people look at law as a guaranteed job. You get articles and then you work a couple of years. Well, you get four years out, and the doors start closing. I took the Canadian Securities course right after first year, and that was where I was going to go. I look at my friends who became brokers at that time. Things are different [for them]. You can't always do it the same. Given the market and the success they've achieved and the differences in our lifestyle, I think maybe the path not taken may have led to a better tomorrow. But, as you can see from my satisfaction rating [three, or somewhat satisfied], I don't mope over it.

Hank finds that he's on a treadmill, things never stop: "I worked in private industry before I became a lawyer, and there are always times when you have a lull. You don't seem to get that [in law] as much; or, if you have a lull, you're worried." Harvey dislikes the hours of work, and unreasonable expectations of clients "in terms of completion dates, and the amount of work to be done and at what cost. And also pressure from the partners to bill, whether it's expressed or not. You know it's always a concern."

Murray finds the pressure to work long hours "tough on family life." Leon thinks that his generation is "more concerned about family time and spare time" than income, and that there will be changes in the long hours of work: "We don't need to work that hard. There's no reason to set our goals that high. It's not necessary."

For Oscar, the solution is to gain some perspective about hours:

The hours get to you from time to time. But I think you have to have some perspective on it. The trick, when you don't have a deal on, is to walk away at two in the afternoon or take Friday off. It's difficult to train yourself to do that; if you can do that, it's much easier to strike the balance ... I find when I'm not happy with what I'm doing, it's because I've been grinding away for too long, and that just means I need a break. It's not because I don't like practising law, it's just spending too many hours inside these four walls.

Stewart dislikes the economic pressures and the need to hustle business:

I think particularly in a small firm, there's a lot of economic pressure. You pretty well have to [work hard] in small firms. I don't know, maybe lawyers in smaller firms are turning into the modern version of used car salesman. You have to be out there hustling clients, taking people out to lunch – we take insurance adjusters out and claim managers, realtors. That's something I'm not comfortable with – glad-handing people and trying to hustle business. I guess I'm not a good salesman. I'm too reserved to do that comfortably. So I don't like that aspect of law, particularly.

Confrontation and Adversarial Work

Eighteen percent of the women and 8% of the men did not like the adversarial nature of their work. The respondents' thoughts on the adversarial system and the adversarial nature of themselves and other lawyers are discussed in Chapter 5.

For Jillian, who deals with her own life in a non-confrontational manner, it is difficult to get involved in someone's personal problems. Similarly, Viola dislikes dealing with other people's personal problems and the confrontation that these problems lead to: "I'm being asked to play a role in someone else's life where I don't feel I belong, and in a confrontational way in which I don't feel comfortable, because I don't handle my own problems that way. It's just all wrong for me." Viola explained why she wants to get away from the "adversarial stuff":

I find it really eats at me. I mean, I do a hearing and I win, and I still feel sick, and it's always been that way. And in court too, I'd win and I'd feel sick, and if I lost I didn't feel very good. It was never the decision – the decision was probably fair. I never won something I thought I shouldn't have won. It's not that. It's just the process to get to it. Telling some sixty-year-old man, "You know, I think you're overweight. Do you think that might be contributing to your problem?" I mean that. My first trial back in 1989, I thought I was going to commit suicide, all this stuff. I don't like digging into somebody's stuff.

For some lawyers, it is the conflict that permeates all aspects of their job that they dislike. Sometimes Laura finds the conflicts with her clients (telling them what they can and cannot do), with lawyers on the other side, and with lawyers in her firm (over ideas of how things should be done) excessive. Similarly, Paula commented:

Sometimes I get sick of the confrontation, and if it goes on for too long and you don't get a break from it, it becomes a question of "Why am I getting up in the morning to go argue with people?" Sometimes I enjoy it, sometimes I don't have a problem. And I don't mean legal argument, I mean just witnesses asking, "Why do I have to be here? I don't want to be here." And people just dissatisfied all the time. And you're arguing with people, and that I don't like. I get sick of that. And sometimes I wonder whether or not it's a productive career. [Arguing with people] instead of producing something or creating something. Is this a creative way to live my life? [Interviewer: So you don't know whether you would do it ever again?] No, I don't know. I have often wondered whether or not I'd do it over again, if I shouldn't have just gone and gotten a MBA or turned to the diplomatic core.

Tina dislikes the arrogance and egos that are created through the posturing in the adversarial process. Patrick finds that the "over-adversarial colleagues" with whom he deals are not serving their clients' best interests.

Lawyers Have a Poor Reputation
Sixteen percent of both the women and men did not like the reputation of lawyers or the jokes told about lawyers. The downside to being a lawyer, according to Sandra, is "the lawyer's reputation as a shark, somebody you have to watch out for, somebody you can't trust, who can weasel their way around the law and get you off on a technicality." Emily dislikes "people's reaction when you say you're a lawyer, a sleazy, money-grubbing lawyer." Gene does not tell people that he is a lawyer, unless he is asked. Lawyers

are viewed as "socially non-productive. They make work, they're too highly paid, a gilded monopoly."

Kevin hates what he perceives to be the perception of 99.9% of the public who do not deal with lawyers on a regular basis:

> If you talk to anybody – as I say, 99.9% of the public – about what they think about lawyers, if they have negative views, most of those people's experiences with lawyers are limited to a time in their lives when they were charged criminally, a time in their lives when they were going through a divorce. Those types of experiences have not been the kind that leave friendly imprints on their minds, and as a result they're not going to think kindly of lawyers. They're going to think, "I got ripped off by my wife, she took me for everything. And all I got was a bill from my lawyer." And so they don't see the system working for them all that well. That's one of my dislikes about being a lawyer. I wish people would understand. A lot of times people don't realize that success or failure sometimes hinges on them and the merits of the case.

Leon dislikes "the aspersions that are cast on lawyers all the time, because he thinks they are largely unfair." He continues: "It's just like any other profession, there are good ones and there are bad ones. It seems that there's a tradition of making fun of lawyers and casting aspersions. All the stuff we've got on television doesn't help, because they misrepresent the legal profession, very seriously. It makes for good entertainment, but it's all sex and power. It has nothing to do with the real practice of law, and so I dislike that part of it." Having made more money per year as a commercial fisherman than he did for his first six years of practising law, Owen dislikes "the perception that all lawyers are rich fat cats." It bothers Fred when he tells people he is a lawyer, and "everybody figures [he is] a slimy, well-paid slug."

Unpleasant Clients

Fourteen percent of the women and 20% of the men disliked the unrealistic expectations put on lawyers, and the unpleasantness of some of their clients. Jessica finds that clients in a wills, trusts, and estates practice are not "necessarily the most agreeable." Family law and criminal law clients can also be demanding, as Elizabeth and Olive reveal:

> At times your clients don't let you have any life at all. They're angry if you don't want to deal with phone calls at ten-thirty at night or catching you on the street. I've been shopping with a friend and had someone come up to me and start blurting out their entire family matter in front

of my friend. I had to pull him [my client] away and say, "Look, this isn't appropriate." [He said,] "Why can't I get you in the office?" [I responded,] "I'm sorry you're going to have to try." I find that disheartening, and occasionally I have to do my shopping out of town, it's so frustrating. I'm pretty much the only lawyer in town doing family law – legal aid anyway – and it does mean the avalanche comes my way. You get stopped on the street, you get stopped in the malls; you cease having your own life, and sometimes you have to get quite hard.

The demands – people sometimes don't appreciate that you're a criminal lawyer and you're in court all day. You're not there to answer their phone calls, and they think that you're like a barber shop – three chairs, no waiting, and that you have no other clients. The demands from even one client are difficult to deal with, and sometimes you just have to cut loose, and let them find someone else.

Some of the lawyers dislike dealing with fees. Alex finds bartering with clients "very unbecoming." Jack hates "squabbles over money." Although it does not happen often, he dislikes it, because he thinks he issues fair accounts, and his clients get good value for their money. Gerry dislikes "this business of lawyers' fees, people always think you're trying to rip them off." To him, "There seems to be a consensus out there – a large portion of the people will try to chisel you down, whether you price your services at half of what you should charge, or whether you charge more than you should, a great percentage of people out there will try and chip away at it." This is one of the things that might cause him to quit the practice of law. He does not understand why "people ask you to assume responsibility or liability for all the difficult high-risk type situations. They expect you to advise and stickhandle it through, and pop the puck in the net. They look at it and say 'Oh, well, that looked easy.' When you succeed and you make it look simple. That's when you've done your job, and I don't think there's a great public awareness of what it is that lawyers do. I think that's unfortunate, and I think it grinds lawyers down." Likewise, Keith does not think that clients "appreciate all the work you do for them, and it's difficult to show them or explain to them. The bill is always too high, or you didn't do it fast enough. On the other hand, there are clients who are very happy, and that's rewarding."

Dislike of the Profession and Other Lawyers
Twelve percent of the women and 8% of the men disliked lawyers or the profession more generally. Karen dislikes dealing with unreasonable lawyers who do not arrive at the best solution for everyone, "because they like to

go to court and fight." She feels guilty because the process is expensive, and not always productive, and many of the clients cannot afford it. She continues,

> Sometimes, it doesn't sit right with me. I'm sitting in the senior partner's office and he's picking up the phone and talking on ten other files, but you know that he's charging the first client for that whole time. It just doesn't sit right. It's become too much of a business, and I just don't like that part of it. Even the court system frustrates me – you don't always get justice. You win, but you don't win, because the person has no assets or, you know, one spouse runs off with the children and you never see them again even though you have custody and you just fought for two months [to get it].

Susan dislikes "being around too many narrow-minded, chauvinistic lawyers and, if one is a lawyer, there's a tendency to have to associate with a lot of them." Wendy thinks there "are some real scum-buckets out there. There are some lawyers who I don't think are human beings. You can be very adversarial, but you can still be a person." She provides the example of a lawyer who would not agree to a trial adjournment shortly after a tragic death in her immediate family:

> I wasn't looking for major sympathy, I was looking for common courtesy. If he'd phoned me and told me that something terrible had happened to him, I wouldn't have to phone up my client to get their consent to adjourn this thing, I'd just say, "Of course." Now, I ended up getting it [an adjournment] anyway, but certainly not with his cooperation. And that kind of person, I'd run into his type, people who were using my own personal pain as leverage, thinking that maybe ... prompting me to settle the thing for some ridiculous sum of money. I called his bluff. I looked at him and thought, "Why do I deal with these people? Do I ever want to run across someone like him?"

Jeff does "not particularly enjoy the company of lawyers socially." He "perhaps naively expected it to be a more contemplative, intellectual community than it turned out to be." Lawyers are not "as inspired or inspiring company" as he expected. Rather, it turns out that law "is more of a locker room fraternity" than he anticipated. Vincent is more blunt about what he dislikes: "Stupid lawyers. Stupid, as in not necessarily agree or disagree, just thick. People who don't get the point, who don't do the work, who are intellectually lazy and it shows. And the same with judges because there are members of the Bench who are intellectually lazy."

Facing the Gritty Side of Life

Eight percent of the women and 4% of the men disliked dealing with the negative aspects of life. Flora finds it hard to deal with conflict all the time. She admits, "It sounds stupid because you say, 'Well, why did you become a lawyer?'" Megan dislikes the responsibility "for someone else's crises," and Rebecca dislikes the fact that everyone is "working toward the negative":

> Somebody comes in, and they're unhappy because something bad has happened to them or they want to do something bad. Nobody is ever happy at the end of the day, because of some kind of compromise – whether it's the judgment or a negotiated settlement that is a compromise – and everybody is sort of but not really happy at the end of the day. And I didn't like dealing with some of the people I had to deal with who, even when it was completely unnecessary, would cause a power struggle, just for the sake of having a power struggle. It's unnecessary.

Although Paul likes the practice of law, he dislikes the conflicts he has to deal with all of the time. He is also frustrated by

> the backward notions of a lot of the people that you're dealing with, judges for example, and you have to work within the legal system, which is often corrupt and stupid. That's frustrating. Your clients are often people you don't have a lot of sympathy for, but you're obligated as a lawyer to represent their interests anyway, unless a moral problem develops and you can't morally represent this person. I wouldn't turn anyone away just because I don't like them, but you do have to deal with a lot of scummy clients. That, in a way, doesn't give you a lot of control over your life.

Advice to Those Contemplating a Career in Law

Although the question was not initially in the interview schedule, as the interviews progressed, I could not resist asking some of the respondents what advice they would have for students who are thinking about going to law school, or whether they would recommend law as a career.[13] A number of the respondents recommended that students find out more about law before devoting four years of their lives (three years at law school and one year of articles) to studying it. For example, Karen had this advice:

> If you have a chance – if you know anyone or if you can volunteer for a month or hang out in a lawyer's office – you should. You should see what it's like, follow someone around, and see what they do. It isn't just going into court and having glamorous arguments. It's having ten files all on your desk and everyone calling and saying, "Have you done this? Have

you done that?" and four senior partners all wanting you to put their lists of documents together. You know, it depends on where you are, but it's not always a glamorous profession, and especially if you're in a big firm and you're a junior lawyer. I urge them to think about what a lawyer does day-to-day, and if that still appeals to them, great. But if they're looking for certain things, have it [their expectations] tested with reality and make sure that's something they want.

Similarly, Zeke suggested that potential law students "sit down with a lawyer to find out what the practice is all about." Although Zeke is happy with his income, not all lawyers are "fabulously wealthy." Some lawyers "grind it out day-to-day," have all the headaches that go with the job, and do not get paid very well. According to Zeke, if you are not paid well for your work as a lawyer,

> really, it's not worth it. You may as well go do something else so that at the end of the day, when five o'clock rolls around, you can leave and know that you're not going to have to even worry about it until you show up the next day. I think people should realize that maybe twenty years ago law was a ticket to become extremely wealthy, but it's not that way anymore. There are lots of lawyers, it's competitive, and you have to work. What you bring in, you've earned. There are people out there who don't have any work, who have graduated from law school and can't find articles, or get let go after articles, and I think that would surprise people who want to become lawyers – the excessive number of lawyers.

Law school was not what Riley expected. He thought that it would be more like graduate school, "where there was a focus on individual development and room for discussion of individual ideas." He was disappointed to find that it was more like high school: "You have all these courses structured, and you move about as a horde from class to class, and you go down to your lockers as a horde, and the gossip spreads like high school." Although he enjoyed the academic world, he finds that practising law is "not nearly as glamorous" as he expected. He has far less control over his practice and his life, and far more stress than he expected. He recommends that students know why they are going into law, and then talk to, or spend some time with, people who actually do the job: "See what they do, and all the routine drudgery – preparation of pleadings and answering letters from clients who are unhappy with their bills – all those routine things you don't think about before you go to law school." He would not discourage people from going to law school, but they should know what they are doing, and "separate the myths from reality." Law is not practised as it is seen on television.

Simon and Ted suggest that people think twice about going into law, because there are lots of lawyers, and the legal profession is becoming more and more competitive. It can be a difficult career path. When asked whether they would recommend law, a number of respondents said they would not. Conrad explained:

Absolutely not. Absolutely, positively not. Lawyers are like rats – there are just too many. They graduate something like 350 lawyers a year, and you have to think the average person looking in the yellow pages at all those lawyers' ads ... How often does a normal person need a lawyer in his or her lifetime? Maybe to draft a will, if they get divorced, or if they're in a car accident; corporate people, more often. There are just too many lawyers. The system is going to collapse under its own weight eventually. Even now, when I was looking for a job, there were people looking for lawyers who had completed articles and had a typing speed of a certain amount per minute because they wanted to use them as paralegals and stuff. When I was at ICBC (I'd been called to the bar), I worked for $24,000 a year when I started. And I know lots of other lawyers who went to ICBC for a similarly low wage – at least you were making $24,000 a year and you weren't having to work seventy hours a week to get it. I don't know whether any recommendation I could give would ever change people, because the one thing I know about lawyers, about their character, anyone who is ever interested in law school, no matter what you say to them about things being bad, they always feel that things will be different for them. They're better, they're smarter, they're luckier; they won't end up in that boat like everyone else. They remain undeterred in their quest for a degree.

Fred thinks that law is a double-edged sword. There are lawyers who make more than $300,000 a year; however, on the whole that is not true. He has a theory about the people who are making lots of money:

My theory on that is that when you're making that kind of money, you have no life. Your life is your work and, if you're a woman, you're probably not married. But if you're married, you have no kids, you dote on a niece, you have tons of toys – the place at Whistler, the fancy car. And if you're a guy, you're probably divorced. But if you're not divorced, you have an empty marriage. And if you have kids, they see you as a trough – private school, fancy car. You and I see them at university, and they just treat dad like dirt. They're just not normal. Some are well balanced. I guess I thought at some point, will I be like them or will I be like the other people? I think people should know about that. Most lawyers don't make a lot of money, and it gets a bad rap in the profession.

Wesley was pessimistic about the chances of someone succeeding at law, given the number of lawyers:

> Going back to another question about going back and doing law, one thing I was unaware of was the chance of success. And these numbers aren't accurate, but [reflect] a perception that I hold and many of my class-mates held. Of the 2,000 people that applied to law school, 200 got in. Of the 200 that got in, 150 were able to find articling positions; seventy-five were able to stay in the law after that; twenty to thirty today are still practising, so that would automatically lead to the conclusion that [the success rate] is twenty out of 2,000 [1%]. Percentage wise it's a silly risk to be taking. Now the numbers I have given you are skewed, they're not accurate, they're approximations, but they give you a percentage. If you do this route, you've got a 1% chance of success, or you can do something else if you want to invest the eight years to do it. On a risk/return basis, I don't think you can justify that, but I didn't have a clue at the time.

Ray would not encourage people to go into law. From his perspective, the "market is flooded with lawyers," and universities should decrease the number of law graduates. Having said that, he adds, "It's difficult to find good quality and experienced lawyers."

Law is not something Vincent would do now. It is not as much fun as it was five years earlier, when he started practising law. Law school has become so "hyper competitive" he doesn't think that he would be admit-ted today. Yet the higher standards do not produce better lawyers:

> The ability to write examinations doesn't determine that you're going to be good or even competent. So it seems an awfully specific, unrealistic training. When I look back on it, I had fun. I liked law school, but I've been out for two years doing everything from bussing and washing dishes to being a waiter, to being a ditch digger. I look at law school now, and you've got these people who come straight out of high school, straight into university, straight into law school, straight into articles, straight into the workplace, divorced entirely from reality, brilliant, but a disaster when they start to practise. And there are too many of them. If you're going in because you want a nice secure career, forget it. You make a hell of a lot more money selling real estate, and it's probably more secure. Why sweat blood for three years just so you can come out and be unemployed? If you want money and security, go to med school.

Alex would discourage people from going into law, because he is "getting tired of the lawyer bashing." People do not understand or appreciate what lawyers do:

But, I tell you, as soon as we do something wrong they're on us. They don't like to pay for anything, but as soon as something goes wrong – they just don't appreciate the services rendered. I don't think they understand. It's part of our job to explain to them what we do, but they don't want to hear that, because they think you're charging for it. They just want the cheapest work you can do, and I'm getting tired of it. And I charge them less than the norm, so I'm never going to get rich doing this.

Georgina, who went to law school by default to get out of another area she was unhappy in, thinks that the "worst reason to go into law is that there is nothing else to do." The stress and the hours are not worth it. Her advice: "Become an optometrist if your goal is to make money. There are better jobs with more money and less stress." If she could do it again, she would go into the medical profession. Vera would also recommend the medical profession, because it is a more friendly profession and more open to part-time work. She finds her workplace rather depressing: "The people I work with don't give a shit about me personally. They really don't. Some of the partners will pay lip service to you, and ask how you are doing, and stuff like that; but you just come and go ... I think if you went and asked every partner what my kids' names are, they'd have difficulties, although those same guys will tell you all about their problems with their wives, with their kids, and what's the latest trauma ... But it's not reciprocated, so it's not a personal relationship."

Sybil would recommend neither law nor medicine. She lives in constant fear of being sued. She adds, "At least I know that the only grief I will have ever caused anybody will be money; but a doctor, you're playing with lives; that would be worse."

Sandra, one of the older respondents, recommended that older women be encouraged to go into law:

I think a lot of them are afraid to, partly because it's so intimidating to get into law school, but I think they have a lot to offer. I'm not talking about having to be in your fifties, I'm talking about people in their forties. Those that maybe had that aspiration, but then decided to have a family and stayed home and didn't do it, and then are afraid to get back into it. I found people helpful. Nobody has been trying to block [my return to law school] in any way. I have had lawyers say, "What the heck are you going to do that for?" But they're in a place in their own lives where they're getting disillusioned with, or bored with, law, and they can't see why anybody would want to start out at this point in life and get into what they feel is now a rut. [Interviewer: Is law something you would recommend?] Yes, I think if a person has the abilities and the motivation, I think it would be good. I think as job-sharing becomes more available and more effective, and as firms are more open to taking on more women, and as we try to deal with non-discriminatory clauses seriously, as long as we're not sixty-five, we're not going to be discriminated against so far as the Law Society is concerned. So I think that there's the opportunity to work, but to get into a smaller firm in which you can job-share. My own feeling would be that if a young woman lawyer had five or six years of experience or more and decided she wanted to stay home and have children and only work part time – to have an older woman, who maybe does not have the legal experience but had the time, who didn't have the pressures that small children put on you, [the two together] would be a good combination, because you could pick up for each other. I don't see that happening.

Sally thinks she would recommend law to some people – "people who are prepared to work hard, and who have a thick skin." Although it depends on the type of law lawyers are in, she thinks that law is for people who are prepared for the stress and personal sacrifices, because "there aren't enough hours in the day to be able to do everything well." She would like to see more flexibility, job-sharing, and a reduced workweek. However, she does not think this will happen without changed expectations for both women and men.

Nicole thinks that law is more difficult for women than for men. However, that does not mean that women should avoid law. Rather, "it means they should go into it in larger numbers." She feels "somewhat guilty" about getting out of the profession: "Maybe more women should be making demands, rather than saying, 'Okay, I'll leave. Goodbye.'"

A number of lawyers who work in smaller centres said they were great places to work, but chuckled about recommending it to others, because they did not want to increase the competition. Elizabeth explains:

The more competition we have out here, the more difficult it will be to do as well as we are, so I have a vested interest in keeping the population of counsel here down. However, I would sincerely encourage anyone to branch out – the bars are smaller, the sense of camaraderie is great, and the willingness to assist new counsel is incredible. It seems to be inexhaustible – far better chance of advancement; some difficulty in adjusting. I'm a big city girl, I grew up in [a large city], I lived in [a number of large cities], I'd never lived in a small town. The first year was difficult for me and my children; however, once we adjusted and started getting more involved in outdoor activities ... I truly love it up here now. I get down to the Lower Mainland when I can, go shopping and what not. I have no reservations about encouraging people to get out of the Lower Mainland.

Concluding Comments

The women and men in this study were similar in the two most frequent reasons they gave for going to law school; approximately one-third of the women and men went to law school because they had a keen interest in law, and one-third of them went to law school by default, with nothing better to do. Those lawyers who went to law school because they had a keen interest in law were more satisfied with the practice of law (58% of the women and 81% of the men) than those who were just looking for something to do. Only 33% of the women and 47% of the men in the latter group were satisfied with the practice of law. Similarly, lawyers who had a keen interest in law were more likely to predict they would be practising law five years from the time of the interview (68% of the women and 94% of the men), than those who were just looking for something to do. Only 47% of the women and 82% of the men in this latter group thought they would be practising five years from the time of the interview. However, when they were asked whether or not they would do it over again,[14] only 68% of the women and 69% of the men who had a keen interest in the practice of law said they would, and 47% of the women and 71% of the men who were just looking for something to do said they would do it over again. Half of the twelve women and four of the thirteen men who were dissatisfied with the practice of law overall would become lawyers if they had to do it over again. Five of the dissatisfied men were uncertain whether they would do it again. Career choices are obviously complicated decisions. However, as one might predict, those who go to law school out of interest, as opposed to because of having nothing better to do, are more likely to be satisfied with the practice of law.

There were some differences. The men (24%) were more likely than the women (10%) to go to law school to broaden their education or gain more control over their lives. Money was mentioned more frequently by men (18%) than women (10%), and pressure from family was mentioned more often by women (12%) than men (4%). The women (16%) were slightly more likely than the men (10%) to identify commitment to improving society or helping people as a reason for going to law school. However, it is important to remember that the respondents were not given a list of possible choices. Such lists affect the type of responses one receives.

Overall, the men (62%) were more satisfied with the practice of law than the women (50%); however, given the historical exclusion of women and the finding by other studies what women remain "fringe dwellers" in the legal community, perhaps the surprise is that the difference is not greater. A similar proportion of women and men in this study liked the following aspects of the practice of law: the challenge and satisfaction, a forum in which to interact with people, and knowledge and intellectual stimulation.

A similar proportion disliked the stress and responsibility, the hours worked and the pressure to bill, and jokes about lawyers. However, the women (18%) were more likely than the men (8%) to dislike the adversarial nature of the work.

While women and men go into law for similar reasons, their experiences once in practice, discussed in Chapters 3 through 6, are less similar.

3
Fitting In

Women lawyers work in an environment in which "the vast majority of members of the profession recognize the existence of gender bias in the profession."[1] Bias in employment opportunities takes place during hiring, during access to future employment opportunities, and during access to areas of practice. According to Madame Justice Wilson, "advancement is still controlled by men and perceptions of how women lawyers are different continue to impede their progress."[2] Studies consistently show that women lawyers make less than their male contemporaries, and that women are less likely to become partners in their law firms.[3]

This chapter examines where the respondents in this study are fitting into the established legal profession, three to seven years after they were called to the bar. What is their work history? How much money do the women make relative to the men? Where are the respondents in their rise to partnership in a firm? How many hours do they work? What are their future plans? Are they interested in being appointed judges?

Educational Background

The women and men who were interviewed for this study had similar educational backgrounds, except that the women were more likely to have clerked with a judge for part of their articles (16% of the women, compared with 4% of the men). Eight percent of the women and 10% of the men had earned graduate degrees in addition to their bachelor of laws, 74% of the women and 72% of the men had other bachelor degrees, while 18% of the women and 16% of the men had only bachelor of laws. Most of the respondents received their law degrees from the University of British Columbia (60% of the women and 64% of the men), or the University of Victoria (22% of the women and 14% of the men).

Work Histories

Only 54% of the women, compared with 76% of the men, had been practising law continuously since their call to the bar. This is somewhat surprising, given that lawyers who had been called at the same time as my respondents, but who were no longer practising law at the time I drew the sample, were excluded from the population before sampling (see the discussion of my sampling method in Chapter 1). Of those called between 1986 and 1990, 34.1% of the women and 25.6% of the men had already left the practice of law when I drew the sample in 1993. Of those I interviewed, 8% of the women and 18% of the men had not practised continuously because they had spent time looking for a position.

In terms of the number of full-time jobs practising law since their call, the men were more likely than the women (40%, compared with 26%) to have had only one such job. Forty-four percent of the women and 34% of the men had had two full-time jobs practising law; 28% of the women and 26% of the men had had more than two full-time jobs practising law. The women (12%) were more likely than the men (2%) to have had one or more jobs that, although not practising law, were law-related. This reflects rather a high degree of mobility (more so for women than for men), given that the respondents were all early in their legal careers (called between three and seven years).

Reasons for Leaving

The thirty-seven women respondents who had worked at more than one job since their call to the bar gave the following reasons for leaving their positions:[4] a falling-out or difficulty with people they worked with or for (35%), economics of the firm (32%), less stress, looking for balance (32%), tired of work (30%), moved to a better position (27%), discrimination (16%), no control over work (14%), and the adversarial nature of work (3%). The thirty men who had worked at more than one job since being called to the bar gave similar reasons: a falling-out or difficulty with people they worked with or for (47%), moved to a better position (40%), economics of the firm (23%), no control over work (27%), tired of work (23%), less stress, looking for balance (7%), adversarial nature of work (3%).

Some of the respondents, such as Kristine and Lois, moved on because of "difficult bosses." Nicole did not like the "crazy, crazy hours" she was expected to work, in a "patriarchal firm" with a "lot of unhappiness." The managing partner, who made all the decisions,

> would make inspections, believe it or not, around the office at six o'clock to make sure that people were still at their desks. I found that bothersome. I felt that I was there as a professional. Obviously, I was doing whatever it took to do my job right. I didn't need him checking in on me. It was very, very important to be seen there in the evenings and on weekends, just to be seen in the evenings and on weekends, and they had crazy things ... This one particular individual loved to go out for dinner

with his partners or associates, whoever would join him, to the Vancouver Club or some expensive restaurant. They always paid, but it would be an enormous meal, a two-hour dinner. It would take you out of the office for two hours ... and then going back to the office and working until ten or eleven at night. It was just stupid. It was very important to do that with them. It affected your chances of being kept on as an articling student, and being in the group as an associate. So I didn't like that. On the other hand, most of the people there were lawyers I really liked.

Similarly, Sybil had a "crazy boss," who would set appointments for her at six-thirty in the morning and six at night, just to make sure she was there. She hated the hours, and the fact that her boss "gouged people ... He would bill twenty-four hours in a day."

Olive hated her first job. She was getting paid less than summer students, and "they worked us like dogs." The lawyers she worked for had bad reputations, so that everyone who dealt with the firm "put everything that had ever happened in a phone conversation into a letter confirming it, because if it wasn't in a letter, it didn't happen." The lawyers were "very sharp and not to be trusted completely." Olive felt she was "getting tarred with that brush" and so, when she ran into another opportunity, she left the firm. Opal left a firm because she "hated the place." One of the partners did not speak to her for two years, because they had a debate about a particular topic, and he did not like the way she spoke to him. The firm eventually disintegrated, so she realized it was not just her, but that the firm was having problems.

Bruce left his first position because of the hours, the pressure to work more hours, and some of the partners. Carl left his first position after two years because his "bosses were dicks." Although he enjoyed his second job, he left it after two years because of personality conflicts. Now, not happy with the practice of law overall and his hours of work, he is satisfied with the control he has over his work as a sole practitioner, sharing an office. Gerry had a falling out with his employer at his first job, and he was "turfed." He is very happy with the group of lawyers he presently works with. Ian left his first position because of a dispute over his salary, and he wanted more independence. He now enjoys being on his own, so that he can make his "own decisions and not be answerable to anybody else."

Patrick took the first job that was offered to him after articles, because "times were economically tough." However, he did not like the environment at the firm. He left because of "a dispute over my value, unenjoyable working conditions, and lack of pay." Now, as an associate in a small law firm, he is satisfied with the practice of law and the control he has over his work. Although his income has increased, he gives it only a "four" on the satisfaction scale, mid-range on a scale ranging from very satisfied to very dissatisfied. Vernon left his first job because he thought he could do better financially by moving. He more than doubled his salary working the same hours at his second firm. He left this position because he did not like the partners, especially the ethics of one of them. Now associated with two lawyers, he is very satisfied with his income. Although still dissatisfied with the lack of balance he finds in his life, he realizes that much of his practice is "self-driven," and he could scale down and earn less.

A number of respondents had left jobs because of the bad economics of their firm, or the fact that their firm was falling apart. For example, Angela left a securities firm when the "market crashed and work dried up." Laura's articling firm gave her a two-month extension after articles, and then she worked for a firm that did contract work for the Insurance Corporation of British Columbia. She was laid off when ICBC cancelled its contract with her firm. Neil was laid off from a job with an eighty-five to ninety-hours a week that he hated. Now an associate in a small firm, he is working fifty hours a week, and is satisfied with his hours of work and his income (which is $12,000 a year lower than his income at his first firm).

Some of the women and men left their firms for better money or better positions. Betty moved from a low paying, disorganized firm to a firm that offered her more money. However, she was then terminated from this position because of a disability that she developed. Iris was doing mostly family law in a small town, when she was approached by a former colleague to move to a larger centre and set up a practice. She felt she was "going to get stuck with family law forever," so decided she would give it a try. Later, for lifestyle and other reasons, she returned to the town and found a different area of law to practise in. She now enjoys the practice of law, but would be happier with the type of law she practised if she were more "on top of it."

Rosa met a lawyer through some business her parents were conducting, and accepted a good deal in a small partnership. The cost of buying into her previous firm ($120,000 to $150,000) was prohibitive. She is happy with her hours of work (approximately forty-five hours a week) and the control she has over her work; however she is very dissatisfied with her income. She adds, "There are some extremely misleading pictures on what lawyers are making. Because I made some lifestyle decisions, it has affected my ability to earn a comparable income." Zackery moved from Crown counsel to a small firm with which he could do criminal litigation. The firm was looking for someone, and there was potential for advancement. He is very satisfied with the type of law he practises, and the control he has over his work.

Some of the respondents simply tired of the work they were doing. Donna left her first job at a large firm for a number of reasons. She was working "a tremendous number of hours – often seven days a week, and many nights until ten o'clock." Initially she liked the job, but she "gradually became disillusioned with it" and "felt used." She continued, "I didn't have control over the amount of work that I did. I didn't have control over the type of cases that I worked on. I didn't feel appreciated. I didn't feel properly compensated. I didn't feel that I had the opportunities within the firm that my ability should have entitled me to." She is making much more money now as a sole practitioner sharing an office, and she is very satisfied with the control she has over her work. However, doing primarily litigation means that there is sometimes too much work, and sometimes too little.

Holly has worked with four law firms since being called to the bar. She left her first job because she was not getting the "exposure and hands-on experience I wanted." She left her second job because the firm went through a restructuring, and had a bad mix of personalities. She left her third job because of a bad experience, and because she wanted control over her life: "I didn't want to be seen as a number, and I didn't want to be seen as so many dollars per square foot, and I didn't want to be a dog for other people. I was tired of the downtown work-till-you-drop." She is now much happier with her hours of work and the type of law she practises, but positions the "practice of law overall" and the "balance with her personal life" at "four," mid-range on a scale ranging from very satisfied to very dissatisfied.

Adam did not like anything about his first job, except for the money. He "didn't like the nature of practice, didn't like the partners, and didn't like the hours. The only thing I liked about it was the money. Every other aspect I disliked." A normal week was sixty hours, "a hellish number." He is now very satisfied with his hours, the type of law he practises (administrative), the control he has over his work, the balance with his personal life, and even his income. Fred left a department in a large downtown firm, because he was told he would not get the vote of the partner who ran the department. He did not particularly like the job. While the money and experience were good, he did not have much contact with clients, and he had no control over his work: "I did what I was told." It was not a big loss – "the partner was insane" – and everyone but one lawyer in that department had left. No one had stayed for more than three years. Now, working in one of the outlying municipalities for a firm with two locations, he is satisfied with his hours of work (forty-five hours per week) and the balance between work and his personal life. He makes less money, but he is very satisfied with the type of work he does. His present job allows him to make enough money, raise a family, and "have a life."

Rob liked the people at the firm he left, but he found it unrewarding to simply deal with a large number of people moving through his office – a "retail practice." He is much happier now, because his present job provides him with what he thought the practice of law was going to be, "working with the same people, and being a part of what they were doing." He now deals with three or four clients on an ongoing basis.

The women and the men gave similar reasons as to why they left their positions. However, the men were more likely than the women to mention a falling-out (or that people were difficult to work with), that they were moving to a better position, or that they wanted more control over their work. The women were more likely to mention that they were looking for less stress (more balance), and the existence of discrimination, as reasons for leaving their jobs. The quotations from the respondents show the variety of reasons these lawyers moved on from their earlier jobs, and that similar concerns were expressed by women and men, although not always in equal proportions.

Where the Respondents Work and What They Do
Approximately three-quarters of the women (74%) and the men (76%) worked in Vancouver, or other parts of the Lower Mainland, at the time they were interviewed. The men (50%) were more concentrated in downtown Vancouver than the women (40%). Sixteen percent of the women and 14% of the men worked in other cities with a population of more than 50,000. Six percent of the women and men worked in locations with populations between ten and fifty thousand, and 4% of the women and men worked in towns of under ten thousand.

In summarizing reports from law societies across Canada, Madame Justice Wilson stated that women were under-represented in private practice and over-represented in government positions.[5] Similarly, in this study, 62% of the women and 90% of the men worked in private firms, and 24% of the women and 6% of the men worked for government (this included one woman and two men who worked for government administrative agencies). Six percent of the women and none of the men in this study worked as corporate counsel (another area identified with the over-representation of women). The differences between the women and the men in this study are even greater than those Wilson summarized.[6] It appears as though there may be a trend for more women to move into government positions. This proposition is supported by the data from Fiona Kay and her associates. In 1990, approximately 11% of the men in her sample and 16% of the women were in government positions. In 1996, when she re-surveyed the same group, 11% of the men and 19% of the women were working for government.[7]

Type of Law Practised
In the two areas in which respondents most frequently practised,[8] women were more likely to practise family law than the men (20%, compared with 14%), and work in wills and estates (10%, compared with 4%). Men were

more likely than the women to practise real property (30%, compared with 10%), corporate-commercial (24%, compared with 12%), do civil litigation (38%, compared with 32%), and act as criminal defence counsel (16%, compared with 10%). Madame Justice Wilson writes that "it has been suggested that women are segregated into certain areas of practice, that they are being channelled into family law and estate practice, and are unable to fully penetrate corporate or general litigation practice."[9] This study confirms that suggestion.

In the concentration of their practice, 88% of the women and men spent 50% or more of their time in the area in which they practised most frequently, and 40% of the women and 20% of the men spent 100% of their time in one area. It is unclear what impact this greater specialization by some women has on their careers. However, of the twenty-eight women who spent 90% to 100% of their time in one area of law, 75% were satisfied with the type of law they practised,[10] and only one expressed dissatisfaction.

The respondents gave a variety of reasons for practising the type of law that they did. The most common factors were personal interest (30% of the women and 34% of the men), the availability of clients or the demands in the market (22% of the women and 26% of the men), and their previous experience as an articling student (20% of the women and 24% of the men). Others were slotted or pushed into their areas by employers (10% of the women and 4% of the men), some just fell into their areas of practice (6% of women and 12% of men), some respondents were avoiding courtroom appearances (10% of the women and 6% of the men), and other respondents were looking for more flexibility and less stress in their present areas of practice (8% of the women and 10% of the men).

When I asked the respondents what they believed their personal strengths were for their particular type of practice, I was able to code 129 responses from the fifty women, and 122 responses from the fifty men. Table 1 shows the skills that were mentioned by four or more women or men.

While women did not specifically mention their non-adversarial skills, such skills could easily be considered to be included in "people skills" and other skills women attributed to themselves. Other strengths mentioned by the respondents included the ability to remain detached, common sense, the ability to handle stress, an interest in the area practised, their non-aggressive approach, maturity, training as an articling student, thick skin, knowledge of a language in addition to English, and so on.

Career Advancement and Mobility

In a prior survey of the legal profession in British Columbia in 1990, the most frequently identified type of bias or discrimination against women in the legal profession was career advancement, identified by 75.5% of the

Table 1

Respondents' personal strengths for the practice of law

Personal strength	Number of women	Number of men
People skills	21	11
Analytical ability	10	10
Empathy and compassion	9	5
Advocacy skills	8	7
Prior experience or knowledge in the area	8	8
Time management skills	8	5
Communication skills	7	–
Ability to deal with details	7	4
Problem-solving skills	7	–
Writing skills	7	–
Persistence or aggression	7	–
Good business sense	–	4
Non-adversarial abilities	–	4
Total number of responses	99	58

women and 43.7% of the men. In that survey, when asked about the opportunities to advance in their firms, 41.1% of the women and 14.9% of the men said that men had a much better or slightly better chance of advancing in their firm; 29.4% of the women and 50.8% of the men thought there was an equal chance of advancing for women and men.[11]

When the 100 lawyers who were interviewed for this study were asked whether they thought there was bias or discrimination against women in the legal profession today that restricts their career advancement,[12] 88% of the women and 66% of the men said "Yes." Only 4% of the women and 18% of the men said there was no such discrimination against women. We return to the issue of discrimination in Chapter 4.

Income[13]

Studies have shown that women do not make as much income as men practising law.[14] Various theories have offered multifaceted explanations for these differences.[15] Human capital theory explains differential income between women and men by suggesting that women do not invest as much in their education and training as men. Kay and Hagan point to a number of problems with this theory, including the fact that research consistently shows that women get paid less for their investments in human capital than men.[16] Dual labour market theories suggest that the marketplace discriminates, in that women are placed in or choose peripheral or secondary positions (low paying, dead-end jobs), rather than the core or primary labour market positions which provide for higher incomes and greater security.[17] According to Kay and Hagan, neither of these theories "consider relational aspects of the division of labour (i.e., ownership, supervisory authority, discretion in controlling monetary resources)."[18]

Kay and Hagan test these theories using the concept of "mobility ladders," and a class taxonomy which is "grounded in ownership relations, number of lawyers in firm or office, authority, participation in policy-making decisions, work autonomy, and hierarchical position."[19] They tested their theory using sophisticated analyses on lawyers' income, from data they collected in 1990, from Toronto lawyers who were called in 1975 or later. The authors found an interaction between gender and experience, in that income for men rose much more rapidly than for women as careers progressed. Their results suggest that "earning differentials remain after one takes into account differences in credentials, positions, and organizations. Men are rewarded more for their human capital acquisitions. Men reap greater income rewards from experience and from elite law school education than women."[20]

The Appendix explains the statistical analysis that was done on the data in this study. The figure and table in the Appendix clearly show that women may make slightly more than men by the third year of their call, but their incomes do not rise appreciably, whereas the incomes of men lawyers increase sharply as they become more experienced. In fact, the offsetting Sex-by-Seniority interaction is so great that by about three-and-a-half years of call, the positive sex effect for women is completely negated by the negative effect of the interaction. It may be that, in the legal profession at least, women not only run into a glass ceiling, but in fact they start out very close to it. The finding that there is a gender effect on income of even such a homogeneous group as lawyers called from three through seven years is probably not surprising. Even in the most conscious of professions (something the law is apparently not), gender bias in remuneration persists, often to the astonishment of those in a position to deal with it. What *is* surprising is the clear interaction between gender and seniority, in a group that differs so little in seniority.

These results confirm the findings of Kay and Hagan[21] in their survey of Ontario lawyers, that there is an interaction between gender and experience, in that income for men rises much more rapidly than for women as their careers progress. This study did not, however, replicate their results showing effects of size of firm and hours worked.

Time in Present Position

The women respondents had been at their present jobs for an average of 25.6 months (a median of fifteen months) when they were interviewed, whereas the men had been at their present jobs for an average of forty-one months (a median of forty months). Table 2 shows the average time the respondents were in their present jobs by year of call. The table shows a trend to an increase in disparity between women and men, the more senior they become. Men called in 1986 and 1987 had spent substantially more time in their present positions than the women called in those years. As might be expected, there was less disparity for those most recently called. Looking at the women as a group, there was little difference between the women called four, five, and seven years in how long they had been at their present position.

Ten of the seventeen women (59%) called in 1986 and 1987 had been in their present position for less than eighteen months ("short term"). The other seven had been in their present positions between forty-five and seventy-four months ("long term"). In contrast, only two of the nineteen men called in 1986 and 1987 had been in their present positions for less than eighteen months, and fifteen (79%) had been in their positions between forty-eight and eighty-nine months. The other two had been in their present positions for thirty-six months.

In comparing the women with short-term and long-term careers in law, marriage and children do not distinguish them, as one might predict. The women with long-term careers were more likely to be married and to have children (although the numbers are small, and it is difficult to generalize about children). Six of the ten women with short-term careers in law, compared with six of the seven women with long-term careers, were living in married or equivalent relationships. Only two of the women with short-term careers and three of the women with long-term careers had children.

There was little difference between the women with short-term careers and the women with long-term careers in their perceptions of and experience with discrimination. Eight of the ten women with short-term careers thought there was bias or discrimination against women in the legal profession, one thought there was bias but that it was not overt, and the tenth said there was none. Six of the seven women with long-term careers said there was bias or discrimination against women in the legal profession, and one was ambivalent. Seven of the ten women with short-term careers

Table 2

Average number of months respondents were in their present job by year of call

	Year of call				
	1990	1989	1988	1987	1986
Women	17	25.8	27.3	33.9	26.8
Men	26.5	23.1	32.3	54.4	69.2

had experienced discrimination (two said it was not overt), one had not, and two did not know. Five of the seven women with long-term careers had experienced discrimination, one had described what appeared as discrimination but she did not call it that, and one had not experienced discrimination. Most of the women with careers in law, both short- and long-term, not only thought there was discrimination, but had experienced it.

One of the differences between the women with short-term and long-term careers was that the women with short-term careers had practised in large firms. At least six of the ten women with short-term careers had practised with large law firms on a partnership track. One, who had excellent reviews throughout her three years on the job, was told, "While there are no guarantees, we're happy with you and would be pleased to make you a partner." Six months later she was informed that she was not going to be made a partner. When asked whether she had any idea why that was, she responded:

> No, but that's an interesting question. No one has come right out and been honest and told me why I'm not going to be made partner. What they have said is, "It's nothing to do with your work, we like your work, you're popular," and all those sorts of things, "You'll get great references." So, I've never been told why. I can speculate and say that perhaps the truest reason is that I just don't have enough of a client base of my own to be able to support myself as a partner, because my experience and what I'm good at mean that I'm not a rainmaker. I don't bring in clients. My skill is in putting in the billable hours and working under a senior partner who refers the work to me, and I do it and he has the comfort of knowing that it's done well and the client will be happy. I don't have much of a client base of my own, nor do I make an effort to be involved or pound the pavement for it. And nowadays, in a downtown law firm, even partners have to account for their own economic viability. In a different economic climate I may have been made a partner, because the firm believes that good people shouldn't be let go. There's no point in hashing that out, they don't want to say, whatever it is. I know what I'm capable of doing. I know how people regard me in this firm and, if that's the case, then I'm better off not being here. So, I went out to look. I'm leaving.

This respondent was on the partnership track. She was working fifty-hour weeks, six days a week, sometimes until three or four in the morning, sometimes seven days a week. She loves the law and devotes all of her time and energy to it. It is one of the reasons she was still single and childless. Her move out of private practice means she is no longer on a partnership track.

A second woman with a short-term career had left a large firm after five years, one year away from being considered for partnership. Initially, she enjoyed the work but then "gradually became disillusioned with it, and began to feel used." She comments, "I didn't have control over the amount of work that I did. I didn't have control over the type of cases that I worked on. I didn't feel appreciated. I didn't feel properly compensated. I didn't feel that I had the opportunities within the firm that my ability should have entitled me to." She worked such long hours she could not count them, but they amounted to "significantly all of [her] life." When she left, she had no idea whether she would have made it to partnership:

> It was hard to tell at the time. It's not in the firm's interest to make everybody a partner. They need more associates than partners or they won't have the financial leverage that they get from working all the juniors' asses off, so, I don't know. I can't say whether I would have been offered a partnership or not. I know that people I worked with were satisfied with my work, but that's not what decides whether or not you become a partner. I came to the practice of law much later than most people, so I didn't expect to fill as junior a role within the organization of the firm as my years of call would indicate. I didn't realize before I got in there that it was as lockstep as it is, and I thought there would be more opportunities for compensation based on merit or advancement based on merit.

A third woman with a short-term career had practised two-and-a-half years with a large firm and found that the partners were more comfortable dealing with male associates, the "plum cases" went to them. She left because there was "too much of a pecking order," and she was not getting the experience that she wanted. A fourth woman with a short-term career had practised with a large firm for seven years, but left because it was "male-dominated." A lawyer's life revolves around the hours he or she can bill, and this woman felt that it was difficult for women to build up a practice; most of the women in the firm had left. I asked her what kind of woman would fit into this firm. She responded, "A woman that had absolutely no other life, who was one of the boys." A fifth woman with a short-term career had practised with a large firm for three years, working sixty-five to seventy-hour weeks, from eight in the morning until seven in the evening. She hated the hours and the lack of control over her life. A sixth woman had started at a big law firm, was laid off, and then was invited back one-and-a-half years later at a reduced salary. She was uncertain as to whether she was now on the partnership track, or whether she was a permanent associate. Since it was not important to her to know one way or the other, she had not tried to clarify her position.

None of the seven women with long-term careers practised in a large firm, and only four of them were in private practice. One was in partnership with her husband, and the other three practised as associates in firms with five to eighteen lawyers. Only one was interested in partnership; however, she was looking elsewhere for partnership (something she wished she had done some time ago, rather than sticking with "the devil" she knew). One woman was looking to move from a shared arrangement to a position as an associate, and another was looking to move from being an associate to sole practice.

Where Do They Want to Be?

To gain some insight into career aspirations, I asked the respondents whether they thought they would be practising law in five years, and what type of working arrangement they wanted to have if they were practising law. Twice as many women (16%) as men (8%) said they would not be practising law; 68% of the women and 78% of the men said they would likely be practising law; and 16% of the women and 14% of the men did not know for sure.

Only 50% of the women, compared with 70% of the men, wanted the same working arrangement in five years. Twenty-six percent of the women and 42% of the men worked as associates in law firms, and only 8% of these women and 2% of these men wanted to be associates in five years. Thirteen male associates, and only one female associate, aspired to partnership.

When they were interviewed, only six women (12%) and ten men (20%) were partners in law firms. Three of the women partners (half of them) were in partnership with one other lawyer – their spouse – the other three women were in small firms (two in firms with fewer than five lawyers, and one in a firm of fewer than twenty lawyers). In contrast, only one of the male partners was in partnership with his spouse. Five of the ten men who were partners worked in firms with twenty or more lawyers, three of them for firms with fifty or more lawyers.

Only 18% of the women, compared with 48% of the men, were interested in being partners in five years (this number included the women and men who were already partners – all of them still wanted to be partners five years from the time I interviewed them).[22] Looking more closely at the three women who wanted to be partners, one wanted to move into a small partnership from a sole practitioner, office-sharing arrangement. The second, who worked as an associate in a large firm, was thinking about children, as well as partnership in her firm within three years:

> Regarding women partners – it's not something that I get concerned about because I feel that if I'm going to be admitted, I'm going to be admitted on my merits, not on whether I'm a woman or a man. I haven't seen anything in the admitting processes that would cause me any concern. [Interviewer: Do you think you'll still be practising law five years from now?]

That's a hard question to answer. My mindset now is that if I have a child, I'd like to spend some time at home with that child, and since I'm not getting any younger, chances are that five years from now I'm likely to have a small child. Yes, subject to the caveat of spending more time at home with my child and, even if I'm at home, I may try and work something in part time. It depends on the kid.

The third woman was looking at partnership in a firm of four to five lawyers; however, there was a person three years her senior who had still not been asked to become a partner. She is presently looking elsewhere, and regrets not having moved when she had an opportunity.

Fourteen men aspired to partnership, in addition to the ten men who were already partners. Seven of the fourteen worked in law firms with twenty or more lawyers, and seven worked in law firms with fewer than fifteen lawyers. Of the seven men who worked in law firms with twenty or more lawyers, all but one saw nothing hindering their ascent to partnership in their present firm. The remaining lawyer thought that a change in the political landscape affecting the firm's agency work might affect his partnership opportunities. Of the seven men who worked in smaller firms, six were looking for partnership in the firm they were with, and the seventh man was a sole practitioner looking to move to a partnership. Of the six men who were looking to become partners in their firms, four saw nothing that would hinder their partnership aspirations, one thought he would make partnership if he did not "screw up," and another thought that lack of clients could affect his ability to become a partner.

This study confirms, in simplistic detail, what other studies have found through sophisticated data analyses. Women do not become partners at the same rate as men, women are more likely to remove themselves or be removed from partnership track than men, and women appear to have to perform better than men to achieve partnership. In some cases, no matter what women do, they are not considered partnership material.

Kay and Hagan analyzed two data sets from Ontario: a study completed in 1990 of a disproportionately stratified random sample of lawyers called between 1975 and 1990, and a re-survey of these lawyers in 1996. From their 1990 study, the authors conclude that "men are about 92 percent more likely than women to be invited to partnership ... *This finding supports more anecdotal studies and suggests that, regardless of experience and other background characteristics, men have consistently better prospects for partnership than women.*"[23] By 1996, things had not improved for women in the partnership arena; men were 110% more likely to become partners than the women.[24] According to Kay and Hagan, men gain more benefits from doing partnership activities: "First, human capital variables predict the probability of partnership better for men than for women. Years of experience and specialization status have significant positive effects upon the probability of partnership for men, but not for women. Billing high hours and working late hours are important to the partnership prospects of men, but for women it is additional hours worked as overtime, evenings, and weekends that yield advantages in the partnership tournament."[25]

Kay and Hagan have explored a number of different explanations for the differential partnership success of women and men. As with their work on differential income, they use human capital theory and structural discrimination. In the latter case, "the organization of law practice and work structures within law firms are exclusionary to many women and unaccommodating to the increasing diversity of lawyers."[26] The authors have also added social capital (from the work of Pierre Bourdieu and James Coleman) to their theoretical perspective. Social capital refers to the relationships and connections that individuals have (that is, who you are and who you know becomes important). One not only has social, cultural, and economic capital, but one has to play these cards correctly in the "partnership tournament."[27] Unfortunately for women, the right social capital is hard to come by. Even if women have inherited social capital (the right parents), developed networking capital (the right contacts), achieved time-dependent social capital (the time to network), and accessed practice-setting capital (the right firm in size, number of women, and geographical area), they still are less likely to become partners than men. Their social capital is less valued than that of men. Another factor may be operating, as well. Studies on discrimination illustrate that often decision makers discriminate by seeking "social similarity among people being selected for positions."[28] If being a woman is part of the social capital that a woman brings to a job, it is little wonder that the other social capital she brings offers her "less currency in the partnership tournament."[29]

All but one of the men on partnership track whom I interviewed were comfortable that nothing would stand in their way. The only man who expressed any doubt stated that the firm's agency work could disappear, depending on the government in power. The women who had been on partnership track before I met them had either been told they were not going to make it (but would be given stellar references), or were leaving because they did not think they would make partnership, or did not feel welcomed in their firm. Kay and Hagan summarize four ways, discussed by Lamont and Lareau (1988), that women might be excluded from partnership based on social capital. Women might simply eliminate themselves from the competition for a variety of reasons (uncomfortable or unfamiliar with the culture; desire for more flexibility). Women may be eliminated or leave because they are required to do more than others (double, triple, and quadruple shifts). Women may be relegated to less desirable work. Finally, women may be directly excluded by discrimination. It appears as though all of these factors were operating in the professional lives of the women I interviewed.

As a woman who articled in both Alberta and British Columbia, and who had no interest whatsoever in working for a large firm, much less becoming a partner in a large firm, the obvious question that comes to my mind is, Do women define success differently, or do they simply desire different types of careers? This question is also raised by Kay and Hagan,[30] and by many critics of the work on women in the legal profession. This question is extremely difficult to answer. The women I interviewed, who were leaving or had left partnership track positions, were extremely successful women. They were positive about their moves and they were not looking back, at least not during the time allotted for my interviews. There were also men who had left the "rat race" of large firms because they had no interest in becoming partners in large downtown firms. However, there did not appear to be any men who, on the verge of partnership, were being told that they were not going to make it. Ten percent of the women I interviewed (but none of the men) were dissatisfied with their opportunities for advancement in their work.[31] I do not think that it would be stretching the data to suggest that there are women who define success as partnership, who appear to have all of the qualities of partners, but who are still not winning the partnership game.

Aspirations to the Judiciary

In 1993, Madame Justice Wilson reported that women were under-represented in the judiciary. At that time, in British Columbia, 13% of federally appointed judges and 19% of provincially appointed judges were women.[32] According to Statistics Canada, 13% of all judges in Canada were women in 1986, and this figure rose to 20% in 1991, and to 21% in 1996. Between 1994 and 1997, 35.8% of the 212 federal appointments were women.[33]

Respondents in my study were asked whether they would like to be a judge sometime in the future. Although none of the respondents mentioned judgeship when they were asked what type of work arrangement they would like in five years, 30% of the women and 24% of the men said they would like to be a judge in the future, whereas, 44% of the women and 56% of the men said, "No." The remaining respondents were not sure, did not know or, in the case of three women, did not expect to be in the legal profession in five years, and therefore did not aspire to being a judge. When asked why they would not want to become a judge, the two most common reasons were that there was too much responsibility and stress involved in being a judge (mentioned by eighteen women and seventeen men), and that they would not like the social isolation that goes with being a judge (mentioned by eleven women and eighteen men). Other reasons included a lack of desire for the job (eight women and seven men), lack of a litigation background (seven women and eight men), a reluctance to listen to what they would have to hear (five women and seven men), a lack of desire to stay in practice long enough to become a judge (five women and four men), a feeling they would not be any good at it (four women and three men), and insufficient objectivity to sit as a judge (one woman and four men). One woman did not want to play the distasteful games that she believed it would take to become a judge.[34]

The most common reason for the respondents to be interested in being appointed a judge was that they thought they would make good decisions, and had a good sense of the law (nine women and twelve men). Seven women and four men were attracted by the academic side of being a judge; ten men and two women liked the benefits that went with being a judge (for example, steady income, pension); eight men and four women thought being a judge would be less stressful (better hours, no time sheets, no clients calling at night); three men and two women thought the prestige or recognition was attractive; four women and three men saw it as a positive career change; one woman and two men wanted to see the courtroom from another perspective; and three women would consider being a judge because they thought there should be more women judges.

Are They Fitting In?

Both women and men lawyers identify similar strengths when it comes to practising law, and they seem to leave legal positions for similar reasons. However, women are more likely to work in government positions than men, and are not evenly distributed across areas of legal work. They earn less money than men, and they spend less time in legal positions.

The majority of the respondents (88% of the women and 66% of the men) thought bias or discrimination against women in the legal profession restricts their career advancement. Previous studies of partnership opportunities have painted a bleak picture for partnership opportunities for women. This study confirms that bleak picture and also illustrates that a much higher proportion of women than men have no expectation or, perhaps, aspiration of becoming partners in law firms. Whether this can be characterized as their "choice" is addressed in Chapter 7. Chapter 4 addresses two of the major barriers identified by women as barriers to equality in the legal profession – discrimination and sexual harassment.

4
Discrimination and Sexual Harassment

Gender bias and discrimination in the legal profession have been documented throughout the world.[1] Numerous studies have also been conducted in Canada.[2] Some of the studies that Madame Justice Wilson relied on in her Report to the Canadian Bar Association had asked lawyers about their perceptions of gender bias or discrimination in the legal profession; others had asked about the lawyers' experience with it. For example, in the Saskatchewan survey, 92% of the women and 12% of the men had experienced sexual discrimination and, in Ontario, 70% of the women and 6% of the men had experienced such discrimination. In the survey of active members of the Law Society of British Columbia, 98% of the women and 83% of the men were of the view that there was some bias or discrimination against women in the legal profession. In the survey of members of the Law Society of Alberta, 97% of the women and 78% of the men thought there was some bias or discrimination against women in the legal profession.[3]

The most frequently cited form of perceived gender bias in the British Columbia and Alberta surveys was in relation to career advancement – identified by more than 75% of the women and more than 40% of the men in British Columbia and Alberta. Attaining partnership was the next most frequently identified sphere in which women were discriminated against, cited by more than 60% of the women, and more than 30% of the men in British Columbia and Alberta. In 1996, Fiona Kay, reporting on her study of Ontario lawyers, stated that "25% of the men and 61% of the women felt men were more favoured in attaining partnership; 27% of the men and 70% of the women felt men were favoured in general career advancement."[4]

The 100 interviewees in this study were asked whether they had ever been discriminated against in the legal profession on any of the grounds set out in the Law Society's Rule[5] and, if so, whether it was by other lawyers, judges, or clients. They were then asked about any professional or personal consequences of the discrimination.[6] This chapter examines their responses.

Experience with Gender Discrimination

Sixty percent of the women interviewed said they had been discriminated against in the legal profession on the basis of their sex, while 4% of the men said they had been discriminated against on the basis of sex. The women lawyers were most likely to experience discrimination from other lawyers (77% of the thirty women experiencing discrimination), then from judges (33%), and then from clients (27%). One woman did not know whether she had been discriminated against by clients. She commented, "I suppose I would never know whether a particular client didn't come to me because I was female."[7]

Discrimination by Other Lawyers

Forty-six percent of the fifty women respondents encountered discrimination from other lawyers. One woman was discriminated against in salary: "My salary has been affected at different firms that I have worked at, just because I'm female and have been single. Salary is at the forefront. There is a perception among older men, the partners who are deciding your salary, that I'm single, I'm female, I don't have as many obligations, financially I don't have dependants, therefore I'm willing to take less money. I think that has affected the salary offers I've been given."

However, need is not always a factor. Another woman, who had billed substantially more than the others of her experience, was stunned when she discovered that a summer student was being paid more than she was, because he was from a wealthy family, and the firm was hoping he would stay with them and bring in business. He did not stay.

A number of women explained how their opinion was given less weight, or how they were not taken as seriously as the men:

> Well, I went through a large firm, and I feel as if I'm as bright and capable as any of the males who were my senior, and I didn't have a particularly good experience there. I don't know how much of that relates to my being female, but I attribute at least some of it to that, and maybe to the type of female that I am, because I noticed that females who were submissive and who were inclined to say, "Yes, sir, you're right, sir," got along better than I did. I was more inclined to say what I thought. There's no doubt that it was a men's club I was in, and it was blatant. The guys would go around at lunchtime sticking their heads in the doors of other lawyers who were males and saying, "Do you want to go for lunch?" It wouldn't occur to them to stick their head in my door, you know, or [to invite] other women. So that's just one slight example of it, and that didn't affect my career, but in my experience there are lots of lawyers who, within the firm, would tend to discount the opinions or suggestions,

when they were working on a case or matters within the firm, if they were coming from a woman.

I think that there's a lot of subtle stuff, that people don't listen to you in the same way, that women in general have a tendency to be less authoritarian. I suspect that men are more likely to say very firmly, "This is the way it is," whereas women are more likely to say, well, "Let's be a little more cautious." And so you're not given the same degree of credibility. I know that there is – I can see it in the people here that I work with – there's a deference to some of the men. They just don't give the same validity to my knowledge and experience as they do to a man's, even when that man is telling them that I'm much more of an expert in that area than he is. But it's not as outrageous now. Most of the discrimination happened before I became a lawyer.

Social opportunities are sometimes a double-edged sword for women. This may be why the homosocial bonds that cement opportunities for men often undermine opportunities for women. One woman felt excluded from "the loop," in that she was not invited for lunches or a beer after work, while another felt that she was working in "the old boys' network, in which if you're not out playing golf, you're not out winning clients." Another commented:

In the beginning there used to be a lot of the old boys going out for lunch and coffee, and they would never invite me along. That has changed over the course of time, but I had to be aggressive about butting in on some of the old boys going out together. I think that I conquered that aspect. For the other women in my office, there's still no excuse for them not being at the same levels of seniority. I think my superiors know we're not happy about that. I don't know what will happen. It's a real hot issue here, and there's a lot of it [gender discrimination].

For some women, the allocation of work is a problem. One woman worked in a "a firm of old boys." The men did the trial work, which was more interesting, while she was in the library writing memos. Another woman found that senior partners were more comfortable dealing with male associates, so the "plum cases went to the males." There were other female litigators in the firm who felt the same way she did. Two women were not given clients because the clients would not have been comfortable with, or were viewed as not wanting to deal with, women. One respondent commented, "Well, you know, I thought, that's fair, I probably wouldn't have liked them anyway."

Some of the men saw women being excluded from work:

When in private practice, it was difficult for women to get good solicitor's work. The solicitors wouldn't give them work, they didn't want to work with them, and they justified it by saying clients didn't want to work with them. Because solicitor's work tends to be more clubby work, it was easier for it to happen. It's easier for women to get files in litigation, they could be discretely parcelled off, they were for small amounts and, once you were doing the litigation, it became easier to advance and establish a track record in court and get the good files. You could do *pro bono* work, which could get you a high profile, whereas solicitor's work depended upon the whims of those above you on the ladder. Even in the litigation area, the firm I was at, the most-senior litigator didn't like working with women, tried to avoid it, and so did one of the other four most-senior litigators. Even in litigation, it was probably more difficult for women to stay on. It wasn't impossible. There were women who were partners who did well, but they tended to be women who came from elsewhere – who had somehow built up a practice elsewhere – and then were wooed into the firm. They were parachuted in. They didn't depend on the other partners in the firm for their advancement.

One respondent, a lone woman lawyer in the office, had to lunch with the lawyers, whereas the male associate could go home for lunch with his wife. The respondent was being "checked out," to see whether she fit in. The ceremonial scrutiny was not required of the male associate: "He was accepted as one of the boys already." Any socializing with the staff was seen as "some kind of mutiny, or not knowing my place in the hierarchy." Although she did not mind drinking "with the boys," she was glad to have left the firm.

At an articling interview, one of the women was told that she was lucky to get an interview, because she was a woman. She was told about the one woman the firm had hired who had become pregnant eight months later. He made it clear to her that she would not be hired: "He told me right then and there I wasn't going to get the job because I'm a woman. He asked me all about my personal life, and said that it sounded far too stressful to be able to devote enough time to the office."

One woman had to deal with lawyers who attempted to bully her, and who made "real sexist comments," but she dealt with it, by either teasing the person in response, telling them it was "entirely inappropriate," or getting "pissed off." She added, "But sometimes the statements were so outrageous I just laughed and said something like, 'You can't really think that that asshole statement is going to intimidate me?' They were just so dumb." To her, it was not a big issue. Another woman was called "babe" by a lawyer. She too dealt with it (by telling him she did not appreciate it), and the offensive lawyer was apologetic. Another woman disliked the paternalistic attitude of the partners. She commented, "It's like I moved 5,000 miles across the country to leave my father ... and yet I have two of them right here at my doorstep. There's a paternalistic attitude, as if they have to help a little bit more because you're a woman, you're the weaker sex. That's the sense I have."

Two men said they had been discriminated against on the basis of gender. One wanted to move to government, but was told that the government does not hire from majority groups as a matter of policy. Another man commented on his treatment by a woman lawyer: "Just because I'm a male, she thinks I'm an animal for defending this guy. I mean she's a zealot; anybody who would defend someone charged with sexual abuse (it doesn't even matter how minor), they're just creeps, obviously."

Discrimination by Judges or Masters

Twenty percent of the women respondents, but none of the men, reported discrimination by judges on the basis of gender. Some judges were condescending and patronizing; however, the men lawyers did not appear to receive the same treatment. One woman remembers a judge who was invited to the law school to give a talk. Later, in the hallway, he told her she was "taking up a position in the law school that a man would be better able to take and follow through." He asked her whether she was aware that she would make more money if she "went and married [her]self a doctor or a dentist and stayed home and had kids." These forms of gender harassment were probably more damaging in the past; however, such behaviour can still have a devastating effect on women.

One woman described a judge who was well known for his strong prejudices:

Male over female, older over younger – about the only time when he isn't insulting to a female practitioner is when he's got another female practitioner. If he's got both of them, he'll take the lesser of two evils, which is usually the elder. She'll be given a certain respect. [Interviewer: How is he insulting?] [He'll say] "I don't need to hear from you," "sit down," various other forms of comments to that effect. The one I'm thinking about right now is something I've heard from another case. There was a woman representing an accused, Crown counsel was male, the other accused's counsel was male. The judge in his chambers was willing to listen to both male attorneys but basically told the woman to sit down and shut up. I had him on a number of matrimonial applications, and he was rude.

Another woman relayed an incident from a friend of hers, who had just returned from court:

> She was almost in tears, she was so frustrated and upset. She had the distinct sense that the judge was behaving in a paternalistic way, that he would not have behaved [that way] with a male lawyer. She was so frustrated, she wondered whether she was doing her client a favour acting for them or not, being a female, if her client would have been better off having a man in front of that particular judge instead of her. I don't know, every judge I go before brings to the job his or her own biases and prejudices, and all that. I haven't experienced it with female judges, but I certainly have with some of the male judges, and particularly the older ones. If there's a male lawyer appearing for one client and a female for the other, they'll give less weight, less credence to what the female is saying. They'll be more inclined to accept the arguments of the male. "He must be right if he's male." They probably never [consciously] go through that thought process.

When asked whether there was discrimination in the legal profession that restricted women's career advancement, 12% of the women (but none of the men) mentioned judicial attitudes. It should be kept in mind that the respondents were not asked whether women were discriminated against by judicial attitudes. When that specific question was asked of respondents in the Alberta survey, 54.5% of the women and 21.7% of the men identified judicial attitudes as a field in which women were discriminated against in the legal profession.[8]

Discrimination by Clients

Sixteen percent of the women respondents, but none of the men, said they had been discriminated against by clients. One woman had a problem with middle-aged business clients who did not take her seriously. They would call her "sweetheart, that kind of stuff." She was not sure whether it was discrimination, or whether it was "just the way they were brought up." She added, "The fact of life is that some middle-aged business men just have difficulty with the fact that I'm younger and I'm a woman. Some of them find me attractive, and they just have a hard time thinking I have anything intelligent to say to them." Another woman was sick of clients calling her "dear," a term she was sure that her male colleagues did not hear from their clients. A number of women thought that their clients would have preferred a man lawyer. One female client, to the lawyer's amusement, thought that a man would be more aggressive.

When asked whether there was discrimination in the legal profession that restricted women's career advancement, 12% of the women and 8% of the men mentioned clients. Again, the respondents were not asked this specific question but an open-ended question about discrimination, generally. In the British Columbia survey, 23.1% of the women and 4.9% of the men who were specifically asked said they had been denied an opportunity to work on a file (in the previous five years) because a client objected to them doing so on the basis of gender. In the Alberta survey, 49.7% of the women, but only 14.2% of the men, had had such an experience.[9]

Ambiguities Surrounding Discrimination

Three additional women said they were probably discriminated against on the basis of gender, but it was insufficiently overt to pin down. One commented,

> I don't feel that the practice of law is a friendly place for women, although it may be changing, and I am pleased to see that. It's a function of a number of things: the profession is conservative to begin with; once one starts out in practice there are great, great pressures to conform, and what you are conforming to is a set of ideas and values of senior people in the firm, who are men because of the configuration of the profession, who are conservative.

> Not overtly – the discrimination that I expect happens is on the subliminal level, which is that people are people and they grow up with certain beliefs, prejudices, and biases which will govern how they act. For example, if a lawyer doesn't want to deal with a woman, doesn't want to deal with a woman [of colour] in particular, then he or she would simply not refer a particular file or a particular client to me. There's no way I can know that, or suspect it even, because in a law firm the senior partner has the luxury of delegating a file to any one of a number of associates, all of whom are equally bright. It may be as simple as [the fact that] he or she doesn't like the colour of my hair and won't refer a file to me. Is it because of race, or because I'm a woman, or [is it that] he just doesn't like me? You don't know that. So it's hard for me to say that I have ever been the victim of overt discrimination. Most people who get past law school know that it's uncouth, bad manners, to make racist, sexist remarks in public to a fellow lawyer, within the same firm certainly.

> I think a lot of times, if there is discrimination, not just in law but in life, it is not overt, so you don't go out and say it right to their faces.

Others just did not know whether they had been discriminated against, or whether they would call it discrimination. One woman was not aware of discrimination, but realized she may not see its occurrence: "It's like when you go to rent an apartment, and you're a black fellow aged nineteen, and the manager says it's rented. You don't know whether the apartment is rented or whether he's reacting to you." Another woman had been asked about her plans for a family, and more recently in an interview with five men, she was asked whether she had any problems with being interviewed by five men: "I thought that was totally outrageous. They wouldn't ask the guys that. So I don't know that I would call it discrimination ... And it is unfortunate, but discrimination? No, not to the extent I would go to the Law Society. But sometimes I feel that I may not be advancing to the extent that I should. That I'm being treated differently by my client than a male lawyer would be."

One woman said she did not find the legal profession a problem, or think she had experienced any discrimination, even though the law was "still an old boys' club," and she knew other women who had been discriminated against. Another woman had not experienced discrimination, but thought it was because she had chosen not to go through interviews with large firms, or perhaps she was "just lucky that way." Another woman said she had escaped discrimination because she was single.

One woman felt she had had some concessions because she is female; for example, it was okay to cry if stress got to her. Another woman thought she had been given some advantages because she was a woman; however, when she was asked what she meant, she commented: "Well, the first firm I was at ... there were no women and there were two articling students, me and another male. And I honestly believe that the firm was desperate to get a woman because of their lack of women ... We were both kept on at the end of the day, but if we had been equally competent, I think they would have taken me just because they wanted to get some women in the firm, so that was an example in which I felt that I was being benefited by my gender."

Then she continued,

You know, I've heard the same stupid jokes and stuff that everybody has, but it doesn't bother me, I've never taken any of that personally. I suppose overall it sets women back, but it's never affected my ability to practise. I think that there's definitely built-in discrimination in the system, in that the partners in the downtown firms are all men who have women at home doing everything and, as a result, their expectations are that that's how everybody should work. And there are a lot of men out there who are prepared to work that hard because they have the support-staff-at-home thing. Women just can't, because if they want to have a family or something, they just can't work those crazy, crazy hours. So, I think there is built-in discrimination in the whole system that doesn't allow women to get ahead as easily as men.

Despite the ambiguity some women experienced, one of the men commented that he would be surprised if there was no discrimination against women lawyers:

> There is in most sectors of our society, and the legal profession is not, in my experience, a progressive sector of our society. It is one that has historically been controlled by white able-bodied males, mostly of privileged backgrounds. That's changing, but I would be surprised if there wasn't a significant amount of discrimination. I don't have any difficulty believing the information I've read in the reports. There's nothing in there that's inconsistent with my experience. Certainly, when you look at the representation of women at various levels in law firms, they do seem to be under-represented at the higher levels. I think the profession has been slow to develop maternity leave policies. I don't think there are any law firms that have in-house daycare or anything progressive like that.

Discrimination on the Basis of Family or Marital Status

Ten percent of the women respondents and 2% of the men said they had been discriminated against on the basis of family or marital status. While 74% of the women and 76% of the men were living in a married or similar situation, only 26% of the women, compared with 50% of the men, had children. Furthermore, only three women (6%), compared with 44% of the men, had children under the age of ten years. The effect of law on the respondents' decision to have children is discussed further in Chapter 6.

One woman was asked in a job interview whether she planned to have children, which she found inappropriate, and another had to endure comments about working part-time. One woman, with reasonably good grades and a "sterling work record," described her experience while looking for articles:

> I went into a firm, and it was a woman interviewing me – a woman who was married with kids. At that point I was a single mom. Her question to me was, "How do you think you're going to work for a firm and take care of your child?" I managed to get through law school doing it, I have good support behind me, I'll do what I have to do. There was no question in her tone, in everything she said, that she didn't think that I could do the same job as a single male who played racquetball instead of going home and taking care of a kid. The firm I ultimately articled with was no problem at all. They knew I had a child. I think that there's a perception that if you're a single mother, you can't devote yourself as completely to the job as some law firms expect you to do. That's why I ended up choosing the firms I did choose, but in part because the lifestyle was an important part to me. I needed to know that I could go home to my kids. They're

very important to me, and I wasn't going to give up my family just because of a job.

One man thought he may have been discriminated against on the basis of family status (he had a relatively large number of children) when applying for articles, but he thought it could also have been because of race.

Discrimination on the Basis of Race or Ethnic Origin

Respondents were not asked about their race or ethnic background, however I noted that 10% of the women and 2% of the men were from racialized groups, and an additional 6% of the women referred to their ethnic background. One of the respondents was Aboriginal.[10] Five women and one of the men said they had been discriminated against on the basis of race or ethnic origin. One woman had to put up with jokes about her ethnic background at several interviews. She commented, "I mean, I don't have a chip on my shoulder, but a lot of this stuff is there." Another said, "I sometimes get asked whether or not I'm Jewish, because my last name is one that could lead people to that conclusion. I see no purpose for that question, other than some prejudicial attitude."

Some were uncertain about the effect of their race or ethnicity: "Some places I am sure didn't hire me because I'm female. I'm sure that some places I interviewed at for articling and associate positions took one look at my last name [which revealed my ethnic background]. I'd like to think that if people didn't want to hire me, they didn't want to hire me because they just didn't like me, so it's hard to say." One woman commented that it was "very refreshing" not to be discriminated against because of her race, and another commented: "[I was discriminated against on the basis of] race, not so much overtly, but it has definitely been there. On cases, I've had partners say, 'Well, you should work on this case with us because they're of your kind.' It was said in jest. I wouldn't say it has been much, but it's there."

One man indicated he had been discriminated against on the basis of race when he applied for articles. However, his race has now become his strength, as he works for clients in his community.

One woman summarized her views on discrimination in the legal profession: "I also want to say that I'm not a person with disabilities, and I'm not a person of colour, but I'm offended by the paucity of women and men of colour and women and men with disabilities in the profession. I think it's grotesque that the numbers in the profession are so predominately white and able-bodied." Other respondents talked about what they perceived to be the case for lawyers from particular racial and ethnic backgrounds. One woman described the experience of an East Indian man (with a last name that did not reflect his East Indian identity), who went to several job interviews during which the lawyers at the firm looked shocked to see him: "It was a pro forma interview when they found out that he wasn't white, but that he was East Indian." Another woman did not think that lawyers from different races or ethnic origins were treated the same as everybody else, and that their opportunities to advance were not as good. She added, "I don't seem to encounter many, so that indicates to me that something is missing there." Another woman reflected on the fact that there were no persons of colour in her office: "I guess in its own way, that's a real form of discrimination as well." One woman thought that racial minorities were ghettoized as were women. They are "forced into practices that specifically represent the race they represent, or working with clients that are the race they represent." She did not think that the full range of practice was open to them. While one man thought that Aboriginals had a difficult time finding articles, one woman thought there was reverse discrimination in the sense that Aboriginals "already have a foot in the door that the rest of us don't have."

One man explained the battle his firm was having trying to retain Chinese lawyers:

> We've been battling with the Chinese lawyer factor. We've tried to hire Chinese lawyers, we've not done well; we've not been able to keep them. We've had five or six, but it must be because of our client mix. We don't have a lot of Asian clients, and we tried to develop an Asian practice. You've got to have Asian lawyers to do it. That has offended people. We had one person who spoke very good Chinese who isn't Asian, and he wasn't good enough for that clientele. We've had three Chinese women lawyers, all of whom wanted to work substantially less than the target – in fact, so much less that it had to be considered half time – and the consequence of that was, not because of their race but because of their desire to work less, we had to turf them. Unfortunately, it looks like a race and sex thing, but I cannot say that it was. I know what their hours were. I know what they wanted.

The controversy over issues of race in the legal profession is illustrated by the inability of the Canadian Bar Association's Working Group on Racial Equality in the Legal Profession to present their views in one report.[11] However, the dissenting voice wrote, "a meaningful commitment to the struggle for social justice demands that we respect a multiplicity of voices and perspectives."[12] Both reports contain a number of recommendations to improve law school and the legal profession for racialized groups. These reports and others have recommended ways to improve the position of Aboriginal peoples in law school and the legal profession.[13]

Discrimination on the Basis of Sexual Orientation

Although respondents were not asked about their sexual orientation, during the interview, three women disclosed that they were lesbians.[14] One woman described the sexism and homophobia of law school:

Once, in law school, I was subjected to extreme sexism and homophobia, by my classmates predominately, although there was a percentage of professors who were misogynous and sexist, particularly about issues such as rape, abortion, and rights for gays and lesbians. Whenever these subject matters arose in class, I would literally recoil internally, because it was a fairly safe bet that someone, whether it be the professor or classmates, would make comments that were truly offensive. Women, in the women's caucus in which I was, were subjected to taunts of lesbianism, which of course in my case were true, and lots of other name-calling. The student newspaper aided and abetted this by publishing incredibly sexist and misogynist articles, to which the school did not adequately respond by preventing or calling for retractions or apologies. The school didn't respond to my needs as a lesbian. It promoted only heterosexual events, by having grads and balls in which students were encouraged to bring their husbands or boyfriends or girlfriends of the opposite sex. Heterosexuality is terribly invalidating to someone who does not fit the majority. I assume that the same was true or worse for men and women of colour and men and women with disabilities.

She also experienced invalidation as a person at work:

When I was breaking up with my partner and essentially going through a divorce, I was devastated, and I was not out as a lesbian at work. I remember how devastated I felt, and how completely afraid I was to say something to people, for fear, this amorphous fear, that if I came out, they wouldn't hire me back, they wouldn't like me, I wouldn't get good files. I mean, there's just a myriad of concerns that a person has in that position of subordination, and I remember I would go to the bathroom ... to cry because I didn't want to be seen. I didn't want to have to explain to people why I was so upset. I think it's another instance of the institutional – or the entrenched – discrimination, the fact that people are not comfortable being who they are.

Homophobic statements strike at the core of one's being, and are difficult to deal with, whether one is "out" or not:

A homophobic statement was made in my presence, and at the time I wasn't out to those people. I was just outraged, I was appalled, I just couldn't believe it, because I had chosen conscientiously to article at a progressive firm, a presumably conscientious firm, and here they were saying incredibly homophobic things. It's an incredible feeling to be treated that way, and not feel like you can respond, and I see myself as an articulate person. I'm now out but I'd still have a hard time saying something in response. Not because I'd be afraid of being out, but because when one is affected that personally, it's difficult to amass the resources to deal with that kind of offence and also respond. It was one of the reasons I left a few weeks early. It wasn't the kind of place I wanted to work. I felt alienated. I felt disgusted with their values and their views. I was seething. At some core level I was angry at myself, because I wasn't able to say something to them, and I decided to cut my losses and my time there.

Another lesbian commented that she had to endure homophobic comments at work until she came out: "That seemed to put a lid on it. I was present when revolting jokes were told. Now that I've come out, those jokes don't get told, at least in my presence, and that's good." However, she added, "There are a lot of assumptions about heterosexuality – being married, having kids." It is difficult to "float around in that environment, and not fit into those categories."

How does one deal with a comment about "those types of cases," when one is a member of the group targeted by the comment?

While working as a lawyer, the organization was handling a couple of test cases on sexual orientation, and I was not counsel on record for either. A new case came into the office, the clients had approached me directly to represent them. I raised it with the executive director who said, "You know, we can't do too many of *those* cases." It was an issue. I was appalled. We represented the same clients year after year after year, and we do those same [types of] hearings every two to three months. So this issue of representing "those types of clients," or doing that type of work, didn't seem to arise as a criterion for [that] work, yet it did seem to arise about the work we were doing on sexual orientation.

One woman, who did not reveal her sexual orientation, was asked about her personal life in a job interview:

And I said, "I'm not sure I want to discuss that with you." And one of the partners said, "Well, are you gay?" And I said, "You can't ask that question even if you're just joking. It's offensive." He said, "No, actually it's relevant." And, I said, "How could it be relevant to hiring me?" He

said, "Well, we might have to think whether we want a gay lawyer working for us. [This] is a small community and word would get out." I never
answered. I said, "Well, I guess you'll just have to guess." That would have
been a point of contention for them.

There were other respondents who thought that there was discrimination against lawyers in the legal profession on the basis of sexual orientation.
Although there is a new section of the Canadian Bar Association for gay
and lesbian lawyers, one woman thought that there would be good reason
for gay and lesbian lawyers to fear discrimination in opportunities for
advancement. She added, "I think it's a macho atmosphere, and they
wouldn't want to disclose it, and they would certainly not want their
clients to know it." Another woman thought there would likely be discrimination in her firm, because she has "never been around such a group
of homophobes." One man thought that coming out in a large firm about
one's sexual orientation would be the "kiss of death."

On the other end of the spectrum, one woman commented, "We
have homosexuals in our office and that doesn't appear to be a problem. I
don't see any discrimination there." One of the men used to think there
would be discrimination on the basis of sexual orientation; however, he
had abandoned that belief because of what is going on in his own office.
"[Interviewer: What is going on in your office?] Well, we have some people
who have a sexual orientation that is not heterosexual. [Interviewer: And
they are 'out' in the office?] They're not like Svend Robinson, with a public announcement. [Interviewer: People know?] People know, and it's fine.
[Interviewer: It's not a problem?] Right. I'm not sure that they would
answer the question the same way, but that's how I feel."

One woman observed how one of her clients had been treated, because
of how others perceived his sexual orientation:

No one will admit it, but there was a client that came into one of the firms
I worked for, who outwardly appeared very feminine. I don't know
whether or not he was gay, I didn't care. But the male lawyer who saw
him first didn't talk to him long, and thought, "Here, you talk to him,
this would be a good case for you to handle." Had the lawyer talked to
him and found out what case this guy had, he would have taken it. But
I think he did, in fact, turn him away because he was uncomfortable dealing with him. He wasn't turned away from the firm entirely, but he was
definitely turned away from that lawyer, for what was his perceived sexual orientation. So I think it happens. I think it is more likely with male
lawyers. They all tend to be a little homophobic. I know of many lawyers
who find a way not to take cases. I don't think I know any gay or lesbian
lawyers. I'm sure there are plenty, but I didn't happen to run across them.

Although some lawyers would probably be uncomfortable if they had to practise with a lesbian or a gay man, one man lawyer did not think that it would be a big concern:

> I think that's a concern among the older practitioners, not among the younger because, frankly ... And even some of the older ones in our firm (we have a conservative partnership), but even when I look at the most conservative of them, I don't know that I could point to anyone in my partnership and say they'd go nuts if we hired someone of a different sexual orientation, or if it were discovered or if one of our big clients was [gay]. [Interviewer: What would the reaction be if one of the lawyers came out of the closet?] You would probably get a few jokes and some concern. Ultimately it would be fine. I'm sure there'd be some who would be bothered by it, but overall, I don't think it would be a problem.

Lesbian and gay lawyers have made presentations to the Law Society of British Columbia's Gender Bias Committee, which concluded that: "Because of their sexual orientation, gay men and lesbian women must overcome major hurdles to enter and become successful in the legal profession. Homophobic barriers force most homosexuals to deny their sexual orientation, rendering them invisible to their colleagues."[15]

In the late 1980s, lesbian and gay lawyers started to organize and to challenge the discrimination that exists in the law and the legal profession. In 1987 and 1988, lesbian and gay law students and professors organized Queen's Law Lesbians and Gays (QLLAG), and held the first Conference on Lesbian and Gay Rights in Canada at Queen's University in Kingston in 1990.[16] In October 1992, the Second Pan-Canadian Conference on Lesbian and Gay Rights, *Out Rights/Les Droits Visibles* was held in Vancouver. Today, the Lesbian/Gay/Bisexual/Transgender Issues Section of the Canadian Bar Association, BC Branch, meets on a regular basis, and has its own Newsletter (*Triangle*). In 1997, at the Canadian Bar Association Mid-Winter meetings, the Sexual Orientation and Gender Identity Conference (SOGIC) was established, and it now has subsections across Canada.

Discrimination on the Basis of Age

Ten percent of the women and 8% of the men said they were discriminated against on the basis of age. Some of the older women respondents were discriminated against because of their age. One woman was told by a firm that they did not want to hire anyone who had been employed in other capacities. They wanted lawyers "fresh out of law school." However, she managed to find a job in which the firm treated her with a great deal of respect and took advantage of her experience, because clients were comfortable dealing with her. Another woman commented:

It's not smart to go into law as an older woman with kids. I had lots of interviews, I had good references, and I did well in my articles. I'm older than the senior partner who was interviewing me, and he was intimidated. Then he tells me, "You know, you're just not lean and hungry enough for a law firm." This is true, because they want a workhorse. They want a junior lawyer who is going to be there until midnight every night, doing a lot of work for them so they can go home to their families. So they love the young men with the babies, because those guys are there to slave, and that's very clear. They don't value an older woman's life experience. They don't value a lot of things that are valued in [other professions]. There's a real bias against older, aging women.

Some of the younger women respondents thought their youth was a factor. While a junior in litigation, one woman was overlooked as if she "wasn't there":

I don't know whether that's because of my race or my sex, as opposed to my youth. For example, one time I was appearing in contested chambers, and I was there representing a party which was taking no position. I was there to monitor the case, and when the time was right, to announce I had no position. The lawyers representing the other interests, all men, just ignored me, as if I was invisible, even though I was clearly sitting at the counsel table, gowned, and I was appearing as a lawyer. The judge was really nice. After these guys had all spoken, none of whom had acknowledged me, he turns to me and asked "Ms. [name], do you have anything to say?" I was pleased, and I stood up and said we took no position. I thought it was really nice of him. He too could have done like the other parties, ignored me. I know it was minor, but to me it was the attitude. I just don't think it was proper. If I were in their shoes, even if they were not representing a major party, you still make a point of ... It was bizarre. I don't know whether they thought I was a secretary sitting there, or what. The judge made a point of drawing attention to me, and asking me if I had anything to say. To these male lawyers, they were so oblivious to that. So what? Maybe as a female, a more junior person, I noticed it. It's just a reflection of how we're brought up sometimes. If you're not a WASP, a male WASP, then somehow you're lesser.

Four men said they had been discriminated against based on their age. One was told that his age, being young, was a "potential bar as far as a quick advancement in the profession." Three men felt that judges discriminated against them, because judges gave more weight to lawyers who were more senior. One commented: "Arguments being treated flippantly because it is a young lawyer who is advancing them, who is going up against senior counsel. That has happened on occasion. Sometimes it has ended up in the Court of Appeal, so it's gratifying to be right. That's fairly trivial; I can't think of anything else. Just at the trial level. I don't do that much Court of Appeal." When he first started, he thought that older lawyers had a handicap because they were unfamiliar with the *Charter*. The court assumed "that you were an old warhorse who couldn't learn new tricks."

Discrimination on the Basis of Disability

Respondents were not asked whether they had a disability.[17] None of the women and only one of the men reported having been discriminated against on the basis of disability. The man was not sure whether it was because of his age or his disability: "There were times when I had some suspicions, but nothing overt that I could put my finger on. My sense, after law school when I was looking for an articling position, was that both my age and my disability were marks against in some firms. Obviously in others it wasn't at all a problem, and I don't have anything concrete to point to as proof. I wouldn't have felt confident enough to lay a complaint, for example, but I did have that suspicion."

This man was the only respondent who was visibly disabled. There were a number of respondents that talked about the inflexibility of the profession to deal with disabilities that were less visible – injury from car accidents, illness related to stress, and so on. However, none of these respondents said they were discriminated against on the basis of their disability.

David Lepofsky recommended twenty-seven specific actions that law schools can take to ensure that people with disabilities have equal access to the practice of law and to the services of lawyers. These recommendations include appointing a senior faculty member as coordinator to facilitate access to services at law schools, and the creation of a committee to "identify barriers to access in the law school admissions system, teaching processes and student evaluation methods, and to recommend to the Co-ordinator methods by which these barriers can be removed."[18] Lepofsky suggests that disabled law students be offered a faculty and student mentor to "function in a more individualized and informal counselling role." Law schools should allow students to complete their degrees over longer periods of time than the three years required at most law schools; some law schools now offer part-time law degree programs. Lepofsky also recommends changes to the law school curriculum and student legal aid clinics. Many of the recommendations also apply to other disadvantaged groups.

The Effects of Discrimination

For the most part, the respondents who thought they were subjected to discrimination did nothing about it.[19] Some women spoke to others: "React? I've never really done anything. The clients aren't mine. If they were mine, I'd tend to be more forceful with them. It also happened earlier in my career, when I was a little less confident, and a little less willing to make a client angry. I did mention it to the senior lawyer on the file, and they spoke to the client and said, 'She wouldn't be on the file if she couldn't do the work.'"

Some of the women responded directly to the offender. One told the man he was "archaic," and that she hoped he would retire before she had the opportunity to go to court. Another woman was angry, and did not want to work in a place where she was not treated well. It played a part in, but was not an overriding reason for her decision to leave private practice. A man who was discriminated against on the basis of race became angry, and wondered whether his education had been worth all the effort.

Perceptions of Bias

Respondents were asked whether they thought that bias or discrimination against women in the legal profession today restricts their career advancement.[20] Unlike the earlier surveys, they were not given a list of possible forms of bias, but were left to come up with their own.[21] In response to the question, 88% of the women and 66% of the men said "Yes." Only 4% of the women and 18% of the men said there was no discrimination against women.

Lack of Accommodation for Family

Lack of accommodation for family, or questions about family plans, were the most common forms of discrimination against women in the legal profession, mentioned by 60% of the women and 42% of the men.[22] Such discrimination could take place at the time of hiring:

> One of the questions I've always been asked, whether it was for articling interviews or associates, was whether I was planning on having kids. I have always been assured, "Oh, it wouldn't matter all that much, but we just have to know." Given that women bear children, you have to make an important decision as to how you're going to fit it in, if at all possible. If not, you're constantly against this battle of partners looking at you and thinking, "She's not going to be around long. We'll just give her this responsibility, and she'll go out and get pregnant." This is always in the back of partners' minds.

A man thought that a lot of firms were reluctant to hire women, because they might leave "for career reasons, or lifestyle reasons, or they may become pregnant" and disrupt their practice. One woman explained the recruiting process at her firm:

> It's still predominantly a male profession, despite the fact that women are entering law schools in equal rates. In recruiting, we try to be fair, we never ask students questions like, "What are your plans?", "Are you married?", "Will you have kids?". We just don't think that's appropriate. But there's no denying that given two candidates of equal value and experience and qualification and everything else, that the thought does occur (and this discussion comes up internally) "Is so and so likely to stick around, or is she likely to go to Paris, or do her master's degree, or have kids?" That becomes a possibility. It's talked about as if, so and so, the male, will likely be a long-term, hard-working lawyer. And it's true, you have to acknowledge that, with women, the experience is that they're more likely to sacrifice career for family, whereas men are not expected to do that. So, in economic terms, it's harder for law firms to make that investment in a female, because the investment, which is expensive in the first few years, may never pay off if she takes off after three years and says she's dissatisfied with the profession, and says, "I want to go and do in-house counsel, or I want to do my master's, or I want to go to Paris, or I want to get married and have kids." The men don't do that. Men can have kids and have a family and still practise law. Even the brightest women in this firm have decided to go part time and raise kids. But she will never be partner as long as she's part time. Even though we talk about part-time partners, the reality is that male partners feel, "Why should I support part-time partners when I put in 100%? It's your choice to have kids, why should we bear the burden of it economically and everything else?" That's not an unusual complaint you hear from the lawyers. And it's not just from the male lawyers either; sometimes it's female partners who chose not to have kids or have not married and they say, "Well, I've sacrificed, I never expected any special treatment going through, why should you?"

For some respondents, the extra responsibility of child care is a strong disadvantage for women, given the hours expected at law firms. One woman said that with the "double burden of children and family and household responsibilities, it was physically impossible to work the number of hours firms expect you to work, as well as meet those other obligations, which the men don't share fairly." Another commented,

> I know of many men who are married and have kids, who aren't even asked about that, in terms of their interviews, whereas the women tend

to be, because it's still accepted that it's the woman who's responsible for those children. "If the kid gets sick, who's going to get called, mommy or daddy?", they want to know. I think that, hopefully, that's going away, because with more and more women in the workforce, the reality of the situation is that people do have families. Do you want to rule out great portions of the population who are highly competent, intelligent people because they may have other demands on their time on occasion? It seems ridiculous to me. I wonder how much those women have had to forego to get to that point. If I wanted to take maternity leave, had I continued to work, the man who started the same time as I did is going to be surpassing me on taking that time. He's not going to face the same impediments in order to have both his home life and his work life.

Some of the respondents recognized that women were simply leaving the profession, or working in smaller firms, because of the lack of accommodation for family life. One woman stated that most of the women she went to law school with were not working in downtown law firms, because these firms are slow in dealing with policies about children and expected hours of work: "There's not a chance for a family and a partnership. There's probably not enough women in the downtown law firms to provide for a circle of support to keep them in the firms."

Some of the women and men saw the issue of family status as one that applies to both women and men, but as discussed more fully in Chapter 6, perhaps not equally. One woman knew young men lawyers who were "simply fed up, and want to take more time and be with their families." Another commented:

I think just the nature of the profession, the long hours, it's difficult for women to combine it with family and household responsibilities, so inevitably you can't compete with the men in terms of billable hours, and that's going to automatically ruin your attractiveness as a partner, for raises, for getting some files. I think that's automatically a big difficulty. I think a lot more women too – perhaps it's my perception – I think we're generally more resistant to wanting to give 100% of our lives over to a job. I don't think we necessarily accept that approach as readily as a lot of men do, but I think even the men are rejecting that more and more.

Although there were respondents who thought that some men also wanted more time to spend with their families, one woman thought that some of the young men were part of the problem:

It's a real status thing for the men to be fathers. But if they find out you're a mother, they don't want you because it's a liability. I sensed in many interviews that I should be telling them that I'm not planning on having more kids. I think that's a big issue: hire someone, you train her, she gets pregnant, and she goes off to raise her family. I find that all this stuff with gender bias is given lip service, but it's so deeply embedded in the presumptions, in the whole psyche of the male world, that we're just playing with the icing on top of the cake. I don't harbour any delusions. If my daughter chooses quality of life and law, she'll have an uphill battle. I don't think we've resolved it. In fact, what I find now is that the younger men are more biased than men in [their forties]. I was shocked at some of the stuff from these patriarchal puppies. These young men are extremely biased. I guess I lived in a world, before I went to law school, that was liberal; and we weren't touched by the corporate world. We were laid-back, open-minded people. You come into law, and ... I didn't realize the amount of sexism that is so ingrained in the corporate world. I expected a fulfilling, fun job, but then you realize what's there.

A number of respondents were of the view that women with children had difficulty advancing in the legal profession. One woman simply said, "Women with a family are doomed and aren't going anywhere." Another described the process to partnership: "During that seven-year term, don't expect to get pregnant if you want a partnership offering." However, one woman, who did not have children and did not plan to have children in the next ten years, had seen women manage in the profession with one child; but after their second, they were "out of the profession":

They can't seem to balance the needs of the two children. I'm not sure if that's within the profession or just society as a whole, so how you attribute that I don't know. I don't think there's enough flexibility in the profession. It doesn't allow for mothering because you have to bill, say, downtown, where you have to bill 1,800 to 2,200 hours a year. How in heaven's name are you going to do that and still be able to spend any time with your children? And so, what choice do you have? You're not making the hours. That affects the fact that you're not going to be able to make the raises. You're not making your overhead, and then they don't want you around. So, eventually, you're going to be booted out.

Some women with children had difficulty advancing, but they were not sure whether it was discrimination or the "facts of life." One commented:

I think there is [discrimination] in that if you're of child-bearing age, [you have to ask the question] "Will the firm invest in you?" because they're not sure how long you'll stay. There is that discrimination, and I don't know how you get around it, because the firm obviously has the economic situation in mind. You're an investment and they're running a business, yet the person has their own personal fulfilment, social, family life in mind. I think those things will always be on a collision course in our capitalist society, or in any society. I see it there. I see it in women who come back in after taking time off to raise children. It's far more difficult to advance. That's true in any profession, and it would be true in the medical profession, or any other. It's just a fact of life. So how much of it is just the realities of things and how much of it actual discrimination, is difficult to say.

A number of the respondents did not see how women with children could advance in the profession, as long as they were required to work the long hours many firms demanded. The women who did manage to "do it all" did not impress some of the respondents. Two women observed:

I've seen it come up with people who have had children and tried to become part-time partners. I think it's tough for women in large firms to succeed in that respect, if they have children. Women can succeed if they become like men, which is what they [men] expect. But if women want to stay home with their children a few days a week, I think it's a tough battle. It is in the big firms, no matter how liberal they say they are, they want their people there, and they try to espouse what they're supposed to espouse ... You can see that it's not happening. I mean women with children are leaving big firms all the time. You don't see a lot of women with children, and the ones you do see have two nannies and a husband who also earns a good income, and they can afford that. That's not the norm. Those are the ones who the firm holds up and says, "Well, look at [name], she's got children, she works five days a week." And the response is "Yes, she has a husband who's a doctor, she has two or three shifts of nannies every day, she comes in at eight because she's a solicitor and leaves at five." Well, great on her, but try doing that in litigation. You can't. I don't know that it's that they haven't dealt with the issue. I think some men resent the fact that women ... they think it [maternity leave] is a holiday during which you've been off for six months, you've stayed home and had children. I do think there's a bit of that, and I think they resent the fact that someone can be there three days a week. It must be that, because otherwise they'd be changing more. What's the problem with someone being a part-time partner?

The attitude that there's only one way to do it – and that's be a workaholic – means that if you're going to have children, you're restricted, generally. Or you have a full-time nanny, or two nannies, and you never see your kids, so there's no balance there. I think there is a systemic bias against women. I mean it's simple, why should everybody have to work fourteen hours a day to get the job done, if you can hire two people to do the job? Often, we're faced with the attitude that this is the way it's always done, this is the way it must be done, rather than, let's figure it out. A lot of lawyers, colleagues, and friends in other firms are leaving because of lifestyle. They don't want to do it anymore, but there's no flexibility within their existing organizations. They're setting up on their own because they want to have a different situation, so it's a lack of flexibility that has to be addressed.

A respondent, who saw a client in between nine-minute contractions with her second child, was not impressed with the demands of law firms:

I think that the legal profession is a difficult profession for women to be in. It's expected, especially in the larger centres, that you're available to your firm twenty-four hours a day, seven days a week, and that's impossible if you want to have a family life. When I was articling, two partners were women, and one was not married and didn't have children. The other had two children. We were told by I don't know how many lawyers, that this particular woman, although she had two children, went into labour with her Dictaphone, and was back to work two weeks later, and that was what we were to strive for [laughter]. I think that if you're willing to be a man, then you're not restricted, but you can't show any sign for desire for motherhood or anything like that.

One woman did not think women were discriminated against if they agreed to work like a man and put in long hours. However, if discrimination included not being allowed to bring your own values into the workplace, "as far as the time dedicated to the job," then women were discriminated against, especially if they had family obligations. Another summarized law firms' lack of flexibility: "You either have to work according to their standards, or you don't work." One woman would have stayed with a law firm if it had been more flexible; however, she was not willing to work "sixty or seventy or eighty hours a week."

According to one man, maternity leaves put women at a disadvantage:

I think that women are discriminated against, both in terms of advancement and areas of practice. The family thing isn't so much discrimination as it's one of those hard realities. The fact of the matter is that the more experience you have, the better the lawyer you become, and there's simply no way to compensate for that. If you're someone who wants to try and balance career and family, that means taking six months off three or four times, or two times even, over a three- or four-year period – that puts you at a disadvantage. It's just a time thing. You're now two years behind your colleagues. By the time you count winding-down time and winding-up time, it's costing you a year each time. It would be altruistic to say that that's a price that you shouldn't have to pay. But the reality is that I have a year more in school than you have. The only way that you can catch up is if you work that much harder than I do. Over a longer period of time, that year will become less and less significant. But if that year is early on in your practice, then it's significant, and it does tend to be earlier on in the practice. So you might be at a 10% or 20% disadvantage, and I don't see any way around that. It's like taking a year out of school, and that's a hard choice. And then you get into the more difficult decisions of, is one of the members of the family going to stay home, or work part time, and things like that. That has tremendous career impact as well.

For some, the problem was really with the clients. A woman who practised criminal law stated that her clients get impatient when she is not there for a day: "So if you want to have a baby and take six months off work, you're going to come back ... and your practice could be wiped out." A man described the demands of his practice, and the impact it would have on the women and men who are not prepared to work the hours clients demand:

The fact of the matter is that we have people who demand us to be here seven days a week, twenty-four hours a day, and she [a woman who retired from partnership to work part time], and hats off to her, she said, "No, that's not for me." And I've said that. I've been cut out of work, you know. So that's just a harsh reality, and that gets back to my earlier point that calculating hours only makes sense on a yearly average, because I'll do overnighters. I'll work for thirty-six hours straight, sleep for four or six hours, and come back for another twenty-four. You know we do that. Women in our firm have not been good about doing that. Many men have not been good about doing that. So to me, that's not a gender issue. It just happens to be that all of our women have not been good about doing that. But we have many men, and I get to that stage that, for religious reasons, I don't work [on one day]. That upsets a lot of people here and it keeps me off of files. That's a ground of religious discrimination but I don't view it as religious discrimination. For me, that's empowering. I can say "stuff it" and survive.

When asked whether he thought that might be discrimination on the basis of religion, he responded:

No, why would it be? We have a clientele that says we need you to

accomplish this project in this amount of time and if that means working seven days a week, then that's the deal. That's a market decision. If
we don't want to do that we can say "No." [Interviewer: Maybe you work
better if you work six days a week?] There's no question that we do; however, it may be negligence not to work seven days. [Interviewer: So, the
client drives you?] Yes, there's no question. It's a hard, hard time. Last
year I took two days off, and I have let it be known that I'm not happy
with that situation, and I'll do everything that I can not to do that again.
So I do weird things like come in on another day and work until midnight, while everybody else has gone home that afternoon so that they
can at least enjoy part of the day with their family so that I can have my
day, because that's important to me and my family. My wife and I both
hold the same religious values. Now, is that discrimination? If that is,
that's a bizarre view of discrimination because for me that's entirely a market decision. We had a choice to say "No." We elected not to, and the
price we'll pay is that some people will not be able to work on that file,
and that "some people" is me. It will also exclude many women. It will
exclude just as many men. It will exclude more men, frankly, but it will
happen to exclude more women as a percentage of the total volume. I
view neither of those situations as discrimination – that's the market.

When brought back to the question of whether he thought there was
bias or discrimination against women in the legal profession today that
restricts their career advancement, he had this to say:

I'm told that there is. [Interviewer: Do you believe it?] I believe that there
is. I have a hard time seeing where it is, because I view so many things
– maybe it's my economic bias, you know – I view so many things as
being market-driven, and if that's the market, if we don't want to respond
to it, we don't have to. It's a free and democratic society. In terms of career
advancement, there's no question that women are prevented from advancing, but it's not because there's a deliberate policy to do it. It's because,
in my view, we have a philosophy that says that the client drives us, so
women say, "I'll only work this much because I have other goals and ambi-
tions." My hat's off to them. I salute them for wanting to do that. I wish
that I had the guts to do it. I feel that my family would suffer if I made
that decision, because we don't have another financial provider in the
family. We have one-and-a-quarter caregivers in our family. That's the way
we have apportioned our jobs. So, yeah, I believe that there is. I assume
others are concerned about this notion that men are going to have to
subsidize women's practices. I know that it's a huge issue, it's an undercurrent of thought, and so I hear the arguments from those people, to
the effect that, "I'll leave the profession before I have to go and subsidize

somebody's practice so that they only have to work half-time. I'm killing myself and my family is suffering so that I'm going to subsidize somebody." It just doesn't make sense. I understand that argument. I'm faced with that argument, and if I have to do that, it's going to hurt me twice as bad as most people here because they have double incomes. It's going to hurt me very hard, so I'm sympathetic to that undercurrent. At the same time, I'm sympathetic to women, and to men who can't speak, because there are men who want to restore some balance to their life, and that really has to do with time.

Some respondents believed that things were improving, and that firms would have to adjust to women in the workforce. One woman, who did not have children but expected to have a family in the next ten years, thought things were getting better, as more women were graduating, and at the top of their class:

If they want to continue to have the pick of the top people in a law school class, they'll have to start accommodating women's needs. It's a problem. My practice commands that I exit myself from my life for four to six weeks. Fine, now I'm single, and I don't have kids. But if I have a baby at home, I can't do that. The demands are still going to be that I do that. So I either change my line of practice, or I go home and feed my kid, and come back and work till two in the morning. Women are still forced to make more compromises than the system. It's a problem.

However, she is of the view that firms are going to have to take "a good hard look at the bottom line, job-sharing, accommodating family needs," and recognize that lawyers have responsibilities outside the office. Although she acknowledges that the firms are not there yet, she blames part of it on the marketplace:

If we tell a client, "No, we can't close a deal in four weeks because all the people staffing it go home every night at seven," they're going to turn around and find a firm with which the staff, for example, is all guys with no families, who work until two in the morning. The marketplace won't permit that kind of accommodation. It's not all the firm's fault. The practice of law has evolved to the point that it cultivates workaholics, and there's an expectation from senior members of the firms that they had to pay their dues, so why shouldn't you? A lot of them are male who, ironically, have wives who stay home with the kids because they're financially able to do that, and they have the expectation that you'll do what they do, or what they have done.

One man thought that some progress was being made in the legal profession because discrimination on the basis of gender is a high-profile issue in the profession:

> But as far as the profession, as a profession, is responding to the imperatives to remove those prejudices, you just have to look at the profile of various partnerships around the city and the makeup of those partnerships. How many are women and how many are men? And how enlightened is the thinking about accommodating maternity leaves? All of those issues are all wound up in these issues. There's obviously room to grow within the legal profession, but the legal profession is a great big ponderous conservative beast and it moves more slowly in these regards than other institutions do, but I think there is some movement. I think that there are enclaves of backward thinking. I think that there is also clear progress being made, in terms of affirmative action posturing that has been taken by people in authority in the legal profession, so you'll see some positive change in those areas. But I also think that there are pockets of resistance that need to be pursued. The fact is, at this late date, you still don't see the distribution of the sexes looking like it ought to in a law firm. I think concerns about people stepping out of the profession for periods of time to raise children, and so on, lead law firms to still make that decision. My perspective on that is that if you have talented and capable people, whether they're male or female, they're an asset worth developing and encouraging to grow within the law firm, and it's a small price to pay to accommodate those people if you're developing that talented person who is going to make a long-term contribution to your joint enterprise. So, I think it's now contrary to the self-interest of law firms to exclude some from the body of people who have been assisting them and helping them do what they do, for reasons that have nothing to do with their talent and ability.

One woman thought that there was discrimination, but thought perhaps that women were leaving because "they are just smarter than men, and realize they don't want to spend sixty hours per week working in this crazy profession, or women are going into government far more than men."

A man, who did not have children and did not plan to have any, thought that the solution to raising children and making the workplace more fair to women was "a redistribution of responsibilities between men and women,[23] rather than institutionalization of child care," although he had not completely resolved the issue in his own mind. From his perspective, there were already enough laws that encourage people to have children. Another man thought that firms were becoming more flexible; however, in his situation, as with a number of other men lawyers, either spouse would stay at home to raise the children, and generally it would be the woman. One man, whose wife was expecting a child, did not see how he could possibly continue his practice unless he lived a more traditional lifestyle. After describing a hectic practice in which he encountered few women, he stated:

> The only way I'm going to be able to do this is if we have a more tradi-tional home life, in which I don't take primary responsibility for child care, because there's no way I can do this job and do that. Clients phone me at home, and on the weekends, and at night all the time. They want an answer, they want it now. I get called back from vacation because of project work, I have to be willing to come back and do the project. As I said, the trick is to be able to take some time off later. But that arrange-ment is not conducive to raising a family, so if you're going to take the primary responsibility for child care, it's difficult to practise the type of law I practise. I don't know whether that's discrimination. If someone had to point to something and say, "Yeah, there's something there," if you think that all aspects of the profession should reflect the gender balance of those coming out of law school, there has to be something there, because it's so skewed. But I can't point to any incident, or anything in particular, other than speculating about the role of women in society.

He thought that the lifestyle of his practice in the securities industry did not lend itself to the demands of child-rearing and child-caring responsi-bilities: "I don't know whether it's the chicken or the egg, or something more fundamental than that, but in our society women just don't find it possible to make the necessary sacrifices."

One respondent stated that a woman in her firm had quit because the firm was not prepared to accommodate her needs arising out of young chil-dren. One of the male partners commented to the respondent, "I don't know what's wrong with you junior lawyers. In my day, I had a wife at home who used to take care of all those things and free me after work all the time." The respondent added, "He's completely alienated from both of his kids, and he doesn't see the connection."

Some of the respondents did not think that there should be concessions for women with children. A woman who was planning to start a family commented:

> I don't believe that a woman should have less billing hours just because she has children at home. I'm sorry, either you can do the job, or you can't, and it's just that way. This is all run by clients, and if you aren't there and the clients can't reach you because you're working fewer hours

because of your children, the firm is going to likely lose that client, and that's not fair. These are people who have worked long and hard, and who often work long hours to make the kind of money they've got, and to establish the kind of practice that they've got. If we want equal treatment, we've got to have equal pay for equal work. If you can do it, you get the pay. If you can't do it, then you can't expect equal pay, and you can't expect equal opportunities. You've got to be able to sit there and find a way, find some other way, of having your child taken care of. I know lots of females who have nannies, both lawyers and non-lawyers, and I personally have absolutely no idea how they possibly do it at all. It's incomprehensible to me, and my hat goes off to them. But I resent the fact that they've had the choice, made the choice, or been lucky enough to have children. But I have to carry them on my coat sleeves, and my work has to prop them up because they have the benefits that I don't have. I've got the work, and they've got the benefit, the kids. It's not fair. And that's discrimination.

Another woman, who had two small children, was not entirely comfortable with the idea that it might be discrimination for firms not to pay maternity leave full time:

Because the bottom line is, if you have a man who is going to be working there for six months bringing in $100,000 in billable time and the woman isn't, and you're having to pay them both, it's a huge strain. Just the reality is a huge strain, so I don't know. I think the system, the way it's set up, makes it difficult for women to have a family life. But I think for women who are willing to "play by the rules," and come back, you know, a week after they've had their baby, and be there sixty hours a week, if they're prepared to do that, then I don't think there's a problem. Most people aren't prepared to do that once they have a family.

One man sees problems for women, but thinks things are changing. His firm has a maternity policy, and a number of lawyers are having children. It seems to be working, and he has not seen any horrible problems to this point. He thinks that society and clients are coming to accept the fact that professionals have lives outside their offices.

Professional Advancement
Career advancement (attaining partnership, access to managerial positions) was the second most frequent form of discrimination against women, identified by 38% of the women and 28% of the men. One woman was convinced that the older male lawyers "simply don't want a female partner." They have excuses like, women will leave the profession, or they

can't make the tough decisions: "If they can make the tough decisions, they are such ball-busting bitches you don't want to be associated with them. It's unfortunate but I think it happens more often than not." Another woman stated:

> It comes down to the old boys' network – men feeling more comfortable with men – and if you're a woman you always have that as a barrier. In terms of career advancement, particularly nowadays in the private bar, the private world, people are hungry; they want people who are going to go out there and get clients, and getting those clients generally means courting or schmoozing up to people in [high] places. Those people in [high] places tend to be males who tend to be more comfortable with other males. So it affects your advancement, because you don't have the client contact, you don't have the exposure, and you're not bringing in as much business, which affects your career advancement.

Two women thought that women had to be better than men to advance in a law firm. Another thought there was "still a lot of tokenism." Women could be made partners, but there is no commitment to advance women. A man had heard that women in large firms are sidetracked from partnership – "the old guard protecting their turf."

Assignment of Work

Twenty-six percent of the women, and only 6% of the men, identified assignment of work as a form of discrimination against women in the legal profession.[24] One woman commented on the "ghettoization" of women lawyers and their work by the Legal Services Society, which is more responsive to the male lobbyists in the criminal bar than to the women in the family bar. Another described how she was expected to practise family law: "That's something I truly hated. I did it, but I hated it." Another commented on the "pink-collar ghetto" in family law.

When Mary Jane Mossman, a law professor at Osgoode Hall Law School, spoke in Vancouver at the Clara Brett Martin dinner on 27 January 1989, one woman in the audience described family law as "the shit box of the legal profession."[25] A more scientific assessment of the status of family law, by Kay et al., shows that it ranks tenth out of sixteen areas of practice ranked in prestige by respondents, ahead of criminal law, which ranked twelfth.[26] Kay found evidence that women were less likely than men (11%, compared with 15%) to practise corporate-commercial law (which ranked second in prestige), and less likely than men (15%, compared with 23%) to practise civil litigation (which ranked third in prestige). Too few women practise in tax law (ranked first) to make any generalization.

However, the "ghettoization" of women lawyers was not only as to the type of law practised, but also as to what type of work women did in the law firm. One woman respondent in this study described the division of labour in the law firms: "Remember when all teachers were men, and then women started? Then men were all the supervisors? In law, women are in the law firms doing the work, the men are jogging around Stanley Park. The young men get to meet the clients, and the women go to the library to do research and run the files. So what they've done is created a little work ghetto, in which the women do all the work and the men go out and have all the fun."

Another woman described the division of labour at the offices of Crown counsel, and thought perhaps it was the "old boys' network" in operation: "From colleagues and friends I know that even in our own branch, for a lot of female Crown counsel, their opportunities for advancement are limited. It's an old boys' network, and there are lots of anecdotes in which women are ghettoized, and forced to prosecute in youth court, or sexual assault." She suggested that things appeared to be slowly changing – she knew a woman appointed to management. Unfortunately, informal political games needed to be played in order to be promoted, including going out for lunch with the senior males. That, however, was difficult without an invitation from these men.

In some cases, it is the attitude about what women are good at or not good at that impedes their movement into some areas of practice: "A disproportionate number of women practise in the family law area, and part of that is because there is an expectation that women are more suited to that because they are women. They understand that kind of stuff. So when you make your choices when you are newly called, you make choices based on the demand and where you can make a living." Another woman lamented: "I think that women are wrongly seen as being less able to be adversarial. And when they are adversarial, they are not regarded the same way as men who are being adversarial. I have heard too many off-coloured jokes about women lawyers; men lawyers not being referred to in those same ways. And I suspect that those attitudes got in the way of career advancement when people are within firms, and that when people are being chosen for partnership probably, although it is not a personal concern of mine."

One woman described how friends have had problems with the treatment they received from male partners in their firms: "It was frustrating for them. They didn't get the work they wanted. They didn't get the positions they wanted. So they were frustrated, and moved on to other things. I know [discrimination] exists out there. I've never personally experienced or seen any of it, because I've never had the big firm experience." Rather than watching it happen, women in one firm brought the issue up at their firm: "We had a session in which the women lawyers presented their opinions about discrimination, or the experience with discrimination in the law firm, and brought them to the partners. Some of the partners, who weren't as defensive as others, said, 'Yes, that's true, we don't give the women the kinds of work we give men. We just naturally think, especially in the areas of criminal work, that's for a man. There's a different comfort level in working closely with a junior associate who's the same gender as you.'"

Feeling Opinions Are Valued

Twenty-two percent of the women and 6% of the men said that women were discriminated against by having insufficient weight given to their opinions.[27] According to one woman, "Because you're a woman, people don't think you have the credibility. Japanese businessmen want a man as their lawyer, even though the woman is smarter. They don't care, they generally just want a man." Other women see it as a problem that is starting to disappear:

> I think it's becoming less so now than it used to be, with more and more women entering the profession, but I see that a woman who presents an argument generally has to make sure that her argument is a sound argument and she presents it in a good manner, in order to be heard by whomever the argument is directed at. I've seen men sometimes present a half-hearted argument and be listened to, and they didn't have to fight to get a response.

> I don't see it happening with my peers to a significant degree at all. I think it's largely a function of the change in views of society, which have been dramatic over the last ten, twenty, and thirty years. And I see older members of the profession, primarily male, who don't treat women with the same confidence in their abilities, because of their sex. That is, generally they don't have confidence in their ability to deal with clients, and sometimes that's justified when you have old male clients who don't want to deal with a younger female lawyer. Confidence in their ability to function as a lawyer is the primary thing. It's improving, but yes, there still is.

Hiring

Ten percent of the women and 12% of the men mentioned "hiring" as a form of discrimination against women in the legal profession, which restricts their career advancement.[28] One man attributed this to law being a service industry. His firm's large commercial clients were largely male, and in that type of business, a relationship is probably the most critical aspect of attracting and maintaining clients. You can have all the reputation in the world, but if you aren't friends with that person and have a personal relationship with them, you're not playing on a level playing field with the guy that does. Because that's such an important aspect of attracting clients in an incredibly competitive atmosphere, if you have a male lawyer and a female lawyer who are equally talented in terms of their legal abilities, chances are you're going to take the male lawyer because his ability to bring in work from the business community is greater than the female's capability, just because business remains dominated largely by men. That's my own personal view of it. I'm not speaking for the firm.

Another man theorized about the reasons for discrimination against women in the legal profession: "I think people tend to hire people that remind them of themselves when they were young. People tend to want to duplicate themselves or the group. They tend to look for someone who's like everyone else in the group, because more men are making those decisions, I think there's more of a natural inclination toward men. That's putting it nicely. There are also a lot of dinosaurs out there who still aren't comfortable working with women."

Other Comments on Discrimination Against Women

One woman held the view that the culture of the legal profession discriminates against women:

So much of it isn't overt, and the people who are doing it don't understand that they are. If they were confronted with it, they would be more surprised, especially the old boys' network. They'd say, "Oh, I play golf with so and so because he's my friend." Nobody says you guys can't play golf or join your own league. There's a lack of appreciation that creates barriers. Some of the barriers are imposed by the client – lunching the client is a common thing to do. When I had lunch with male clients, some men are uncomfortable with that because they don't know the protocol. The expectation is that if you're a male lawyer lunching with a client, then of course you're going to pick up the tab. The comfort level isn't there. Only time will take care of that.

Another commented that the double standard in society works against women:

I think that their personal lives are probably scrutinized more than men. I think a promiscuous, drinking man is tolerated and enjoyed, because he tells great stories every Monday morning about waking up who knows where, with who knows who. But if a woman did that, they'd be appalled. There was a female articling student who had a short relationship with a first-year lawyer, and everybody talked about her lack of judgment. What was he doing? I agree it was a lack of judgment, but what about him? So, I think there's still a little double standard, as far as that kind of behaviour.

One woman was not sure that she was being understood when she talked about the lack of flexibility in law firms:

I discussed it with people before I left, because they were surprised I was leaving. I kept saying, "You know, you guys just don't get it. I don't want to be a partner, but there's no option for that here. I have to want to be a partner. Like I have to want to have the goal of sitting around, divvy-ing up the money, and I don't want that. I'm prepared to work hard. It's not an issue of not working hard, but I don't want what I'm supposed to want. So why can't I just be off that track, and not be required to bill 1,800 hours a year, because I don't want to do that? Why can't I work like a regular person, you know, if there's a trial I'll work hard, like I always do, but why do I have to want it?" They haven't turned their minds to that fact. No, they don't have that concept in that firm, and in most big firms, not yet. They have some research positions, which is different ... I had people come and try to change my mind and tell me, "No, you think you don't want to, but you will." Well, I know what I want, and I don't want this, it doesn't interest me, but they don't get it – not yet. I think they will down the road, because people are leaving, tons of people are leaving.

One man said there was discrimination against women, but thought that things were changing:

I think there's a time lag in the legal profession. I don't believe there's that much sexual discrimination. I think there is in terms of partnership, there's a natural time lag, and there have been advances in social attitudes in the last twenty years. Undergraduate and law school, it was fifty-fifty; I can't conceive of discrimination on that basis. But I read about it, and I am aware of it. I have a lot of colleagues that have concerns about it, but at the same time, I think that the legal profession is enlightened. The heart of, maybe one of the structural elements of discrimination, is in terms of lifestyle, and in terms of women reaching a certain age, in terms of child-bearing, and not have the support for that. And I think that's applicable to young fathers as well; at least, that's what I've heard from my colleagues.

Another man was less optimistic:

> There are an awful lot of dinosaurs out there, and we have one or two in this firm. There are attitudes out there. You go to a closing – nineteen guys in blue suits and black shoes and white shirts. There's an attitude there, and that is reflected in the senior levels of the profession. So I'm sure that, as a profession, there is room to work on it. As a firm, we're good, but as a profession there's still an awful lot of senior lawyers out there who need an attitude adjustment. And there are one or two in this firm.

Perceptions That Discrimination Does Not Exist

Two women (4%) did not know whether there was discrimination, because they had not been in the profession long enough. One had not practised long enough, and the other commented,

> Oh [there is] probably discrimination against women, but I didn't have a big problem with discrimination myself, and I think there are a lot of women out there doing well, either setting up their own firms, or managing themselves well within the firms that they're working in. So I frankly think there is a lot of attention by the Law Society on discrimination against women, and I think there has been a lot of attribution of women leaving the profession to discrimination on the basis of sex. My own experience is that is certainly not why I left the profession, and I don't want it all laid at the door of discrimination. I worked in a firm ... where the senior partners were men. They were paternal, there's no question about it, but I certainly felt like I had every opportunity that another junior in the firm had. They were paternal, they called me "dear"; but I didn't feel like it was limiting my opportunities.

She then volunteered her opinion on women who are leaving the profession:

> My own feeling for why women are leaving in droves, or leaving at a greater rate than men, is because I think that women have that option. I don't think that most of us, at least in my generation, were brought up with the idea that they would be a lawyer, and that that would be their identity for the rest of their lives. I think women in my age group [late twenties] felt that we had flexibility to be what we wanted to be, and we feel the option to leave law if it isn't satisfying for us – job satisfaction is maybe more our guiding factor. I think that men are still socialized a lot more to become a professional, and not to abandon that lightly. So I think it's much easier socially for a woman to say, "This isn't for me, I'm out

of here," than it is for a man. My own experience is that men were as dissatisfied with the practice as I was, many of them were, but they just didn't feel they had the option of leaving, which I felt I had. I think there's a lot of miserable men out there, they just don't have the social support to say, "This isn't for me," because men don't do that. They don't have that option. Possibly they were the only income earner, which makes it even more difficult to leave. A woman is more likely to be a supplementary income, or a second income, as opposed to the only income. There are exceptions, of course, single parent families and things like that, which are more likely to be women, but I think there is more the social pressure [on men]. I've taken a lot of flak for leaving law, but not as much, I'm sure, as if I'd been a man.

Two women were somewhat ambivalent as to whether they thought there was discrimination. One thought there were places in which there was gender bias, but that it is the choices women make that disadvantage them and "cause them not to advance." She added, "There's still an old boys' network there. Women's choices cause them not to advance, not the firm, maybe society, but not the firms. There is nothing the firms can do about it." She also held the view that gender bias was just a "sexy topic," and none of the women she had talked to had ever encountered gender bias. The other woman worked for herself, and so it was difficult to say whether there was discrimination against women. However, she had articled with a man who was "very sexist." She added, "As far as getting appointed to the Bench these days, the suggestion is that it is easier if you are a woman to get appointed to the Bench, you know. I don't know whether I agree with that, or whether there is some positive discrimination going on, but it's about time, anyway." Earlier she had commented, "I'm sure a lot of women are precluded from advancing because of their marital status, or the fact that they might be having children."

One woman did not see any discrimination in the legal profession, although she had been asked in an articling interview whether she planned to have children, and she did not think that the question was appropriate. Finally, one woman, who considered herself a feminist (but not a "rabid" one), found that the backlash from the Law Society's "intrusive" work on gender bias was resulting in more discrimination against women. Firms were fearful of hiring women, and the workplace was becoming more unpleasant.

Eighteen percent of the men did not think there was discrimination against women in the legal profession. However, some of these men recognized a problem that they thought was, or would be, remedied. One did not see much discrimination within law firms, but thought that there was still an "old network of clients who may not feel comfortable with women lawyers." He was optimistic that as his generation moved into management the problems would be alleviated, and the criterion would be merit, not colour or sex. Another described the old boys' network:

There is still, I think among the male lawyers, a perception that females are apart – I don't want to say inferior because I don't think it is inferior, but they're different, and as a consequence they are treated differently. And I guess the best analogy is the old boys' network. I think that in many cases, in terms of being equal, there is not a level of comfort with having women involved on a close personal level, I suppose. As a consequence, they are isolated outside of some of the political workings of the firm, as opposed to, not the business work, but in terms of decision making. They have an input, but the problem is in terms of the actual power of the decisions that go on. I think that they're more or less excluded from those, in terms of what area of practice, what clients to approach, how to deal with those things. I think that's something that still needs to be worked out.

When asked whether he thought bias or discrimination against women in the legal profession today restricts their career advancement, he had this to say:

Not any more. I think, in fact, that the programs that are put in place have enhanced equality. I know that there are a lot more female judges being appointed. I think that the pendulum has been swinging back, just not far enough. I think that there's a recognition and a movement toward levelling the playing field. If they're given the opportunity and said they don't like it, fine. I tend to think that there's a presumption that there's no interest or they don't have the ability, which I don't think is the case. What I see happening a lot, in terms of the hiring of people, is that the political things can sometimes be a constraint. Whereas [with the] "Let's go for a beer after work with the junior lawyers" [type of thing], the females aren't traditionally seen as fitting in that well with that type of thing. The ones that succeed seem to become "one of the boys."

Another man stated that he would be shocked if there was discrimination against women in the legal profession:

I'm not saying there's not discrimination, there may be discrimination, but I don't think it's as widespread as those reports make it out to be. I certainly didn't ever get the view, when I was at law school, that they were treated any differently. The top three students in our class were female. The gold medallist the year before us was female. Clearly they're not being discriminated against in law school. I don't see it. Those students were highly sought after by firms for articles. I'm not female, so obviously I can't comment on how females perceive it, but from where I sit, I don't see that as a problem. If it truly were a problem, I'd be shocked because it just doesn't happen.

Some of the men who said there was no discrimination against women recognized the inflexibility of the practice of law, and the clients, in dealing with women who have children:

It's not the profession, it's that the practice and the clients dictate what we're talking about. I'll digress a second. If you look at women and the graduation age, they are, let's say, twenty-eight or so, and then you add six years to that while they're senior associates – they're thirty-four or thirty-five. At that point they tend to be, if they haven't before then, having children because women are the ones who have children. If they choose to do so, that puts them in a problem with the practice. I don't think any firm can deal with the fact that your clients have a relationship with you. Every good firm has lawyers, a lot of lawyers, who have their own clients, and they're the reason the clients come. It's a personal practice, and if you leave for any period of time, you lose some of your clients. The firm could lose some of the clients, and the firm can deal with that either by putting someone else in your place, but then that person ends up with a relationship, and you can't just yank them out and throw them out in the cold when you're back, or the clients leave and find someone who will be there for them when they need them, and who they like.

According to this man, the problem is with clients:

Client expectations have changed recently. They're much more demanding – the age of fax and modems, and "Do it now." You've got to be there, and I think a problem arises with people leaving the practice. It would happen if I left the practice, if my wife had a child at that time. Once you're a partner it's different, and the firms, in a way, are ready to deal with it because, for one thing, you're a partner and it's harder to get out. In other words, if you go to that position and announce you're going to have children, there's not much they can do about it. It's a big step to get rid of a partner. But even then, I think problems arise, but it is dealt with, because they can't fix it as easily. In other words, they may lose some clients and may have less of an income from you, but they're going to have to live with it. With an associate, if they lose a client, you know that's terrible because you need the clients to justify your partnership. You see, it's a chicken and egg thing. You need the clients to show them that they should bring you on as a partner, and if you don't have them because you left, you won't be a partner, or they can hire another associate, because there's lots of people lined up behind you.

In addition, he was not prepared to suffer what he saw as the consequences of a woman taking time off:

I'd be upset as a lawyer if firms allowed a female associate to take a year or eighteen months off, and then I had to be there to cover for her and all her clients, and not be able to build up my practice during that time, and give it all back. Or, if they just allowed her practice to wither and then brought her into partnership with me, and yet she was paid as I was, and she was working fewer hours because she had fewer clients. In other words, it's a merit kind of practice. I just would be upset if her lack of clients or more time off didn't have some effect, because I could take a year off, but I won't because, if I do, my practice will suffer. It's as simple as that. You've chosen your job, and it's unforgiving, although different firms have tried different things, but not with much success.

According to one man, "single parents have a tough row to hoe," as do women who want to have children. Although he had not seen any women with difficulties, he could well imagine the "absolute horror" a female lawyer with a family would go through in these circumstances. Some of the men were more negative about the adjustments expected of the legal profession:

Yeah, yeah. I'm getting tired of it, because I don't care. Do you know what I mean? You come into this office, you're going to be a lawyer. I couldn't care less who you are, and I'm getting tired of hearing about it. Instead of just doing it, we're talking about it, and I hate talking about things when it's better just to do it. The goalposts in my game have changed. Women have been very clever. I don't mean this in a conspiratorial sense, it's just my way of describing it. Here we were all thinking about equal status, equal opportunity, and everybody was convinced that that made nothing but sense because it does, of course. But as I say, the goalposts have changed. Now that's not the case anymore. Now we're talking about shared workweeks, short workweeks, extended maternity leaves, and all of these kinds of things. So the way I describe it, it has gone from being equal status to special status, and I find that problematic. I don't think I should be treated any less equally than women should. Now, I have requirements for budgets and hours related to this firm, and they're fairly onerous. Those budgets and those expectations for hours and money, and things like that, should be the same for women and men. The other thing that I find hard to fathom is how all of these wonderful things are supposed to happen in a business environment, because businesses succeed or fail based on how productive their people are. If your work expectations are lowered, there's no way you can compensate that in terms of a reduction in salary.

He went on to provide an example:

Let's say I've just had a baby, and I come back from maternity leave, and I've decided that I only want to work three or four days a week. This is the office space, this is for me. It's going to exist regardless of how many days of the week I work. So, theoretically, if I'm going to be working three days, we should just be able to divide my salary by three-fifths, but it doesn't work that way. What you would probably think a fair way to remunerate, but it doesn't work that way because a person, if you want to do the math and I'd encourage you to do it, if a person is going to occupy this space and meet the expectations that a person working full time would, the difference between what the firm loses out of its own pocket [and my salary] is not equal to two-fifths of the salary. In fact it is far in excess. So it's a net loss to the firm. So, for example, when gender bias reports come out and recommend among other things, as I recall, a short workweek when that is desirable for a particular person, they're placing a fairly onerous requirement on professionals and business. The business aspect is important, and that's not a productive way to go about doing business. [Interviewer: Do you think that people working three out of five, or two out of five days, might be more productive than working full time?] It's just got to be the most inefficient way to do business. You can't have two people working on the same files, on different files, and who's going to respond to the phone calls for the person who's working on those files? It doesn't work that way. If you canvassed lawyers in this firm, I suspect they'd tell you that they've got to be at their desks most of the time, because the clients want to perceive that you're there. Most clients think that they're the only client you have. You can say, "I've got a fifty-day trial coming up tomorrow," and they'll say, "Oh, that's going to be interesting, but can you get this to me by the end of the day?" They don't care about what else is going on in your life. They want to be responded to.

When asked whether any part-time people worked at his firm, he responded: "Right now all but one of our legal assistants are on four-day workweeks. ['But not your lawyers?'] That's not true, there are two lawyers in this firm who are on four-day workweeks. Don't you have a follow-up question? ['Are there any plans to institute part-time workweeks?'] No, no. The question that I thought you were going to ask is yes, they are both female. ['You caught me on that.'] There you go."

One man held the view that the rules were the same for men as for women. There was no discrimination against women, as long as they were prepared to make the same sacrifices as men. He knows male lawyers who, because of the demands of their job, are rarely home. One man commented that women may have worked harder than men with the same academic background, but they did not face discrimination.

Two men just did not see any discrimination against women:

I know it's not politically correct to hold this view, but I don't see it. The argument could always be made that because I'm not female I wouldn't experience it. But I don't see it, in the sense that I have yet to come out of court thinking to myself that the only reason I won that application, or the only reason the judge went my way, was because I'm male and the other lawyer is female. I have yet to think that this is going to be easy because this is against a female lawyer. I may say to myself that I am perhaps better prepared than this other lawyer, but only because of their method of preparation, which has nothing to do with their gender. We have good female lawyers, we have bad female lawyers. We have good male lawyers, we have bad male lawyers, in the sense that some pay more attention to the practice, and they are just better at their job. I don't see it. Certainly in our firm, two of us were brought into the partnership, the other associate was a female and she's now a partner. We have had a number of summer students who are female. We have a female articling student at the present time. I don't see a bias here one way or the other. We look for people we think are going to fit into our firm and fit into the type of practice that we have here, which is not downtown Vancouver. We want people who can relate to people, whether male or female.

Sexual discrimination? I don't believe it. I don't hear it from the people I work with. It's such a crock. I don't know what goes on in big firms; I have no idea. I don't see it myself, and it's not complained about by women lawyers. The ones I see who are in firms are doing just fine, just the same as a guy. In a big firm they don't get to practise law.

Another man who did not see any gender bias or racial discrimination suggested that the people at the Law Society did not have enough to do.

Five men (10%) were somewhat ambivalent about whether women in the legal profession are discriminated against. One had heard about it, but had never seen it. He was aware that Madame Justice Wilson's report talked about discrimination, and from what he had read, apparently there was.

If it existed, he held the view that it should not. Another man thought that some women make "this thing a big deal," and some "just ignore it and just get on with life." His wife, also a lawyer who was pregnant with their first child, "doesn't make too much fuss about sexual discrimination." He adds: "With this maternity leave she does have a dicey issue, but she holds her ground. She deals with it as any other issue, and stands up for her rights and the protection of the laws that apply to her. She doesn't let it get in her way either." He also provided an explanation for perceptions of discrimination:

> You know what I think happens? Sometimes you get a man who dislikes a woman lawyer, and he'll over-generalize about women, "Oh, you know, women lawyers, blah, blah, blah," or also religion or colour, that stuff. I think that's just simply a mistake about what it is that happens to bug the person. I think that's carried over. But my experience is that the same lawyers, when they go to evaluate candidates, I don't think that lawyer chucks out the applications by women. I think there are fewer applications by women lawyers. [Interviewer: So you don't know whether there is bias or discrimination in the legal profession that restricts their career advancement?] [He laughs] Well, I'm sure there is, but it's hard for me to say. If I look at things and how they work from day to day, I have a hard time saying that, pointing out many lawyers who are just basically ... I mean they might be a little bit sexist, but I think that when it comes to dealing with another lawyer or opposing counsel, I don't think that they ... well, you hear stories, but in terms of what I see as an issue, I don't see much of it; and I think if we had three candidates for an associate position, I don't think a woman would get the short shrift just because she's a woman. We have women students here all the time, summer students; I think that you need a personality you can work with. We had a couple of positions, but ... the women were not suitable candidates, not because they were women. We ended up with a male in the end, but then I look at other positions, summer positions, they're usually women. We're a small firm and the lawyers have to do many things; they have to get the work done, bill, and collect, you have to be a jack of all trades. In terms of the women I know who are practising law, I don't know ... I think I know more men who are like that. The women I know tend to like to take the case and do the work, and then to leave it like that, but I don't know that's so much a problem. I don't see that so much as a male problem. I mean, certainly if there was a woman who fit, that's the type of lawyer we need in this office, whether it's a man or a woman, I don't think it would make any difference. As far as I'm concerned, I don't really care.

Another man worked with female associates who had read the reports on gender equality and said that they were happy that those type of things were not happening at their firm. This man did not think that it was an issue with lawyers his age: "I'm prepared to acknowledge that half a generation up there that's a concern. You know, I've had more women professors, I think, than men. I respect them equally, provided that they can teach well in their areas. I've been negative to both men and women when I haven't got a competent education – equally with counsel on the other side. I respect counsel for what they know, not who they are, and I routinely get upset only when I feel somebody just doesn't know the legal issues, not a gender that's different."

One man did not know whether it was discrimination, but recognized that women who want to have children are "put in a difficult position":

I don't know whose fault that is, but law is a business just like any other business. If you're going to have a child, you can't work the number of hours that are needed to be profitable within the firm, and consequently some accommodation has to be made. I think that hurts women more than anybody. It's awkward, because I know a number of firms have structured arrangements, that if you wish to work less, then you're paid comparably less. That's generally acceptable to everyone. Other firms that I know, this was an issue at the Canadian Bar Association meeting in Quebec, it was contemplated that work expectations for women, or childbearing women, should be reduced without reducing their income, and all that's going to mean is that people or firms will not hire women, because it just doesn't make economic sense. So, I'm not sure whether that's discrimination, but it certainly affects advancement and job hiring and things of that nature.

When we returned to the question of whether he thought women in the legal profession today experience bias or discrimination that restricts their career advancement, he continued:

"Restricts" is a tough one. There's certainly no problem in women getting articling positions, and there's no problem in having them asked back to be associates, and there's no problem as they advance through their junior years. I think the difficulty arises, and it's twofold: the first is that business is still a fairly male-oriented environment and, to become a partner in a law firm, you have to be able to attract clients, and there are very few clients that women attract. I think, in some ways, that's because law is more progressive. For example, my wife is a MBA, and she went to interview with banks, and she was told by a number of Schedule A banks that there are no women above manager. So she said, "I'll not go to the bank." So she became a CA, which is the easy way out, but it's just reality. So, the first thing is the inability to attract clients, which is necessary to become a partner. The second is the "having a baby syndrome." I think firms are coming to grips with it, but only in the way that there's got to be an accommodation in which, for a period you realize that you are generating 'χ' dollars less, so you're taking out 'γ' dollars less, to the extent that is acceptable to both parties, I think firms will be able to deal with it. But the last thing a firm is going to want to do is be told you have to ... it's just creating a subsidy, and I don't think anyone wants to pay for a subsidy.

Upon being asked whether he thought firms would be prepared to allow a man or a woman to work 20% less for 20% less pay, he responded:

I don't think the numbers would be 20%/20% because, for example, if I only work four days a week, they're still paying rent for this, they have to amortize the furniture, they still have all the technology, equipment, the overhead per lawyer, which is significant. I don't know what it is in the firm – say $140,000 – the overhead would stay approximately the same while the revenue would go down 20%, so the net profit would be less than a 20% decrease. I know one firm that just entered into an agreement for a four-day week for 65% of pay, and that, I think, is more the economic ratio.

I asked him whether it was a figure that was possible to calculate:

By negotiation, I don't think you can say this is what it is. And it all depends, if someone is going to share a secretary, you can reduce the overhead. If you give them a smaller office, then you can reduce the overhead, but it's pure dollars and cents, that's all it is, I think everybody recognizes. Certainly here, women are half the brains and, in law school, women tend to be the best students. We're actively trying to recruit women articling students because they're bright. When you come on to the business, it's got to make sense from a business point of view. So I think the accommodation can be arranged, but it's going to be different for everybody. I don't think you can brand all women with that view, because there are some who don't want children, there are some who don't want to get married, there are some who want to have full-time nannies (and there is one lawyer couple in town who have three nannies – one for day, one for night, and one for weekends). And if you're willing to do that, you can work all you want, and it's not going to affect your bottom-line contribution at all.

Another man, who left a firm because he could not live up to the firm's expectations, and the expectations he had for himself in terms of his family life, identified discrimination as it relates to family status, because "private firms are in business to make money." He continued:

> In some ways you can look at that and say that my firm wasn't overly flexible in terms of accommodating my desire to have a family life, but in many respects it was my own assessment of the trade-off that I was making that influenced my decision, and I see that among many of the female lawyers who I have practised with as well. The firm I was with before was a small partnership, and there were far more female associates than there were male associates – most of them young and most of them single or married without children. I think that it has been my perception that women have tended to face what is being described as discrimination – I haven't resolved it in my mind, but I don't necessarily know whether it's discrimination or not. What I see a lot of times is that it's a demanding profession, much more demanding than most jobs that you could get elsewhere, and I think if you have something else that tugs at your time in your life, you're bound to be unhappy in law. If it's discriminatory in the firms for them not to accommodate that, then I guess there has been discrimination, because I think firms are not generally willing to make great accommodation.

The firm had made some accommodations for him in terms of his family. The partner he worked with would ask the respondent whether it was inconvenient for him to handle a matter. He never felt that there was pressure to take on files or issues that interfered with his family commitments at the end of the day. He worked forty-five to fifty hours a week, but was not prepared to meet the expectation of eighty to 100 hours a week when a big file demanded it. He recognized that law is a competitive business, and if "you can't run or skate as fast as the next person any more, for whatever reason, there is always somebody else right behind you willing to do so." Law does not provide one with the "luxury to be able to go at a slow pace."

Two men (4%) commented on reverse discrimination, or discrimination that works both ways. One thought that women, although they may not have any advantage in large law firms, had an advantage when it came to being appointed to the Bench, although he did not think this was necessarily a bad thing. Female prosecutors enjoyed the same advantage as male prosecutors, in which seniority, not merit, are grounds for promotion. When asked whether female defence counsel had any problems, he commented: "I don't think they do. It may well be some old judge kicking around who may discriminate, but by and large, you have to realize that there are a lot of women as Crown counsel who appear in the court all the time, and as a result the trails have been blazed. In all my time in court I have never seen any sexist comments from a judge. I'd be interested in what others have to say about it."

Experience with Sexual Harassment

Twenty-five years ago, the term "sexual harassment" was not in our vocabulary. The first examination of this issue in Canada was by Constance Backhouse, a Canadian lawyer and law professor, and Leah Cohen, a Canadian journalist.[29] They described sexual harassment as "an expression of power." The problem was named,[30] and sexual harassment moved from a private, unspoken domain to the public domain.[31] Although lower courts and tribunals in Canada grappled with the issue of whether sexual harassment was discrimination on the basis of gender under human rights legislation in the late 1970s and early 1980s, it was not until 1989 that the Supreme Court of Canada overturned the Manitoba Court of Appeal's decision,[32] and found that sexual harassment was a form of discrimination. Many human rights acts now include a reference to sexual harassment; however, if legislation does not prohibit sexual harassment, it will be included in provisions which prohibit discrimination on the basis of gender.

The first studies on sexual harassment focused on the workplace and colleges and universities.[33] A recent issue of the *Canadian Review of Sociology and Anthropology* was devoted to examining the issue of sexual harassment, "Where We Were, Where We Are, and Prospects for the New Millennium."[34] It includes articles on sexual harassment in public places such as streets, transit systems, shopping malls,[35] public housing,[36] and sports settings for female athletes.[37] Another article compares Canadian working women who reported being sexually harassed at work (in a telephone survey) with those who had filed harassment complaints with the Canadian Human Rights Commission.[38]

By the time the interviews for this study were conducted in 1993-94, the terminology surrounding sexual harassment was firmly embedded in our legal culture; however, there were controversies over its interpretation that still exist today. Respondents were asked whether they had ever been sexually harassed in work-related situations, including professional functions, since entering the legal profession as an articling student.[39] If they had been, they were asked to elaborate on whether the harassment was by other lawyers, judges, or clients. They were also asked how they reacted or responded to the harassment, whether the harassment or their response adversely affected their career, and whether the harassment affected them personally.

Respondents Who Experienced Sexual Harassment

Thirty-six percent of the women interviewed had been sexually harassed since entering the legal profession.[40] As for who is doing the harassing, 34% of the women interviewed said they had been sexually harassed by other lawyers, 12% had been sexually harassed by judges, and 10% by clients. The nature of the harassment included sexual innuendo, looks, gestures, so-called "jokes," and jokes for embarrassment value, persistent unwanted "flattery," sexual propositions, excessive compliments about what they were wearing and suggestions as to what they ought to wear, physical descriptions and names ("big tits," "broads," "baby"), pictures of scantily clad women, partners "hanging all over you" at social functions, being pinched and grabbed, "playing footsie" at a social function, attempted kisses, and comments about weight.[41]

For some, it was the atmosphere created in the firm. One woman said she was "livid" about the sexist behaviour at the firm with which she articled:

> The young guys couldn't see it. Every Friday afternoon, the articling students and partners would go to a strip joint. Some didn't think they could say "No." The women were back at the office working, while the men were at the strip joint. The secretaries hated the arrogant and sexist lawyers. I was floored by the fact that there was no support from the younger men. One associate, who was there for two years, was thinking of lying, and saying she would not get married or have a family. [On top of that] women weren't getting interesting work. Men didn't want to work with women; women weren't seen as intelligent as men. I was hired to keep up appearances, "Here's a woman. We hire them once in awhile." Sexual innuendos, clients coming on and not recognizing the professional relationship.

Reactions to Sexual Harassment

Reactions to sexual harassment varied and seemed to depend upon how much power the women had in relation to losing their jobs or being ostracized. A number of women explained:

> My reaction varied depending on my position. Sometimes I said I didn't appreciate it. Sometimes I said nothing, or tried to ignore it. It depended on how I felt at that particular moment – what my relative position of power was to the other person, and what consequences I thought might result if I said or did something.

> I ignore it, the only way to keep my job. I never condone or ask to participate in it. [Interviewer: What if you complained?] I'd be fired. I'm lucky, why throw it away? I can deal with them by ignoring them.

> I just tried to avoid it, to avoid them. I didn't feel there was the ability to

complain, and that was more related to just differences in power, or a perception that you wouldn't be taken seriously by those you complained to.

It made me angry but, when you're an articling student, especially, you have no power whatsoever. You have to get through your articles, and then you can go off and do what you want. I eventually put up and shut up. I wasn't happy about it. I guess I practise more of an avoidance strategy. Most of it wasn't sufficiently serious that I had to do anything about it, so I took the easier route, I guess.

It was only a few days after I was called to the bar. I wasn't going to tell him where to go. So I was disappointed in the absolute non-support [from my male colleagues]. And of course now I wish it would happen to me again, because I would have a totally different tack and reaction. [Interviewer: How would you react now?] I'd call him on it. I'd have no qualms about doing it. But as I said, I was by myself, and I had no friends at this function. It was just a few days after my call, and I thought, "Man, do you want to toast your career right now?"

With the clients, I set them straight. Other lawyers hid behind the joke, and said "That's not appropriate," and laughed. I didn't indicate how upset I was until later, when I was no longer an articling student.

Others were more assertive, but for some there were consequences. One woman told a man, who wanted to have sex with her, to "hit the road." It was effective; however, it meant that she was not hired by the firm. Another woman was uncomfortable doing it, but told the man that he was wrecking his life doing such ridiculous things. Another made herself quite clear, so the offenders thought twice. Initially, one woman thought that the harassment just "came with the territory," but then later, when she thought about it, decided it was not appropriate. However, she thinks that it is the way that person is, and he is "probably never going to change."

One woman was quite vocal about the sexist behaviour of the men. At first she was really upset, and would end up staying away from work, breaking into tears at home, and asking herself if she was to blame. Eventually she talked to someone in charge, and the person was supportive, and told her she did not have to put up with the behaviour.

There were an insufficient number of responses to analyze my respondents' reactions to sexual harassment in terms of, for example, their employment relationship to the harasser, the type of harassment, its affect on their job and their person, and so on. However, the study by Crocker and Kalemba did examine some of these variables. They found that 53% of the women responded to the harassment directly ("reporting, speaking to someone, retaliating or confronting the harasser") and 46% took an indirect approach ("ignoring the problem, not responding, taking the [sexual harassment] as a joke [only 1% did this], avoiding the situation, or changing [their] behaviour"). Nine percent of the women left the situation, and 2% quit their jobs. The other variables illustrate some of the power dynamics in women's responses to sexual harassment. Women were more likely to confront co-workers than their supervisors or clients, and were more likely to leave the situation or quit their jobs when harassed by supervisors. In fact, leaving a job was "used almost exclusively by women who were harassed by someone in a position of authority."[42] Sexual harassment by supervisors also had more of a negative effect on the women. The authors also found greater similarities in women's responses to clients and supervisors, than in their responses to clients and co-workers. In discussing this finding Crocker and Kalemba suggest that clients have something in common with superiors that "deters women from responding directly and causes a similar level of adverse effects." Although clients are not seen as having formal power in organizational power theory, "they may have access to some other source of power that mirrors the effects of formal organizational power. The target may be as dependent upon a client as she is on a supervisor for her continued employment or economic success."[43] This has interesting implications for women lawyers whose contacts with clients are often crucial to their success as a lawyer.

The Effects of Sexual Harassment
Research on the effects of sexual harassment shows that it has a chilling effect on women's working environment, threatens their personhood, and results in psychological problems. However, it also takes its toll on business, costing millions of dollars in absenteeism and loss of productivity and employees.[44]

Some of the women in this study dealt with the harassment, and some received an apology. However, as one commented, "There's always a personal toll." The effects of harassment include depression, embarrassment, anger, irritation (being "pissed off"), and distress. Comments by the women included:

> Having to endure any of these types of comments, or the threat or promises of reprisals, is chilling, not to mention wearing.

> [I reacted] with embarrassment, with mixed feelings of wanting to maintain some professional standard and relationship. There were angry feelings ... depression.

I was distressed at the time. I thought I handled it very well, and I didn't tell anyone for a lot of reasons. It wasn't important to me. I was quite distraught, but not for long, because I thought I handled it well. It was just an incident.

I think that something like that can't help but change the relationship, at least the way you view that particular relationship. I had always seen it as a professional relationship, and suddenly everything was overturned somewhat in my mind. I didn't see the need for that. I get along well with the people that I work with at all levels ... Personally, I felt insulted, and I felt as though, in my professional capacity, the respect with which I expect to be viewed had been lowered. I think to that extent, I think personally and professionally, I found it disturbing.

Other women had managed to diminish the effect:

I have an attitude toward [harassment]. It didn't affect me to say, "Go to hell" to him. I just felt it was the right thing to do. I can write it off, and did so at the time. It has crossed my mind to raise it, to set a precedent as to what should happen. It happened quite a few years ago but it's still on my mind.

I thought it was totally inappropriate. I didn't think of it as sexual harassment, I guess, in that it was a isolated incident, and nothing like it had ever remotely occurred to me before, and knowing what I do in my conversations with other women, it wasn't way up there on the scale of harassment, but it was someone that I worked with, and I felt that it did to some extent alter the relationship. Obviously, there was something going on that I didn't know about. It was an incident that was isolated and controlled, and I spoke to someone else in the organization about it, and they had been aware of it, but that was the extent of it. It hasn't reoccurred.

It didn't bother me too much, because I'd been told that he was a boozer. I was more disappointed in the non-support from the older members at the bar that were there. That's what bugged me more. I just thought what a bunch of brown-nosers. They don't have the moxy to stand up to somebody doing that. And of course now, as I say, I wish I had, but I thought because they had been around longer, they should have. But I mean, I didn't hold him in any respect, so it didn't bug me too much. I still think, "What a twit."

Certainly the one occasion when I was told it wasn't my place [to correct this person], I was angry, and I felt personally affected by it. And many of the incidents of that nature I find quite forgettable. They may irritate me or disturb me for a while.

One woman discussed the Law Society of British Columbia's *Discipline Digest* case with one of the partners. He asked her why she was showing it to them. She responded, "Because you're the firm associate liaison, and you should be aware of these things." He asked, "Well, do you think there's sexual harassment going on in the office?" She relayed the rest of the conversation:

I told him shortly after I started here, I walked past an associate's office, and he yelled out, "Hey, [name] is your hair really [colour]?" I looked at him and said, "Well, I'll never tell." The partner, who was in his office, said, "Well, all you have to do is just ask her to drop her pants and you'll find out." And I looked at him and said, "You know, in some circumstances that would be considered sexual harassment." And everyone got upset and flustered, and I said, "Maybe if you circulate this [*Discipline Digest*] bulletin, maybe those types of stupid comments won't be made." And, he said "Maybe you should put it into a memo to the partners." And I said "Oh yeah, right. Oh sure, that's something I'm going to do. I've been here less than six months, and I'm going to be the one who sends out this sexual harassment bulletin; get a grip!" So, there's no sexual harassment in this office.

Ambivalence about Sexual Harassment

Ten percent of the women were somewhat ambivalent in their responses to the question of whether they had every been sexually harassed since entering the legal profession – one said she had not been directly or overtly subjected to it, and four described behaviour that they recognized the others might consider sexual harassment, but that they did not consider to be sexual harassment. Three of these women excused the behaviour. One, who was often asked by male clients, "What's a nice girl like you doing not married and having kids?" described them as "totally well-meaning, but clueless." She continued:

They don't mean it as a put down or harassment. But I just thought, "You never ask guys, 'What's a nice male lawyer like you doing, not married, not having kids?'" I laugh, or just say I'm too busy, or haven't found the right person. But the fact is that it shouldn't even be an issue. And it's not because they don't think I'm a good lawyer, they think I'm a perfectly good lawyer. They find it incomprehensible that someone who is not Quasimodo would choose to go into law and not get married and have kids. And, yet the same question never arises with male lawyers, and that reflects a certain attitude in society that is not conducive to women being in the profession. You shouldn't have to deal with comments like that on any level. What I choose to do or not do in my personal life is none of their business. Of course, I can't tell them that. They're perfectly well-meaning. They don't mean to offend you.

Another respondent made it clear she did not appreciate inappropriate sexual joking. When asked whether she would describe her experience as a form of sexual harassment, she responded:

No, because I know the individuals. It's behaviour that, if someone else heard about it, would be in one of those Benchers' Bulletins, and come out as a sexual discrimination and harassment. When you know the individuals, and they're of the old school, that's more or less the way things are. They make joking, stupid remarks, without thinking. They make those offhand sexist remarks, because they've made them for fifty years. It's not going to stop because I call up five committees, so for me it's just saying, "Listen, I don't appreciate that."

In the midst of some tough negotiations, a man lawyer commented, "I want you to understand that this is nothing sexual, this is nothing personal, but you're a bitch!" The respondent burst out laughing. Others might have reported the offending lawyer. However, she held the view that, "If I were a man, he would have called me up and said, 'You son of a bitch.' Would that have been discrimination? If we're going to get out there and be equals, then we're equals. I just thought it was funny. But what he did, he would have done to a male."

Respondents Who Did Not Experience Sexual Harassment
Among the 54% who said they had not been sexually harassed was a woman who was called "hon" and "sweetheart," but described herself as having dodged sexual harassment because she didn't "fit the mould."[45] Another, who said she had never been sexually harassed, said that the reason was that she did not "easily feel harassed," and that her attitude of not putting up with it resulted in it not being a problem. Another could not imagine anyone making an inappropriate suggestion to her, because she is viewed as an "aggressive female." One older respondent, who had been harassed in a previous career, assumed she had not been harassed in the legal profession because of her age. Another had seen and heard about sexual harassment in other firms, but worked for a small firm with which it did not occur. One situation of which she was aware bordered on sexual assault, and she thought the police should have been called.

Sexual harassment appears to be widespread in the legal profession.

However, some women do not view it this way. One woman viewed the legal profession as a potential opportunity for relationships to develop, and one described how some women lawyers use sex to get what they want in the law firm. Here are their comments:

> Well, it's not harassment if you're happy about it. This is one of those grey areas. Sometimes, especially if you're going to law school with a bunch of people, you get to know them really well, and sometimes you date them. So there's a certain amount of flirtation going on at various times. It's hard to say then, after that. The problem with the word "sexual harassment" is that it really is in the eye of the person allegedly being harassed, because if it's welcome, then they're not going to proceed with charges if it was perceived as flirtation. I can honestly say that I've not received any unwelcome advances, or anything like that, or had any lurid jokes told. People are good. I've been flirted with, but I didn't mind.

> I think that what you're going to have to do is look at the overall environment. It's my knowledge that sexual harassment in the workplace with regards to lawyers is more in the reverse. Young female lawyers are willing to sleep with the partner. It goes just as much one way as the other.

Male Respondents Who Reported Sexual Harassment

Only 4% of the men reported being sexually harassed. One man had been sexually harassed by a female member of the support staff. He found it annoying and uncomfortable, but successfully avoided the harasser and there were no adverse consequences to his job. The power relationship, which exists between women and their harassers, was not present in these circumstances, and still the man was annoyed and uncomfortable with the harassment.

The other man broadened the definition of sexual harassment as follows:

> It depends on the definition of sexual harassment. I would advocate a fairly broad definition. Where I used to practise, they'd say things about women, or gay and lesbian people, which I would find objectionable. In some instances, I would say something, in others I wouldn't. Some [comments] would be included in the definition of sexual harassment – making those comments after an objection has been expressed. A partner took us out to lunch. At one point he stated, and this is word for word, that "women were biologically unsuited for the practice of law" (meaning they have babies and things and that's what they should be thinking about). We expressed our strong disagreement with this view and marshalled arguments that the best students in our classes were women, but he just wouldn't have any of it. It was clear-cut to him. I'm confident that he

wouldn't see that as sexual harassment, but he was the partner, he was my boss, he made comments that I found objectionable, and I expressed my objection to them. Under some definition, that would count as sexual harassment. I know he wouldn't see it that way, and I suppose I didn't see it that way. I was just annoyed with the whole experience.

One man had concerns about the uncertainty surrounding what constitutes harassment:

There are clearly scenarios that are completely inappropriate, which obviously come under sexual harassment, but in fact would be much more than just sexual harassment, but the commencement of it would be sexual harassment, and go from there. Those things are clearly unacceptable in any workplace. The difficult part of this is the huge grey area in which, and you hear people saying this jokingly, they're scared to tell a joke or to comment, for fear that someone may misunderstand or take offence. I think that has an unfortunate effect on a workplace. Or, perhaps I'm naive, in the sense that I think that people should understand where the line is. Certainly, certain comments are clearly inappropriate ... and those are the kind a person should make when they are out with the guys at the pub. But you don't do it in mixed company. But it seems to me that if you take this [the rule] to the full extent of what it seems to suggest, you may make it a sterile place to work, where people walk around like robots, there's no personality anymore. There's so many things you can't touch on.

He then talked about what he called the "double standard":

If you have a female lawyer or staff member who is one to tell jokes, I can't see anything happening because of that. The problem always seems to arise when the male says the joke or makes the comment. You never read about the opposite circumstance. I can think of a number of female staff members who are just as upfront with comments that are said in a joking manner, and people take it as that. As I and a few other lawyers have commented, "If we'd said that, and it was the other way around, it would be considered inappropriate."

Two men did not mind the flirting that went on by secretaries and other staff. Another commented, "Like any profession, sex makes the world go around. That's just the way it is." Other men, however, were uncomfortable with the office flirts, but realized that women had a much tougher time dealing with harassment:

It's difficult to conceive of a man being sexually harassed, or inappropriate advances being made. Society doesn't view a man as being capable of being sexually harassed, unless it's by another man. But the notion of a male lawyer complaining because a secretary finds him attractive just seems odd. With the policy in place, maybe it won't seem so odd. Generally speaking, the more powerful person is harassing the less powerful, and using the imbalance to get what they want. With the policy in place, there's a potential for disciplinary hearings as a result of it, that may have some effect. The downside, of course, is when you have a power imbalance, you have less of a likelihood of someone coming forward. It's difficult for support staff, most difficult for associates and articling students. Support staff – the general perception is that if you're a competent, skilled paralegal or legal secretary, then you can say, "Take this job and shove it, I'm not working here any more," and you can go out on the street and be working within two weeks.

However, associates did not have that same comfort:

If they walk out of a firm alleging sexual harassment, they're going to have a hard time finding a job. That's the general belief, and I don't think it's unwarranted, especially if they're in a specialty area. If a four- to five-year call associate is being harassed by a partner, working in a specialized area, that senior partner is going to know everyone who works in the field, and there will be questions asked. There's an awful lot of room for damage. It may well not come to pass. Odds are it won't come to pass, and lawyers are supposed to be intelligent enough to know that if you start stabbing people in the back, you're going to get your ass sued into the ground. There's nothing I love more than a wrongful dismissal suit, but that's not much comfort to an associate who has a house to pay for, and it's no consolation when you believe that if you raise the complaint, you won't work in this town again. Your belief may not be warranted, but that's irrelevant to the belief. There's a lot to get in the way. It's going to take some gutsy people, and it's going to take some gutsy determinations from the Law Society. You don't want the Clarence Thomas/Anita Hill scenario to be re-enacted. I certainly wouldn't want to be raising a sexual harassment complaint against the senior partner, or against a fellow associate. That wouldn't be something I'd enjoy doing. I have to wonder whether I'd be taken seriously – How do I prove it? What's my credibility going to be like? What's going to be left of it? I can't see it being much different for a woman. The fears would be stronger for a woman.

One man had a great deal of empathy for women, having been harassed as a waiter in his earlier career:

[I remember] working in restaurants when I was a kid and getting my bum grabbed by people. It happens to males, too, and particularly to younger ones, for the same reasons that it happens to younger women. They're perceived as not being as powerful and easier to take advantage of. But nothing happened to me to the extent of any permanent damage, just enough to make me irate. When harassment happens to anybody, particularly of a sexual nature ... I don't like sexist jokes for example. When I was a teenager, I remember how confused I was because no one had ever done anything like that to me before. But I think if you talk to most people, most have some incident, but they just bury it. These things can make you sensitive, or they can make you intolerant, but intolerance didn't happen because I didn't suffer any permanent damage, just enough to realize that it made me feel terrible. Now that I think about it, it makes me mad, because I know that the people were doing it just for a laugh.

One man had his own policy:

I've told 90% of the women here, "You know, I like to make a lot of jokes, and sometimes I like to tell off-colour jokes. I'd like you to know that if anything I say offends you, I want you to tell me immediately. I tell jokes to make people laugh. If it upsets you, that's not my goal, and I want to know, and I want to know right away." I usually say, "I'd prefer you not to scream across the hall, 'You pig,' but I still want to know." [Interviewer: And that works?] I think it does. Nobody has ever come up to me and said, "You know, that's disgusting. I never want you to say that again." But I think the advantage of having such a small environment is that people get to know me, and they're not threatened by me. But I still like to say it at the outset, because if you get a new legal assistant – she's twenty-two years old and just out of legal assistants' school – I don't want her to think because I'm a lawyer and she's on practicum that she has to put up with however offensive I want to be. I want her to know that she should be comfortable saying, "You know, I don't want to hear that," if that's what she feels. I've never had anyone do that, but I still like to let them know that that's there, so they don't feel intimidated or uncomfortable.

As one of the reviewers of an earlier version of this book asked, "Would she be likely to feel comfortable complaining?" If not, then his tactic may simply normalize his conduct and perpetuate a chilly climate for women in his office.

Ridding the Legal Profession of Discrimination and Sexual Harassment

Sixty percent of the women interviewed for this study said they had been discriminated against in the legal profession on the basis of gender, mostly by other lawyers, but also by judges and clients. Furthermore, 88% of the women and 66% of the men thought bias or discrimination against women in the legal profession today restricts their career advancement. Some of the lawyers also talked about discrimination on the basis of race, ethnic background, sexual orientation, and disability in the legal profession; however, it is more difficult to quantify this behaviour because of the low number of people from these groups. The most frequently cited form of discrimination against women was lack of accommodation for family commitments, followed by discrimination in career advancement, and then assignment of work, and appropriate weight not given to their opinions. Thirty-six percent of the women interviewed had been sexually harassed since entering the legal profession, most frequently by other lawyers but also by judges and clients.

Change could take place at four different levels, at least. First, individual law firms could, as Bisom-Rapp suggests, take the gender bias reports "seriously and to heart": "Instead of directing energy into litigation prevention strategies, firms should evaluate and revise the current conception of lawyering that disadvantages many women. Among the many components of that task, one stands out as paramount: to end the assumption that the lawyer is a male without significant family responsibilities. Women will never be equals in the legal profession as long as a 'pregnant attorney' is a contradiction in terms." She is of the view that law firms have two reasons to promote greater diversity. First, "lawyers are the gatekeepers of the justice system" and, as such, should be "trailblazers in promoting equality." Second, "if they hope to remain competitive in attracting and retaining corporate clients, many of which have had far more success in diversifying their law departments, firms must 'reflect the diversity of the clients they serve.'" Bisom-Rapp believes that law firms "should pursue full integration because it makes good moral and economic sense."[46] Bisom-Rapp's views on the issue of family responsibilities, and the role they play in the lives of women and men lawyers, are discussed in Chapter 7.

Second, law societies could introduce anti-discrimination and anti-sexual harassment rules. Even though federal and provincial human rights legislation and rights under the *Charter of Rights and Freedoms* enshrined in the *Constitution Act, 1982*, prohibit discrimination based on sex, and sexual harassment is discrimination based on sex, self-regulating professions still have an interest in dealing with such matters in-house.[47] The Law Society of British Columbia did so in 1992, and other law societies across Canada have done the same. The rules came into force in British Columbia just before I conducted the interviews for this study, and a couple of questions about their effectiveness were added to the interview schedule.

The respondents in this study were much more optimistic about the anti-sexual harassment rule than they were about the anti-discrimination rule. Sixty-six percent of the women and 70% of the men thought that the anti-sexual harassment rule would be effective, whereas only 23% of the women and 38% of the men thought the anti-discrimination rules would be effective.[48] The difference may be partly due to the fact that sexual harassment is easier to detect than discrimination, in areas of hiring or advancement in the legal profession. Another factor that may have been operating at this time was the circulation of a case of sexual harassment, by a lawyer of another lawyer, to all members of the Law Society. The Law Society had dealt with a complaint of sexual harassment in a public forum, and lawyers were talking about it. It raised both the awareness within the profession and increased its sensitivity to issues of sexual harassment.

Many of the concerns respondents in this study expressed about potential litigation because of the British Columbia Law Society's rules were probably alleviated by the introduction of an ombudsperson who works to educate lawyers about the issues, as well as investigate and resolve complaints on an informal basis. I have pointed out the irony in the Law Society's establishment of an informal system that could be used instead of its own self-regulating system.[49] However, it is true that informal resolution mechanisms have many advantages over prolonged, polarized litigation. According to Gail H. Forsythe, the Law Society of British Columbia's first ombudsperson, informal resolution provides a number of advantages. It is quicker, cheaper, and avoids escalation and bad media coverage. It allows for working relationships to be maintained rather than destroyed through the litigation process. It allows for education and closure on issues, and those without funds have easier access to informal resolutions.[50] In her first year, Forsythe delivered training sessions to more than 400 people, and responded to more than fifty complaints.[51]

Third, discrimination and sexual harassment lawsuits can be taken outside the legal profession and into the courts. Such litigation in the United States has received widespread publicity in Canada. Susan Bisom-Rapp has analyzed the effectiveness of anti-discrimination laws in the United States, in light of the litigation prevention strategies used by firms to ward off discrimination lawsuits.[52] She concludes that the preventive strategies alter the discourse used to describe the decision-making process in a firm, but do not change the actual outcome. Bisom-Rapp is of the view that the limit to anti-discrimination laws can be found in the anti-litigation tactics used by defence lawyers who "capture" the laws and use them for their own purposes.[53] The most common anti-litigation tactic is to recommend that firms develop written performance reviews, which, as Bisom-Rapp describes, are couched in "a discourse of gender and racial neutrality," and which "mask continuing conditions of inequality."[54] According to Linda Krieger, discrimination prevention and case law operate on assumptions designed to deal with overt discrimination, and "greatly constrain the ability of anti-discrimination law to address unconscious bias, 'today's more prevalent type of discrimination.'"[55] For example, there is an assumption that the discrimination takes place at the time of the decision (as opposed to throughout the career of a candidate), and there is an assumption that decision makers are capable of actually expressing the reasons for their decisions. According to Bisom-Rapp, lawyers are not experts at detecting gender stereotyping and unconscious discrimination, but rather they are experts in "discerning the kind of evidence that makes a legal finding of discrimination likely." The effect of prevention strategies is that they increase the "likelihood that law firm decisions can be defended, without altering the factors that contribute to women's systemic disadvantage."[56]

In addition, anti-discrimination laws are not effective in combatting the "institutional and ideological forces that contribute to gender disadvantage" in the legal profession.[57] Performance decisions are too complex to be assessed as to whether race, sex, sexual orientation, or disability did or did not influence or cause a particular decision. According to Bisom-Rapp, evaluations that try to erase gender differences (the goal of litigation-prevention tactics) obscure "both the problems facing women attorneys and the political solutions to them."[58] Having expressed her pessimism about anti-discrimination litigation and its prevention strategies, Bisom-Rapp suggests that judges in discrimination cases pay more attention, and take judicial notice of, "basic, commonsense facts in everyday life, in discrimination cases." Documentation by firms of their hiring and promotion practices should be scrutinized carefully, not taken at face value.[59]

While it is important that law firms and law societies lead by example, they still operate within the broader society. The task of eliminating discrimination and sexual harassment from the legal profession needs support from outside the profession. This fourth level of change is raised again in Chapters 6 and 7.

Whether the Law Society of British Columbia has succeeded in reducing discrimination and sexual harassment has not been established. However, from the prediction of the respondents in 1993-94, when the policy was first introduced, it may be that the sexual harassment policy is more effective than the anti-discrimination policy. Although some lawyers thought that some grey areas surround sexual harassment, for the most part, sexual harassment was seen as more obvious and easier to detect than discrimination. In addition, the "personal preferences" that some see as part of discrimination, do not manifest themselves with sexual harassment. While discrimination and sexual harassment pose major barriers to women's equality in the legal profession, the stereotype of women as "reluctant adversaries" also causes them some problems. Chapter 5 examines this issue.

5
Reluctant Adversaries

The adversarial system has faced a barrage of criticism over the years, although some have noted that the "rhetoric in praise [of it] flows freely in the prose of many legal insiders."[1] There is no agreement on how to define the adversarial system, however. Some writers distinguish it from the "players" or adversaries in the system. For example, Davis and Elliston suggest that the phrase "adversarial system" is used in at least three senses, the first two having to do with the system, the third with the participants: 1) a system in which two opposing parties present their interests for resolution, 2) a system in which judges play a passive role in hearing evidence and deciding the fate of litigants, and 3) a "style of lawyering." They see "style of lawyering" as independent of the adversarial system itself.[2]

Landsman suggests that the adversarial nature of lawyering is a recent phenomenon,[3] and he defines the characteristics of the adversarial system, without reference to the style of lawyering: 1) the existence of a neutral and passive fact finder, 2) party presentation of evidence, and 3) highly structured rules to govern the hearing.[4] Belliotti incorporates both system and "player" characteristics into his definition:

(A) formal proceedings; (B) contending parties who are responsible for focusing the disputed issues, investigating facts, and presenting information and evidence (... "partisan presentation"); (C) neutral and passive fact finder ... ; and (D) principles of professional responsibility which govern the conduct of the lawyers who represent or constitute the contending parties: (i) *principle of detachment* – a lawyer is neither responsible for her client's goals nor allowed to comment personally on the intrinsic merit of her client's cause or version of the facts; (ii) *principle of zealous advocacy* – a lawyer must work assiduously and forcefully, within the legal and professional parameters, to increase the likelihood that her client will prevail.[5]

Critics of the adversarial system find no empirical and little logical support for it. Belliotti examined seven common justifications or rationales for the adversarial system:

- truth
- protection of individual rights and the curbing of state power
- individual autonomy
- "lawyer as friend"[6]
- ritualistic expression of societal values
- dispute resolution
- pragmatism.

He concluded that "no convincing justification has been advanced which argues persuasively that our adversarial system has independent value or that it serves important societal objectives better than any other existing or possible legal systems."[7] Rhode observes that there is no evidence that the adversarial system reveals the truth, and it is not "intuitively obvious that truth is more often revealed by self-interested, rather than disinterested, exploration."[8] Even Landsman, who set out to defend the adversarial system, ended with an unequivocal statement that the adversarial system is not appropriate "when the parties must continue to work or to live together in intimate contact or in a cooperative relationship." In addition, "the adversary procedure may exacerbate rather than resolve tensions and may not foster the compromise essential to the restoration of harmony. For this reason, disputes between labor and management and between family members in an intact family unit, for example, should usually be resolved in nonadversarial proceedings."[9]

Finally, he suggested that it is "sensible to utilize nonadversarial methods when all the parties strongly desire speed, simplicity, and economy in adjudication."[10] He does not leave a positive impression of those who use the adversarial system. New legal ethics scholars in the United States are critical of the "hyperadversarial, amoral character of much American legal practice."[11] Although Canadian lawyers may differ from their counterparts in the United States,[12] there is still a concern in Canada about how legal ethics should or might temper the extreme adversarial approach seen in some cases.[13] Despite the criticisms of the adversarial system, and recommendations for alternatives, including negotiation, arbitration, or alternative dispute resolution, or restrictions to the adversarial system,[14] some countries with inquisitorial systems have moved toward an adversarial one.[15]

Feminist critiques of the adversarial legal system are numerous. Eve Hill outlines three of them. First, it claims to be based on "objective" criteria, which feminists argue are really male criteria. Second, the adversarial nature of resolving disputes assumes that one or the other litigant is right when, in fact, the truth may lie somewhere in between.[16] This is sometimes described as the abstract rights approach (the male approach) versus a preference for reconciliation (the female approach). Third, the legal system's approach starts with a rigid hierarchy of actors and rights, whereas the female approach prefers to work on communication and relationships, using hierarchy as a last resort.[17]

Feminists are equally critical of some of the alternatives to the adversarial system for failing to meet quality-of-justice standards. For example, negotiation can be "competitive/adversarial/hard" or "cooperative/problem-solving/soft," and when negotiation is competitive it can have as many drawbacks as (or more than) the adversarial system. According to Hill, "the competitive approach is the traditional approach to negotiation. The cooperative approach has come to light more recently."[18] Mediation is criticized because it fails to prevent inequalities of power from affecting the results.[19] Arbitration usually focuses on a win/lose outcome and therefore mirrors the adversarial system.[20] Textbooks on alternative forums of conflict resolution provide adversarial strategies for achieving the best results for clients.[21]

The increasing number of women entering the legal profession has led to studies and commentaries on the adversarial player, the question of how women, as "reluctant adversaries,"[22] react to the system, and how they might actually change the nature of the legal profession and the legal system.[23] Foster suggests that people in the United States think of lawyers as advocates – gladiators, ready for combat.[24] He concludes that women law students deal with the adversarial system in one of three ways: 1) some adapt to the system, taking on the role of the adversary and playing the "macho adversarial game," 2) others reject the adversarial system and try to change the rules, and 3) still others simply "grimace and bear it."[25]

I became sceptical of the conclusion that women were more reluctant than men to be adversaries when I surveyed non-practising members of the Law Society of Alberta in 1991-92, and found that women were less likely than men to cite the adversarial system as a reason for leaving the practice of law. When asked to indicate reasons they were not practising law, 36% of the women and fully 46% of the men called to the bar in 1978 or later (and 27% of the men called before 1978), indicated that the adversarial nature of the work was a factor.[26] However, interviews of family law lawyers in the Lower Mainland of British Columbia showed not only a diversity of approaches for women and men, but also some differences between the women and men. On a scale ranging from very conciliatory to very adversarial, 72% of the women and 39% of the men rated themselves as conciliatory, while 6% of the women and 28% of the men rated themselves as adversarial.[27] Of the eighteen men interviewed, ten took the hired-gun approach to a moral conflict, also known as "maximum role identification,"[28] and eight of the eighteen women interviewed gave priority to personal standards, also known as "minimum role identification." One woman took the maximum role identification and one man took the minimum role identification.[29]

This chapter examines the approaches that the respondents in this study take to the practice of law, and their perceptions of the effectiveness of the adversarial system. First, it discusses the strategies the respondents reported taking to the practice of law, on a conciliatory-adversarial continuum, and their perceptions of their approach, relative to other lawyers they encounter. Second, it examines their views on how women and men compare on the continuum. Finally, it discusses their opinions on the effectiveness of the adversarial system in resolving disputes.

The Conciliatory-Adversarial Continuum

Respondents were asked to place themselves on a continuum in terms of how they practised law, ranging from very conciliatory to very adversarial.[30] They were then asked how, on the same scale, they would describe most lawyers they encounter in their work, and whether they would describe women and men differently.[31] This section discusses the respondents' views of their own approach to the practice of law, and some of their views on the adversarial approach of lawyers generally.

Sixty-two percent of the women and 54% of the men described themselves as conciliatory, or as lawyers who would start at the conciliatory end of the continuum.[32] In other words, the majority of women and men describe themselves as conciliatory, despite our adversarial system. This should not come as a surprise, if we differentiate between an adversarial system and an adversarial approach to the practice of law. Only 12% of the women and 14% of the men rated themselves as adversarial, or as someone who started at the adversarial end of the continuum. Sixteen percent of the women and 12% of the men claimed to work in the mid-range of the continuum, and 8% of the women and 20% of the men said their approach depended upon the circumstances of the case.

The fact that more women than men described their approach as conciliatory is consistent with some of the literature. However, it is interesting that approximately the same number of women and men describe themselves as adversarial or starting on the adversarial end of the continuum. The role of the reluctant adversary is not limited to women. In addition, more men than women seemed to keep their options open and take whatever position works in the circumstances. This may be because the men had more variety in their practice and were less likely than the women to be working only in one area (see Chapter 3). Upon closer examination of the lawyers who kept their options open, three of the four women and eight of the ten men spent only 75% of their time or less on the area of law they practised the most. The variety in their practices probably required some of the respondents to keep their options open; for example, one woman did family and criminal law; another woman and a man did criminal, family, and immigration, and one of the men had a general practice.

Very Conciliatory Respondents

The explanations that the women and men gave for their conciliatory approach varied, falling into five categories:

1 The conciliatory approach is best suited to the type of law the respondents practise.
2 It is more compatible with the respondents' personalities.
3 It is the best way to achieve desired results.
4 It was developed or learned from mentors.
5 One can more easily start at the conciliatory end, and then become more adversarial, if required.

Conciliation Suits Their Area of the Law

Some respondents distinguish between the role of a solicitor and the role of a barrister, or they stress that they practise in an area that is conciliatory in nature, although they were not always in agreement as to which areas of law were more conciliatory. In addition, there is no uniformity among barristers or among solicitors. Among the twenty-two women and twenty-seven men who identified themselves as primarily barristers, 59% of the women and 33% of the men said they were conciliatory, or started on the conciliatory end of the continuum; only 23% of the women and 22% of the men described themselves as adversarial or as starting on the adversarial end of the continuum. The men (44%) were more likely than the women (18%) to practise mid-range on the scale.

Solicitors were more inclined to be conciliatory, but men more so than women – 71% of the 14 women and 88% of the 16 men who identified themselves primarily as solicitors were either conciliatory, or started on the conciliatory end of the continuum. The women (21%) were more likely than the men to practise mid-range on the scale. One woman and none of the men started at the adversarial end of the continuum.

The need to maintain an ongoing relationship (for example, a business relationship) often requires a conciliatory approach. Business lawyers see themselves as deal makers or facilitators, not deal breakers, and as such, take a conciliatory approach to their work. For example, Barbara sees her job as a solicitor as one of "bringing people together." People who enter into deals together "are going to have to relate to each other for a long time, so you try to be more conciliatory." Similarly, Nancy, who works with developers and land purchasers, finds that it is the way to get deals done: "If I take an adversarial position, the deal won't close, and that is everybody's loss. It's more an area of practice in which you tend to work together to try and close a deal." According to Hank, his work as a solicitor requires that everyone work together, as most of his clients do not want to go to court. He adds, "It's a matter of just looking after them that way, not taking them somewhere they don't want to go." Other solicitors had similar explanations. Daniel, a solicitor who sees himself as a facilitator, takes a conciliatory approach because it preserves the relationship his client has with others:

> In the areas in which I practise there is often a continuing relationship among the clients involved. That's one factor that comes into play, and I feel it's my obligation to foster a working relationship. Misunderstandings can jeopardize that. So when I approach a situation, I try to ensure that there's adequate communication, and sometimes a lawyer's involvement can be problematic in that regard, by virtue of the fact that there's another step in the chain of communication. So I like to try to think of myself as a facilitator of communication. I like to listen as well as I can to both sides. I find that, generally, most clients are more willing to perhaps sacrifice some objective to conclude a deal successfully. I find generally that people are more conciliatory, so I like to facilitate that.

Ian works in conveyancing, in which it would be very unusual for the parties to be in an adversarial situation. For the most part, his work involves "win/win" situations. Similarly, Oscar, who works in the securities area, finds little room to be adversarial:

> If you think of the typical securities transaction, the underwriter agrees to buy the shares at a price (for a commission), and the size of the commission is something for which the two sides are obviously at odds, but that's a narrow question, that's a business question. The form of the average underwriting agreement, "A deal's a deal," varies very little. These are almost standard documents. There's almost an acceptable form to all of this stuff, so it's not like many transactions in which a solicitor has to closely negotiate a document from start to finish, with every representation or warranty argued over. The representations and warranties that are made in these agreements are standard. Things you argue over are very limited. Once you've got past that initial question of what is the price at which this deal can be done, everyone is working on both sides of the deal toward the same end, and that's getting the bloody document through the securities commissions with a minimum of fuss, and getting the thing closed as quickly as possible. If you take an adversarial approach, you

won't achieve the client's objective of getting that done. It doesn't matter if you're acting for the underwriter or the issuer, your job is to get that prospectus through the commission as quickly as possible, and you're just part of the team that's working on it. So the situation requires you to be fairly conciliatory, and just try to get the job done. If you're adversarial, you won't get very far.

As a corporate and business lawyer, Mark's job is also to bring the parties to a conclusion that is satisfying to all of them:

I see it first of all as being less adversarial than litigation, by definition. We're usually working on business deals, and as long as my client's interest is being protected, I just prefer going the route of being conciliatory, rather than being adversarial. I only become adversarial if there's a need for it. If there's something that the other side is doing, whether it be the lawyer directly or the other lawyer's client that is affecting our interests and my client's interest, or somehow affecting how I am doing my job, then I'll become more adversarial as well. But I guess I start off with the belief that we're all working toward one goal, and I try to facilitate that.

Some of the respondents see the conciliatory approach as suitable for administrative law, and even criminal law. In fact, some lawyers find criminal law more conciliatory than family law. Douglas, a barrister, explained: "Most criminal lawyers are conciliatory. Most lawyers are professional, and willing to try and work things out and help other counsel (even if they're on the other side). Family practitioners tend to be more adversarial (especially females, they want to create a fight when there isn't a fight). I've had to actually say to the court 'I'm trying to settle this, but this lawyer won't even pass it on to the client. Yes, she can have access, we don't have to be here to fight about access. SHE CAN HAVE ACCESS! Why are we fighting?'"
Vincent finds criminal law more conciliatory than civil litigation:

In the civil area, it's a matter of: Is it financially worth while going to trial? There's an awful lot of bluffing and, generally speaking, I don't much like the civil bar – they're not civil, they're an absolute pain in the butt to deal with, and they're far more adversarial than virtually any criminal lawyer I have dealt with, Crown or defence side. In criminal work, generally speaking, it's not the client that's paying. If you're on for the Crown, Ottawa is paying. If you're on for the defence, legal aid is paying. So there is less of a monetary pressure. From a defence viewpoint, I'll probably get castigated by every defence lawyer who catches wind of this, but the basic rule of thumb is that clients are usually guilty, which makes it much easier to be conciliatory. The client has done it. It's basically, Can the Crown prove it? Or, if you have a decent shot at running a good defence, you don't have all that much to lose. There's nothing worse than an innocent client to defend for the stress levels. It's very satisfying if you win, but it's not much fun if you lose. Innocent people do get convicted. Being adversarial doesn't seem to accomplish much, it just seems to get everyone ticked off and gums up the works.

In the context of discussing other lawyers, Elizabeth and Nicole commented on the adversarial nature of family law practice:

Most lawyers [in criminal law] here are exceptionally conciliatory. We have a chance to sit down and have a cup a coffee and hammer something out. I don't see the same thing in family, and that's one of the reasons that it's so unpleasant to be in that area. You can try to be reasonable, but some of the counsel are exceptionally adversarial. They take positions that they know their clients cannot get, and you say to them, "If we take this to court, you know and I know that the judge is not going to order no access, I mean let's be reasonable." [Interviewer: Are family lawyers more adversarial than criminal lawyers?] Yes, sometimes to the extent of being offensive. There are not that many lawyers here. I have run across four who I would put in that category, but given the small numbers we are dealing with ... I just cringe to find I have to deal with them, because I know it's going to court no matter how reasonable my position is going to be. I'll just tell my client we're going to court on it, because I can talk to counsel, but it's not likely we'll be able to work something out, not because my client is being unreasonable, but because I know the position the other side will take will be instantly, "No, too bad." I've been known to say some family law lawyers are a bunch of assholes, and I've never said that in the other context.

In my first year, I practised almost exclusively family law, and I found that the family bar is extremely adversarial, and, as a result, I was turned off by it. I think that there should be mandatory mediation in family matters, because people spend too much – not just money, but they totally destroy any relationship that they might have had on a friendship basis with their spouse by going to a lawyer. But then, I've done a lot of personal injury law, and I've found, by and large, most of the lawyers practising in that area are very conciliatory. I've had a good experience with that bar.

Antagonists, and even supporters of the adversarial system, criticize its

use in the area of family law. Even though there is often a need for es-
tranged and former intimates to maintain ongoing relationships (because
of children), the adversarial system heightens conflict and thwarts those
ongoing relationships. One might be left with the impression that the
adversarial system is reserved in the family law area for the benefit of those
who do not care about the consequences of their actions, and who have the
time and the money to harass those who do not. It is ironic that the criminal justice system, the bastion of the adversarial system, is often one in
which the Crown and the defence negotiate and compromise.[33] Family law,
often seen as unsuited for the adversarial system, is where lawyers may be
the most adversarial. As suggested in the literature cited at the beginning
of this chapter, this adversarial approach may not change simply because
the parties are in mediation or negotiations.

However, some lawyers use the conciliatory approach for family law –
women much more so than men. In the current study, six women (12%)
and two men (4%) identified themselves as spending 60% or more of their
time in the family law area (Hotel in her study of family law lawyers in the
Lower Mainland of British Columbia found that 72% of the women and
39% of the men in her study rated themselves as conciliatory, and 6%
of the women and 28% of the men rated themselves as adversarial).[34] All
six women family lawyers in my study said they work at the conciliatory
end of the continuum, while the two men took an adversarial approach.[35]
Holly and Vera (two barristers) each explained their conciliatory approach
as follows:

> I believe, especially in a family context, that when the lawyer steps out,
> the family still has to be together, especially when there are children
> involved. So it's better for the family and for the children if you can work
> to bring the people to a point of conciliation. The more adversarial you
> are, the less likely it will be that these people will be able to work things
> out for themselves in the future, that they'll be able to deal with their
> children without animosity. I find that it works best if you can bring the
> two sides together, and to that end I work to be conciliatory.

> I pride myself by saying "one" [very conciliatory], because I try very much
> to keep it out of the court system. I don't have great respect for lawyers
> who want to get into court that fast. I don't have a great respect for a lot
> of the judges, and the system in general. I don't have a great respect for
> it having the capability for resolving family matters, which often involve
> children and emotional issues.

Karen, who had left private practice, described the approach she took
before she left as very conciliatory because she was doing family law:

My own approach was that half of those people should have been in mediation. But unfortunately, it depends on who's on the other side, and a lot of the lawyers I dealt with in family law were the most unreasonable people I have ever met. I couldn't believe how adversarial they were. They took on the persona of their client, and a lot of them were female lawyers. It was just hopeless, just completely hopeless. I was so fed up with them all. I believe that there are two sides to every issue and when your client comes in, you take their side, but you don't necessarily, I mean, I never stepped into my client's shoes and said, "She's right," or "He's right, that's it." I said, "That's one side." What you have to do is develop the best approach and reasonably solve this. That was my approach to family law.

For some, such as Rosa, it is the client who tries to force her approach. She has referred clients in the matrimonial area to other lawyers, because "regardless of what they are entitled to at law, what is in their best interests, they want to screw the other party." While this might provide them with "some emotional gratification down the road," she has reservations about taking these clients or maintaining their approach.

Three of the women respondents were defence counsel: one took a conciliatory approach, one an adversarial approach, and one said it depended on the circumstances. Of the six men respondents who were defence counsel, three took the conciliatory approach or started at the conciliatory end of the continuum: one worked the entire range, and two were mid-range on the scale. The one woman, who worked for the Crown, took a conciliatory approach, as did one man. The other man who was Crown counsel was in the middle of the scale. Olive's experience, as defence counsel, was,

that if you push a certain case, you may be able to take advantage of the Crown because they're inexperienced or because they've screwed up somehow, they hadn't looked at the file. In that particular case, that may be to your client's advantage, but in the long run, your reputation is all you've got in this business and if you, how shall I say it, screw the Crown, you'll live to be screwed, and they'll all look at you and never trust you again. So I don't take a very aggressive approach generally, and I tell my clients that. If they want someone who's going to fight tooth and nail, and possibly get everybody in the courtroom angry, but it looks like they're doing a good job, then they can go somewhere else. It's not my style.

Paula, a Crown counsel, worked at the conciliatory end of the continuum,

because the whole thing is to ensure that justice is done. You don't have a personal stake in something, so you're not a six or a seven [very adversarial]. Also, I don't know how you could keep up this pace remaining very adversarial. And then obviously you're not going to be able to come to an agreement on every file, either dropping it or taking a plea or agreeing to settle, so you can't be a one or a two [very conciliatory]. There are obviously times when you're just going to have to say, "I'm sorry, we have no choice, we have to go to trial," which, to me, is not saying you're adversarial.

Ivan did not consider himself to be aggressive, but liked to think that he was a firm prosecutor. When asked to elaborate on how he was firm, not aggressive, he responded:

Several factors – one is your own personal style of getting a result, and I prefer it to be a more civilized exercise. I look to senior lawyers who are known as being effective, and yet aren't brawlers. They're more surgical in the use of their professional technique and have a foundation of decency for their professional practice. So that's the personal style aspect of it. The other is what your objective is. The luxury of being a prosecutor is that your objective isn't necessarily to win, it's to get the just result. If you feel that you can properly stay a charge or go for a light sentence, that isn't incompatible with your role. So your ego isn't on the line, whereas in civil litigation there's more of a focus on win or lose, and who won and who lost, and to what extent did you get more than you deserved.

The need to maintain an ongoing relationship was given as an explanation for a conciliatory approach in administrative law by both Pamela and Opal. Opal attributes this to the ongoing relationship among the parties in labour relations: "You have to look for solutions that don't foster alienation, and so it's in the interests of everybody that problems try to be resolved, as opposed to litigating."

Conciliation Suits Their Personality
Some respondents describe the conciliatory approach as "their way" of approaching the practice of law, or as more suited to their personality, whether it is because they are "friendly and easy going," or "not adversarial at all." For instance, Heather described herself as "very conciliatory, because I'm a direct person. I'm not saying there's anything wrong with being adversarial, but it's not my style to be manipulative." However, this direct approach can cause problems: "I'm also more likely to assume that the other person is behaving that way, which is not always the best thing to assume."
Nicholas sees himself as less adversarial than a lot of the lawyers he deals with:

I find a lot of the practice of law is too adversarial and, quite frankly, I think a lot of lawyers are real jerks. Lawyers fight over the location of a discovery, whose office it's going to be in, whether it will be in their territory, silly things like that, and I don't care anymore. It's just not worthwhile. I don't like going to chambers, and when I go to chambers and see other people in front of judges bickering about stupid things, that embarrasses me. That part of the practice of law turns me off. I think I'm trying to get more and more conciliatory, and just get down and deal with the issues. Sometimes, for tactical or other reasons, you're in a real dog fight; but generally, unless it's worth fighting about, I'm not going to bother.

Having described their personal approach as conciliatory, some added that this did not mean that they could be pushed around, and that they were prepared to match their opponent, should the circumstances require a more adversarial response. Gail, a barrister, and Jessica, a solicitor, explained:

I'd think my approach is more toward a conciliatory approach, because I tend to be a reasonable person to deal with. I don't take adversarial positions unless there's a strategic advantage to it. I'd probably say two or three [closer to the very conciliatory end of the scale]. I'm perfectly prepared to go the maximum on something when I feel we have to take that approach, but I think a lot of lawyers tend to sweat the little things, and I don't do that. I try to cut through most of the crap that leads up to a trial, and get the documents, make whatever disclosure I'm going to make, and just go on the issues.

Well my approach to most situations is, "Let's work it out," as opposed to "Wait a minute, what's going on here?" I think in most cases that approach is more productive, but on occasion the "Wait a minute, what's going on here approach" is warranted. My personality is more to one side than the other. I don't like getting embroiled in a conflict if it can be avoided, but I think on occasion it's warranted.

Two women had some doubts about their preference for a conciliatory approach to practice; in fact, Jessica thought it might be to the detriment of her client to the point that she would get a second opinion. I asked Nicole why she described herself as a one [very conciliatory]. She responded, "Because I'm not an adversarial person, and I don't like confrontation." She generally tries to find a mediated solution to problems and realized when she went into law that her "personality was probably not best suited to the practice of law."

Riley had left litigation because it was not suited to his personality. He found that he was being more adversarial than he was comfortable with. Leon left litigation for similar reasons:

I think I'm three to four [somewhat conciliatory]. One of the reasons I got out of pure litigation practice was that I found my personality was not well suited to a very, very adversarial position. In a lot of cases, if you've got good quality counsel, you can have a lot of fun and still be very adversarial, or reasonably adversarial, and still protect your client properly. But there are a lot of people out there who don't view it that way, and that I find to be distasteful. I don't like that ... You have to make sure you're getting for your client what's important, and of course you have to find out from your client what's important and be prepared to make sure that he gets those things covered. But, on the other hand, I think I view myself as a negotiator and a deal maker, as opposed to a deal breaker, and if you're too adversarial you're a deal breaker. It's as simple as that.

Conciliation Achieves Results
Some respondents believe that the conciliatory approach is simply the best way to achieve the desired results. Laura, a barrister, does not believe "that you get anywhere by being very adversarial." It is not necessary "to brow-beat your opponent or the lawyer on the other side, or their client, in order to get what you want." She thinks that both parties would be happier with a settlement, rather than "something dictated to them through the courts." Likewise, Rosa, another barrister, feels that "in the long run, it is always more cost effective for a client to get things settled as quickly as possible, for the least amount of money."

Carl believes that being adversarial could ruin the relationship he has with an insurance company, and "it actually hurts the client, rather than helps the case." Fred also thinks that you get further when "everyone is reasonable and rational ... You can attract more bees with honey than you can with vinegar, you know, that attitude." Murray's clients "don't want to end up with a fight. All that does is waste their time, and it makes for excessive legal fees, which is in no one's best interest." However, he runs into a problem when the other side picks a firm with adversarial lawyers. He adds, "if my clients are going up against or involved with someone from [those firms,] I tell them up front it will probably double the legal fees. In some circumstances, they've requested that the other side change law firms."

Rob explained his approach:

That's actually a very difficult question to answer, because you can take a very conciliatory approach and be very adversarial in terms of getting what you want. That's what I do. I tend to get very close to what I want, but I do it in a very conciliatory way. In other words, I try to convince the other side why what I want makes sense. And I usually succeed in doing that. When you say that you're very conciliatory, that suggests that you're giving the farm away all the time. The answer is that you can get what you want, you can win and be conciliatory in your approach at the same time. [Interviewer: Would you say that you're very assertive about getting what you want for your client?] Yes, in a conciliatory way, in a commonsensical way. If you know why it is you need something, and you can explain it to the other side, they'll usually give it to you. I deal with a fairly small group of solicitors in the city and, because we deal with each other over and over again, we've developed relationships and ways of dealing with each other.

Respondents Learned Conciliation
Some respondents developed or learned the conciliatory approach from mentors, or others who demonstrated that the conciliatory approach was more appropriate to achieving the desired results. Lois explained:

> I was very lucky. When [name] took me over as almost a mentor, he taught that this is the way you do it. If you can do someone a favour, you do it, as long as it's not going to hurt your client. I have no problem adjourning something, other than trials, of course, if it's for the convenience of counsel, knowing full well that I can call this person, the same lawyer, and say "My week has just gone down the drain. I need to adjourn this, let's do it in a week or two," and it's served me very well.

Start with Conciliation and Adjust if Required
Some respondents start at the conciliatory end of the continuum, and become more adversarial if required. Donna starts off trying to be conciliatory. If that does not work, she becomes more adversarial. She does not think of herself "as being adversarial for the sake of it." She explained:

> I'd rather try to get along, but the nature of the litigation practice is that you have people who are already involved in some dispute they can't resolve themselves. So I think litigation lawyers tend to be gladiators. They go out and do combat. That's what they do. Often when I'm acting for a plaintiff, I'm dealing with ICBC, and if I start off dealing with them in a very conciliatory or what might be seen as a submissive role, I'm going to get walked on, and so is my client. So, I have to exhibit some substance, but I make it clear, I think, to the adjusters I deal with, that I don't want to fight for the sake of it, and that I'm prepared to be cooperative if they are. Sometimes you meet a brick wall on the other side.

Sometimes it's clear that there's not much opportunity to be conciliatory. You fight from the beginning, and that's what you're into. I'm up for a fight, if I have to fight.

Edward starts out being a conciliatory defence counsel and, if it does not work, he becomes adversarial: "I subscribe to the doctrine you can catch more bees with honey. It is my practice to fire off letters to Crown counsel inviting them to stay the charges, or some alternative disposition that I feel is good for my client, and if that doesn't work I get very adversarial. Part of the reason is so that perhaps next time they will perhaps be more apt to respond to my initial efforts. I don't get as high as seven [very adversarial]; I range from three to five [in the mid-range]."

Sixty-two percent of the women and 54% of the men described themselves as conciliatory, or as starting on the conciliatory end of the continuum. For these respondents, this approach was the best for achieving what their clients wanted. Although the reluctant adversary is not confined to women lawyers, a small number of women and men take the adversarial approach to law.

Adversarial Respondents

Only 12% of the women and 14% of the men described themselves as adversarial, or as someone who starts at the adversarial end of the continuum. Some of the respondents who described themselves as adversarial claimed to be following their client's instructions (by contrast, none of the lawyers who said they were conciliatory were so at their client's instructions). The respondents' other explanations fell into four categories and were similar to the explanations given by the conciliatory respondents:

1 The adversarial approach is best suited to the type of law the respondents practised.
2 It is the best way to achieve desired results.
3 It was developed or learned from mentors.
4 One can start at the adversarial end and become more conciliatory if required.

The Adversarial Approach Suits Their Area of Law

Some of the respondents attribute their adversarial approach to the type of law they practise. Although Carissa does mostly corporate-commercial, she has been involved in litigation in which "there is a winner and a loser," and "one side walks away with a judgment and the other side has to pay." Therefore, she had to "start off at the far end, being very adversarial." This is partly because the other side assumes that "whatever position you take to begin with, won't be the most that you're striving for." Now that she does solicitor's work, she still describes herself as a four or a five [mid-range on the scale], closer to a five [somewhat adversarial]:

> I assume that the client is paying me because they need me to do something for them. If the parties are truly conciliatory, they don't need lawyers, they'd come to you with a perfect package and say, "I just want you to document this," but that's not what happens most times. When you have a buyer and seller, their interests are adverse, in the sense that one person wants to sell and get the highest price, and the other person wants to buy and get the cheapest price. The reality is that the goals are different, and your job is to make them think that it's not as different as they might think initially.

This is an unusual approach for a solicitor, and Carissa was the only respondent to take it. Theresa, a criminal law practitioner, explained why she is adversarial: "Because the areas I tend to practise in tend to necessitate that. I am defending individuals against the state, and the state takes an adversarial approach to the individuals. In my view, if you want to be an effective advocate, you have to be adversarial. I am quite happy to be conciliatory when it works for my client, to make deals with the prosecution when I can, or make deals with immigration officers when I can; but, unfortunately, most of the time that is not necessarily going to be the most effective approach."

Although other criminal practitioners are adversarial, many of them are conciliatory in their approach.

The Adversarial Approach Achieves Results

Some respondents thought the adversarial approach was the best way to achieve the desired results for their clients. Wendy, who was no longer practising law, describes herself as "quite aggressive":

> Nothing particularly frightens me off. I'd be a five [somewhat adversarial] heading toward the adversarial end of the scale. It had something to do with that upper hand that I was talking about before, though my ultimate goal was often to settle a matter and have it all taken care of. I had to appear to at least be taking that adversarial position so that the person on the other side believed that I was adamant, and that I wasn't going to be moved, and that I'd be glad sitting in court. And it's either one of those things that you can or can't do. Some lawyers I knew would never go to court, and it was a terrible downfall for them, because they didn't have any bargaining power whatsoever. They had no leverage. So I guess I leaned more toward adversarial, even if my ultimate goal was to come up with some agreement. I came across as about as adversarial as you

could get, I'd imagine. At the same time, I think that prompted a lot of respect from other lawyers; no one tried to take advantage of me. Some tried, but it didn't work very well.

Jeff describes himself as a mid-range on the scale because of the nature of the civil litigation work he does. In a recent case, he fought hard on procedural points: "These sorts of skirmishes occur quite regularly, and so there is a strong adversarial character to the litigation itself. I think this is true for all parties. No one's instructions are to give ground anywhere, for fear that some momentum may develop that leads them in the wrong way." However, he does not think that he is "gratuitously adversarial." He recognizes that "there are times when being adversarial can work against your client's interests, and work against your own effectiveness as counsel," and he hopes that he recognizes those situations, and "adopts a non-adversarial posture when it is called for."

According to Vernon, also mid-range on the scale, there is a downside to going to court; however, that is the system in which he works for his clients, and he has to deal with other adversarial lawyers:

> The value of having the court system is that you can get a final resolution. A woman was just in here, and her husband is a maniac. We're going to trial. If it weren't for the trial process, she'd never get anywhere. And we haven't been able to get anyplace with him, and he won't cooperate no matter what. So I think that it's good that she can get something ultimately through the court, and that's why she's here to see me. She's not here for counselling and I don't do counselling. I do the court side [of the matter]. The way I view it is just to try and get them through with the least emotional damage, as well. I see myself as being willing to negotiate or conciliate, but ultimately it's an adversarial process, so I weight it a little off-centre of going to court and fighting it out. I'm quite willing to do that, if that's what's required ... I think it leans mainly toward the adversarial. In fact, I think that one of the main difficulties I feel emotionally in being a lawyer is dealing with some of the other lawyers, some screaming maniacs who are in town that make life much more difficult than it ought to be, even in terms of what it is we're doing. Standing in the shoes of the client, fighting out the same battle with me is just a waste of time. It doesn't help the client, it doesn't advance them.

Respondents Learned the Adversarial Approach
Flora learned the adversarial approach from her principal during articles:

> I articled for [name], who always impressed upon me, no matter what you're there for, whether you're negotiating or mediating or going to trial

or in front of an administrative tribunal, you're there to get the best deal for your client, so never forget that fact. You're there as a lawyer, no matter how casual and nice the thing is. That was drilled into me ... I suppose I'm never very conciliatory, that's being naive. I think as lawyers we're here to protect our clients. I suppose if you're Crown counsel, you can't be very adversarial; but I act for plaintiffs. I probably start out as a five [somewhat adversarial]. I'm very good about giving all my affidavit material, disclosing information; that's one thing I was trained to do. I think it's much fairer, because if you don't, you just end up adjourning it. It happens a lot in family law – lawyers get a forty-page affidavit as they walk into chambers. You end up with an adjournment, so nobody's any further ahead. When acting for a client, obtaining a restraining order, I'm a seven [very adversarial]. This woman and kids need protection – you can't be conciliatory in those circumstances. There are aspects of family law for which I think mediation is far better. [I think], "Why waste your money on a lawyer? The law is fifty-fifty. Go see a good tax accountant." I don't say this to clients, but the law is fifty-fifty. [I think], "If you go through two years of litigation, this is all you're going to get. So go and see a good tax accountant and save your money and do something reasonable about the kids. Don't be a jerk about the kids."

Start with the Adversarial Approach and Adjust if Required
This approach is illustrated by Kevin, who recognizes that his adversarial tendencies have to be tempered with a conciliatory approach when necessary:

I know you used the word "generally," but I think it's important to make this point, because a good lawyer, in my opinion, will vacillate. There are times when you have to be very adversarial, and there are times when it's better to be very conciliatory. If you're taking care of your client's interests, as you should be, you should be flexible enough to know which approach is better in which circumstance. I would say that, in terms of whether I'm adversarial in how I practise, I would lean toward the adversarial side. [Interviewer: But you would practise all the way from one through seven [very conciliatory to very adversarial]?] Certainly I would, depending on the circumstances. One of the worst situations that you can ever be in, in my view as defence counsel in commercial litigation, is a situation in which the other side can push you all over the place, and you have no standing, you have nothing to say, and you've got to take it, and that's horrible. Now that has nothing to do with your client, or anything else. It's a personal ego thing, that kind of problem. In those circumstances, even though you have these adversarial tendencies generally, they don't get you anywhere. All you do, if you're adversarial in that situation, is you're going to achieve a bad relationship with the other lawyer, and that's all you're going to achieve, so there are circumstances in which it doesn't pay to keep fighting and be adversarial.

Similarly, Dorothy tends to be adversarial, and knows that people see her as adversarial. She can, however, adjust if the circumstances require it:

I have a tendency to treat each case individually, as they come before me. In some cases I would take a seven, or a very adversarial stance, and in other cases I would take a one, or a very conciliatory approach. That can be, even within the same type of practice. I have dealt in one case with two parties in a matrimonial scenario in which there were allegations of physical and mental abuse, in which a very adversarial approach was the only way to get things done, and that meant several applications in chambers for orders. We obtained all of our orders and were successful in the end. A conciliatory approach would never have worked on that file, and that was a front-end decision I made with my client when we talked about the kind of person I would be dealing with. On the other hand, in one case in which we had several applications that seemed to be floundering, we never seemed to be getting anywhere, I said to the other lawyer let's sit in a room with our clients and just talk about this, which we did. That case was completed and resolved, and finalized with a consent order on related issues within seven days of our meeting. I think it depends on the case. Generally, I tend to be on the more adversarial end, and people would perceive me as that.

Frank likes to start from an adversarial position, although he can be "both very conciliatory and very adversarial – it just depends on the circumstances, as to when a conciliatory approach is required, and when an adversarial approach is required."

I issue writs quickly and I commence litigation quickly on all of my files. I tell my client that once we get into the litigation, the eventual goal is a trial, and we proceed with the case as if it's not going to settle. So that's the mindset I like to start with, put that into my client and myself. That's how we approach it, and do our investigation and gather the evidence. But I also say to my clients that it's my belief that if you have that mind-set the chances of settling are much higher, and the reason we take that approach is so that we can settle.

Clients Want the Adversarial Approach

Some respondents take the adversarial approach in response to their client's instructions. Flora, who learned the adversarial approach from her principal, explained:

I want to see what my client wants. It depends on what instructions I have. What does "very adversarial" mean, I mean beat up the other lawyer? [Interviewer: How would you think of it?] I don't know, a real asshole, pardon me ... I'm not a jerk. I've just done a file in which I settled an ICBC claim. This is what my client wants, and I think I did quite well. We got the average range, and I don't feel bad about what I got for my client. I think if I had gone to trial I probably could have gotten more, but I might have gotten less. It's a crapshoot ... I'm fair to the other lawyers ... but I think you have to, especially when plaintiffs come to you, and as plaintiff's counsel [Interviewer: You have to start at the adversarial end of the scale?] Oh, yeah. A client comes in and says, "I want a real bitch", you know you have to play the game. You can't be too wishy-washy ... And yet I'm looking at courses on family mediation. Philosophically, I think I'm probably a four or a five [somewhat adversarial]; but if my client or I have an adjuster who's off the wall, I'll be a seven or a six [very adversarial].

It is interesting that few lawyers see their clients as dictating their approach on the scale ranging from very conciliatory to very adversarial,[36] and this might indicate that the lawyers in this study did not see themselves as the hired guns of their clients.

Mid-Range Respondents

Sixteen percent of the women and 10% of the men work in the mid-range of the continuum. Some thought that the mid-range was the best way to achieve their goals. Melanie tries to be conciliatory with the other side and at the same time keep her clients' needs in mind. However, if the other side pushes, she will become more adversarial: "Sometimes you have lawyers on the other side of litigation files that are just jerks, and I don't like to get like that, I can be firm, and, as I say, dig in my heels, but I'm not going to be sharp in my practice. I don't believe in that. It's unethical, I feel, and it's not necessary in dealing with people."

Likewise, Simon works in the mid-range and tries to resolve issues. He tries to get the best for his client, particularly in the family area, "without going to the real adversarial type of position." He took a course on negotiating that took a "principled approach," and he tries to deal with issues in that way.

Iris worked the mid-range, and had learned not to be too conciliatory. When asked what she meant, she commented:

I felt that probably, with clients and with other lawyers, I was walked on, and I didn't like that part of it. I've come to be able to stop that behaviour with clients and, to a lesser extent, with lawyers, but I'm working on that as well. I'm a calm type of personality, and I don't get easily excited. My inclination is to just approach everything as calmly as possible, and try to diffuse anybody who's raging out of control. So I'd probably place myself in the mid-range, but not much higher [towards the adversarial end of the scale] in dealing with people.

Approach Depends on the Circumstances and Type of Case

Eight percent of the women and 20% of the men said that their approach to the practice of law varies with the circumstances of the case, or the type of law they are practising. For instance, some take a more adversarial role in criminal law, and a more conciliatory approach in family law (unlike some of the earlier respondents). Elizabeth is very adversarial when it comes to criminal defence work: "The Crown has to prove their case, period. You can only be conciliatory in areas that are not going to impact negatively on the client, and so any admissions you are going to make have to be carefully thought out. If they are not in issue, I have no objections to making those kinds of concessions. You have an obligation which is different from family law, and that is why I am far more aggressive in criminal law. It's up to the Crown to prove its case."

However in family law, she describes herself as a mid-range on the scale, or somewhat conciliatory.

> Family law is different in a sense. You're dealing with people's lives, but not necessarily their freedom. What you want to do is find out what's best for them, best for the children. You still are an officer of the court and have to consider the best interests of the children, and sometimes the best interests of the children aren't necessarily the best interests of your client. You have to explain that to your client, who may not be particularly happy about the situation. You try and work out some balance. You explain to them what their rights are, and try and work out so that they have those rights as best you can do it. However, if the gentleman is abusive of the child, you may want to get supervision, as far as access is concerned. He has to clearly be able to understand that. You have to be able to approach the other side and say, "Look, we want the access, we understand there's a difficulty, we're willing to make some concessions. Here are what the concessions are, but we're going to have access whether you like it or not."

Fiona's approach also varies with the type of case she has. If she is dealing with a criminal matter she can be very adversarial,

> because it's not a personalized matter. Often, you're dealing with the state, with the police, or Crown counsel, and they're officers [of the court]. So you're not personal with the Crown counsel or police officer, but you have to be very adversarial, and serve your client's best interests. An example

is that Crown counsel tells you they have given full disclosure, and they probably have. They're acting in good faith, and give you what they have. [Then] you get your police officer in cross-examination, and you say, "Officer, did you take notes?" "Oh, yeah." Crown counsel hadn't said that. So then you're in mid-trial and you've found out ... so I find it has to be a mindset that's quite adversarial. You must aggressively pursue every avenue to the benefit of your client. If you just presume, and take a conciliatory attitude or approach from the beginning, you're not going to get anything.

When it comes to family law she can be conciliatory, but it depends on the lawyers she is dealing with:

I find that lawyers in the Lower Mainland are extremely aggressive, and I hate to generalize, but they are. But with other lawyers, you can take a more objective and reasoned approach. Sometimes you can't. That's why I say it's shaped often by the counsel you're dealing with. I'm qualified to do mediation, and I'll do that whenever I can. I don't get much of a chance ... I like that approach. If you asked somebody I've worked with as counsel, they'd probably describe me as a six or a seven [very adversarial]. [Interviewer: How would you describe yourself?] Probably a three [more conciliatory], but it depends.

Although Megan claims she is very conciliatory in family matters and mid-range on the scale in criminal matters ("because you don't fight every case"), she rates herself as very adversarial when she deals with the Immigration and Refugee Board. When asked why she was very adversarial with the Refugee Board, she responded: "It's a very adversarial atmosphere toward the client. They [refugees] are all presumed to be liars right off the bat. They are all treated as if they are criminals, and they are in a vulnerable position, so you have to struggle hard against them."

For others, too, it depends on the area in which they are practising, and the nature of the matter. According to Adam,

there are some cases in which the conciliatory approach is inappropriate. The saying is, "While it's fine to have half a loaf, you don't want half a baby." In environmental matters, the subject matter often involves ethical or moral values and, in those circumstances, it's not always appropriate to have a conciliatory approach. On the other hand, about the regulatory work, we're in front of the same tribunal, the same group of lawyers, representing the same group of clients over and over and over again. There a lot of matters are dealt with on a conciliatory basis.

Paul breaks it down into the various areas of law:

With criminal law you have to be very adversarial, though I wouldn't put myself on the far end of the continuum, because I'll cooperate with the Crown if it's in the best interests of my client. There's always a position you have to take in the best interest of your client. I'd say I would probably be right dead in the middle. [Interviewer: What about family law?] In family law, I'd probably try to be on the conciliatory end. That's the way family law should be practised although a lot of practitioners don't do that. I'd say more between two and three [towards the conciliatory end of the scale]. [Interviewer: What about immigration law?] Once again, not as adversarial as criminal – maybe a three [somewhat conciliatory] for immigration. It's not always in the best interest of your client to be that adversarial. On the other hand, if I were practising civil litigation, I'd probably be closer to a seven [very adversarial], because that's the nature of civil litigation. And when I say "civil litigation," I mean lawsuits, disputes of individuals over money or contracts.

For some respondents, their approach depends on the circumstances of the case, what the client wants, and the lawyer they are up against on the other side. Georgina is very conciliatory if she doesn't respect what her client wants and very adversarial if it is important to her client's interests. Jack finds that his approach is "dictated by others," although he dislikes the adversarial approach: "When I am dealing with someone who is very adversarial, it makes me question the whole process. It makes me often question what I am doing, because if I am dealing with someone very adversarial, the process can be so harmful that you question whether your client should even be involved in it."

In summarizing the lawyers' approaches to the practice of law, the majority (but more women than men) took the conciliatory approach, and thought that it was the best way to approach cases. To some extent, the adversarial approach appears to be reserved for those who were not sufficiently civilized to resolve their own disputes. Less than 15% of the respondents said they took an adversarial approach to the practice of law.

Comparisons with Other Lawyers
Despite the low number of lawyers who identified themselves as "adversarials," 64% of the women and 40% of the men saw themselves as more conciliatory than the lawyers they encounter in their work. Only 6% of the women and 4% of the men felt they were more adversarial than other lawyers they encounter in their work. Twenty percent of the women and 48% of the men viewed themselves as similar to other lawyers they encounter in their work. The rest maintained that it depended on the area of practice and other factors.

A number of other themes emerged, many painting an unflattering view of lawyers who take the adversarial approach to the practice of law. Donna, who sees herself as more conciliatory than other lawyers she encounters in her work, comments:

> I wouldn't describe many lawyers as very conciliatory because most of the lawyers I deal with are litigation lawyers, and their clients are already into a dispute when we get involved. Things that are in litigation are hard to resolve so that everybody is a winner. There's generally a winner and a loser, and every lawyer hopes that his client will be the winner. So, if you're very conciliatory initially, I don't know that you're likely to come out ahead. I think most of them are somewhere in the middle, probably. And most of them are prepared to be adversarial. I think that most of the lawyers are probably more adversarial than I am. I think more of them are prepared to be assholes, for the sake of it, than I am. But I don't know. I heard from another lawyer that someone I had litigated against told this other person that it was the most confrontational piece of litigation he'd ever been involved in his life, so, I don't know whether I have a realistic impression of how I conduct my cases. [Interviewer: How did you find him?] I thought he was very adversarial, and I thought I was doing what I had to do.

In addition, lawyers who are seen as adversarial are sometimes seen as not necessarily doing their clients any favours. In fact, some respondents think some adversarial lawyers are actually "milking" their clients. Melanie commented:

> If there's a way to work out a resolution in a relatively conciliatory way, then great, that's to be preferred, because it's more efficient. You don't waste a lot of money for your client. I think, actually, some of the litigation lawyers in town who are very adversarial are trying to milk files. They're trying to get as much money as they can out of them, so they'll bring on motions unnecessarily, or they'll be difficult to deal with unnecessarily. I think it keeps them in the fray, and it keeps the bills high. It's a cynical point of view, but I guess that's how I feel.

Opal thinks that some lawyers are "out to make the most money they can off a client. Things tend to take longer than they do with other lawyers, and there is not much likelihood of settlement."

Fred, who sees himself about the same as other lawyers he encounters in his work, realizes he is generalizing, but he finds most litigators to be more adversarial, to the point at which they "sometimes overlook the best interests of their clients, in the sense of getting good value for the result. In other words, they say, 'I will win at all costs.'" He feels that 70% of the solicitors he deals with are very good, and "30% are just very difficult, and sometimes the deal falls apart – either because we don't work well together, or they don't work well with anyone – one of the two."

There was no consensus as to whether more experienced counsel were more conciliatory or more adversarial. Lois felt that while there are exceptions, more experienced counsel are easier to get along with. She has had more difficulty with junior counsel: "I feel sometimes their adversarial approach comes out of not knowing, so they'll say 'No' off the bat, because they don't know what they should do. Whereas much more experienced counsel sit there and they realize there is no problem in delaying a discovery for two days, either for my convenience or my client's convenience. Experienced defence counsel will realize the judge is going to weigh all those factors. Junior counsel don't seem to understand the importance of that kind of fact scenario on a plaintiff and on a judge."

Similarly, Vincent thinks junior litigators, who "seem to have bigger chips on their shoulders," are more difficult to deal with. More senior litigators "don't have to prove anything. They are just easier to deal with." Tony suggested that lawyers in mid-career were the least cooperative:

> It goes in phases. I have had periods of my practice during which I have gotten cooperative counsel, and almost all my files are working with cooperation on both sides. I have gone through phases during which I can't expect any quarter from the other side, and not the slightest courtesy. Overall, I don't think I have a clear impression of where it breaks down. I find among the younger practitioners there's a cooperative attitude. I find the more senior practitioner tends to become cooperative. I've found people to be markedly uncooperative between about the fourth or fifth year of call and the eighth or ninth. I have my own suspicions, it may have to do with the fact that by the time you're into your fourth or fifth year you're more comfortable about your own expertise and knowledge and confidence. And it may be at that point that someone's true character comes out. That may be done away with, especially in Vancouver, as lawyers are specializing more and more. You end up practising in a small circle of lawyers, and if you develop a reputation of being very adversarial, that gets around, and you're not going to get cooperation. Your practice is going to become more expensive to your client, and more difficult and stressful to you. I don't think, ultimately, that makes sense. And I suspect what happens is that between the fourth and eighth year of call, people realize they can't practise that way, or decide to leave, or are ousted in one manner or another. That's when I find the highest incidence of lawyers who are uncooperative, but there are exceptions. I have recently had an experience with some junior lawyers who, I don't know why, take a very

adversarial role, in terms of how they want to run litigation and that's fine. I'm prepared to practise with whatever I'm faced with on the other side.

Yvonne was in the process of leaving the practice of law, partly because she finds most lawyers to be very adversarial. Her approach is to say, "Here's the situation. Let's not make it worse for our clients. Let's just try and work this out reasonably." Then she gets "dumped on" by the adversarial lawyer who comes back with "If you do this, we're going to do that."

Daniel, who sees himself about the same as other lawyers he encounters in his work, believes that people might gravitate to areas of the law with which they are most comfortable. Solicitors are deal makers, who are trying to reach a consensus, and he finds that most of them practise at the conciliatory end of the continuum.

Holly views herself as more conciliatory than other lawyers she encounters in her work, and sees adversarial lawyers as living up to an image, or demonstrating a learned response:

In general (and I know that I'm generalizing here), lawyers tend to be more adversarial than conciliatory. We're used to competing through school – do well, get in the top 10% – competing to get into law school, writing the LSAT, getting grades so that you can get a good articling position (whatever that means) and get into a good firm. Then, even beyond that, you're still fighting with the lawyers on the other side. In general, it attracts a fairly competitive group, or people who are used to competing and achieving and doing well, and they don't like it when they lose. I think a lot of lawyers look at each case as if it's a test of their own ability, which in some ways it is. But I think the thing to recognize is that, in some cases, there's just no winning, no matter what you do. Sure you can make the result a little better, but in some cases it's not a winner, period. It's just based on facts, and has nothing to do with the law or your ability. I think a lot of people lose sight of that.

Carissa, who sees herself as more conciliatory than other lawyers she encounters in her work, said that adversarial lawyers are more successful in practice:

In general, lawyers tend to be more adversarial, but there are some very nice, calm, conciliatory people, but they don't generally (and I hate to generalize) achieve the same level of status or power in a law firm, certainly in a major downtown firm. Somehow, the notion of being nice is that you're not someone to be taken seriously. You can't be a power-broker, you must be one of these lightweights who like to go home at five, and have a nice little family, and people can walk over you. There's even a little bit of that in interactions with staff – people who yell, or have a reputation for being difficult, or who yell and scream if it's not done properly – will get their work done first. It's just plain simple, no one wants to be yelled at. And people are living in fear of being yelled at, so they're going to do your work first, regardless of how much you might like the other person, who's nice and gentle and pleasant to you. A lot of people don't want to be in conflict positions. So being loud and obnoxious and demanding does bring its own reward sometimes, you know.

Overall, few respondents viewed themselves as adversarial, and many had uncomplimentary remarks about those who are adversarial. One is left with the impression that there may be an image or myth of the adversarial lawyer. However, 64% of the women and 40% of the men see themselves as more conciliatory than other lawyers they encounter in their work. There could be a number of reasons there is such a disparity between the proportion of lawyers who see themselves as more conciliatory and those that see themselves as more adversarial. First, this sample was limited to lawyers called between three and seven years. Perhaps the more adversarial lawyers are more senior. This seems unlikely, as many respondents thought that lawyers became less adversarial as they aged (although some also thought that older lawyers were more adversarial than younger lawyers). Second, we are more likely to remember negative experiences than positive ones, and most of the respondents who described lawyers who were more adversarial did so in less than flattering terms. Third, as at least one woman indicated, maybe she just did not have an accurate idea as to how other lawyers viewed her. Respondents may be inaccurate in assessing how others perceive them.

Gender Perceptions of the Conciliatory-Adversarial Continuum
When respondents were asked whether the women and men lawyers they encountered in their work differed in their approach, 38% of the women and 6% of the men said that women were more conciliatory in the practice of law; 26% of the women and 26% of the men thought that women were more adversarial than men; and 28% of the women and 48% of the men thought that women and men were about the same on the scale ranging from very conciliatory to very adversarial. The remainder of the respondents could not generalize, for a variety of reasons – interaction with no (or too few) women, too much variation, and so on.

Women Are More Conciliatory Than Men
The image of women lawyers as more conciliatory than men did not prevail among the respondents, especially the men. Only 38% of the women,

and a mere 6% of the men, thought that women lawyers were more con-ciliatory than men lawyers. It may be that lawyers have a greater expecta-tion that women will be more conciliatory than men, and their responses reflect, in part, their perceptions of the women lawyers they encounter.[37]

For some women respondents, other women lawyers are easier to work with, and less confrontational, than men. For example, Deborah finds that women "engage in discourse; they are more open; it's easier to resolve dif-ferences. Men are more adversarial and confrontational." According to Sally, "Women tend to start out as problem solvers, as opposed to running off to court to get *ex parte* orders, and setting things for trial. Men tend to resort to court more frequently." However, she finds that there are a lot of "extremely conciliatory men who are wonderful to deal with, but some just start from the position that winning at all costs is the goal, and it is diffi-cult to respond to that in a way that protects your clients' best interests." Other women reported that men engage in more posturing than women. Amy expressed her displeasure: "I have to endure extreme behaviour by male counsel – raised voices, intense gesticulation, loud voices, some things which I thought were sharp. There are male counsel who have a reputation for this behaviour, whereas women, when I first make contact (usually tele-phone contact), there is a much calmer demeanour, and usually we seem to strike a chord which allows us to have a conversation about the substance of the case."

Holly thinks women tend to be more conciliatory than men. When asked to explain, she responded:

> There seems to be less posturing when you're dealing with women. They tend to be solution-oriented, and not courtroom-oriented. They don't need to strut their stuff in the courtroom. In fact, the women tend to want to try and work something out. There are a couple of female lawyers in this community who are quite good that way, and if they can resolve something without going to court, they'll generally do it, although they're slow at getting around to doing things. Most of the time, I find that the male lawyers tend to, you know, "See you in court."

Similarly, Iris found men lawyers to be more adversarial in that they "tend to get more excited about things for no real reason," whereas she can talk things out with the women lawyers and does not have "to listen to somebody yell at the top of their lungs."

Angela theorized that women's conciliatory approach is "a function of socialization. Women are more willing to give and take; men more likely to hold to their position." Ursula also thought that the dividing line was more male/female than solicitor/litigator: "I hate to sound like a sexist, but it is the way it works out. I think men are socialized for one position and women are socialized to facilitate ... I mean, it is not all along sexual lines. Lawyers in general tend to be cocky. Big egos, you know; that's what makes for a good lawyer. I think so it is the nature of the game. You have to be self-confident."

Some women think that women's conciliatory nature is the result of fear or avoidance of negative labels, or their perception that it is necessary to mask their adversarial nature. However this puts women in a bind, as they had to have been somewhat assertive to get where they are. Carissa explained:

Women, to begin with, are not overtly adversarial because there's a label attached to being adversarial and a woman, and that is, "You're a bitch." I don't know what the word is for men, no one ever calls them that. You hear it from staff, even fellow associates, that someone is a bitch. So no one wants to be called a bitch, even if it does mean that sometimes you do get your work done a lot quicker than when you're a nice person. So women are not as overtly adversarial to begin with. And, I think by nature, women don't want to be seen as adversarial, so they start off being closer to the conciliatory end of the continuum. But in general I think that the women in law are probably not typical of women in the rest of society, because if you were to take a poll and ask women in law about their background, you'd find that most of these women have come from backgrounds in which they've been expected to achieve. Either they're the eldest or they're the only child, and there are lots of expectations placed on them. They have been told that they can do anything that a man can do. And that's the only reason they go into law, because otherwise they'd go into teaching, or into nursing, or accounting, all of which are nice, stable, and esteemed professions, but they're not as groundbreaking, or as unusual, as women entering into law, or medicine for that matter, or engineering. These women are different from women in the rest of society, because we have been taught that it's okay to buck the norm – you don't have to get married and have kids by the time you're twenty-three. And we're used to fighting twice as hard to get to the same place as men, to even be accepted. So for me to say I don't think women are as adversarial as men may be a falsity in itself. We probably do have it in us, we just learn to mask it better and think it's less socially acceptable for women, so therefore we don't like to come out clawing and be overtly adversarial.

She provided an example of how it is sometimes important to meet the expectation that women are less aggressive:

I've had a client call me a tight-ass. He wanted an opinion done right away, and I told him, "I needed these documents signed because I can't give my opinion without your certificate saying that you, acting on behalf of the company, have told me these things. I'm not going to give you my opinion until you sign it." He was frustrated, because he wasn't getting what he wanted. He told me I was a tight-ass, "You don't need all those documents, and I can go to any other law firm and they can give me an opinion without all those documents." And, I said "You just go ahead and do that. Once you get me the documents I can give you an opinion." I just ignored his comments, but I felt like calling him all sorts of names ... After that, he was nice to me. But I thought, "I don't have to put up with this. If it weren't for the fact that this was a client of the firm, and it was my job, I could tell you where to go." But it's the attitude. He'd never call a male lawyer that, even though he'd be just as frustrated. So that's what we have to put up with. We can't afford to, at least I don't think so, that as women we cannot afford to go into hysterics, or start crying or saying, "Gee, you're being a sexist pig." That's just the nature of law. It's a hard thing to juggle. By nature, I don't think we want to be adversarial, but on the other hand we've learned that in order for you to get anywhere, and to be respected in the profession, sometimes you have to be, probably more times than you like.

Several explanations were suggested for men's adversarial posture. Melanie, for instance, thinks that some men have "too much testosterone. It's like a substitute for football or something for them. They have to win everything, and they don't want to be seen losing face." Although Dorothy meets some fairly adversarial women in family law practice, she believes "men are more adversarial, just because they are dealing with a woman." She takes a straightforward approach in dealing with other lawyers, and tells them they are "being ridiculous, and that has a tendency to get men's dander up." She adds, "So, maybe it's me." Emily claimed that "men are more competitive, almost an issue of personal pride that they establish their credibility, that they make their point heard, whether it was necessarily going to get us anywhere or not." And Tina has found that men "tend to get more entrenched in a position, whereas women would be more flexible at hearing new positions, or a little more open to discussion and conciliation."

Women Are More Adversarial Than Men
An equal number of women and men (26%) reported that the women they encounter in their work were more adversarial than the men. Some respondents thought that the more senior women were more adversarial than the junior women. Barbara's theory was that these women "had to fight a lot harder" than she did to establish their careers, and "it has become part of the way they are." Similarly, Laura thought that the more senior women,

who "had to fight their way to be lawyers, have to prove that they are just as good as the men." Murray shares this view. There are a number of women in his area that "have a terrible reputation of fighting, and just not trying to get things resolved." They tend to be "the ones who are in their forties at this stage, and had a much more difficult time in becoming accepted in the law than women now." Karen reported two bad experiences she had had recently, that made her life "hell"; both were with women:

> I hate to stereotype, but there are a few women in family law, more senior ones, who I think are particularly bad for taking on the issues of their client. Everyone else is wrong, and they tell you, in no uncertain terms, all of the bad things that your client has done, based on what their client has told them, which I don't think is very professional. It's good to understand what your client is going through. That's fine, in terms of dealing with your client, but when you deal with the other lawyer – I mean I had this woman tell me, "Your client is a complete asshole. He's done this, this, and this, he's just a jerk." And that's the way every conversation would go. I'd always say, "Listen, I don't want to get into that, you can think what you want, and I don't think it's professional, and let's get to the issue." I mean, it used to come up quite often. It's surprising, and I wouldn't think that person was doing a service to the client.

The more adversarial nature of junior women is sometimes explained as women having to prove they are tough in a man's world, or compensating because they are women. Lois, for example, has had to intervene in cases in which her male partner was up against a junior woman counsel, because it had turned into a "little kitty-cat fight." Similarly, although Olive does not see much difference between women and men defence counsel, she finds that some of the junior women prosecutors are quite aggressive, probably because "they are afraid of being taken advantage of."

Wendy believes women, herself included, to be more adversarial than men:

> This is going to sound so sexist, and I'm not sexist. I think there was a tendency on the women's part, and I can't speak for all of them, to overcompensate a little bit for the fact that they were immediately perceived as being not as strong, and not as adversarial, as the men were. I'm [rather short] on a good day, and when I started, I was reasonably young, and people always thought I was an articling student when I walked into court, even when I was a lawyer, until I talked, and then they realized maybe that wasn't the case. But I was little, and I think I tried to overcompensate for that. So I think, overall, with the major exceptions again, that women lean toward the adversarial side. They have more to prove.

Nicholas also finds women to be more adversarial. This may be partly because the ones he encounters tend to be more junior – having been called to the bar only within the past one to three years. When asked why he describes them as more adversarial, he responded:

> They just seem to be less willing to give in. One example, I guess this has happened to me a few times, and to other people I've talked to, that when you're in chambers, or you're in a trial in a real fight, during the breaks and at the end of it, with most men, I'd hope you still can be friendly and casual while you're waiting for the judge to come into the courtroom – you could be chatting about this and that. A lot of women, they never turn off the adversarial thing. It's there whether you're performing before the judge or not. I've had occasions at the end of a chambers application in which I've tried to say something to the woman and they storm out. I've never had that happen with a man. I've had that happen three or four times with women.

Lois and Kevin also find that the women they encounter are less able to "turn it off," and they take things more personally:

> I can go in and bite your head off in the discovery room, and do my job protecting my client, and I'll still go for lunch with you. It's a job, and a lot of them can't turn it off, and that's my personal beef this month. There are some people who just can't turn it off. We go in, we do our battle, we walk out, we're friends again. They just don't seem to be able to do that, and from some of the senior counsel that I've gotten to know through my partner, that's almost become second nature to me. I feel like it's almost given me a second leg up, because I have a more seasoned style of practice. Of course, I think experience is probably a great deal of it. I've dealt with more male counsel than I have with female counsel, and there have been some female counsel who I've had absolutely no problem with. It's just a few of them that get, I don't know how to put it, they get personal and bitchy about it. They don't leave it at the office. I'm not explaining that properly, and it's not a lot of them, but I'm sensitive to it because it reflects badly on me as female counsel.

> Oh, here we go. Well, as a matter of fact – and I'm going to be as fair as I can about this – I think I've encountered a difference personally. I have no idea whether that's true generally, but I have found (and I suspect actually that it may be partly my own shortcomings, as a matter of fact, and I'm willing to admit that), but I've found in many instances in which I had a female lawyer on the other side, people had their dander up more, it was more tense a relationship. That hasn't always been the case, but I

would say that it would be more likely with my female/male relationships than with my male/male relationships.

Kevin then volunteered an explanation:

I think that it would be a combination of things. I think it would be a combination of women not feeling as secure in the practice as men do, or maybe they're not made to feel as welcome as men are, and that may be a part of it. But the other part, I think, would be my own, as I said earlier, shortcomings, and (I don't even know how to explain it) but I sometimes feel differently when a woman is around on the other side. Well, for women in this firm, though, it's quite different. You wouldn't bat an eye about anything. I never even think twice about it, but I have noticed one thing in my practice, in my experience related to male/female things, and that's when a woman is on the other side of the file ... And I've never been able to figure out what that is, but those are my thoughts on it.

Megan sees no difference in immigration law, but thinks women are more adversarial in family law, especially with issues of violence. "The men, occasionally, play it down," and so she finds men "ironically" more conciliatory. Similarly, Frank finds no difference in personal injury law, but feels that women are less conciliatory in family law. They "are more adversarial, and more apt to take unreasonable positions." In the same vein, Owen thinks that: "Women in criminal law tend to be a little more hard-nosed, they have a thicker skin than women in other areas of law that I've seen, generally because they are dealing with crimes of violence, sometimes, or miscreants of some kind or another who have probably run afoul of the law. So I'd say that most women are a little tougher than the average male colleague in criminal law, and I think that they would have to be, at least for the foreseeable future."

When asked why he thought that was, he responded: "Well, it's a rough arena out there, and there still is, less of it now, there are certainly way more female criminal lawyers than there were ten years ago. I think there's a good sense of collegiality between male and female in the bar in the criminal area. We don't hear the snide comments that you sometimes might hear uptown in the Smithe Street litigation. I think there's more respect, and there are certainly way more women on the Bench in all venues. In Provincial Court, certainly way more."

Gerry had just finished dealing with a female lawyer who was very adversarial, so he thought it might have been a "bad time" to answer the question: "As a matter of fact, the men I don't find to be as adversarial as a lot of the women. I'm disappointed to say that. There aren't as many women practising law, so you have a smaller group to select from. ['In what way are women more adversarial?'] In these negotiations, do you argue principle or do you argue position? She was position-oriented, and to actually get behind the principles which underscored her position was exceedingly difficult, and she took grave offence to any challenge on my part."

Leon and Mark described similar experiences:

This is not universally true, but I do find that if I run into a tough lawyer who I think is too adversarial, and doesn't necessarily do their client a service, it tends to be female more often than male. [Interviewer: And in what way are they more adversarial?] It's the whole tone of the negotiation, and it's the kind of things they take issue with, which I'm not sure – I'm not always convinced that they are that important. And it's more the way that they take issue with things. It's a tone thing a lot of the time, and also just the way that they go about negotiating – sometimes it tends to be very adversarial.

I don't want to answer this in a clichéd way. I don't know what the reasons are for this, but I would say the women or female practising lawyers are a little more adversarial than the men. Not too much more, I'd place them at a four or five [the more adversarial end of the scale] rather than a three or a four [at the more conciliatory end of the scale]. [Interviewer: What is it about them that makes them more adversarial as opposed to more conciliatory?] I mean, sometimes you get into a situation in which compromise is required. I've had a couple of deals in which – again I don't know whether it's the lawyer that's projecting this or just some bad luck with the particular lawyer's clients – but there doesn't seem to be as much of an air of compromise. I think in other situations in which I would have been able to resolve it easily that I haven't been able to do that on a few occasions.

Do Women and Men Take the Same Approach?

Twenty-eight percent of the women and 48% of the men thought that women and men were about the same on the scale ranging from very conciliatory to very adversarial. This response produced few comments on the approaches taken by women and men, as the respondents did not see women and men as differing.

Women Are More Extreme

Three of the fifty men felt that women were more likely to be found at the extremes of the scale – either very conciliatory or very adversarial. For example, Fred claimed that the women he deals with are more conciliatory than the men, "but then again the ones that aren't can be very adversarial. It's like they are polar." To the same effect, Tony reported that he does not run into many women in his practice, but the few he has are "very cooperative counsel or very uncooperative counsel. I rarely find that you get anything in the middle." Conrad also sees women "at the extremes. They are cooperative and reasonable or it's like psycho-bloodlust. Fewer women are in the middle."

Is the Adversarial System Effective?

Respondents were asked whether they thought the adversarial system was effective in resolving disputes.[38] Twice as many men (40%) as women (20%) thought the adversarial system was effective. An almost equal number of women (22%) and men (18%) said it was not effective. Forty-eight percent of the women and 32% of the men thought the system was effective in some cases. Six percent of the women and 10% of the men saw problems with the adversarial system, but did not think there was a better alternative.[39]

The Adversarial System Is Effective

Of the women (20%) and men (40%) who thought the adversarial system was effective, explanations varied, but generally fell into one of six categories:

1 It resolves disputes.
2 It clarifies issues and gets to the truth.
3 The option of going to court is effective.
4 It provides remedies for the otherwise disadvantaged.
5 It is effective, but there are other ways to resolve disputes.
6 It is effective, but it is subject to abuse and misuse.

Resolving Disputes
For some of the respondents, the adversarial system provides a means of resolving disputes at times when nothing else works. According to Donna, "Cases end, files are closed. If you don't mediate or arbitrate or something, you litigate, and the judge will decide if the parties can't agree ... So if things don't get resolved, the court will resolve it." The adversarial system would not be necessary if "everybody were able to see everything in a perfect light. But they see through their idiosyncrasies." Likewise, Conrad believes that the system is effective; for example, "If I can't make the adjuster be reasonable, or from his point of view he can't make me be reasonable, well at least you have a final arbiter." Paula expressed surprise that

the adversarial system actually seems to work: "Sometimes I'm shocked at the end of the day that things went as well as they did for everybody. I think it works."

Clarifying Issues and Getting to the Truth

Some of the respondents endorsed the argument that the adversarial system helps clarify the issues and gets to the truth. Carissa, a solicitor, explained:

> In some ways, I still believe the adversarial system is good. It allows each side to bring forth the best arguments, and it forces them to play all their cards. By starting at opposite extremes, sometimes it's easier to get toward the middle if both sides see that they have had to give up something along the way. And, ultimately, it's getting your case heard and airing your grievances, in a way, that's sometimes good. It's just like sexual assault victims, even though they know they can't win, it's just having it out in the open, and having people acknowledge it happened, rather than keeping it a secret. While traumatic, it's also healing at the same time, and there's something to be said about the open court system, and making it public, which makes it real and acknowledged. For example, in [some societies] it's shameful to air your grievances in public. It's considered bad manners, uncouth, you just don't do that. But that means a lot of secrets are kept, and a lot of grievances are buried, and people don't feel that justice is done. Today in the Canadian legal system, you have travesties of justice from time to time, but I think it's the air of secrecy that bugs people – especially in Canadian society. Karla [Homolka] and Paul [Bernardo] Teale: big hoopla that this is all a secret court, and it does cause people to wonder, "What's she saying about her husband, and how's she implicating him?" You get the sense it's not fair, "Why should she be entitled to that secrecy, whereas he won't have the same luxury?" There's something to be said for the public's right to know what's going on.

Bruce expressed confidence that "no matter how unreasonable a position is in litigation, once you get into the courtroom and both sides go at it, so to speak, the truth usually emerges. It's not the most pleasant experience for the litigants, but in terms of final results it's effective." Similarly, Kevin described the adversarial system as effective, because there has to be a mechanism for resolving disputes,

> otherwise you'll have anarchy and chaos. The way the process works is that, through the adversarial system, you have people throwing the truth

against each other, in effect, and you have an independent person, a judge, who sits there and decides which one makes the most sense. When it comes down to issues that require those types of findings of fact, many times it boils down to the question of credibility. There are always credibility issues in every trial you go to, every time a witness takes the stand, the question of credibility comes up ... The biggest weaknesses in cases are the credibility issues. I think the trial process is the best way to sort out those credibility issues. The second you get into somebody's credibility, you want somebody there who can comment on it and say, "You're not credible." I think it works.

However, Kevin also thought there was a problem with the adversarial system, because "it makes a difference which counsel is involved. There is no question of that. So justice is served better to somebody with a good lawyer than it is to somebody with a lesser lawyer. There is no question about that fact. At the end of the day, a good lawyer is available, theoretically, to everyone. If you don't choose one of them, I guess you do so at your own peril."

Although Jack thinks the system works, he would prefer a system in which the judge becomes more involved. He suggested that this would be particularly appropriate in custody applications, in which interim orders, which are often resolved on the basis of unreliable affidavits, become permanent orders because "money runs out, and the stamina of the client runs out as well." A more active judge at the interim order stage might solve some of these problems.

Going to Court Can Be Very Effective

Some of the respondents thought that disputes are often resolved because of the threat of going to court. Bargaining in the "shadow of the law"[40] is an effective means of resolving disputes, provided counsel are not too keen on going to court. Tony, for example, thinks the system works well, if people bargain within it: "If you have got competent counsel on both sides, you both know what the result is likely to be in court, if not for certain, and you can come to the table with common framework, in terms of what you think the ultimate result will be." The fact that the adversarial system is "hanging over you" is effective. Similarly, Zachery finds that the adversarial system "is a loaded gun to your head," and "it gets people to jump. Otherwise, I could see things just going on forever. It puts a stop to it. I don't know whether it is the most effective way, but it certainly resolves disputes."

Despite these endorsements, there are still reservations about the adversarial system. Ted argued that while it is effective, it is also quite expensive:

Most of the personal injury cases that I've been involved with have settled before they've gone to trial. The positions of the parties tend to be far apart at the beginning. Someone may present a claim that they say is worth $100,000, and you look at it and you think it's worth thirty or forty, and the next few months up to the trial are spent trying to reduce the difference between the parties and quantifying the damages. I don't know whether the system tends to amplify the differences between the parties, in terms of their expectations of what is a reasonable settlement, or whether the system tends to bring people who are of divergent views closer together over time. It's probably a little of both, depending on the counsel involved.

Providing Remedies for the Otherwise Disadvantaged

Zeke believes that the adversarial system is effective for resolving disputes between less powerful individuals and more powerful companies:

Yes, it's always encouraging when you have two sides who can sit down and be totally honest and say, "Let's just resolve this instead of going through this," and both are happy. Unfortunately, I don't think that's very realistic in most cases. If you're dealing with insurance companies, who have policies to limit exactly how much they're going to pay out, they're not prepared to offer what judges are offering, so we have to look at that and say, "How can we settle for something less than we would get in court?" So on that basis, I think the system is effective, because it provides certain litigants, who don't have the power that bigger companies have, an opportunity to go to court and have the court rule on it.

Finding Other Ways

Some think that the system is effective, but that there are alternative ways for resolving disputes, such as mediation. Jeff, for example, thinks there are times when the adversarial system "is necessary, and it's the best"; however, "there are lots of situations in which a non-adversarial approach would be a better approach for a better prospect or result."

Avoiding Abuse and Misuse

Many of the respondents who thought the adversarial system was effective also thought it was subject to abuse. For instance, Barbara thought that some members of the profession "take it too far": "That's why we have protracted litigation, and that is why our court systems are jammed up. There are all sorts of suits filed in court that never should have been filed. People can take 'Everyone is entitled to their day in court' a little bit too far. But, generally it works quite well."

Nicholas thought the adversarial system was effective; however, he thought it could be more effective,

> if people fight more on what really is there, if they get rid of the silly things, like whose office the discovery is going to be in, or some of the other things. If someone is a day late delivering a report, and you're not going to let it in, you argue in court about that, knowing full well that the judge is going to let it in anyway. It's the unnecessary confrontation that hurts the system, but if you can just get right down to it, and agree that this is where we're going to have our fight, our disagreements, the system works very well.

According to James, the adversarial system is effective in arriving at a "relative truth," but he does not think it is effective in what it does to the individuals involved, and the profession as a whole:

> You know, frankly, we get used by clients who only feed us a certain amount of information, so that we can accomplish their objectives. Well, I don't like being used like that. Some lawyers are more cavalier about that than I am. Others are less so. I don't like it. I've been put in a position of feeling like I have to do it, because of my relative lack of seniority. I don't like that at all, but, you know, I've lived with it, I've reconciled it in my own mind. Now that I'm gaining more experience, I let that happen to me less frequently.

Reasons the Adversarial System Is Effective

Forty-eight percent of the women and 32% of the men thought the system was effective in some cases. For some, it depended on the area of law; for others, the types of cases. Some thought it was effective, but not as effective as other means of resolving disputes. Still others saw it as effective in some cases, but subject to abuse.

The Adversarial System Works in Some Areas of Law

Although a number of respondents thought the adversarial system was effective in the criminal law area, but not effective for family law, there was no consensus among the respondents. Susan tries to have rational discussions and reach agreements in most of the disputes she works on. However, in criminal law, "there is such a presumption of innocence and whatnot, and defence counsel does have the right to raise technicalities and whatever to advance her or his case." Thus, she is not sure "how we could get away from the adversarial system in criminal law," other than by the use of diversion and other alternative measures. Megan does not think the adversarial system works with family law matters, but added that sometimes "it is necessary." For criminal law, she thinks it works very well, except in sexual assault cases, in which she thinks it is inappropriate. What would she do for such offences? She suggests more of an "investigative procedure." She does not do sexual assault cases, because she does not want "to be involved in cross-examining a woman about things that I consider to be irrelevant."

Valeria thinks the system works for money disputes, but that "it doesn't seem to have the capacity to get the real story from people in family law, even personal injuries and Native legal disputes." In the same vein, Alex explains:

> It's more successful in areas in which you don't have the personal side coming into it. That's why it's not successful in family law. I spend most of my time in family law actually being a counsellor, not doing much law. Typically, I get on the phone with the other lawyer, and we end up talking more about things other than law. So often, there's so little law. What those people need is not lawyers, they need counselling at that point, and I don't think a lot of lawyers know how to deal with the emotional side of family law. It's effective in commercial matters. Part of the adversarial system is forcing things along, and sometimes with mediation and arbitration, there's not the immediacy of dealing with problems. Even in the adversarial system it can be so spread out, but if it's dealt with properly, it gives people time to compromise or resolve their positions.

Theresa thinks that the adversarial system is effective for criminal law, because "the state is taking an adversarial approach to an individual." She also finds it effective in the immigration field, "because it is an extremely arbitrary system." She explains: "You can sometimes obtain cooperation, but that tends to be on an individual level rather than on a system-wide level. So it is a little harder to categorize immigration, just because the decisions by the immigration officers can be so individualized, because it is administrative law. They are supposed to exercise and have a lot of discretion, in fact it is a violation of legal principles for them to fetter their discretion. So, it is just harder to classify."

However, Paul thinks that the adversarial system is not effective for immigration law. He thinks there should be a "much more relaxed" administrative decision-making process for refugee cases,

> more of an inquisitive, inquiry type situation, in which everyone gets to participate, and everyone knows what the issues are, and it's not just ripping the individual apart in cross-examination – that's what happens now. So it should be a little more open, and definitely should be a lot

less court-like. Nowadays it's like these people walk into a courtroom and there are people on platforms that they have to look up to, and have to be cross-examined in front of, and they're obligated to make their case in front of these people, who are like judges, and it's not the best system for this kind of case.

Barry had just settled "a messy estate" through mediation at the time of the interview: "Both sides just hated each other. The adversarial system would have cost hundreds of thousands of dollars, but we went to three-day mediation and settled. It depends on the type of case. The adversarial system is good at uncovering the facts, because you have to do that for your client. But sometimes it's not the best approach. When you get people's backs up against the wall, sometimes they don't think rationally. They do something to spite the other side, as opposed to looking at the net present value of the lawsuit."

Stewart does a fair amount of mediation with insurance companies, which like to mediate if they can. He has yet to be involved in a mediation that did not settle, and thought that we could probably get by without the adversarial system, except for the odd case that did not settle. He also thought that the adversarial system was inappropriate for family law:

> I think some kind of mediation, or basic common sense, should be used, especially when it comes to custody and access to children. When you're fighting about assets, then you could just as well do that in the adversarial system. When you're talking about custody and access, I don't think the adversarial approach works very well. When I was up north I did a fair amount of legal aid, and you have kids, eighteen or nineteen [years old] with children, and I'm sure that a mediated settlement would serve their needs a lot better than being dragged into court. Inevitably, when you do get into court, it becomes a mudslinging contest. I remember one case, we were arguing about whether the kid's underwear was always in the suitcase whenever he came back from visiting his mother. And this struck me as absurd. I mean, here we are discussing custody, and we're arguing about something as petty as this. The judge probably wasn't even listening to us by that point.

The Adversarial System Works in Some Cases

For some respondents, such as Deborah and Fred, the adversarial system was effective if they had to respond to someone who was adversarial. However, the problem with the adversarial system, according to Fred, was that it is an "all-or-nothing" proposition. People either get more than they would otherwise, or nothing at all. Holly thought that the adversarial system was effective, if the parties are far apart or if the law is uncertain:

I think it's necessary in some cases, because sometimes people are so far apart that there's just no way that you're going to come to a settlement. I've found that both parties, in the few cases that I've taken all the way through trial in Supreme Court, have had a very good case, and it's been a tough decision. Say, for example, there was a case of joint custody, and the mother wanted to move [out of Canada] and take the children, and the husband, also a good father, wanted to remain in the Lower Mainland. The cases weren't clear on that kind of thing. Both parents were good parents, and both of them offered slightly different things to the children that the other parent couldn't offer. In that case, you can't say to your client, "You're going to lose," and therefore persuade them to settle. You can't predict the outcome, and there's a lot at stake. Sometimes you just have to take things like this to trial. And for that, then, yes, the adversarial works as soon as you have an independent person listening. I've had that happen a few times. I find that the ones that go to a full trial, usually at the Supreme Court level, are usually ones that are irresolvable issues. The problem is that the law is not predictable, and because it's unpredictable, it's left in the hands of the judges.

Similarly, Harvey expressed the opinion that the adversarial system is for people who cannot come to resolutions on their own. However, he thinks that more effort should be spent on exploring alternatives: "Certainly [litigation] is a cost-consuming matter, which will hopefully deter people from pursuing it. I think it's difficult in that a lot of times when you have people on either side, you may have on one side as a client a person who is very adversarial, and a person on the other side who is very conciliatory, and I think that creates a great deal of difficulty for the legal profession, because I think there are a lot of people out there who would expect conciliatory efforts to be made, and they are frustrated with what may happen."

Keith likes to "work things out through arbitration, and things of that nature." However, "somewhat strangely," when he drafts leases, he does not like to add arbitration clauses:

I find, normally what happens when the parties reach a breakdown, they have to have an adversarial approach to it. Now, at least initially, if within that adversarial approach they can find some compromise, I always try to promote that, at least for the clients to look at, to consider whether there's some ground for compromise, because I don't see the conciliation part always as appropriate. Normally, whether it's family law or civil disputes, the hostilities are such that they're not in a position that they're going to sit down and resolve it. I'd like people to do that, but we're dealing with individuals who don't see the grey, they see the black and white, I guess.

When asked whether litigation was sometimes useful for reaching settlements, he responded:

> That's often when they realize that there's cost involved. They realize that there are certain risks. I think that's why a lot of cases settle, they begin to see all the delays and everything else. They say, "Okay, let's get realistic." And that's maybe why I don't like to see [arbitration clauses] in leases, because then somebody is going to hold up an arbitration clause just as a matter of strategy. Say we've got to go through arbitration, and then nobody is satisfied with the arbitration report. At least if they're heading for litigation, they end up in a situation in which they begin to see some of the risks and costs involved.

Neil also finds that the question of costs can prompt a settlement: "I frequently find myself saying, "Okay, you're right, but it is going to cost you $40,000 to prove that you're right, and for a $10,000 claim, why don't we try to work this a different way?"

For Tina, the adversarial system works best if the parties do not have to continue working together. However, in labour law, in which the parties "must develop a working relationship, a true adversarial process can be very destructive." She added, "When you have a real winner and a real loser, I think that can be very destructive of an ongoing relationship."

The Conciliatory Approach Is Better
Some respondents think the adversarial system is effective, but that other means of resolving disputes are better. Betty, who thinks it is effective "to a limited degree," said:

> We try to encourage mediation. Ultimately it helps my clients. They're making the decisions, as opposed to a judge, and they get to sit at a table and say to ICBC "I know you don't believe me, but I'm really hurt." This more conciliatory approach is better. However, ICBC has brought in a bunch of new policies – "No crash, no cash" – and that simply necessitates taking a lot of these cases to court. In that respect, a great number of people want their day in court, and in that sense the adversarial system is good. They don't want to think that their lawyer and ICBC's lawyers are friendly. People are always shocked when I approach the other lawyer in court and say, "Hi, how's it going?" They don't want us to be friends. They want their adversarial lawyer to be tough and aggressive.

Karen maintains that the best system depends on the context. Family law clients should go through mediation, especially if there are children involved: "It is more conducive to an ongoing relationship that is beneficial to the children," although there can be problems if one party is dominant and the other can be intimidated. She continued:

> I also think that some lawyers don't encourage [mediation], and they do a disservice in that respect. I don't think every dispute can be resolved that way, but I lean toward mediation and alternative dispute resolution – it should be used more for most things. I think most things are people problems at the end of the day, and if you have the individuals sit down, and you have someone who's good at [mediation], I think a lot could be solved. I had one case in which I was working with a senior member of the firm. It was a liability issue, and all the other lawyers were quite reasonable. The lawyer I was working with doesn't do mediation: he loves his day in court. I kept pushing and pushing, and all the other lawyers wanted to mediate. So I finally got him to go, and by the end of the day we had reached an agreement. He felt good about it, but by the next morning, he hated the whole approach. He was never going to do that again, and how did I rope him in to it? We never would have won in court; there was no hope, but he was so determined to go in there and do his stuff. I think we provided good service to the client, but he couldn't see it that way. The only reason I think he agreed in the end was because he had double-booked two trials at the same time, and he wasn't sure how he was going to deal with it. It was the sort of thing we should have done a lot sooner and cut down the client's bill.

No Alternatives, Despite the Problems

Six percent of the women and 10% of the men saw problems with the adversarial system, but could not think of an alternative that would work any better. Although the adversarial system is becoming "more costly and more cumbersome all the time," Daniel has yet to see a better alternative for resolving disputes. Likewise, Edward cannot think of a better alternative; however, he does think that there "should be more alternative measures – circle sentencing, a corrections program on victim offender reconciliation." For Jillian, the system does not offer what her clients are looking for:

> It may be as effective as anything else. I'm certainly not a big fan of the adversarial system. My own experience was that most of the clients who came to me didn't really have a legal problem, they had a personal problem, they had a problem with a relationship. The disputes that escalated to litigation were generally the ones in which the personal relationship had broken down. One of my real dissatisfactions with law was that I couldn't provide a solution to that. Those parties either needed to get back together and try and hammer something out, or they needed to both come to terms with what had happened in the relationship and move on.

So I felt I wasn't offering the customer something that they were satisfied with, and I wasn't satisfied as a result.

The Adversarial System Is Not Effective

Twenty-two percent of the women and 18% of the men said that the adversarial system was not an effective way of resolving disputes. Their comments reflect many of the criticisms of the adversarial system found in the literature:

1 It is too costly.
2 The wealthy and the lawyers benefit.
3 It is too time consuming.
4 There is always a winner and a loser.
5 There are no satisfied winners.
6 The system creates or encourages conflicts.
7 Negotiations and mediation are more effective.
8 Judicial bias can create problems.

The Adversarial System Is Too Costly

Heather stated that the adversarial system is not effective, because it is "expensive and time consuming." She provided an example of a three-week trial which cost lots of money, and concluded, "We won, but so what? We'll probably break even at the end of the day." In the same way, before Adam left private practice, he found himself telling clients,

> "Why pay me so much an hour to deal with this when the person you're dealing with was a few months ago your partner, your best friend, or a business relation, and something has happened. You want me to sue them for $20,000. Why don't you call them up and say, 'What about $10,000?'" And it was always, "No, no, no, it's a matter of principle." So they'd pay me a lot of money to litigate matters, and someone else would pay another lawyer to litigate matters, and eventually it would make it to trial, and someone else would pay a judge a lot of money to deal with it. The number of resources needed to settle disputes was disproportionate to the subject matter.

Derek reported a similar view of solicitor's work: "I find with bigger firms there is too much of that approach, and taking a position from the start. I think they try to cover their ass more, so I think they take more of an adversarial approach. I find that with the bigger firms, they have more of an attitude, 'This is the way it's done because that's the way the firm does it.' No, I don't think it is [effective], if one of our objectives is to cut clients' costs and reach an agreement."

Lawyers and the Wealthy Benefit Most

Some respondents think that the adversarial system is most likely to benefit lawyers and the wealthy, rather than the less well to do. Flora explained:

> You get into litigation, and you get into a chess game. If there's an imbal-
> ance in power between the two parties, the person with a lot of money
> can go to the Supreme Court of Canada. So it's not going to resolve the
> problem. Then when it's people fighting over kids and there's no abuse –
> it's just the principle that "I want the kids" – litigation doesn't help at
> all. It's who can afford the most expensive lawyer. One person is on legal
> aid, and the other one has a sophisticated practitioner. The legal aid lawyer
> gets papered with all kinds of forty-page affidavits and doesn't even have
> a secretary. The litigation system favours the wealthy, favours the people
> with connections. That's life, but life's not fair.

Jessica claimed that the adversarial system is "non-productive," in that:

> It encourages lawyers to exacerbate matters. It's a waste ... well, I shouldn't
> regard it as a waste. Lawyers profit from the fact, in the estate area, that
> the estate is depleted, in terms of legal expenses and so forth. I think
> some of our legislation encourages this. *The Wills Variation Act*, I think,
> is a dreadful piece of legislation, in terms of the way it's been applied.
> The estates area is an area in which emotions and hostilities can get the
> better of people, and they don't act in a rational way.

Oscar thinks the adversarial system is "a ridiculous way to resolve disputes," in that "the only people who make any money off it are lawyers."

The Adversarial System Takes Too Much Time

Vincent stressed the inefficiency of the adversarial system in the criminal
law area: "It takes too long; it is not tremendously effective at doing what
it is supposed to do. If a trial is the pursuit of truth, then that is certainly
not the case in criminal law. From a defence perspective, truth is the last
thing you want, and from a Crown perspective, nine-tenths of the battle is
just getting the case called, which is not tremendously effective." However,
he saw few options available in the criminal law area.

Both Parties Cannot Win

According to Melanie, the adversarial system is not particularly effective:

> There's always a winner and a loser in the adversarial system. Like when
> you're going to court, you both can't win. I think a more mediated or
> negotiated solution is better. I mean, to some degree, that's adversarial in

itself, but the whole point is – "How can we meet both of our interests and come to a middle ground that's satisfactory for both?" – and I find that's much quicker and it's cheaper. There are occasions, though, when you just have somebody that's so unreasonable, or your client doesn't have any choice, and the adversarial system does work, necessarily so.

Tim thinks the adversarial system "causes more ill-feeling in the long run than it resolves." However, "short of a significant change in human nature," he does not see any way around it.

The Winner Is Often Unhappy

Riley believes that often, "both parties come out unhappy" with the adversarial approach: "If it goes through to litigation, certainly the loser is always unhappy. The winner is often unhappy, because they have monstrous legal bills to pay. They don't usually feel terribly vindicated, in that they knew they were right all along in their own minds, and all they can see is a waste of money and time, as you know it can take years to resolve a dispute."

Similarly, Adam claims that clients are not particularly satisfied with what they get out of the process: "They seemed to expect that when their legal dispute ended they would feel better, and that doesn't happen by and large. So it doesn't give the clients what they want." Sybil also finds that "there is an expectation that wrongs are going to be righted, and that if you win in court, everything will be better, and you will be completely compensated. That never happens; I don't think it gears us for a peaceful world."

Sally thinks that court proceedings, especially family disputes, are complicated times for clients:

Clients are vulnerable when they come to see you. I don't think that anyone deliberately whips a client up into a frenzy so that they start court proceedings, and I'm not saying that there aren't circumstances in which you don't have to immediately go to court. But it's such a complicated time for people, that when you combine that vulnerability with upset and the emotional aspect, I don't think people are happy with the results, because nobody wins. You spend a lot of money, and somebody else makes the decision. That may not be something that either of the parties are comfortable with, even the winner.

Encouraging Conflict

Nancy thinks the adversarial system brings people to a standstill, and "they become adamant about their positions." Similarly, Murray finds that the system "tends to pit interests against one another, rather than trying to find common goals or common solutions. Whether that's in the labour process or in commercial transactions, I think the result is the same, a great deal of effort is wasted unnecessarily."

Negotiation and Mediation Are More Effective[41]
Oscar maintained that he is not a litigator because "litigation is absolutely the worst way to resolve a dispute possible." His preferred method is "to sit down and make everyone talk it through, more of a conciliatory approach." He recognizes that "if someone does not want to participate, that's a lost cause and you have no choice but to go to litigation." But litigation, in his view is "the absolute worst thing you can do." He elaborated:

> I've never been involved in something that has had to go to litigation. Because of dollars involved and time pressures involved at my level, people cannot wait two years to litigate something. If you're an issuer and you're doing a $20 million issue, and a dispute comes up as to what's meant in the underwriting agreement, you can't wait two years with $20 million. You have to resolve it in the next hour and press on, and the business pressures are such that the issuers don't want to take it to court. On the underwriters' side, if they ever took one of their clients to court, they'd never get another piece of business from another issuer in town. So again, business pressure is such that it just doesn't result in lawsuits. There are few securities lawsuits in Canada. Down in the United States, securities law is one of the most active areas for litigation, and that's because of the differences in the court system, differences in the securities legislation, and, I don't know, maybe differences in the temperament of people involved. You can count on your fingers of one hand the number of times in a year that there are lawsuits coming out of a securities transaction in Canada. [Interviewer: Do you use arbitration for resolving disputes?] It doesn't get there. The businessmen solve the problem and press on. If you're involved in a multi-million dollar transaction, and when there is that much money at stake and it's in the middle of trying to get the transaction done, there's just no time to do anything other than fix the problem and move on, and everyone involved in the process recognizes that. You almost never even have to go and talk to the litigators. I almost never have occasion to speak to the litigators, which is I guess different from the experience of a lot of people; but it just doesn't come up.

Even those who thought the adversarial system was not effective recognized that there were times when it had to be used. For instance, Flora realizes there are problems with mediation:

> I'd never recommend it to a woman who's been battered. I mean, forget

it, we're going to trial. There are cases in which I've seen people got married young and now they're fighting over things and are equal as far as their power and personal power is concerned. I think mediation is ideal for that. You say "Listen, the father has a right to see the children. You have to set up a schedule and think of the kids first." Why tie up chambers? Have you ever been in chambers before Christmas, or before school holidays? I mean they're fighting over, you know, "I don't want him to pick up the kids until five in the afternoon on Christmas Day, but he wants them at three in the afternoon because they have to drive to Seattle." The judges sit there with this look of incredible patience, and these lawyers are getting paid $200 per hour to sit there and argue. We're crazy as a society. These things could be resolved if you sit them down and say, "This isn't reasonable, you're doing this and this, now go away." But the stuff I've heard is unbelievable. I was there once and this couple couldn't agree over the old record collection (Beatles, Beach Boys), and the two lawyers had these forty-page affidavits. The judge asks, "Where are the records?" One counsel had them in a box, so he hands them to the judge, and the judge lifts the box and says, "You take one, you take one." Here we are in the Supreme Court of British Columbia, and everyone was just rolling. This is the kind of thing that's going to litigation. This is ridiculous. It was the funniest thing I've ever seen in my life. It was unbelievable. There's no point in being adversarial. You have to look at the case and the circumstances.

Judicial Bias[42] Creates a Problem

Adam identified a problem with presenting cases to judges who have little empathy for the disadvantaged, but he feels that the adversarial system is still useful when displaying strength:

A lot of what I do is work on behalf of causes that tend to be disadvantaged in one way or the other. I use the adversarial system and go in front of judges who aren't by and large sympathetic to these causes. They'll just ignore the law in order to give the decision to the side they think should win. So, there are all sorts of reasons I'm not happy with the adversarial system. Nonetheless, I'm here doing law that's very adversarial. The fact that I don't think the adversarial system works well doesn't mean I don't see that there are advantages to it, particularly for the types of groups I work for. Sometimes you have to use it, too, as a display of strength, or maybe even a rationality to the other side, to say, "Okay, if you won't deal with our concerns in a reasonable way that will result in the best for us both, let's go to court, let's be mutually destructive, and maybe next time you'll behave differently."

Similarly, while Vernon thinks the adversarial system "gives an ultimate resolution," he does not consider it an effective system:

> Well, it's an imposed decision that is arbitrary to the whims of the judge, and without having judges who are particularly sensitive to any of the underlying issues, or the dynamics of family, or why things are the way they are. There are a few good judges for family law, but very few. One of the best is a female judge just appointed here, and she stands head and shoulders above any of the others, and she was a really adversarial lawyer. Everyone was wondering what was going to happen, but she's proving to be just an excellent judge.

Most Lawyers Are Reluctant Adversaries

Only a small number of lawyers rated themselves as adversarial, or as someone who started on the adversarial end of the continuum in their law practice. Both women and men were more likely to take, or to start with, the conciliatory approach to their practice – the women (62%) more so than the men (54%). Furthermore, less than a quarter of the women and men who identified themselves as barristers took an adversarial approach to their practice. Few lawyers see themselves as the "hired gun" of their clients, ready for adversarial battles. The majority of women and men who practise law are "reluctant adversaries," who feel that they serve their clients' interests best by not being adversarial. In addition, many of the adversarial lawyers are seen as doing their clients a disservice.

A number of the respondents talked about how the adversarial approach is not appropriate for resolving disputes between people who have to continue their relationships be they business relationships or continuing family relationships following separation or divorce. It is interesting that the stereotype of women as reluctant adversaries, or as more conciliatory than men, directs them to family law, but not to business law. Why are women, as conciliatory deal makers, not encouraged, rather than discouraged, from practising business law? Obviously, other factors operate when some doors are open and others closed to women practitioners.

Although the adversarial system is often justified on the basis of the competing rights of the accused against the state in criminal law, many of the lawyers working in this area are seen as more conciliatory than the lawyers who work in the family law area, and some of them described themselves as taking a conciliatory approach to criminal law. Why are lawyers cooperative when their clients are up against the state on criminal charges? It may be, as one respondent suggested, that defence counsel start to assume that those who are charged are actually guilty. The system works for those who are guilty, while defending the innocent is a harrowing experience. Duncan Kennedy has suggested that people at the "lower end of the social order ... tend to be much more manipulated, culled out, directed, oriented and controlled by their lawyers, by contrast to the higher status people."[43] This is an issue dealt with in much greater detail in other studies.[44]

Lawyers appear to be aware of the adversarial approaches of some of their colleagues, and some respondents have suggested to their client that a case will take longer and cost more because of the lawyer on the other side. Perhaps clients should be encouraged to ask lawyers about their "style of lawyering," as part of the information they may want before hiring a lawyer. However, there is always the possibility that lawyers may not have an accurate perception of their own approach. Sixty-four percent of the women and 40% of the men saw themselves as more conciliatory than the other lawyers they encountered in their work. Only 6% of the women and 4% of the men saw themselves as more adversarial than the lawyers they encounter in their work.

Female lawyers do not meet the stereotypical expectation that they are more conciliatory than men lawyers, or perhaps the expectation that women are more conciliatory results in them being seen as failing to meet that expectation. Only 38% of the women and 6% of the men thought that women were more conciliatory than men, and a little more than a quarter of the women and men thought that women were actually more adversarial than men. Obviously, the respondents' perceptions depend upon which lawyers they encounter in their work. However, one might ask, what would the ideal world look like? Do the stereotypes of women as caring and men as better adversaries create a problem for women in the legal profession? Would women be more equal in the legal profession if the lawyers thought that the women and men they encountered were about the same on the scale ranging from very conciliatory to very adversarial? These are difficult questions to answer, but this study lends support to the proposition that women are no more reluctant than men, when it comes to being adversarial in the practice of law. Rather, few lawyers of either gender take an adversarial approach to their practice, dispelling the myths of the adversarial male lawyer and women as the reluctant adversaries.

Despite the prevalence of reluctant adversaries among the women and men who were interviewed, only 22% of the women and 18% of the men thought the adversarial system was not effective. Clearly, these respondents distinguished between the adversarial system and their "style of lawyering." The men were more categorical about the effectiveness of the adversarial system than the women but, other than that, there was little difference. Many of the respondents who thought the adversarial system was effective were also of the view that not everything should be decided in a courtroom. The adversarial system included the benefits of negotiating within the "shadow of the law."

While the majority of the respondents endorsed the adversarial system, the majority also were opposed to zealous advocacy within the system. Lawyers do not have to adopt an adversarial position in order for the adversarial system to work. In addition, most of the lawyers who were either adversarial or conciliatory were also prepared to move to the other end of the scale if it suited their goals. Some lawyers did not identify with either end of the scale but rather worked the mid-range (16% of the women and 12% of the men), and some (8% of the women and 20% of the men) said their approach depended upon the circumstances of the case. This finding is similar to the one by Wilkinson et al., who found that "practitioners operated on a continuum of roles, acting as counsellor and then as hired gun rather than choosing one role over the other."[45] However, in this study, most of the lawyers were "reluctant adversaries," who thought that their clients' interests were best served without taking an adversarial approach for their clients. The stereotype of women as reluctant adversaries, and therefore perhaps not suited to the practice of law, bears little resemblance to the reality of how law is practised and how lawyers view each other in their practice.

6

The Balancing Act: Careers, Co-Habitors, Children, and Chores

Women who enter the paid workforce, particularly women in male-dominated occupations such as law, face discrimination in the workplace (see Chapter 4). However, the greatest barrier to equality in the paid workforce may actually come from the inequality and subordination that they experience at home. In exploring the relationships between housework and women's subordination, Chris Kynaston writes, "given the current, virulent antifeminist backlash and the existence of ongoing labour restructuring that threatens to push many women back into their homes, both as paid and unpaid labourers, it becomes increasingly urgent to lay bare the exploitative dimensions of housework and, in particular, to highlight how this type of privatised female labour upholds and nourishes the patriarchal *status quo* and critically undermines the achievement of gender equality (citations omitted)."[1]

According to Kynaston, the exploitation of women's labour at home leads to "gender inequalities in access to things such as leisure, household [that is, financial] resources, sleep, and good health."[2] Although a "minority of couples" have renegotiated the distribution of housework, the so-called "bloodless" revolution, in which men would take on their share of household tasks as women entered the paid workforce, has never occurred. Rather, "gender inequality became more deeply entrenched as women were increasingly forced to assume a 'double load' of unpaid domestic work and paid employment."[3]

In contrast, Margrit Eichler believes that there has been some shift from the patriarchal model (in which wives are responsible for all unpaid family work and service and dependent upon their husbands for economic support) to an individual responsibility model of the family (in which the assumption is that women and men are equal and therefore equally capable of performing either the economic function previously performed by men or the care function previously performed by women). The latter assumes gender equality; however, it is rare that women actually perform as men in the economic sphere, or men actually perform as women in the caring sphere.[4] As Eichler writes, "it is a well-documented fact that women all over the world do most of the unpaid housework and caring work, while at the same time doing a substantial portion of the paid work."[5] As a result, "it is hard to resist the conclusion that women are being exploited, especially those who are themselves engaged in paid employment or who are married to men who have retired from paid employment."[6] However, Eichler reports that there has been a "remarkable change," in that most men today recognize that they *should* contribute more to household tasks by "helping." However, the concept of "helping" means that women are still responsible for household and family management, and it perpetuates the patriarchal model. There is little recognition of these managerial tasks in the family sphere, whereas in the paid workforce managerial tasks are well rewarded.[7] The shift in men's attitudes (whether it be toward household tasks or child care) "seems to be almost entirely at the normative level rather than at the behavioural level."[8]

There is no doubt that the public/private divide has been challenged and continues to be challenged.[9] However, as Susan B. Boyd states, "the sexual division of labour remains largely intact, within both the heterosexual family and the paid workforce."[10] Privileged female lawyers are no exception.[11] Strong social, economic, and gender forces pull women into the home, while their spouses enjoy not only the luxury of these women's labour, but also the benefits of the income that they bring in through their participation in the paid labour force. Williams refers to gender as a "force field" that pulls women into the "domestic caretaker" role and men into the "ideal worker" role.[12] This "veering towards domesticity" is often enhanced by discrimination and harassment in the paid workforce.[13]

This chapter examines the personal lives of the young lawyers who were interviewed. Are they living in a married or similar relationship?[14] Have they postponed a relationship in order to establish a career? Do they have children? Has being a lawyer affected their decision to not have children up until now? Do they plan to have children in the future? Have they achieved equality at home in housework and child care? These questions raise the broader question of the impact that a demanding workaholic profession has on the lives of both women and men.

Balancing Co-Habitation

Historically, some women were forced to retire from the paid workforce upon marriage, or were excluded from some paid jobs because they were married.[15] The attitude that married women do not need to work, do not need a pay raise,[16] or should stay home to raise children, still exists in some workplaces today.[17]

Marriage often presents women with disadvantages in the workforce. Married women are viewed as less committed and more disruptive to their workplace because they may have children and, if they have children, the children will demand some of their time and attention during paid working hours. As a consequence, some women put off marriage and children in order to first establish their careers, and other women remain childless.[18] While some men also put off marriage in order to establish their place in the workforce, marriage often brings men advantages in the workplace.[19] For example, the aura of commitment to paid work follows men who have children. Joan Williams summarizes the sociological literature on the "choices" women and men make:

> [Women's] "choice" to remain childless reflects their knowledge that marriage generally hurts women's careers. In sharp contrast, men need not remain childless to protect their ability to perform as ideal workers. In fact, marriage enhances their ability to do so, as is evidenced by the fact that ambitious young men are pressured to marry, that 95% of men in management do marry, and that marriage generally enhances men's careers. That ambitious women often are forced to choose between work and family, while ambitious men are not, is a dramatic illustration that men and women face profoundly different "choices" [footnotes omitted].[20]

In the mail-out survey of lawyers in British Columbia in 1990, only 69.5% of the women, compared with 83.2% of the men, were living in a married or equivalent relationship. There was little difference between the women and men under thirty-five years of age, but a pronounced difference between women and men in the thirty-five-plus group; only 74% of the women in this latter group were married, compared with 89% of the men.[21] In the Alberta survey, 75% of the women, compared with 83.8% of the men, were living in a married or equivalent relationship.[22] Fiona Kay found similar differences in Ontario – 78% of the women and 89% of the men were living in a married or equivalent relationship.[23] As might be expected in the younger group of lawyers I interviewed, there was little difference between the women and men – 74% of the women and 76% of the men were living in a married or similar relationship.[24] Four percent of the women and men lived in a platonic relationship.

I asked those interviewees who were not living in a married or similar relationship whether being a lawyer had been a factor in their marital status. Seven women and six men said "Yes." The respondents had a variety of reasons why law had been a factor in their marital status.[25] One woman, who practised family law, thought that it had made her "rabidly anti-marriage" and "less open to committed relationships." Continuing a relationship she had been in would have meant abandoning her career and moving, and she did not have time for a relationship with the number of hours she worked. One man thought that his experience practising family law had left him "kind of jaded," but his lifestyle, other interests, and developing a career were probably more important factors in his marital status.

One woman was completely caught up in work and had to consciously adjust her working hours in order to retrieve her personal life:

> The reason [that law is a factor in my marital status] is that there is only so much time in the day, and in the first few years of my practice I worked way more than I do now. I was in the office first thing in the morning, and sometimes I wouldn't leave until three or four in the morning. And I was in there every Saturday and Sunday, because I was starting out and I loved it, and I wanted to do well. The work was fascinating, and I was getting good work. But it became a habit, unfortunately, and I didn't realize it until I'd done it for a while. Then I started to realize, gee, "How come no one is ever phoning me?" I realized I was never home. I was never returning phone calls, I never accepted invitations, and my friends just stopped calling. When that realization came to me, I said, "No, this isn't healthy," ... because it was addictive. Like anything else, you just get used to it; so I had to make a conscious effort to stop myself, and go home in the evenings, or plan things in the evenings, and go out on weekends. For the first little while, I tell you, it was strange. I felt, gee, I shouldn't be here, I have work to do, they need me," and other stuff. It's that feeling that you're needed by someone that draws you to it, and you think no one can do it quite as well as I can. That's ego stroking and all that, but I didn't have time for anything. I didn't have time to do my laundry, or pick up dry cleaning, or pay my bills. I certainly didn't have time for a relationship, and the only people I ever saw were at the law firm. And that's why you see a lot of relationships forming out of work and lawyers – those are the only people you ever see. It's considered a faux pas to date your clients, so you're not going to do that, and the only ones left are other lawyers.

Three women said that they had no time for a relationship, and one just did not see how a relationship would be compatible with practising law. One woman explained her marital status this way: "Men – they want someone to take care of them, cook their meals, and so on. Time – hours put in. Men are needy. No matter how independent they are, and they may be supportive, they always turn out to be needy ... The nature of men – sooner or later they turn out to be needy and can't handle not being catered to."[26]

Her comment may reflect the plight of married women who work outside the home. They "sleep less, enjoy less leisure time, and work much longer hours than their husbands [footnotes omitted]." In fact, some studies show that high-powered jobs "may be the least stressful element in a woman's life."[27]

One of the male respondents in this study wanted to establish a relationship, but realized he would have to cut back on the amount he worked. Two men were single because they wanted to establish their careers first, and two men had relationships break up because of the amount of time they spent at work. One of these men was no longer married because the demands of practice and commuting earlier in his career had had an "enormous impact" on his relationship with his partner.

Three women and five men said that law had not been a factor in their marital status. However, one woman's former spouse blamed law for the breakup of their relationship. She was less convinced: "He just decided that I was making enough money for the two of us and decided not to work. I wouldn't attribute that to the fact that I was a lawyer. He always tried to blame it on the law, but it was the fact that I made a bad choice [by marrying him], and he was a lazy bum. I could have afforded it if it had been worth my while, but it wasn't."

Of the thirty-seven women who were living in a married or equivalent relationship, thirteen had spouses who were lawyers and two had spouses who formerly were lawyers – a total of 41% of the women with spouses. Thirty-four (92% of the women who had spouses) had spouses who worked full time, two had spouses who worked part time, and one had a spouse not in the paid workforce. Of the thirty-eight men who were living in a married or equivalent relationship, four (11%) had spouses who were lawyers. Seventeen (45% of the men who had spouses) had spouses who worked full time, fourteen had spouses who worked part time, five had spouses who were not in the paid workforce, one had a spouse on disability, and one had a spouse on maternity leave. Female lawyers who were living in a married or equivalent relationship were twice as likely as their male counterparts to have partners who were working full time in the paid workforce.

There appears to be a trend in the younger generation of lawyers. The women are no more likely than the men to avoid personal relationships in order to establish their careers, but the people who the women have relationships with are more likely to be employed – and employed full time – and many of their spouses are lawyers. Whether these personal relationships survive the practice of law is unknown at this time. The area in which female lawyers still differ from men is in their decisions about or opportunities for raising children.

Balancing Children

In the survey of British Columbia lawyers in 1990, only 37.9% of the women, compared with 63.2% of the men, had children. Of those respondents who had children, the women had an average of 1.8 children, and the men had an average of 2.3 children. Although there was a small difference between the women and men over forty-five years of age (80% of these women and 85% of these men had children), there were substantial differences in the younger age categories. Only 62% of women, compared with 82% of the men, who were forty to forty-four years of age, had children; 50% of the women, compared with 67% of the men, who were thirty-five to thirty-nine years of age, had children; and 20% of the women, compared with 31% of the men, under thirty-five had children.[28] In the Alberta survey in 1991, only 52.7% of the women, compared with 70.8% of the men, had children.[29] Fiona Kay found similar differences in Ontario – 73% of the women and 82% of the men had children.[30]

In the random sample of young lawyers interviewed for this study, only 26% of the women,[31] compared with 50% of the men, had children. If one counts expectant parents, 28% of the women and 58% of the men had children. Of the thirty-seven women who had no children, only seventeen (including one who was pregnant), or 46%, expected or hoped to have children in the next ten years, and fourteen (37%) did not expect to. The rest thought it was possible, or did not know. Of the twenty-five men who had no children, nineteen (including four who were expecting), or 76%, expected or hoped to have children in the next ten years, and only three (12%) did not. If hopes and expectations are met, this would leave 40% of the women and 12% of the men in this cohort childless. For the women, this is at least double the expected permanent childlessness.[32]

What was interesting in the cohort of lawyers in this study was that only 10% of the women, compared with 48% of men, had had children after being called to the bar, or were expecting a birth at the time of the interviews. Of the few women who had children, most of them (eight out of thirteen, or 62%) had them *before* their call to the bar. Most of the men who had children had them *after* their call to the bar (96%). The difference between the women and men cannot be explained by the variation in their ages. As set out in Chapter 1, the women ranged in age from twenty-eight to fifty-nine, with a median age of thirty-five, and 20% were over the age of forty. The men ranged in age from twenty-eight to fifty-eight, with a median age of thirty-four, and 10% were over forty years of age. Ten percent of the women and 6% of the men were under thirty years of age. It may be that the majority of female lawyers, if they are going to have children at all, have them before they are called to the bar.

However, having children before law school or during law school can have its drawbacks, as Flora explained:

It's not smart to go into law as an older woman with kids. I had lots of interviews, I had good references, and I did well in my articles. I'm older than the senior partner who is interviewing me and he's being intimidated; and then he tells me, "You know, you're just not lean and hungry enough for a law firm." This is true, because they want a workhorse. They want a junior lawyer who's going to be there until midnight every night doing a lot of work for them so they can go home to their families. So they love the young men with the babies because those guys are there to slave and that's clear. They don't value an older woman's life experience. There's a real bias against older women.

I asked the childless respondents whether being a lawyer was a factor in their not having had children at the time of the interview. Seventeen women and two of the men said that it was. Five of the women said that they did not have time to have children, and another three said that they wanted to establish themselves first in their career. One commented:

I thought when I was younger I'd feel ripped off and deprived if I didn't have children. I thought ideally the only way to do it was to have children before I went to law school or reach a position of financial security in which I could do it. I was idealistic about what my ability would be, about being able to find part-time work and that sort of thing. There's just no time, and I cannot perceive a point in time when there will be time or when I'll be sufficiently financially stable to take the time off to have children.

Three women said that they did not have children because they would need a relationship first, and that was affected by being a lawyer. One added that a woman cannot do litigation and have a family. She knew a woman who had children in law school, and who felt like a triple failure: "Failure as a lawyer, failure as a mother, and failure as a spouse – you just can't do it, unless you hire nannies." This respondent's firm does not want her to have children, and they get nervous every time they see her with her nephew. She would not be seen as having the "same dedication" if she had children. Two women said they would have had children by now if they had not become lawyers. Two women said they just could not afford to have children. One could not afford six months off work, although her mother says she could if she wanted to. The other explained:

It's hard to picture how I could be a lawyer and a mother at the same time. That also applied to being a law student and an articling student. And also, because I do mostly legal aid, financially speaking, I wouldn't say my income is great ... I don't know how I could leave my practice for more than a month without losing whatever client base I have. I don't know what I would do for money while I was off for any length of time.

You can't count on being healthy right up to the point of delivery and getting right back to work a month later. It's a combination of financial need, and the conditions of being a sole practitioner, without any possibility of maternity leave from anyone. I have a real concern about what happens when I have a trial the next day and I have a crying baby that night; how I can't put both enough attention into a baby and effectively deal with my clients. It's hard enough without a baby. It's a question that's much on my mind, but ...

Support for the proposition that women in male-dominated occupations sacrifice their desires for children is found in the work of Olsen et al. In their survey of women librarians (a female-dominated occupation) and MBAs (a male-dominated group), they found that 72% of the librarians wanted children, but only 46% had children, compared with MBAs, 81% of whom wanted children, but only 32% had them.[33]

Of the two men who said being a lawyer had been a factor in their not having children, one man had not had time to have children up to this point and the other was too busy establishing his career.

Balancing Child Care

The increasing number of women in the workforce means that many professional men no longer have the support of a full-time, work-at-home spouse, and some of these men are also affected by the changing structure of the workplace.[34] Although there is some evidence that men are increasing their proportion of child care in light of women's increasing participation in the paid workforce, these tasks still fall disproportionately on women. The Conference Board of Canada reported in 1990 that 75% of women, but only 4.1% of men, had the majority of the responsibility for making child-care arrangements, and women were four times more likely than men to stay home when their children were sick.[35] Another study in Canada showed that only 49% of women who work full time and 62% of women who work part time share child care equally with their partners.[36] The 1996 Census found that 64% of wives with full-time paid jobs, compared with only 39% of husbands with full-time paid jobs, spent fifteen hours or more looking after their children in the week before the census. When preschoolers were at home, the percentage of women who spent fifteen hours or more looking after their children rose to 80% and the percentage of men, to 49%. Without preschoolers at home, the percentage dropped to 51% for women and 29% for men. Only 42% of husbands without paid work, compared with 79% of wives without paid work, spent fifteen hours or more a week looking after their children.[37]

In the survey of active members of the Law Society of British Columbia, in 1990, women who worked full time and had children requiring care spent a median of 30.5 hours on such care, whereas the men spent a median of fourteen hours on such care. The corresponding figures for the Alberta lawyers were thirty-five hours for women and fifteen hours for men. Female lawyers in the British Columbia and Alberta surveys who worked full time provided a median of 40% of their child-care needs, compared with 20% provided by men in the British Columbia survey and 25% provided by men in the Alberta survey. The spouses of women lawyers, in British Columbia and Alberta surveys, did a median of 20% of the required child care, compared with the spouses of men lawyers who did a median of 66% of the child care.[38] In 1996, Fiona Kay found even larger differences in Ontario. Women with children spent an average of 41.67 hours a week on child care, compared with 16.28 hours spent by men with children. When she limited her analysis to lawyers who were married with spouses in the paid workforce, the hours spent on child care were 41.93 for women and 16.46 for men.[39] Not surprisingly, women lawyers who share child care with their spouses report less "time crunch stress" than women who handle higher proportions of child care.[40]

It is somewhat difficult to quantify the amount of time spent on child care from my interviews of young women lawyers. Only 26% had children, only 20% had children who were still at home, and only three (6%) had children under the age of ten. In contrast, 50% of the men had children, 48% had children at home, and 44% had children under the age of ten.

Only four of the women had children requiring child care. Three were satisfied with the division of household labour with their spouse, and one was very dissatisfied. The three women who were satisfied with their spouses' contributions to child care had scaled back their practice, or were working part time. Heather scaled her working hours back when her first child arrived and scaled them back again with her second child. She was moving toward a three-day week so that she could spend more time with her two young children and was planning to move out of law and work with her husband in his new business so that she would have more time at home. This was not how she had predicted her life: "I never saw myself as a stay-home mother. My grandmother worked. My mother worked. So I had this image of strong working women all the time. Now that we have a little bit more room financially, we are not rich, but it is not as tight as it has been, the idea of being at home a little more, at least for a few years, is very appealing."

Heather and her husband share much of the child-care responsibilities, except that Heather is 100% responsible for organizing child care, and 70% responsible for time spent with their children on recreational activities. While they share some of the household tasks, most are performed either by Heather or by paid labour. Heather does almost all of the cooking, "unless you call it cooking when he puts his toast in the toaster for breakfast," and she refused to count that.

Vera left her litigation practice and went to work with another firm part time (thirty-five to forty hours a week) after her first child was born. She is satisfied with the balance between her work and family life, because she has managed to keep her part-time position "against threats of losing my job, against threats of having to hire someone else to replace me, and on and on and on." She is satisfied with having scaled back her work and doing the bulk of the child care and household tasks. Sybil was happy to leave her law firm to spend more time with her children. She now works in partnership with her husband, but spends more time with her children and running the firm, than practising law. She is satisfied with the division of labour that she has worked out with her husband.

Twenty-two of the men had children requiring child care. Thirteen were satisfied with the division of labour and nine were dissatisfied, in the sense that they would like to be more involved in the care of their children. Since 41% of the men with children requiring child care (nine out of twenty-two) were dissatisfied with the division of labour because they wanted to be more involved with their children, it is possible that these men would support changes to the workforce so that both women and men could spend more time with their children.[41] While some of these nine men supported changes to the workplace, a closer look at their work and family lives shows little hope for any revolutionary changes.

Hank was reluctant to venture into new areas of practice because they take more work and cut into the time he could spend with his children. He would like to cut back on his sixty-five to seventy-hour workweek, which is tough on his young family. His wife works part time (fifteen to twenty hours a week) in a female-dominated occupation, and both are dissatisfied with the amount of time he has for the children. In five years, he sees himself as cutting down to fifty-five to sixty hours a week. After all, "You have to hold up your end of the partnership."

Jeff hoped to reduce his ninety-five to 100 hour week to fifty hours a week in five years and to work only the occasional weekend. He sees this as an area that the younger generation of lawyers can have some impact:

> We're rising up through the ranks and we can form the profession in whatever image we choose. I'm prepared to exchange some income for the time, but it's difficult to do that by yourself in a large organization. Most lawyers working in large, urban firms have a good income and I think that if they accepted less work and were willing to accept less money, I think it's a great bargain. I think that for the money you're losing, you're gaining something out of all proportion to the salary. [Interviewer: So, do

you actually see that in your colleagues?] Yes, these are things that people talk about and we'll be the senior partners in twenty years, so we won't be able to point to anyone else and blame our circumstances on them.

Kevin is quite satisfied with his sixty-hour workweek when he is at work, but when he gets home he wishes that he had more time at home: "I wish the days were two hours longer. If the day were two hours longer, I would spend the extra two hours with my family. Geez, I wonder what my wife would say if she could answer. She thinks, of course, that I work too much. But I would place myself at two [the satisfied end of the scale]."

He actually increased the hours he worked with the arrival of their child, because he caught a ride to work with his wife who stopped at the babysitter's place on her way to work. In five years, he sees himself working the same type of hours.

Leon, who works sixty-hour weeks, but tries to limit his work to five days a week, was quite satisfied with the balance between his work and personal life. Having children has had a major impact on his hours: "I always make an effort to go home for supper. If I have to go back, I go back in the evening after I put them to bed, or else I work at home. If I didn't have kids I probably wouldn't necessarily go home." Although he thinks that his generation is more concerned about family time and is prepared to have a little less income, he still expects to be working the same number of hours in five years. Being one of the few men who had a full-time wife at home, I asked him what effect this had on the scheme of things. He said it has made a "tremendous difference." After their second child, they decided that his wife would quit her equally hectic job and stay home with the children:

> She was doing both, and it was totally unfair. That kept on until we had our second child. She may go back sometime but she's really, really enjoying staying home. I much, much prefer that she be home. The extra money would mean nothing to me because it's better for our kids. It's just way, way, way less stressful because I'd have to practise law in a different way. She does the lion's share of the work now. If she were working full time, we'd have to find a way to split it more equitably or hire somebody to do it.

I then asked him whether he would end up being a traditional male partner who spends all of his time at the office. His response illustrates some of the forces at work:

> Actually, I hope not because I work to live, not live to work. I really, really enjoy my kids and the best part of my day is coming home – the best

part of my day is not here. I enjoy what I do. People often ask "Do you like your job?" and I say "I like my job, but I get too much of it." I commit to [coaching my children's sporting events] because in this job you're never finished. What you have to do is you just have to leave. If you commit yourself to doing those things, you end up spending time with your kids, and you find out that's worth it. Plus clients are prepared to accept that. You say, "I've got to go, I've got to coach my kid's soccer team." They say, "Okay, fine, you're out of here." Whereas if you say, "I'd like to go home now and spend time with my kids," they look at you and say, "Just a minute, we have to finish that stuff." It's a way of disciplining yourself in a way because you can become sucked in to your clients' situations, and so I purposely made an effort. Plus I'm involved in [other organizations] in the community.

Jack also has a full-time wife who left a hectic paying job to care for their children. They decided that he would work the equivalent of a job-and-a-half or two jobs so that their children would have one constant caregiver:

I'm either at work or at home. So we don't have a two-income family. But I think our kids get more attention. I'd like to spend more time at home, but it makes more sense that there be one constant caregiver. Though I know I'm nurturing with my children, my wife is the better caregiver – that's partly aptitude and partly her mother was a stay-at-home mom. We have made a decision and are comfortable with it, and this is her firm, too. She's not involved in the decision making, but she is involved in the success and everything that happens here. I suppose we're throwbacks to the fifties. But I'm not at all judgmental of other people's ways of dealing with their families. I think I'm fortunate in that I have the kind of a job in which I can work longer hours and eventually make the equivalent of two incomes so we can have someone to be with the kids all the time. My wife can't earn that kind of money in [her profession].

He also wanted to make more money so that they could afford to hire someone to do some of the other household tasks, so his wife could spend more time with their children.

Bob, who works forty-hour weeks and expects to be working the same hours in five years, also has a wife who was "very happy staying at home with the children because that's a decision we both made. That's how we want to do things." However, he realizes that "from time to time, mentally it is not enough. She was with a child all day long and wasn't getting enough outside stimulation," so his spouse now works approximately ten hours a week outside the home. Ray is satisfied with his fifty-hour week and expects to be working the same hours in five years. His wife works two days a week in the paid labour force and they, according to Ray, are both satisfied with their division of labour. Ray would like to spend more time with his children, but was resigned to the fact that his profession does not permit it. Conrad had been quite busy in the time before I talked to him and was working fifty to seventy hours a week, compared with his usual forty-hour week. He liked his firm: "They don't expect you to get divorced and sell your child. They would rather have you go home and meet your family." His wife works in the paid labour force two days a week, and they are satisfied with their division of labour.

Vernon, who described himself as "an older dad," works fifty hours a week and would like to be working a four-day, thirty-five-hour week in five years:

> I have a real struggle to balance all the demands on me among wife, child, family, practice, business, administrative demands, and financial demands. I find it hard to keep it all in balance. I don't feel I give enough to anything. And my highest priority is my family. There's another reason for hesitating to estimate the number of hours I work per week because my wife has pointed out to me that it never leaves me. It's three in the morning and I'm lying there worrying about some file. I'm not sitting in the office, but it's still with me.

Vernon was the only one, of the nine men who wanted to spend more time with his family, who came close to indicating that he might be prepared to move toward what Eichler refers to as an individual responsibility model of the family (in which mothers and fathers are equally responsible for child care and household tasks).[42] Vernon's wife works sixteen hours a week in the paid workforce and would like him to do more of the work around the house. It appears as though, at least in this cohort of lawyers, the profession is not moving toward an equal sharing of paid and unpaid labour. A study of Stanford law graduates found that men who expected to undertake child care planned to devote only 60% as much time as the women to such work.[43] According to Thornton, "challenging the norm that releases men from responsibility for regular child care is an issue in respect of which little progress has been made during the life of second-wave feminism."[44]

Of the thirteen men who had children requiring child care, and who were satisfied with the division of labour, five had spouses who worked full time in the paid labour force, five had spouses who worked part time, and three had spouses at home (including one who was on maternity leave). Of the five men who had both children and spouses who worked full time in the paid workforce, four were of the opinion that their spouse was less satisfied with the division of labour than they were. However, the five men were averaging fifty-six hours of paid work per week, and their spouses (four in female-dominated occupations) averaged thirty-nine hours of paid work per week.

Of the five men who had both children and spouses working part time, four were of the opinion that their spouse was less satisfied with the division of labour than they were. Of the three men with children and spouses at home, only one stated that his spouse was less satisfied with the division on child care than he was.

Although some men still benefit from a full-time spouse, few men with children have the full-time support of a spouse who works full time at home. Nevertheless, men with spouses in the paid workforce still benefit from the fact that women do more than their share of child care and work at home. In addition, the accommodation that women lawyers with children are making is to reduce their work in the paid workforce so that they can spend more time with their children. The accommodation the men in my study appear to be making is to increase their workload in the paid workforce so that their spouses can either reduce or eliminate their time in the paid workforce. A feminist in the Ukraine told Joan Williams that "men did not do 'women's work' and she thought they never would." As a result, the solution to the child-care dilemma was not what the American feminists focus on (trying to get men to do their share), but her "best hope" was "extensive systems of socialized support for childcare, including not only maternity leaves, but also state-run day care centers, child-rearing leaves of up to three years, even (in Germany) a paid day off each month for housework."[45] I will return to this discussion in Chapter 7.

Balancing Household Chores

Studies show that women who work full time in the paid workforce still do between 60% and 76% of the household work.[46] Some studies show that this is the case even in households in which men are unemployed.[47] The 1996 Census found that 51% of wives with full-time paid jobs, compared with only 23% of husbands with full-time paid jobs, spent fifteen hours or more on unpaid work housework or home maintenance. Only 36% of husbands without paid work, compared with 70% of wives without paid work, spent this amount of time on such work.[48] In addition, women do the more stressful types of tasks in which there is low-schedule control, and such tasks are more associated with psychological stress. Buying groceries, preparing meals, and cleaning allow for less control over one's schedule than mowing the grass or making repairs around the house.[49] Some studies have suggested that any move to more equal distribution in household tasks is not because men are doing more but because women are doing less, and the extra work is simply not getting done.[50]

As previously noted, 74% of the women and 76% of the men in my study were living in a married or similar relationship.[51] Of the respondents who had spouses or partners, 32% of the women (but none of the men) said that their spouses were more satisfied than they were with the division of household chores. One-quarter of the women and 45% of the men recognized that their partners were less satisfied than they were with the division of household chores. Some studies have suggested that this dissatisfaction at home "frequently undermines the viability of marital relationships."[52] Inequality in the division of household labour causes women more psychological distress than the amount of work they actually do.[53] However, taking advantage of one's spouse may also cause an increase in psychological distress in men.[54] Because men are working sufficiently below levels that would cause distress, one study suggests that increasing their contribution to household work, to decrease the distress for women, should not result in greater distress to the men.[55]

My interviews found that while some women had children before entering law school or the practice of law, many women who stay in the practice of law put off having children, or do not have children at all. Many of the men who have children also feel the strain of spending more time at work than they would like. This may be the time for the legal profession to rethink the "hidden," or gendered assumptions about the practice of law.[56] These assumptions are revealed by asking a simple question of men that is often asked of women: Is it "practicable for a man to successfully fulfil the duties of husband, father, and lawyer at the same time?"[57] The fact that we do not ask such a question, and that the question seems rather strange, illustrates that the gendered division of labour is still strongly ingrained in our culture. I will return to these issues in Chapter 7.

Balancing Hours Worked

In the surveys of lawyers in British Columbia in 1990, and in Alberta in 1991, both women and men who worked full time worked an average of fifty hours a week. In the British Columbia survey, 23% of the women and 25% of the men worked sixty hours or more a week. In Alberta, 27% of the women and 23% of the men worked sixty hours or more. Thus, approximately 25% of lawyers work sixty hours or more per week. In the interviews for this study, 62% of the men worked fifty hours or more a week (nine of these men worked sixty hours or more a week), and 44% of the women worked fifty hours or more a week (ten of these women worked sixty hours or more a week). Overall, 19% of the lawyers interviewed worked sixty hours or more a week. Although Kay does not provide the equivalent Ontario figures, she does report that women who work in private practice work an average of 53.9 hours a week, and men an average of 54.4 hours a week.[58]

Many lawyers work long hours. In my interviews of young lawyers, the women worked a median of forty-seven hours per week, and the men a median of fifty hours per week. Only 26% of the women and 14% of the men worked forty or fewer hours a week – the hours one might expect of a full-time worker. This expanded workweek, in an economic climate of unemployment, has major implications for women and work. Women, who carry an excessive burden of child care and household chores, cannot compete in a work world that demands excessively long hours. In addition, the excessive hours worked by some lawyers (equivalent to two jobs in some cases) has implications for their health and personal lives (discussed in Chapter 7).

Despite the excessive hours the lawyers worked in this study, only 18% of the women and 22% of the men expressed dissatisfaction with the hours they worked. The nine dissatisfied women worked between forty-five and seventy hours a week (an average of 58.3), and the dissatisfied men worked between fifty-three and ninety-five hours a week (an average of 60.8 hours). However, 28% of the women and 32% of the men expressed dissatisfaction with the balance they had between law and their personal lives. Complaints about the lack of balance between work and personal lives are somewhat more widespread among the men than the women.

It appears as if little has changed for women in the area of child care and housework since the first woman was called to the bar in British Columbia in 1912. In examining the history of women lawyers in British Columbia, in an earlier article, I concluded that: "The typical male lawyer, early in the century, had a full-time wife to cater to him, support his career, and care for his children, home, and social life. To practise law like a man, in early times, meant that women would forego children, and perhaps relationships. Even if these women remained childless and single, they still returned home to their second shift of work."[59]

The structure of the legal profession and our society remains much the same. Although, as Eichler noted, men may realize they should do more of their share of the household work and child care, many do not. The hours they work prevent them from full or equal participation in the private sphere. Women lawyers, who want to practise law and have a relationship and children, still find themselves returning home from their shift at the office, only to face additional shifts of household tasks and management, children, and a husband. It is little wonder that women lawyers end up scaling back their work to accommodate these extra demands, and men lawyers are delighted when their spouses agree to reduce or eliminate their work in the paid workforce so that they, the women, can work even longer hours in the unpaid workforce. "The extra pressure on women with four shifts (and the additional pressure on men who no longer have a full-time housekeeper, child care worker, social planner, and sexual partner) is taking its toll on both women and men."[60]

7
Breaking the Mould

Although the legal barriers that historically prevented women from entering the legal profession have been removed, informal and structural barriers that impede women's full participation within the legal profession still exist today. This study was designed to examine how young lawyers, both women and men, were doing in the legal profession: Were they fitting in or breaking the old mould? There are other possibilities. Many women and men, frustrated with the practice of law, leave it, whereas others grin and bear it. Neither the legal profession nor the paid workforce more generally is particularly suited for or receptive to people who have additional responsibilities such as child care, elder care, emotional care, and home management. Much of the discrimination against women in the legal profession (and the paid workforce more generally) stems from these additional expectations and burdens we place on women in our society; however, it still appears that sexual harassment and discrimination are used to exclude the full participation of women lawyers who have managed to reduce these additional burdens. Although the Canadian Bar Association and law societies across Canada have put much effort into finding solutions to these issues, it may be that, as with the early pioneer women lawyers, the solutions must also come from outside the profession.

Unlike what some popular books would have us believe, women and men are not entirely from different planets. In some respects the women and men lawyers in this study were very similar. For the most part, they went to law school for the same reasons. One-third of these respondents had a keen interest in the law, while another third went to law school by default (they had nothing better to do). However, once they were in the profession, the women were less likely to have practised without interruption than the men, and they were likely to have been in their current positions for a shorter period of time than the men. Although the women and men gave similar reasons as to why they left their various positions, the women were more likely than the men to mention stress (and a need to balance their work and family life), and the existence of discrimination, as reasons for leaving their jobs. The men were more likely than the women to mention a falling-out (or that people were difficult to work with), that they were moving to a better position, or that they wanted more control over their work.

The male and female respondents liked and disliked similar things about the practice of law. More than one-third of them liked the fact that law was challenging and satisfying, and approximately one-quarter liked the fact that law provided them a forum in which to interact with people, and it also provided knowledge and intellectual stimulation. The stress and responsibility of the practice of law topped the list of what respondents disliked about the practice of law (approximately 40%). One-quarter of the respondents disliked the hours demanded by the practice of law, as well as the pressure to bill clients and market their services. Although more men than women (62%, compared with 50%) were satisfied with the practice of law overall, an almost equal number (26% of the men and 24% of the women) were dissatisfied with it.[1] Only 60% of the women and 70% of the men would become lawyers if they could "do it again."

Women called to the bar at the same time as these respondents were more likely than the men to have left the practice of law, by the time the sample was drawn (31.4% of the women and 25.6% of the men).[2] The remaining women interviewed were more likely than the men to predict that they would not be practising in five years. Sixteen percent of the women interviewed, compared with only 8% of the men, made this prediction. Studies have shown that the most common reasons women leave the legal profession are child-care commitments, low pay, and discrimination.

All is not lost for women and men who leave[3] the practice of law. A law degree and a call to the bar are stepping stones to many other careers for non-practising lawyers. Some of the law societies have hosted alternative career forums to help members' transition.[4] Many lawyers leave the profession for more interesting and financial rewarding careers. However, some lawyers leave because of their experience with the practice of law – stress, long hours, and lack of accommodation for their personal lives. Others leave because of drug- and alcohol-related problems.[5] Some of these stress-related problems may be because the legal profession has failed to adapt to the changing structure of the workforce.

Although more women (62%) than the men (54%) described themselves as conciliatory, or as lawyers who would start at the conciliatory end of the continuum, the notion that women are not sufficiently adversarial to work as lawyers is a myth. Only 12% of the women and 14% of the men rated themselves as adversarial, or as someone who started at the adversarial end of the continuum. The role of "reluctant adversary" is not confined to women lawyers; few lawyers take the adversarial approach to their practice, and those that do are often seen as not acting in the best interests of their clients. Despite their (perhaps wise) reluctance to play an adversarial role, most of the respondents endorsed the adversarial system, provided it was not abused or used in inappropriate situations. When other means of resolving disputes were exhausted, the adversarial system is seen as an effective means to bringing a dispute to a conclusion.

Some of the respondents pointed to the top students in their class who were women, and the number of women summer students, articling students, and young associates as signs that women were beginning to fit into the legal profession. However, these indicators are deceptive of any progress at higher levels. For the women in this study, partnerships in large firms were non-existent. The six women partners worked with their spouses or in other small firms. Only one woman associate was in the position to move to partnership in a large firm, and she was unsure of whether this might happen. A number of women, on the verge of partnership, had left their firms with glowing references when they were told they were not going to make it. In contrast, ten men were partners (five worked in firms of twenty or more lawyers) and another fourteen aspired to partnership. Seven of the fourteen men aspiring to be partners worked in firms of twenty lawyers or more, and only one of these had some question about whether he would become a partner (his future depended on agency work from the government, and a change in government would change his prospects). Clearly, there is little indication that women are achieving partnership status in firms even when they set out to do so.

This and other studies have shown that women lawyers earn less than their male colleagues, and they are less likely to be promoted or become partners in large law firms. Various theoretical explanations, which try to account for legitimate reasons for these differences (for example, differential investment in human capital), still find that there is a substantial unexplained component, which is attributed to discrimination in the legal profession (see studies cited in Chapter 3). Lawyers' perceptions of gender bias coincide with the evidence that women still face discrimination from within the profession.

This study and others show that women are under-represented in private practice and over-represented in (and moving into) government positions. Although at one time the public sector was seen as somewhat of a haven for women lawyers,[6] there is some indication that the public sector is taking on private sector values and characteristics, which may limit women's participation in this segment of the workforce. The privatization of what were once public services and efforts to down-size (or "stream-line") the civil service, so that civil servants are working private sector hours (without extra pay), have made these jobs more difficult for women, who perform more than their share of child care and household tasks and management.[7] A recent government report found that, according to the male managers, gender barriers have been removed in the civil service; however, women see "a male-dominated closed shop, where 12-hour days are the norm and childcare concerns are a sign of weakness."[8] In addition, the adoption of private-sector, performance-based evaluations and performance-based pay (bonuses), in order to supposedly increase productivity, have recreated disadvantages to women in the public sphere.[9] The "cultural transformation" of the public service "may have counterproductive effects on gender equality."[10] Susan Bisom-Rapp suggests that the new discourse of performance-based reviews, a "discourse of gender and racial neutrality," masks, rather than eliminates, conditions of inequality, by assuming that the ideal worker is one who has no family or household responsibilities.[11] Or, as Terri Apter summarizes the plight of women in the paid workforce, "workers are wives, yet workers are still assumed to have wives."[12]

Fiona Kay's data from Ontario support the "ghettoization perspective rather than the genuine integration of women" into the legal profession. For example, women are under-represented in partnership positions, and they move 37% more slowly than men toward partnership.[13] According to Margaret Thornton, the bureaucratization of the legal profession is gendered, in the sense that "hierarchical ordering leads to superordinate positions becoming masculinised, with subordinate positions becoming feminised, in accordance with the conventional social script."[14] Women remain "fringe dwellers" of the legal establishment.[15]

Thirty-six percent of the women in this study had been sexually harassed since entering the legal profession – 34% of the women had been sexually harassed by other lawyers, 12% by judges, and 10% by clients. Sexual harassment creates a major barrier to the equal participation of women in the legal profession and elsewhere. In addition, it acts as a form of social control over women and is incompatible with equality in the legal profession. Respondents in this study were more optimistic about the effectiveness of anti-sexual harassment rules than they were about anti-discrimination rules (66% of the women and 70% of the men thought that the anti-sexual harassment rule would be effective, whereas only 23% of the women and 38% of the men thought the anti-discrimination rules would be effective). Sexual harassment was more readily identified and therefore easier to deal with; however, as some respondents also realized, reporting sexual harassment could be a career-ending move.

Numerous studies in Canada and around the world have identified gender bias or discrimination as a major barrier to women's participation in the legal establishment. There is still a widespread perception among the respondents in this study that bias or discrimination in the legal profession restricts women's career advancement (88% of the women and 66% of the men in this study). Sixty percent of the women interviewed said they had been discriminated against. Studies in the United States show that "between two-thirds and three-fourths of the women surveyed indicate that they have experienced some form of discrimination or bias."[16]

Discrimination in the legal profession can come from a variety of sources. Some men with power simply do not like sharing power with women. They view women's role in the workplace as subordinate to that of men. These are men who will discriminate against women simply because they are women. Although there was no measure of this in this study, the proportion of men who fell into this category seems to be small. Most of them are identified as belonging to the "old boys' club," and are thought to be becoming relics of the past. However, according to some respondents, "baby dinosaurs" are growing up to replace them. Some women in this study sacrificed their personal lives and sold their souls to their law firms in order to become partners. They were being let go with glowing recommendations, rather than being invited into partnerships. The men who were poised for partnership, on the other hand, saw little standing in their way. It is difficult to conclude that the legal profession has rid itself of discrimination.

The respondents were not optimistic about the use of rules to curb discrimination. Only 23% of the women and 38% of the men thought the anti-discrimination rules introduced by the Law Society would be effective. They were pessimistic about the rule for a variety of reasons: rules don't change attitudes or behaviour, lawyers will find a way around the rules ("that's what they do for a living"), and the use of the rules may be career-ending and targets of discrimination may be reluctant to use them.[17]

Some of the respondents thought that the solution to discrimination was education. The Report Madame Justice Bertha Wilson chaired for the Canadian Bar Association in 1993 made similar recommendations; however, it also identified a number of areas of resistence.[18] It concluded that "education about the nature of gender inequality in the legal profession is crucial."[19] Following the Report's recommendations, Mary Jane Mossman held forty educational seminars in three Toronto firms between 1994 and 1997 under the Professional Development Program at Osgoode Hall Law School.[20] Following these seminars, she concluded that solutions to gender inequality can be found more readily if they do not challenge the prevailing legal culture ("market-driven and tending to corporatism and commodification"). In effect, if the solutions lie in challenging such a culture, education may have little effect. Mossman was not optimistic that Wilson's challenge to the legal profession about its responsibility to uphold justice could achieve equality without some greater understanding and change to overcome the law firms' culture.

Although discrimination and sexual harassment are major barriers to equality in the legal profession, as suggested in Chapter 6, the major challenge to equality in the workplace may be inequality at home. There are people who think that women are formally equal in the paid workforce, but that they should also be the primary caregivers to "their" children and managers of the household (or managers of the servants), so that men may be more efficient in the workforce.[21] Historically, Virginia G. Drachman found that women lawyers had taken one of three approaches to career, marriage, and children during two periods, the 1880s and in 1920, in the United States.[22] Some took the separatist approach – they would remain single, usually by choice (contrary to popular perception), and devote time to the practice of law. Others took the Victorian approach – they would abandon the practice of law upon marriage. Yet others integrated marriage and work and hired servants to take care of the domestic work. In an earlier work, I referred to this as "partial integration." Full integration involves women integrating a personal relationship and children with a career.[23]

In this study, the women interviewed were no more likely than the men to have put off a personal relationship because of their career; however, only 26% of the women, compared with 50% of the men, had children. Women lawyers appear to be moving toward partial, but not full, integration. For example, only 10% of the women interviewed (compared with 48% of the men) had had children after being called to the bar, or were expecting a birth at the time of the interviews.

Full integration can be achieved in a number of ways. Women could work sixty hours per week at the office, and then become super-mom, super-household manager, and super-spouse for the other seventy-three hours in the week (minus five hours a day for sleeping). Some may be assisted by one, two, or three nannies, thereby allowing them to work longer hours at the office, or to spend more time developing client relations. There is, however, some evidence that the younger generation of women lawyers may not be interested in playing these numerous roles.[24] This appeared to be the case for many of the women lawyers who were interviewed.[25]

Other women may "choose" to sacrifice their careers, in order to fulfil these extra roles (the Victorian approach). It may make more economic sense for women, given their income relative to that of men, to stay at home. Others will "choose" to reduce their time in the paid workforce, by moving to part time. These factors were definitely present in the women who were struggling to make decisions about work and children, and it is definitely a reason some women and men leave the profession. Many women and men simply want to spend time with their children or spouse. In this study, 28% of the women and 32% of the men expressed dissatisfaction with the balance they had between the practice of law and their personal lives.

Why is it that women "sacrifice" their careers, in order to raise children and to ensure that their spouses' careers run more smoothly? Ruth Bloch traced the historical relationship between the concepts "virtue" and "self-interest" in political ideology and concluded that, "between 1780 and 1830, women became associated with virtue and men with self-interest in a dichotomy that crystallized two complementary formulations that linked political and gender ideology; the ideology of conventional femininity (what historians term the ideology of domesticity) and the strain of mainstream liberalism that enshrines the importance of self-interest."[26]

Modern day "femininity" retains many of the characteristics of domesticity. Women are expected to nurture in both the public and private domain. Women's selflessness and humane values are supposed to complement men's self-interest and ambition.[27] Furthermore, "domesticity's polarized dichotomy between affiliation and personal achievement explains why adults who choose to define their lives around relationships naturally do so at the cost of status and power and adults who choose to pursue power and status naturally do so at the expense of those in affiliation with them."[28]

Joan Williams examines the power dynamics that underlie the choices women make about career and children, and the choice rhetoric that is used, pitting women against women:

> The rhetoric of choice masks a gender system that defines child-rearing and the accepted avenues of adult advancement as inconsistent and then allocates the resulting costs of child-rearing to mothers. At the core of the system is a notion of an ideal worker without responsibility for children: a worker absent from home a minimum of nine hours a day, five or six days a week, often with overtime at short notice and at the employer's discretion. Underlying the expectations for the "ideal" worker is the rarely challenged assumption that the accepted avenues of adult power and responsibility are inevitably incompatible with caregiving. Of course they are not: their incompatibility results from a societal choice to marginalized caregivers.

The marginalized caregivers are predominately women, and these women then delegate "their" responsibility to other marginalized women. Many women, with the knowledge that children will hinder their career development, forego children in order to meet the demands of the "ideal" worker. Of the childless lawyers who were interviewed for this study, 34% of the women interviewed, but only 4% of the men, said that being a lawyer was a factor in their not having children. In contrast, careerist men are encouraged to have children, and it often enhances their careers.[29]

It is easy to see how "the rhetoric of choice diverts attention from the constraints within which an individual's choice occurs onto the act of choice itself."[30]

Williams is of the view that when women "speak of their 'choice' to scale back work commitments in deference to their children's needs, they help recreate and legitimize the system of marginalizing caregivers, by enshrining as ideal workers adults without primary responsibility for children. The system blocks mothers from the traditional avenues of power and responsibility and is the key element of women's disempowerment both inside and outside the household."[31] According to Williams, equality requires that the demands of gender equality be aligned with those of domesticity.[32]

The choice rhetoric puts affluent women in a privileged position, and it is then generalized to all women, even those who must work.[33] Williams is not of the opinion that women who say they "choose" to work at home are victims of false consciousness. Such a dichotomy (free choice versus false consciousness), according to Williams, does not reflect reality. Women are not "passive victims of ideology," but rather make choices "within a social context replete with constraints, some of which are disabling, some of which are enabling, and most of which are both, either at different times or simultaneously."[34]

In her more recent work, *Unbending Gender,* Williams tries to inspire social change through reconstructive feminism, by building on the traditions of domesticity – a strategy of "domesticity in drag."[35] For example, she tries to "transform domesticity's norm of mothercare into a norm of parental care with the potential to end the system of providing for children's care by marginalizing their caregivers." Katharine Baker, in a review of Williams's book, feels that Williams is overly optimistic in assuming that men who are freed from paid work will take up their share of domestic work.[36] There appears to be little change in the notion that housework is women's work[37] and breadwinning is men's work,[38] even in the younger generation.

While no one is suggesting that women and men should be denied the opportunity to choose to stay home if their circumstances permit, studies of women's choices, especially when they come to career and family, show some interesting results. Sociologist Arlie Russell Hochschild, in *The Second Shift*[39] and *The Time Bind,*[40] captures the decisions that women make. In her first book, Hochschild, drawing on interviews with and observations of working couples, found that most women were doing more than their "fair share" of work at home and suffered consequences beyond lack of leisure time. They lacked sleep, were more likely to get sick, and were often emotionally drained. Williams summarized some of the research in this area: "Employed wives sleep less, enjoy less leisure, and work much longer hours than their husbands. One study found that wives do seventy-nine percent of the housework. 'Under optimal conditions,' concluded another, employed wives do five times the domestic work their spouses do. A third concluded that husbands of employed wives barely contribute enough domestic labor to make up for the additional work their presence in the household creates. The end result is that employed wives work an average of 144% of the total time of a traditional homemaker."[41]

Not surprisingly, the result is extreme stress. Faced with an excessive amount of work at home, and sex discrimination, low wages, and sexual harassment at work, some women "choose" to work at home.[42]

Hochschild found that in the few households in which men did their share of the second shift, marriages were far less strained than in households in which men were not doing their share. However, she also noted that few women and men actually had the time for this second shift of housework.

For her second book, Hochschild spent time following couples at home and at work, in order to discover how Amerco Inc., one of the most "family-friendly" companies in the United States, was doing with its family policies. Starting in 1985, Amerco began to develop two different types of family-friendly policies. The first type allowed for employees to spend more uninterrupted time at work. This included "high-quality childcare, childcare for sick children, emergency backup childcare, before- and after-school programs, and referral services for elder care, all of which enabled employees to focus better on their work for eight or more hours a day."[43] The second type allowed for workers to spend more time at home. They included shorter and more flexible workdays, part-time work, job-sharing, working at home, paid parental leaves, and family care leaves.

When Hochschild arrived in 1990 to study the company, she soon discovered three things: "First, Amerco's workers declared on survey after survey that they were strained to the limit. Second, the company offered them policies that allowed them to cut back. Third, almost no one cut back."[44] In fact, she found that workers with children worked longer hours than those without children and, by the time she left in 1993, people were working longer hours than when she had arrived.

Hochschild entertained and dismissed most of the common explanations for this phenomenon. She discovered that part-time work was used more by workers who earned less, not more. Well-paid mothers did not spend more time on maternity leave than lower-paid mothers. When she asked workers if they worked long hours because they were afraid of losing their jobs, almost all of them said, "No." Most of the workers were aware of the policies, women more so than men. The workers also believed that the company and senior and middle management were sincere in offering its reduced-work policies. The company also had good reasons for offering the policies: flexible work schedules made them more competitive when they were hiring new workers, and it avoided the "costs of not instituting such policies – in increased absenteeism and tardiness, and lowered productivity."[45]

Hochschild went into this study assuming that home was a "haven from work," and discovered that, for some women, work was a haven from home. One thirty-eight-year-old worker took as much overtime as she could, because when she returned home, she found that her husband had done little in his second shift other than "nap and watch television instead of engaging the children." She felt "she could only get relief from the 'work' of being at home by going to the 'home' of work," where life was less stressful and more interesting.[46] This phenomenon was also found by Reed Larson's study of women and men who were asked to wear pagers. Every time they were paged, they were asked to write down how they felt in terms of happiness, irritability, or anger. They found that the women and men experienced a similar range of emotions, but that "fathers reported more 'positive emotional states' at home; mothers, more positive emotional states at work."[47] Other studies have shown that (for depression and illness) women suffer more acutely from stress at home than stress at work. Work offers women "challenge, control, structure, positive feedback, self esteem ... and social ties."[48] Hochschild found that work had become a haven from home, "a predominant pattern in about one-fifth of the Amerco families, and an important theme in more than half of them."[49] When people change their relationships more often than they change their jobs, "work may become their rock."[50]

While it was not possible to follow my 100 interviewees in their day-to-day routine, some indicated that their lives were strained in the "time bind." More than one-quarter of the women and one-third of the men expressed dissatisfaction with the balance between their work and their personal lives. One-quarter of the women and 45% of the men recognized that their partners were less satisfied than they were with the division of household chores. Sixty-two percent of the men and 44% of the women worked fifty or more hours per week. It is difficult to imagine that this does not create some stress, especially for those without full-time spouses at home.

Hochschild found that the reversal of home and work had other consequences. Workers were using the workplace to socialize and thereby creating "hidden pockets of inefficiency" at work. Their home life was becoming more efficient, as they strove for "quality time" at home – more things were being crammed into shorter periods of home life. Children were not always cooperative. Nine to ten hours a day in daycare was probably too long for them. Some of them rebelled. More and more family work and activities were being "outsourced." Workers found that they were now spending more time on a newly created third shift: the "emotional work necessary to repair the damage caused by time pressures at home."[51] Women were finding that the "emotional dirty work of adjusting children to the Taylorized home and making up to them for its stresses and strains [was] the most painful part of a growing third shift at home."[52]

Women lawyers are not "doing it all." They are dropping out of the legal profession in greater proportion than men. While some have children before entering the profession, there seems to be little room in the profession for women with children. Lack of flexibility in the legal profession for women and men to deal with child care and household commitments – and lack of men's involvement in child care, home management, and chores – are major factors that still affect women's participation in the legal profession.

The fact that some law firms were talking about "quality of life" and "balance" in the lives of their members in the early 1990s[53] may be some indication that women are changing the nature of the workplace. However, the introduction of part-time work, so that some women can care for children, do household chores, manage the household (orchestrate the paid labourers), and work in the paid workforce, while full-time workers (that is, "those committed to law") can work eighty-hour weeks, does not bode well for women in the legal profession. Even if this were a solution, there is still resistance from employers and firms to allowing women to work part time or to job-share.

The male-dominated legal culture does not appear to be welcoming to women and has many disadvantages for men. As more and more women enter the legal profession and the paid workforce, the hours of work have become more and more demanding. Deborah Rhode reports that a few decades ago "lawyers could not reasonably expect to charge for more than 1200 to 1500 hours per year." Now, almost 50% of lawyers in private practice bill more than 2,000 hours per year.[54] One might ask whether there is a relationship between the two. Are hours of work increasing as women enter the workforce, in order to exclude them from full participation? This proposition is not as far-fetched as one might first imagine, if we look at the historical exclusion of women from the male-dominated paid workforce. Experts predict that if there is not considerable change in the distribution of work in the paid workforce and at home, "a considerable number of young women [will] retreat from the workplace because the cost is too great."[55]

Historically, high unemployment was dealt with in two ways. First, it was and still is reduced by removing certain classes of workers from the workforce. Initially, children were removed from the workforce. Children used to work twelve-hour days, six-and-a-half days a week. It was decided that it was in children's best interests to work shorter and shorter weeks, to the point at which now they can be employed only in limited circumstances. After removing children from the workforce, married women were removed, except of course when there was a shortage of so-called "manpower" during the war, when women were called upon to return to the workforce.[56] In those situations, some corporations were so anxious to have women work that they provided them with "nurseries for their children, shopping facilities, hot lunches, convenient banking arrangements, and sometimes even laundry services."[57] In Canada, the federal government introduced the Wartime Day Nurseries Agreement whereby the federal, Ontario, and Quebec governments shared the costs of daycare for mothers who were employed in war industries.[58] During the Second World War, a new town was constructed in Oregon state with "24 hour-a-day child care facilities (including infirmaries for sick children), cooked food services, and public transportation."[59]

After the war, women were told to go back home, so that the men returning from war would have jobs.[60] The federal, Ontario, and Quebec governments ended their Day Nurseries Agreement.[61] Employers made sure that women stayed at home by telling them that if they came back to work, it was full time or nothing. The resistance to part-time work today might have the same philosophy. Women who work part time know that their employers get more work from two part-time workers than from one full-time worker. Still, employers resist what would otherwise make good economic sense. People are also kept out of the workforce for longer periods of time by requiring higher and higher levels of education. Mandatory retirement now removes many people from the workforce based on their age.

There is some evidence that law firms' "adjustments" to bad economic times have a greater impact on women than on men.[62] In a study in the United States, Cynthia Epstein found that before 1990, women associates were becoming partners at a rate of 15.25%, compared with 21.5% for the men. Following the economic slowdown that began in 1990, women were becoming partners at a rate of 5%, compared with 17% for men.[63] Fiona Kay found that partnership prospects for women decreased, relative to men, between her 1990 survey and her re-survey of lawyers in 1996. In my interviews, none of the women were in a position to become partners in large firms.

Removing classes of people from the workforce (whether through legislation, expectations, demands that people work full time or not at all, or other forms of discrimination) is an inappropriate way of dealing with unemployment. Work, in reasonable amounts, has a positive impact on people's self-confidence and their lives. Studies have shown that people who work "report a lower frequency of physical and mental health problems and express positive psychological well-being more often" than those who do not work.[64] Unemployment can literally kill people.[65]

The second way that a crowded workforce can be adjusted is to reduce the workweek and share the work. Sharing the work has less to do with so-called accommodation of women in the workforce, than with creating a more equitable workforce. This idea is not new. In 1933, the United States Senate passed a bill imposing a thirty-hour workweek, in order to deal with unemployment. Senator Black, who introduced it, suggested that it would put 6.5 million jobless Americans back to work, and "benefit industry by increasing the purchasing power of millions of newly hired wage earners." Unfortunately, it was vetoed by President Roosevelt, who later regretted his action.[66] Calls for a shorter workweek (five days) and shorter workdays (six hours) to reduce unemployment also occurred in Canada, but were reject-ed by both provincial and federal governments in the early to mid-1930s.[67]

In the late 1960s and early 1970s, the experts were making predictions about what life would be like by 1985 – predictions that have not been borne out. In 1969, the Conference on Leisure in Canada stated that "the 40 hour week applies to more than 75% of the workers. By 1985, it will have been reduced to 35 hours."[68] In 1971, the experts commented that the workweek in Canada has been reduced "from 58.6 hours in 1901 to 41.1 hours in 1965 ... In the years ahead one hopes that the federal and provincial governments will provide encouragement and leadership for management experimentation with a 3 or 4 day work week and sponsor research on economic, social and psychological implications of growing leisure."[69]

The same types of predictions were being made in the United States. In the late 1950s, experts were predicting that by the early 1990s workers would have "a twenty-two hour week, a six month workyear, or a standard retirement age of thirty-eight."[70] It is interesting to see that the concept of a shorter workweek is still being predicted *for the future*. In 1993, John Robinson and his colleagues at the University of British Columbia predicted that by 2030, Canadians will be working a 27.5-hour week.[71] However, salaried workers in the United States, for example, have increased their workweek from forty-three to forty-seven hours between 1977 and 1997. The number of workers working fifty hours or more a week increased from 24% to 37%.[72]

There are, however, a number of reduced-workweek gurus in Canada and the United States today.[73] Bruce O'Hara, in his book *Working Harder Isn't Working*,[74] examines why we have reached a point in Canada at which 20% of people are stressed from being unemployed and 80% are stressed from being overworked.[75] The proportion of time-stressed Canadian women has increased from 16% in 1992 to 21% in 1998, and the proportion of time-stressed men has increased from 12% to 16% during those years.[76] Excess work results in increased cigarette consumption and drinking (among women), and excess weight (among men).[77] Statistics Canada has estimated that stress costs the workforce $12 billion a year. The effects of long work-ing hours – stress, depression, burnout, and conflicts between work and family – have been well-documented.[78] Along with the overworked, stressed-out employees comes an entire industry of stress-management and "wellness" programs.[79]

Although the respondents in this study were not specifically asked about the stresses they experienced at work or at home, when they were asked what they liked and disliked about the practice of law, 38% of the women and 40% of the men disliked the stress and responsibility that went with the practice of law. As suggested earlier, the hours most of these lawyers worked left little time for anything else.

In response to the predictions in the 1960s and 1970s, O'Hara writes, "Stress management, not leisure counselling, is our major collective preoc-cupation."[80] His solution would be a shorter workweek, and he specifies how that could be done without lowering take-home pay. The more people who are working reasonable hours, the less money that is needed for a number of social programs such as unemployment and stress-related ill-nesses. O'Hara, whose philosophy is, "so long as there is one who seeks work and cannot find it, the hours of work are too long,"[81] started an orga-nization called the Shorter Work Time Network of Canada, a grassroots lobby group for a shorter workweek. While the shorter workweek is sup-ported by labour unions in Canada, the right-wing "think tanks" dismiss it as "nonsense."[82]

In addition, research shows that "much of the loss of self-esteem and psychological stress associated with unemployment stems from the de-cline of income and status compared to one's peers."[83] A country in which people are either overworked or underworked will exaggerate the differ-ences people see and increase their dissatisfaction with their lot in life. This may occur for both the underworked and the overworked. The under-worked resent not having adequate employment, the overworked resent having "their" tax dollars support the underworked. Sharing work also helps resolve a problem that layoffs create: "Some persons have 'too much' leisure and others have 'too much' work."[84]

Some economists argue that working hours declined because of increas-ing pay; historians suggest that it is the decreasing working hours that result in increasing pay. The union workers who lobbied, negotiated, and participated in strikes in the early 1900s for shorter working hours (with its corresponding decrease in surplus labour) knew that a side-effect of a shorter workweek would be an increase, *not a decrease,* in pay. They had a jingle that said: "Whether you work by the piece or by the day / Decreasing the hours increases the pay."[85]

Addressing the situation in the United States in 1991, Juliet Schor,[86] wrote, "if present trends continue, by the end of the century Americans will be spending as much time at their jobs as they did back in the nineteen-twenties." Our only hope is that these predictions will be as wrong as the overly optimistic forecasts of forty years ago. In 1995, Jeremy Rifkin also called for a reduced workweek, in order to share the work.[87] When Rifkin spoke to the British Columbia government in 1997, then-Premier Glenn Clark said he was looking at the shorter workweek as a way to create jobs, but also indicated that it was a long way away.[88]

Studies on decreasing hours of the workweek are largely conducted using people who work for hourly wages in plants and manufacturing jobs – and not using lawyers or other professional occupations, in which a large number are self-employed, and almost none belong to unions. This does not mean that lawyers should ignore what is happening in other sectors of the economy. There are a number of reasons lawyers should heed the philosophy of a reduced workweek. First, as in many other occupational groups, lawyers work too hard. Surveys and interviews show that many lawyers exceed what might be considered a "normal" workweek of thirty-five to forty hours. In this study, only 26% of the women and 14% of the men worked forty or fewer hours a week, the hours one might expect of a full-time worker. Nineteen percent worked sixty hours or more a week. A study in the United States showed that 11% of lawyers worked sixty or more hours a week, and part-timers worked nine to five, five days a week.[89] In 1997, in Canada, employees who were paid for overtime worked an average of 8.5 hours extra a week, and those who were not paid for overtime averaged 9.2 hours of overtime.[90] Many lawyers work days that are almost double what was predicted thirty years ago for Canada, almost triple what was predicted by the American experts. They definitely work more than a three- or four-day workweek that was predicted to arrive in Canada by 1985. In fact, some lawyers who work thirty-five to forty hours or more a week consider their jobs to be part time.[91]

A second reason for considering shorter workweeks is the fact that over-work leads to excessive stress and resulting physical and psychological problems. Lawyers' magazines such as *Lawyers' Weekly*, the *National*, and *Canadian Lawyer*, as well as Law Society Bulletins report that stress-related illness and drug abuse (legal and illegal) are definitely problems in the legal profession. Chemical dependency in the general population is estimated at 10% and, in the legal profession, at 18%.[92] In one study, almost one-third of Canadian lawyers described themselves as problem drinkers.[93] A study in the United States suggested that "the percentage of lawyers with substance abuse problems is twice the national average."[94] The Canadian Bar Association has, through a group called the Legal Profession Assistance Committee (LPAC), put together a program to promote wellness in the legal profession. It is aimed at curtailing problems such as "depression, stress, alcohol and substance abuse, which are at high rates among lawyers."[95] Law societies have also set up elaborate programs to assist lawyers in dealing with these stress- and alcohol- and other drug-related problems. The 16 September 1994 edition of *Lawyers' Weekly* contained twenty phone numbers for support groups across Canada for lawyers, law students, concerned friends, and relatives. Problems that can be addressed are drug or alcohol abuse, depression, marital or family problems, financial difficulty, elder-care concerns, and work and career problems.[96] Stress-related problems and illnesses are a drain on our medical resources and lead to premature death. The only positive outcome is job-creation in the so-called health professions and funeral industry.

These problems are, of course, not limited to the legal profession. The *Vancouver Sun*[97] published an article describing a survey of corporate executives in the United States: 75% thought that burnout was more of a problem today than twenty years ago, 65% of those polled said that managers are working too many hours, 64% said that managers are physically exhausted by the end of the day, and 60% said that they bring too much work home. Another study in the United States showed that more and more workers were "wolfing down lunch at work," rather than taking one-hour lunch breaks: 25% to 30% of the workers took fifteen minutes for lunch, and only 10% took in excess of thirty minutes.[98]

The third problem lawyers need to deal with is the fact that lawyers who work too hard leave in their wake a larger number of unemployed lawyers and students who cannot find articles. They are "work-hogs." In the same edition of *Lawyers' Weekly* dealing with stress, depression, and substance abuse, was a headline article on "Unemployment and under-employment: The harsh reality facing new lawyers."[99] It is interesting that the editors did not make the connection between under-employment and stress on the one hand, and over-employment and stress on the other hand. Rather, the unemployment was blamed on too many graduates, a sluggish economy, and fierce competition, such that some articling students work for nothing. Solutions are framed in terms of decreasing law school enrolment, increasing the articling period, and so on. In 1997, the Canadian Bar Association launched a national study of the unemployment "crisis" facing lawyers. Again, the focus was on limiting law school admissions, or restricting entry into the profession.[100] Reducing the workweek, a positive, equitable way to share the work so that both over- and under-employment are reduced, was not suggested.

The fourth reason lawyers ought to heed the suggestion of a shorter week has to do with the changing nature of the workforce. Lawyers who work excessive hours, and who expect their subordinates to work excessive hours, have refused to recognize the changing workforce. The influx of women into the workforce (including the legal profession) means two things: first, those who have been historically out of the workforce to raise children are now in the workforce.[101] Second, the traditional workweek for lawyers was established considering only men who had full-time wives at home to raise their children, manage their household, and even fill in for receptionists or secretaries who were unable to handle the volume of work. This is becoming less of a reality for men.

As this and many other studies have shown, the burden of home management and chores falls disproportionately on women. Married men do "less housework than they create."[102] Those who have tried to explain the fact that married women do more housework than their husbands by resorting to resource-power theory (he or she with the least amount of power and money does the work) have been unsuccessful, in that "women who earn more than their husbands often do a disproportionate share of the housework."[103] Similarly, researchers have concluded that gender explains more than socialization and gender roles theory and time-availability theory would indicate.[104] Some studies suggest that women and men in marital relationships are "doing gender," that is, a marital household is a "gender factory," in which "housework 'produces' gender through the everyday enactment of dominance, submission, and other behaviours symbolically linked to gender."[105]

Some women wonder whether men spending less time at work would actually do more of the child care and home management and chores. If the effect of a three-day workweek is that women would have four days to do all the unpaid work, and men would have four days to play golf, build model aeroplanes, and play computer games – little will have changed. There is evidence that men with more leisure time and full-time working wives do not devote more time to children and household chores. For example, men who are unemployed or retired do not take up their share of household tasks. Studies of unemployed men show that "the grossly inequitable sexual division of housework that had existed prior to the men's loss of paid employment persisted, almost unaltered, after their loss of paid employment."[106] In fact, unemployed men contributed marginally less to housework than fully employed men. A similar pattern was found with men who retire "unencumbered by the demands of any paid labour, ... retired men nevertheless continue to reap the benefits of their wives' domestic labour whilst offering very little in return."[107] If there is any movement at all, it appears as though a reduced workweek in some European countries has allowed men to spend more time with their children, although they do not take up their share of household tasks.[108]

It was suggested to me by a man that women end up doing most of the housework because they don't negotiate an equal division of labour with their spouses. I must confess it had not occurred to me that this was the solution. However, there is evidence that this is the approach women ought to take, from studies on women in the second-plus relationships. In a study of couples in England, Sullivan found that women in their second-plus relationship with full-time employed men (married or co-habiting) do less housework (76%) than women in their first partnerships (80%). She also cites similar results from studies in the United States. Since the same relationship does not exist for men in their second-plus relationships, Sullivan suggests that it is the experiences of women that make the difference, and that women may be more involved in negotiating housework responsibilities in their subsequent relationships.[109]

The additional leisure time for men may also explain why they have the time to develop business contacts, taking clients out for breakfast, lunch, or dinner.[110] On a more cynical note, some respondents in Epstein's study suggested that women lawyers use their time more efficiently at work so that they can go home to their next shift, whereas men "waste time earlier in the day, or perhaps spend the lunch hours at the gym, and then start working in earnest in the afternoons and evenings" so that senior partners can see how industrious they are.[111] While there was no indication in this study that men were doing this, there were women who were closely scrutinized to see whether they were prepared to spend their "after-work hours" at their desk.

Bruce Feldthusen, in his article on "gender wars," describes men's "right not to know" when it comes to gender issues in legal education.[112] When it comes to children and household chores and management, men assert "their right not to do." According to Rhode, these attitudes among some men "reflect men's privileged status and the resiliency of unconscious bias."[113] Margaret Thornton asserts that the "enfranchisement and entry of women into public life has failed to alter the social norm that caring should be undertaken by women, whether in paid work or not." Such caring, according to Thornton, "includes looking after partners and grown-up children – that is, those who are perfectly capable of looking after themselves."[114]

We can no longer afford to argue for equality in the paid workforce without equality in the unpaid workforce. Carole Pateman's work (in 1988) on the sexual contract clearly illustrated the relationship between the paid and the unpaid workforces.[115] The reproduction of male power occurs through the relationship between these two workforces. Women who cater to the demands of children and spouses, and who manage their lives and a household, are not in the same position as men who are catered to in these arenas. The paid workforce is structured to suit the traditional male worker, who (for the most part) no longer exists. According to Williams, "women who now attribute their difficulties to work/family conflict inside their heads need to begin identifying the problem as discrimination that exists in the outside world."[116] This is not an attack on men; rather "the ways we organize (market and family) work disadvantage men as well as women."[117] As Boyd concludes, "Either the model of full-time work must change, or the public sphere must assume more responsibility for fundamental social responsibilities such as childcare or probably both."[118] Mona Harrington recently suggested, in light of the fact that "the old formulas cannot yield both care and equality," that rather than confine care to the private market (underpaid labour) and private family, it become a national political value.[119]

Both the workplace – its workaholic culture – and the home need restructuring before women can be on equal footing in the legal profession. Once men accept the fact that they too are capable of working in the unpaid workforce, they may more readily accept the fact that women are capable of working in the paid workforce. As suggested in Chapter 4, the elimination of discrimination in the legal profession will have to involve not only changes by law firms and law societies, but also changes to laws and societal norms. As with the early pioneer women in the legal profession, outside intervention may be necessary.

Since economics seems to be such a driving force for many of the lawyers I interviewed, perhaps an economic solution is required. At the present time, employers argue that one overworked employee is worth more or is more efficient than two employees who would share the work. If it costs more in benefits, payroll deductions, and taxes for firms to hire full-time overworked lawyers (who worked fifty to 100 hours a week) than to hire lawyers who worked thirty or forty hours a week, firms might adjust their hiring practices. If sharing the work is social engineering, so is hogging the work. Neither is dictated by economic forces. Society has a vested interest in reducing unemployment and sharing the work. Overwork and underwork both take their toll on our health care services. Perhaps medicare premiums and other payroll deductions for those who overwork should be increased to pay for the increased medical problems of the overworked and of the unemployed and underemployed that surface in their wake. These are the types of solutions that will have to be found outside the profession.

Is the new generation of women and men lawyers restructuring the legal profession? Although it is not possible to arrive at a definite answer to this question, there have been some changes and some "accommodations" for women in the workforce, and men are looking for changes themselves. However, it is unlikely that the major revolution of equality in the legal profession will take place until the "bloodless revolution" takes place at home. Restructuring the old mould of the legal establishment so that women can rush home to their second shift (household tasks), third shift (children), fourth shift (a husband), and perhaps a fifth shift (dealing with the emotional turmoil caused by too little time at home), will not assist women in their quest for equality in the legal profession. The old mould of the legal profession will only be altered when the old mould of the family is altered, so that not only do women "fit the mould" at work, but men "fit the mould" at home.

Appendix:
Income Analysis

The 100 lawyers in this study were measured on a number of variables, including their gross income in 1992 (before taxes, but after deducting business expenses). All but two of the respondents were willing to provide income information. Approximately two dozen variables which might conceptually have been connected with income were selected, including age, gender, and hours worked per week. Preliminary data analyses allowed the elimination of most of these candidate variables, leaving five factors of interest for consideration as predicting income: gender, hours worked per week, number of months in present position, size of firm, and seniority (number of years of call).

The five remaining variables were employed in an attempt to model the best prediction of income. An initial histogram revealed a positively skewed distribution. Accordingly, income was treated as having a log-normal distribution (a common assumption for income). The data were analyzed from a generalized linear modeling approach, using a log-normal distribution for the dependent variable and the identity link function. Initially, a saturated model was fitted with all five candidate variables and with all possible interactions among those variables, as predictors. A series of sequentially reduced models was fitted, dropping one term at a time from the model, according to the outcome of likelihood ratio tests. This process continued until the only terms left in the model were those with observed p-values less than $\alpha = .05$, or terms which included within interaction terms with such p-values. While the original, saturated model had contained thirty-two terms, the final model retained only three: gender, seniority (years since call to the bar), and the interaction between those two factors. Analyses of residuals disclosed no reason for concern about the final model, which was:

$$(Log)Income = 3.5304 + .4508\ Gender(women) + .1416\ Seniority$$
$$- .1306\ Gender*Seniority(women)$$

This equation is graphed in Figure 1, in "real" dollars (that is, exp ["log-dollars"]), and the predicted income of women and men for the five years is presented in the table below.

As Figure 1 clearly shows, women may start off making slightly more than men, but their incomes do not rise appreciably, whereas the incomes of men lawyers increase sharply as they become more experienced. In fact, the offsetting sex-by-seniority interaction is so great that by about three-and-a-half years of call, the positive sex effect for women is completely negated by the negative effect of the interaction. It may be that, in the legal profession at least, women not only run into a glass ceiling, but in fact they start out very close to it.

Figure 1

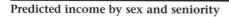

Predicted income by sex and seniority

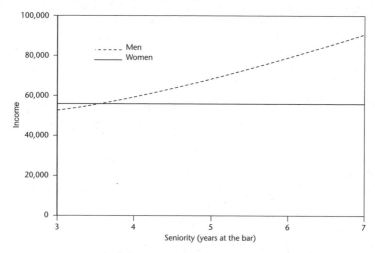

Years to the bar	Women	Men
3	$55,379	$52,206
4	$55,992	$60,148
5	$56,611	$69,297
6	$57,237	$79,838
7	$57,870	$91,983

This analysis is taken from V. Gordon Rose, "OUCH! Banging Heads on the Glass Ceiling: An Examination of Gender Inequality in the Income of BC Lawyers" (Unpublished paper written for a course at Simon Fraser University: Statistics 402, 28 November 1994).

Notes

Preface
1 Juliet Schor, *The Overworked American: The Unexpected Decline of Leisure* (New York: Basic Books, 1991) at 4.

Chapter 1: Introduction
1 "Visible" and "racial" minorities are no longer considered the most appropriate terms to describe people who have been "racialized" by a society. See Joanne St. Lewis and Benjamin Trevino (co-chairs), *The Challenge of Racial Equality: Putting Principles into Practice* (Ottawa: Canadian Bar Association, 1999) at vi for a further explanation.
2 See, for example, Magali Sarfatti Larson, *The Rise of Professionalism: A Sociological Analysis* (Berkeley: University of California Press, 1977); Anne Witz, *Professions and Patriarchy* (London: Routledge, 1992); Keith M. Macdonald, *The Sociology of the Professions* (London: Sage Publications, 1995).
3 Borrowing from Anne Witz, I elaborate on a model for studying the professions in Joan Brockman, "'Fortunate Enough to Obtain and Keep the Title of Profession': Self-Regulating Organizations and the Enforcement of Professional Monopolies" (1998) 41(4) *Canadian Public Administration* 587. The phrase is borrowed from Office des professions du Québec, *The Evolution of Professionalism in Québec* (1976) at 29.
4 Witz, *Professions and Patriarchy* at 39. According to Witz, students of the professions have ignored the professional projects of women.
5 See, for example, Daniel W. Rossides, *Professions and Disciplines: Functional and Conflict Perspectives* (New Jersey: Prentice-Hall, 1998).
6 Ngaire Naffine, *Law and the Sexes: Explorations in Feminist Jurisprudence* (Sydney: Allen and Unwin, 1990) at 100-1, uses this term to describe the acceptable lawyer – "white, educated, affluent and male," but also "masculine" as recognized by the middle classes.
7 This description is borrowed from Margaret Thornton, *Dissonance and Distrust: Women in the Legal Profession* (Melbourne: Oxford University Press, 1996) who uses it to describe women lawyers. I use it in the broader sense to describe those who do not meet the normative "man of law" description provided by Naffine.
8 Witz concludes that women were more successful with legalistic tactics (calling on the state to force professions to open their doors) than they were with credentialistic tactics in gaining access to the medical professions in England (*Professions and Patriarchy,* at 194-6).
9 Lawyers did not, and still do not, have a complete monopoly on legal services in British Columbia. They share some of them with notaries with whom they had major historical battles over who could offer which services: Joan Brockman, "A Cold-Blooded Effort to Bolster Up the Legal Profession: The Battle Between Lawyers and Notaries in British Columbia, 1871-1930" (1999) 32(64) *Social History* 209; Joan Brockman, "'Better to Enlist Their Support Than to Suffer Their Antagonism': The Game of Monopoly Between Lawyers

and Notaries in British Columbia, 1930-1981" (1997) 4(3) *International Journal of the Legal Profession* 197.

10 Constance B. Backhouse, "'To Open the Way for Others of my Sex;' Clara Brett Martin's Career as Canada's First Woman Lawyer" (1985) 1(1) *Canadian Journal of Women and the Law* 1 at 23-5. Margaret Thornton, *Dissonance and Distrust: Women in the Legal Profession* (Melbourne: Oxford University Press, 1996), at 47 describes how ridicule was used in Australia to deter women: "Furthermore, cumulative acts of animosity cemented bonds of homosociability between men." These bonds act to "maintain the sexual binarism and to undermine the role of women in the public sphere" (at 55).

11 Backhouse, "To Open the Way," at 18-19. The controversy that erupted in 1990, over an anti-Semitic letter that Clara Brett Martin wrote in 1915, is discussed by Constance Backhouse, "Clara Brett Martin: Canadian Heroine or Not?" (1992) 5(2) *Canadian Journal of Women and the Law* 263; Lita-Rose Betcherman, "Clara Brett Martin's Anti-Semitism" (1992) 5(2) *Canadian Journal of Women and the Law* 280; Brenda Cossman and Marlee Kline, "'And If Not Now, When?': Feminism and Anti-Semitism Beyond Clara Brett Martin" (1992) 5(2) *Canadian Journal of Women and the Law* 298; and Lynne Pearlman, "Through Jewish Lesbian Eyes: Rethinking Clara Brett Martin" (1992) 5(2) *Canadian Journal of Women and the Law* 317.

12 *In re Mabel P. French* (1905), 37 N.B.R. 359 N.B.S.C. at 361-2.

13 Ibid., at 366.

14 See Lois K. Yorke, "Mabel Penery French (1881-1955): A Life Re-Created" (1993) 42 *University of New Brunswick Law Journal* 3, for the details of French's struggle to enter the bar in New Brunswick and later, British Columbia.

15 J. Sedgwick Cowper, "Confidences of a Woman Lawyer" (1912) 39(2) *Canadian Magazine* 141 at 144. The infamous "Persons Case" (*Edwards* v. *Attorney General of Canada*, [1930] A.C. 124 (P.C.)), which recognized women as persons and allowed them to be appointed to the federal Senate, did not occur until 1930. Other women did try to use their status as a non-person to their advantage. In 1917, the Alberta Court of Appeal decided that a woman could be a vagrant under the anti-vagrancy section of the *Criminal Code* (*R.* v. *Cyr*, [1917] 3 W.W.R. 849). In upholding the trial judge's decision, it also found the magistrate who heard the case, Alice Jamieson, competent to hold her position; see David Bright, "The Other Woman: Lizzie Cyr and the Origins of the 'Persons Case'" (1998) 13(2) *Canadian Journal of Law and Society* 99.

16 Powley was called in Ontario in 1900, the second woman called to the bar in Canada: "Eva Powley, Barrister" (12 July 1900) *The Province* 2.

17 Letter from Oscar Bass to E.M. Pawley [sic], 17 March 1908; MMS 948, Series VIII, Vol. 40, file 14, British Columbia Archives (BCARS).

18 French to Bass, 16 May 1911; MSS 948, Series VIII, Vol. 40, File 18, BCARS.

19 Bass to French, 19 May 1911; MSS 948, Series VI, Vol. 36, p. 767, BCARS.

20 Yorke, "Mabel Penery French" at 36.

21 *Victoria Daily Times* (11 January 1912) at 11.

22 A more detailed discussion of the history of women in the legal profession in British Columbia is found in Joan Brockman, "Exclusionary Tactics: The History of Women and Minorities in the Legal Profession in British Columbia" in Hamar Foster and John P.S. McLaren, ed., *Essays in the History of Canadian Law, Volume VI, British Columbia and the Yukon* (Toronto: Osgoode Society, 1995) 508.

23 For a discussion of the history of women called to the bar in Manitoba see Mary Kinnear, "That There Woman Lawyer: Women Lawyers in Manitoba 1915-1970" (1992) 5(2) *Canadian Journal of Women and the Law* 411.

24 For a discussion of the first women law students and the first woman called to the bar in Alberta, see Sandra Petersson, "Ruby Clements and Early Women of the Alberta Bar" (1997) 9(2) *Canadian Journal of Women and the Law* 365.

25 Jennifer Stoddart, "The Woman Suffrage Bill in Quebec," in Marylee Stephenson, *Women in Canada* (Toronto: New Press, 1973) 90, describes the strong resistance to the Bill, including a comment from Maurice Duplessis, the Leader of the Opposition, that this would "open the door to political corruption" (at 95).

26 Margaret Gillett, *We Walked Very Warily: A History of Women at McGill* (Montreal: Eden Press Women's Publications, 1981) at 305.
27 Married women were not granted many contractual and civil rights in Quebec until 1964: Sandra Burt, "Legislators, Women and Public Policy" in Sandra Burt, Lorraine Code, and Lindsay Dorney, eds., *Changing Patterns: Women in Canada* (Toronto: McClelland and Stewart, 1988) 129 at 146.
28 *Langstaff* v. *The Bar of the Province of Quebec* (1915), 47 R.J.Q. 131 at 139 (emphasis in original).
29 Ibid., at 140.
30 Ibid., at 145.
31 Gillett, *We Walked Very Warily* at 309.
32 Lynn Smith, Marylee Stephenson, and Gina Quijano. "The Legal Profession and Women: Finding Articles in British Columbia" (1973) 8(1) *University of British Columbia Law Review* 137 at 141.
33 Alfred Watts, *History of the Legal Profession in British Columbia* (Vancouver: Law Society of British Columbia, 1984) at 49; F.W. Howay, *British Columbia: From the Earliest Times to the Present, Volume II* (Vancouver: S.J. Clarke Publishing, 1914) at 657.
34 For a discussion of the anti-Asian sentiment in British Columbia at this time, see Patricia E. Roy, "British Columbia's Fear of Asians: 1900-1950" in Patricia E. Roy, *A History of British Columbia: Selected Readings* (Toronto: Copp Clark Pitman, 1989); Patricia E. Roy, *A White Man's Province: British Columbia Politicians and Chinese and Japanese Immigrants, 1858-1914* (Vancouver: University of British Columbia Press, 1989); and W. Peter Ward, *White Canada Forever: Popular Attitudes and Public Policy Toward Orientals in British Columbia,* 2nd ed. (Montreal and Kingston: McGill-Queen's University Press, 1991).
35 After his father retired in 1936, Gordon Cumyow took over as court interpreter, and in 1951 he became the first Chinese notary in British Columbia: Joan Brockman, "'Better to Enlist Their Support Than to Suffer Their Antagonism:' The Game of Monopoly Between Lawyers and Notaries in British Columbia, 1930-1981" (1997) 4(3) *International Journal of the Legal Profession* 197 at 210.
36 Carol F. Lee, "The Road to Enfranchisement: Chinese and Japanese in British Columbia" (1976) *BC Studies* 44. For a discussion of their admission into the legal profession see Brockman, "Exclusionary Tactics"; Dawna Tong, *Gatekeeping in Canadian Law Schools: A History of Exclusion, The Rule of 'Merit,' and a Challenge to Contemporary Practices* (Master of Laws Thesis, University of British Columbia, 1996); Dawna Tong, "A History of Exclusion: The Treatment of Racial and Ethnic Minorities by the Law Society of British Columbia in Admissions to the Legal Profession" (1998) 56(2) *Advocate* 197-208; Gerry Ferguson, "Ethnic and Linguistic Diversity of BC Lawyers" (1997) 55(6) *Advocate* 873-89. For a perspective in other provinces, see Constance Backhouse, "Gretta Wong Grant: Canada's First Chinese-Canadian Female Lawyer" (1996) 15 *Windsor Yearbook of Access to Justice* 3; and Constance Backhouse, "Racial Segregation in Canadian Legal History: Viola Desmond's Challenge, Nova Scotia, 1946" (1994) 17(2) *Dalhousie Law Journal* 299.
37 Daniel M. Paul, *We Are Not Savages: A Micmac Perspective on the Collision of European and Aboriginal Civilizations* (Halifax: Nimbus Publishing, 1993) at 211; Carol Aylward, "Adding Colour: A Critique of 'An Essay on Institutional Responsibility: The Indigenous Blacks and Micmac Programme at Dalhousie Law School'" (1995) 8 *Canadian Journal of Women and the Law* 470 at 482-3.
38 Kim Pemberton, "First Indian Judge Back to Practising Law" (10 February 1995) *Vancouver Sun* B8.
39 Law Society of British Columbia, *Report on the Survey of Aboriginal Law Graduates in British Columbia* (Vancouver: Law Society of British Columbia, 1996) at 1.
40 For some of the problems faced by Aboriginal women in the legal profession and possible solutions, see Sharon McIvor and Teressa Nahanee, *Aboriginal Women in the Legal Profession* (Appendix 11 to the Report of the Canadian Bar Association Task Force on Gender Equality in the Legal Profession, Ottawa, 1993). Recommendations to change the legal establishment for Aboriginals can also be found in Joanne St. Lewis and Benjamin Trevino (co-chairs), *The Challenge of Racial Equality: Putting Principles into Practice* (Ottawa:

Canadian Bar Association, 1999), Chapter 6; and Joanne St. Lewis (co-chair) *Virtual Justice: Systemic Racism and the Canadian Legal Profession,* An Independent Report of the Working Group on Racial Equality in the Legal Profession (Ottawa: Canadian Bar Association, 1999), Chapter 3; Law Society of British Columbia, *Summary and Discussion of the Aboriginal Law Graduates Focus Groups* (Vancouver: Law Society of British Columbia, 1998) at 30-3; and Law Society of British Columbia, *Addressing Discriminatory Barriers Facing Aboriginal Law Students and Lawyers* (Vancouver: Law Society of British Columbia, 2000).

41 "Law Students – Articles" (1949) 7 *Advocate* 15. For the history of legal education in British Columbia see W. Wesley Pue, *Law School: The Story of Legal Education in British Columbia* (Vancouver: University of British Columbia Faculty of Law, 1995).

42 Law Society's Annual Meeting, 1950; MSS 948, Series VIII, Vol. 47, File 67, BCARS at 10.

43 Explained by R.H. Tupper, in a letter to A.A. Moffat, Secretary-Treasurer of the Conference of the Governing Bodies of the Legal Profession in Canada, 19 January 1945; MSS 948, Series VIII, Vol. 46, File 62, BCARS.

44 David A.A. Stager with Harry Arthurs, *Lawyers in Canada* (Toronto: University of Toronto Press, 1990) at 149.

45 Linda Silver Dranoff, "Women in Law in Toronto" (1972) 10(1) *Osgoode Hall Law Journal* 177 at 178-9.

46 Smith et al. "The Legal Profession and Women" at 157.

47 Jennifer K. Bankier, "Women and the Law School: Problems and Potential" (1974) 22(5) *Chitty's Law Journal* 171 at 171.

48 Ibid., at 173. For an overview of the early studies on gender bias in the legal profession, see Joan Brockman and Dorothy Chunn, "Gender Bias in Law and the Social Sciences" in Joan Brockman and Dorothy E. Chunn, eds., *Investigating Gender Bias: Law, Courts, and the Legal Profession* (Toronto: Thompson Educational Publishing, 1993) 3 at 5-12.

49 Stager and Arthurs, *Lawyers in Canada,* at 96-7, quoting statistics from Statistics Canada, which include a small number of students in programs other than bachelor of laws.

50 Joan Brockman, *Identifying the Barriers: A Survey of Members of the Law Society of British Columbia.* A Report Prepared for the Law Society of British Columbia's Subcommittee on Women in the Legal Profession (Vancouver: Law Society of British Columbia, 1991; Appendix 2 at 9-10, in Kate Young (chair), *Women in the Legal Profession* (Vancouver: Law Society of British Columbia, 1991).

51 Statistics Canada, *Census* data from the various years. Also see Katherine Marshall, "Women in Male Dominated Professions" in *Canadian Social Trends* (Ottawa: Statistics Canada, 1987) 7; Katherine Marshall, "Women in Professional Occupations: Progress in the 1980s" *Canadian Social Trends* (Ottawa: Statistics Canada, 1989) 13. These figures from Statistics Canada indicate the numbers of people earning an income from the practice of law. The Federation of Law Societies Membership Charts (for later years) show more lawyers in Canada than the Statistic Canada figures, and therefore there are members who are earning an income other than through the practice of law. The Federation of Law Societies of Canada assesses each law society on the basis of active members, and its statistics can be found at its Web site at <http://www.flsc.ca>. A more detailed analysis is found in Fiona M. Kay and Joan Brockman, "Barriers to Gender Equality in the Canadian Legal Establishment" (2000) 8 *Feminist Legal Studies* 168.

52 In 1973, only 5.4% of law professors in Canada were women, and in 1983 this figure had risen to 15%; Stager, *Lawyers* at 303, quoting figures from Statistics Canada, which include about 5% who teach in programs other than bachelor of laws.

53 Sheila McIntyre, "Gender Bias Within the Law Schools: 'The Memo' and Its Impact" (1987-8) 2 *Canadian Journal of Women and the Law* 362.

54 Diana Majury, "Collective Action on a Systemic Problem" in Carmen Lambert, ed., *Towards a New Equality: The Status of Women in Canadian Universities* (Ottawa: Social Science Federation of Canada, 1991). Also see Bruce Feldthusen, "The Gender Wars: Where the Boys Are" (1990) 4 *Canadian Journal of Women and the Law* 66.

55 Numbers supplied to the author by the law schools.

56 Statistics Canada, *Census* data from the various years.

57 For an overview of these studies, see Kay and Brockman, "Barriers to Gender Equality" at 169.
58 For a scathing feminist critique of this approach to "leaving" the profession see Petra Tancred, "Outsiders/Insiders: Women and Professional Norms" (1999) 14(1) *Canadian Journal of Law and Society* 31.
59 Joan Brockman, "'Resistance by the Club' to the Feminization of the Legal Profession" (1992) 7(2) *Canadian Journal of Law and Society* 47. For an earlier study of the difficulties women had finding articles, see Smith, Stephenson, and Quijano. "The Legal Profession."
60 Joan Brockman, "Leaving the Practice of Law: The Wherefores and the Whys" (1994) 32(1) *Alberta Law Review* 116.
61 Fiona M. Kay, "Flight from Law: A Competing Risks Model of Departures from Law Firms" (1997) 31(2) *Law and Society Review* 301 at 318.
62 Brockman, "Resistance by the Club," at 67.
63 Ibid., at 67-8.
64 Ibid., at 70-1.
65 Brockman, "Leaving the Practice" at 129-30.
66 Kay, "Flight from Law" at 303.
67 Ibid., at 320 and 322.
68 Ibid., at 327.
69 Sandra Harding, *The Science Question in Feminism* (Ithaca, New York: Cornell University Press, 1986); Sandra Harding, *Whose Science? Whose Knowledge? Thinking From Women's Lives* (Ithaca, New York: Cornell University Press, 1991).
70 Sandra Harding, ed., *Feminism and Methodology* (Bloomington: Indiana University Press, 1987) at 183.
71 Harding, *The Science Question* at 76.
72 See Joan Brockman, Denise Evans, and Kerri Reid, "Feminist Perspectives for the Study of Gender Bias in the Legal Profession" (1992) 5(1) *Canadian Journal of Women and the Law* 37. A similar starting point is described by Thornton, *Dissonance and Distrust*, at 47, when she describes women lawyers in Australia as "fringe dwellers in the law," and sets out to explain why this is so. Also see Phyllis D. Coontz, "Gender in the Legal Profession: Women 'See' It, Men Don't" (1995) 15(2) *Women and Politics* 1, who makes a similar argument that the typical lawyer is cast with male, not female, traits; schemas which define success in male, not female, characteristics; and scripts which legitimize male speech, but silence women.
73 For the survey of former members of the Law Society of British Columbia see, Joan Brockman, "Resistance by the Club," and for the survey of members of the Law Society of British Columbia see, Joan Brockman, "Gender Bias in the Legal Profession: A Survey of Members of the Law Society of British Columbia" (1992) 17 *Queen's Law Journal* 91. The questionnaires are reproduced at the end of the articles.
74 For the survey of active members of the Law Society of Alberta see Joan Brockman, "Bias in the Legal Profession: Perceptions and Experiences" (1992) 30(3) *Alberta Law Review* 747. For the survey of inactive members of the Law Society of Alberta see Joan Brockman, "Leaving the Practice of Law: The Wherefores and the Whys" (1994) 32(1) *Alberta Law Review* 116. The questionnaires are reproduced at the end of the articles.
75 Fiona M. Kay, "Flight from Law: A Competing Risk Model of Departures from Law Firms" (1997) 31(2) *Law and Society Review* 301; Fiona M. Kay and John Hagan, "Changing Opportunities for Partnership for Men and Women Lawyers During the Transformation of the Modern Law Firm" (1994) 32(3) *Osgoode Hall Law Journal* 413; Fiona M. Kay and John Hagan, "The Persistent Glass Ceiling: Gendered Inequalities in the Earnings of Lawyers" (1995) 46(2) *British Journal of Sociology* 280; John Hagan and Fiona Kay, *Gender in Practice: A Study of Lawyers' Lives* (New York: Oxford University Press, 1995). Fiona Kay conducted a follow-up survey in 1996: Fiona M. Kay, Nancy Dautovich, and Chantelle Marlor, *Barriers and Opportunities Within Law: Women in a Changing Legal Profession: A Longitudinal Survey of Ontario Lawyers* (Law Society of Upper Canada, 1996).
76 See Susan B. Boyd, Elizabeth Sheehy, and Josée Bouchard, *Canadian Feminist Perspectives on Law: An Annotated Bibliography of Interdisciplinary Writings (1989-99)* (1999) 11(1&2)

Canadian Journal of Women and the Law at 396-415; Melina, Buckley, *Synthesis of Provincial Law Society Reports* (Appendix 4 to Madame Justice Bertha Wilson (chair), *Touchstones for Change: Equality, Diversity and Accountability* (Ottawa: Canadian Bar Association, August 1993); and Gaylene Schellenberg, Melina Buckley, Tshepo Mofitksana, and Susan Zimmerman, *Annotated Bibliography on Gender Equality in the Legal Profession* (Ottawa: Canadian Bar Association, 1993).

77 Mary Jane Mossman, "'Invisible' Constraints on Lawyering and Leadership: The Case of Women Lawyers" (1988) 20 *Ottawa Law Review* 567 at 598-603 discusses invisible structural barriers, and at 593-6, invisible barriers in ideas. She suggests that the former may require outside intervention to increase the numbers and role models for women to fit within male standards, and the latter requires a restructuring of what it means to be a lawyer and a leader.

78 The results are summarized in Appendix 4 to the Canadian Bar Association Task Force on Gender Equality in the Legal Profession prepared by Melina Buckley, *Synthesis of Provincial Law Society Reports* (Ottawa: Canadian Bar Association, 1993), and Madame Justice Bertha Wilson refers to the results in Chapter 4 of her Report, *Touchstones for Change: Equality, Diversity and Accountability* (Ottawa: Canadian Bar Association, 1993).

79 Wilson, *Touchstones for Change* at 55.

80 For a further discussion on methods and methodology see: Joan Brockman and Dale Phillippe, "The Task Force Approach to Studying Gender Bias in the Courts: A Consideration of Feminist Methods and Perspectives" (1991) 16(2) *Atlantis: A Women's Studies Journal* 32; Mary Jane Mossman, "Gender Bias and the Legal Profession: Challenges and Choices" in Joan Brockman and Dorothy E. Chunn, eds., *Investigating Gender Bias in the Law* (Thompson Educational Publishing, 1993) at 147.

81 This sampling approach faces the same critique done by Tancred, "Outsiders/Insiders" on the meaning of "leaving" a profession. It adopts a male definition that excludes many women's experiences.

82 This resulted in eight to twelve lawyers being interviewed in each of the five years of call, representing 16-24% of the women or men called in each year. In total there were 540 women and 904 men called to the bar in British Columbia between 1986 and 1990 who were still on the practising list when the sample was drawn.

83 In a separate study, a random sample of former members of the Law Society from this same cohort were interviewed by Angela McEachern. Some preliminary results were discussed in Angela McEachern and Joan Brockman, "The Exodus from Law: Attractions and Distractions," presented at the Learned Societies Conference, Calgary, Alberta, 13 June 1994.

84 Anglo names are used to further ensure anonymity; however, the few respondents who were of other races had anglo names.

85 Law Society of British Columbia, *Aboriginal Law Graduates in British Columbia* (Vancouver: Law Society of British Columbia, 1996); Law Society of British Columbia, *Report on the Survey of Aboriginal Law Graduates in British Columbia* (Vancouver: Law Society of British Columbia, 1996); S. McIvor and T. Nahanee, *Aboriginal Women in the Legal Profession* (Appendix 11 to Madame Justice Bertha Wilson (chair), *Touchstones for Change: Equality, Diversity and Accountability* (Ottawa: Canadian Bar Association, 1993); Joanne St. Lewis and Benjamin Trevino (co-chairs), *The Challenge of Racial Equality: Putting Principles into Practice* (Ottawa: Canadian Bar Association, 1999); Joanne St. Lewis (co-chair), *Virtual Justice: Systemic Racism and the Canadian Legal Profession,* An Independent Report of the Working Group on Racial Equality in the Legal Profession (Ottawa: Canadian Bar Association, 1999); Law Society of British Columbia, *Addressing Discriminatory Barriers Facing Aboriginal Law Students and Lawyers* (Vancouver: Law Society of British Columbia, 2000).

86 Ethnic variability was also low in Kay et al.'s sample of 1,056 Ontario lawyers called between 1975 and 1990; 92% of the men and 90% of the women responding in that study identified themselves as "Caucasian Europeans," 6% of the respondents identified themselves as Jewish; and 2% as Asian; Kay et al., *Women in a Changing Legal Profession* at 33.

87 Naffine, *Law and the Sexes* at 111.

Chapter 2: Law's Attractions and Detractions

1 James J. White, "Women in the Law" (1967) 65 *Michigan Law Review* 1051. His question asked, "How would you describe your motivation to attend law school on the following scale: (List your motivation with respect to each motive)." Respondents were provided with six motives: 1) desire to help society, 2) desire for prestigious position, 3) continuing intellectual stimulation, 4) good way to make an honourable living, 5) interesting field to know, and 6) good remuneration; and four possible responses: 1) very important, 2) important, 3) so-so, and 4) not important.

2 Bernard F. Lentz and David N. Laband, *Sex Discrimination in the Legal Profession* (Westport, CT: Quorum Books, 1995) at 181. Respondents were asked, "In making a career choice, many things often act in influencing a decision. In thinking about the forces that led you to choose a legal career, which *one* on the following was the most important, which *one* was the second most important, and which *one* was the third most important?" Respondents were given the following factors: family wishes and pressure; financial opportunity; intellectual challenge, interest in social service and helping others; influence of role model; effort to escape economic background; alternative careers not attractive or practical; and other.

3 Ibid., at 180.

4 Respondents were asked, "Do you think that you will still be practising law five years from now?" [If they were ambivalent, they were asked, "How likely is it (0-100%) that you will be practising law five years from now?"] Those who said, "Yes" or gave a probability greater than 50% were coded "Yes." If they said they would not be practising law, they were asked, "Why would you no longer be practising law?"

5 Respondents were shown a scale ranging from a one (very satisfied) to a seven (very dissatisfied) and asked, "How satisfied are you with the following aspects of your work? Practice of law overall." Responses one to three were interpreted as "satisfied."

6 Respondents were asked, "Why did you go to law school?" and not provided a list of possible reasons, as had been done in other studies. These percentages will add up to more than 100%, because some respondents gave more than one reason for entering law school.

7 The lawyers in White's 1965 study ("Women in the Law") were not given any option similar to this response. The only similar response by the lawyers in the study referred to by Lentz and Laband in *Sex Discrimination* was "alternative careers not attractive/practical." Almost half of the women (49%) and men (47%) listed this as one of their three reasons for going to law school.

8 It should be noted that respondents were not asked whether they went to law school to improve society or help people, they were simply asked why they went to law school. If they were provided with this possible explanation, the responses would likely have been higher. Lentz and Laband, *Sex Discrimination* at 181 report that 48% of the women and 38% of men ranked "interest in social service/helping others" as one of the top three factors influencing their decision to have law as a career.

9 Lentz and Laband, *Sex Discrimination* at 181 report that 83% of the women and 78% of men ranked "intellectual challenge" as one of the top three factors influencing their decision to have law as a career. In addition to the difference in the format of the question (choices in their study and open-ended in my study), it may be that my respondents, in the thick of practising law (which is often reported as boring), forgot that they had gone into law for intellectual stimulation.

10 Lentz and Laband, *Sex Discrimination* at 181 report that 14% of the men and 16% of men ranked "family wishes/pressure" as one of the top three factors influencing their decision to have law as a career.

11 They responded one to three on a scale of one to seven.

12 They responded one to three on a scale of one to seven.

13 Since this question was not asked of each respondent, no effort was made to quantify the responses.

14 Respondents were asked, "If you could 'do it over again,' would you become a lawyer?" Those who said, "Yes," "I would go to law school, but not practice," and "Yes, but up until now, no" are treated as "Yes."

Chapter 3: Fitting In

1 Wilson, *Touchstones for Change* at 56.

2 Ibid., at 60.

3 Ibid., at 62-4 and 91-4. Also see Fiona M. Kay and John Hagan, "Raising the Bar: The Gender Stratification of Law Firm Capitalization" (1998) 63(5) *American Sociological Review* 728; and Fiona M. Kay and John Hagan, "Changing Opportunities for Partnership for Men and Women Lawyers During the Transformation of the Modern Law Firm" (1994) 32(3) *Osgoode Hall Law Journal* 413.

4 The percentages add up to more than 100% because some of the respondents gave more than one answer, and some were answering questions in relation to more than one job, having worked at more than one place because of a job move. The thirty-seven women gave seventy different reasons for leaving their positions, and the thirty men gave fifty-one different reasons. A maximum of two reasons was coded for each respondent.

5 Wilson, *Touchstones for Change* at 48.

6 Ibid., see Tables 1 and 2 at 48.

7 Fiona M. Kay, Nancy Dautovich, and Chantelle Marlor. *Barriers and Opportunities Within Law: Women in a Changing Legal Profession: A Longitudinal Survey of Ontario Lawyers* (Toronto: Law Society of Upper Canada, 1996) at 25.

8 Respondents were asked what types of law they practised, and what proportion of their time they spent in the area or areas they identified. It is difficult to determine exactly how to measure this variable, and many respondents had difficulty estimating the amount of time they spent on areas of law. The three most frequent areas of practice were coded; however, only 50% of the men and 32% of the women mentioned more than two areas.

9 Wilson, *Touchstones for Change* at 86.

10 They responded one to three on a scale in which one equals very satisfied and seven equals very dissatisfied. This was similar to the overall sample, as most women (72%) expressed satisfaction with the type of law they practised.

11 Joan Brockman, "Gender Bias in the Legal Profession: A Survey of Members of the Law Society of British Columbia" (1992) 17 *Queen's Law Journal* 91 at 104.

12 The question asked was: "Do you think there is bias or discrimination against women in the legal profession today which restricts their career advancement? [If yes] In what way?"

13 The analyses and conclusions on lawyers' income are taken from a paper written by V. Gordon Rose, "OUCH! Banging Heads on the Glass Ceiling: An Examination of Gender Inequality in the Income of BC Lawyers," for a course at Simon Fraser University (Statistics 402, 28 November 1994). I am grateful to him for his contribution to this book.

14 See, for example, John Hagan, "The Gender Stratification of Income Inequality Among Lawyers" (1990) 68(3) *Social Forces* 835; Fiona M. Kay and John Hagan, "The Persistent Glass Ceiling: Gendered Inequalities in the Earnings of Lawyers" (1995) 46(2) *British Journal of Sociology* 279; Robert G. Wood, Mary E. Corcoran and Paul N. Courant, "Pay Differences among the Highly Paid: The Male-Female Earnings Gap in Lawyers' Salaries" (1993) 11(3) *Journal of Labor Economics* 417.

15 Kay and Hagan, "The Persistent Glass Ceiling" at 280-4; and Wood et al. "Pay Differences" at 418-21.

16 Kay and Hagan, ibid., at 281.

17 Ibid.

18 Ibid., at 282.

19 Ibid., at 284.

20 Ibid., at 303-4.

21 Ibid.

22 This is not out of line with the survey of active members of the Law Society of British Columbia conducted in 1990. Of those called between 1986 and 1990, 2.8% of the women and 5.8% of the men were partners; 14.6% of the women and 39.2% of the men would have preferred to be partners.

23 Fiona M. Kay and John Hagan, "Changing Opportunities" at 443, emphasis in original.

24 Fiona M. Kay and John Hagan, "Cultivating Clients in the Competition for Partnership:

Gender and the Organizational Restructuring of Law Firms in the 1990s" (1999) 33(3) *Law and Society Review*.

25 Ibid., at 541.
26 Ibid., at 526.
27 Ibid., at 529.
28 Ibid., at 544.
29 Ibid., at 544.
30 Kay and Hagan, "Changing Opportunities" at 454.
31 This may seem to be a small number; however 42% of the women and 40% of the men were not in a position in which advancement was relevant. Thus, 17% of the women who were in a position to advance were dissatisfied with their opportunity to do so.
32 Wilson, *Touchstones for Change* at 49-51.
33 Cristin Schmitz, "Fewer Lawyers Applying and Accepted to Bench" (12 June 1998) *Lawyers' Weekly* 10.
34 A maximum of two reasons were coded for each respondent.

Chapter 4: Discrimination and Sexual Harassment

1 See, for example, Bernard F. Lentz and David N. Laband, *Sex Discrimination in the Legal Profession* (Westport, CT: Quorum Books, 1995); Hilary Sommerlad and Peter Sanderson, *Gender, Choice and Commitment: Women Solicitors in England and Wales and the Struggle for Equal Status* (Aldershot: Dartmouth Publishing, 1998); Margaret Thornton, *Dissonance and Distrust: Women in the Legal Profession* (Melbourne: Oxford University Press, 1996); and Clare McGlynn, *The Woman Lawyer: Making the Difference* (London: Butterworths, 1998). Ulrike Schulz (Germany) and Gisela Shaw (England) are presently compiling papers presented at an Invitational Workshop on "A Challenge to Law and Lawyers: Women in the Legal Profession" at the International Institute for the Sociology of Law, Oñita, Spain in July 1999.
2 For an overview of studies in Canada, see Fiona M. Kay, and Joan Brockman, "Barriers to Gender Equality in the Canadian Legal Establishment" (2000) 8 *Feminist Legal Studies* 169.
3 Wilson, *Touchstones* at 56.
4 *Opportunities Within Law: Women in a Changing Legal Profession: A Longitudinal Survey of Ontario Lawyers* (Toronto: Law Society of Upper Canada, 1996) at 88. Kay's surveys were of lawyers called to the bar in Ontario between 1975 and 1990.
5 The question asked was: "Since May 1993, the Law Society's Rules of Professional Conduct have stated that lawyers shall not discriminate on the basis of 1. race, 2. national or ethnic origin, 3. colour, 4. religion, 5. sex, 6. sexual orientation, 7. marital or 8. family status, 9. disability or 10. age. Have you ever been discriminated against in the legal profession on any of these grounds?" The respondents were shown a copy of the Rule.
6 Respondents who had experienced discrimination were asked: "How did you react or respond to it? [Did you or someone else take effective action against the discrimination?] Did this discrimination or your reaction to it adversely affect your career? [If yes] In what way? Did this discrimination affect you personally? [If yes] In what way?"
7 Given the sensitive nature of comments about discrimination and sexual harassment, I have not used the respondents' pseudonyms for these comments.
8 Brockman, "Bias in the Legal Profession" at 759. This question was not asked in the British Columbia mail-out survey. One would expect fewer respondents identifying discrimination in various areas by this open-ended question, rather than a checklist of possible ways of discrimination. This issue is discussed in further detail in Joan Brockman, "'A Wild Feminist at Her Raving Best': Reflections on Studying Gender Bias in the Legal Profession" (2000) 28(1&2) *Resources for Feminist Research* 61.
9 The question was worded slightly differently in the two provinces, which probably accounts for the differences; see Brockman, "Wild Feminist."
10 In the survey I did for the Law Society of British Columbia, 34 women (4.9% of the women) and seventy men (6.3% of the men) identified themselves as members of visible minority groups, by virtue of their colour or race. However, since the response rates were somewhat low (53% of the women and 23% of the men responded to the survey) it is not possible to determine what proportion of the women and men in the larger population of

lawyers are members of these groups. In 1997, Gerry Ferguson, a law professor at the University of Victoria and a member of the Multiculturalism Committee of the Law Society of British Columbia, attempted to determine the ethnic and linguistic diversity of lawyers in British Columbia by using Census Canada data. As he discovered, the estimates that Census Canada makes on the basis of its sample surveys are more accurate for larger groups of subjects than smaller groups. It becomes impossible to estimate, with any reasonable degree of accuracy, the numbers of lawyers in smaller ethnic groups; Gerry Ferguson, "Ethnic and Linguistic Diversity of BC Lawyers" (1997) 55(6) *Advocate* 873.

11 See Joanne St. Lewis and Benjamin Trevino (co-chairs), *The Challenge of Racial Equality: Putting Principles into Practice* (Ottawa: Canadian Bar Association, 1999); Joanne St. Lewis (co-chair), *Virtual Justice: Systemic Racism and the Canadian Legal Profession,* An Independent Report of the Working Group on Racial Equality in the Legal Profession (Ottawa: Canadian Bar Association, 1999).

12 St. Lewis, *Virtual Justice,* at iii.

13 Sharon McIvor and Teressa Nahanee, *Aboriginal Women in the Legal Profession* (Appendix 11 to the Report of the Canadian Bar Association Task Force on Gender Equality in the Legal Profession, Ottawa, 1993); Joanne St. Lewis and Benjamin Trevino (co-chairs), *The Challenge of Racial Equality: Putting Principles into Practice* (Ottawa: Canadian Bar Association, 1999), Chapter 6; and Joanne St. Lewis (co-chair) *Virtual Justice: Systemic Racism and the Canadian Legal Profession,* An Independent Report of the Working Group on Racial Equality in the Legal Profession (Ottawa: Canadian Bar Association, 1999), Chapter 3; Law Society of British Columbia, *Summary and Discussion of the Aboriginal Law Graduates Focus Groups* (Vancouver: Law Society of British Columbia, 1998) at 30-3; and Gerry Ferguson (chair), *Addressing Discriminatory Barriers Facing Aboriginal Law Students and Lawyers* (Vancouver: Law Society of British Columbia, 2000).

14 There are no statistics on the number of lesbians and gay men who are lawyers, and there are few studies that address the barriers they encounter in the legal profession. In 1994, the Los Angeles County Bar Association estimated that "at least 6% and perhaps as many as 10% of Los Angeles County lawyers are gay"; Los Angeles County Bar Association Committee on Sexual Orientation Bias. *Report* (Los Angeles: Country Bar, 1994) at i. If these figures hold true for British Columbia, there are approximately between 500 and 900 lesbian and gay lawyers in British Columbia.

15 E.N. (Ted) Hughes (chair), Alison MacLennan, John McAlpine, Stephen F.D. Kelleher, Marguerite Jackson, and Wendy Baker, *Gender Equality in the Justice System* (Vancouver: Law Society of British Columbia, 1992) at 3-31.

16 Kathleen A. Lahey, "Introduction" (1991) 16 *Queen's Law Journal* 231-5. See (1991) 16(2) *Queen's Law Journal* for papers delivered at that Conference.

17 Little is known about the numbers of women and men in law schools or in the legal profession who have disabilities. Eight women (1.2% of the women respondents) and 17 men (1.5% of the men) in the British Columbia mail-out survey considered themselves disadvantaged by reason of a persistent disability. Six women (1% of the women respondents) and twenty-six men (1.4% of the men) in the Alberta survey considered themselves disadvantaged by reason of a persistent disability. Again, the response rate in these surveys makes it difficult to estimate the numbers of women and men with persistent disabilities in the general population of lawyers in British Columbia and Alberta. It is estimated that 10-15% of Canada's population have a physical or mental disability; David M. Lepofsky, "Disabled Persons and Canadian Law Schools: The Right to Equal Benefit of the Law School" (1991) 36 *McGill Law Journal* 636 at 648.

18 Ibid., at 641.

19 Respondents who said they were discriminated against were asked, "How did you react or respond to it? Did you or someone else take effective action against the discrimination?"

20 The question asked was: "Do you think there is bias or discrimination against women in the legal profession today which restricts their career advancement? [If yes] In what way?"

21 One would expect fewer respondents identifying discrimination in various areas by this open-ended question, rather than a checklist of possible ways of discrimination. This issue is discussed in further detail by Brockman, "A Wild Feminist."

22 In the British Columbia survey, 68.4% of the women and 33.8% of the men thought there was discrimination against women in the legal profession because of "lack of accommodation for family commitments." This was the view of 64.6% of the women and 22.3% of the men in the Alberta survey. In the British Columbia survey, 15.5% of the women and 11.2% of the men thought there was discrimination against men in the legal profession because of "lack of accommodation for family commitments." This was the view of 15.0% of the women and 11.1% of the men in the Alberta survey.

23 I understood this to mean at home; however, this would not be possible without some redistribution at work – see Chapter 6 for further discussion.

24 In the British Columbia survey, 42.5% of the women and 18.4% of the men identified "assignment of files" as an area in which women were discriminated against. In Alberta, 54.5% of the women and 18.4% of the men were of this opinion.

25 Joan Brockman, Denise Evans, and Kerri Reid, "Feminist Perspectives For the Study of Gender Bias in the Legal Profession" 5(1) (1992) *Canadian Journal of Women and the Law* 37 at 51.

26 Kay et al., *Barriers and Opportunities within Law* at 31.

27 In the British Columbia survey, 48.1% of the women and 21.9% of the men identified "other lawyers not giving appropriate weight to opinions" as a form of discrimination against women. In Alberta 59.7% of the women and 20.6% of the men were of this opinion.

28 In the British Columbia survey, 49.2% of the women and 27.4% of the men reported "hiring" as an area in which women were discriminated against. In the Alberta survey, 54.2% of the women and 24.2% of the men were of this view.

29 Constance Backhouse and L. Cohen, *The Secret Oppression: Sexual Harassment of Working Women* (Toronto: Macmillan, 1978). In the same year L. Farley's *Sexual Shakedown: The Sexual Harassment of Women on the Job* (New York: Warner, 1978) was published. Shortly thereafter, came C.A. MacKinnon, *Sexual Harassment of Working Women: A Case of Sex Discrimination* (New Haven, CT: Yale University Press, 1979). Before this, the issue of sexual harassment was sometimes discussed under different terminology. For example, in 1977, Rosabeth Moss Kanter, *Men and Women of the Corporation* (New York: Basic Books, 1977) at 223, described instances of aggressive sexual harassment as "exaggerated displays of aggression and potency: instance of sexual innuendos, aggressive sexual teasing and prowess-oriented 'war stories.'" There were, however, a couple of magazine articles about sexual harassment and the Working Women's Institute in New York and the Alliance Against Sexual Coercion in Boston had examined the issue as early as 1975; see E.L. Weeks, J.M. Boles, A.P. Garbin and J. Bount, "The Transformation of Sexual Harassment from a Private Trouble to a Public Issue" (1986) 54(2) *Sociological Inquiry* 432 at 435-7.

30 For the importance of naming a problem, see Sheilah L. Martin, "Proving Gender Bias in the Law and the Legal System" in Joan Brockman and Dorothy E. Chunn, eds., *Investigating Gender Bias: Law, Courts and the Legal Profession* (Toronto: Thompson Educational Publishing, 1993) 19.

31 Weeks et al., "The Transformation of Sexual Harassment" at 432.

32 In the *Janzen* case, the judges of the Manitoba Court of Appeal assumed that sexual harassment was a sexual encounter. See Joan Brockman, "Social Authority, Legal Discourse and Women's Voices" (1992) 21(2) *Manitoba Law Journal* 213.

33 See, for example, Backhouse and Cohen, *The Secret Oppression;* D.J. Benson and G.E. Thompson, "Sexual Harassment on a University Campus: The Confluence of Authority Relations, Sexual Interest and Gender Stratification" (1982) 29 *Social Problems* 236; B.A. Gutek, *Sex and the Workplace: The Impact of Sexual Behavior and Harassment on Women, Men and Organization* (San Francisco: Jossey-Bass, 1985); B. Dziech. and L. Weiner, *The Lecherous Professor* (Boston: Beacon Press, 1984); Michele A. Paludi, ed., *Sexual Harassment on College Campuses: Abusing the Ivory Power* (Albany: State University of New York Press, 1996), a revised and expanded edition of *Ivory Power: Sexual Harassment on Campus* (1990); M. Stockdale, ed., *Women and Work: Sexual Harassment in the Workplace* (Thousand Oaks, CA: Sage, 1996).

34 Aysan Sev'er, "Sexual Harassment: Where We Were, Where We Are and Prospects for the New Millennium – Introduction to the Special Issue" (1999) 36(4) *Canadian Review of Sociology and Anthropology* 469.
35 Rhonda Lenton, Michael D. Smith, and Norman Morra. "Sexual Harassment in Public Places: Experiences of Canadian Women" (1999) 36(4) *Canadian Review of Sociology and Anthropology* 517. Also see C.B. Gardner, ed., *Passing By: Gender and Public Harassment* (Berkeley: University of California Press, 1995).
36 Walter S. DeKeserdy, Shahid Alvi, and Barbara Perry, "Violence against and the Harassment of Women in Canadian Public Housing: An Exploratory Study" (1999) 36(4) *Canadian Review of Sociology and Anthropology* 499.
37 Vivian Krauchek and Gillian Ranson, "Playing by the Rules of the Game: Women's Experiences and Perceptions of Sexual Harassment in Sport" (1999) 36(4) *Canadian Review of Sociology and Anthropology* 585.
38 Sandy Welsh and James E. Gruber, "Not Taking It Any More: Women Who Report or File Complaints of Sexual Harassment" (1999) 36(4) *Canadian Review of Sociology and Anthropology* 559.
39 The question asked was: "In May 1993, the Law Society defined sexual harassment under the Rules of Professional Conduct as a form of prohibited discrimination. Since entering the legal profession as an articling student, have you ever been sexually harassed in work related situations, including professional functions?" The respondents were shown the Rule and the footnote to the ruling that states,

This reflects the Supreme Court of Canada's decision in *Janzen* v. *Platy Enterprises Ltd.,* [1989] 1 S.C.R. 1252. The Court discusses the issue at 1276-91. The Chief Justice said:

Common to all of these descriptions of sexual harassment is the concept of using a position of power to import sexual requirements into the workplace thereby negatively altering the working conditions of employees who are forced to contend with sexual demands (at 1281).
...
Sexual harassment is not limited to demands for sexual favours made under threats of adverse job consequences should the employee refuse to comply with the demands ... Sexual harassment also encompasses situations in which sexual demands are foisted upon unwilling employees or in which employees endure sexual groping, propositions, and inappropriate comments, but where no tangible economic rewards are attached to involvement in the behaviour (at 1282).

He concluded:

Sexual harassment in the workplace may be broadly defined as unwelcome conduct of a sexual nature that detrimentally affects the work environment or leads to adverse job-related consequences for the victims of the harassment (at 1284).

While the *Janzen* case dealt with sexual harassment in an employment situation, these Rules cover more than lawyers' conduct as employers or employees. They also deal with relations among counsel, among partners, between lawyers and clients and between lawyers and court personnel.
40 Other surveys have found that approximately half of working women have experienced sexual harassment in the workplace; Diane Crocker and Valery Kalemba, "The Incidence and Impact of Women's Experiences of Sexual Harassment in Canadian Workplaces" (1999) 36(4) *Canadian Review of Sociology and Anthropology* 541 at 542. Crocker and Kalemba's study found that in a sample of 1,990 working women between the ages of 18 and 65, 56% had experienced sexual harassment in the previous year (1991), and 77% had experienced sexual harassment in their lifetime. The lower rate of sexual harassment for women lawyers in my interviews may again be because I asked an open-ended question,

whereas, Crocker and Kalemba asked their respondents, "Now, I am going to describe some experiences that women may have with unwanted attention from men at work, and I'd like to know if these things have happened to you." They were then provided with a list of behaviours that had been found to constitute sexual harassment in Canadian legal cases (they are reproduced in their Appendix at 556). In my interviews, another 12% of the women described what others might describe as sexual harassing behaviour, but said they had never been sexually harassed. Under Crocker and Kalemba's definition, this would bring the number of women lawyers who were sexually harassed up to 48%. It may also be that women lawyers do not experience as much sexual harassment as other working women or are less ready to call it sexual harassment, although this latter possibility does not accord with what they should know as lawyers. I suspect that the open-ended versus checklist approach to the question had some effect on the different rates.

41   Since the question was open-ended it was difficult to classify the responses into types of sexual harassment as has been done in other studies. Using Crocker and Kalemba's types (at 547):

1   gender harassment (insulting jokes about women, sexual material displayed)
2   non-verbal unwanted sexual harassment (man leaning or getting too close, suggestive touching, gestures, staring, force or attempted force)
3   verbal unwanted sexual harassment (insulting jokes or remarks about you, questions about your sex life, requests for dates)
4   sexual coercion (hints at job benefits in exchange for sex, threats of job loss or job difficulties),

most of the sexual harassment fell within the first and third category. In Crocker and Kalemba's study, 48% of the women had experienced gender harassment in the previous year, 41% non-verbal unwanted sexual attention, 30% verbal unwanted sexual attention, and 3% sexual coercion. Across their working lives, the percentages for the above types of sexual harassment were: 64%, 60%, 52%, and 10%. For a slightly different categorization see Welsh and Gruber, "Not Taking It Any More" at 581.

42   Crocker and Kalemba, ibid., at 550.

43   Ibid., at 553-4.

44   Sev'er, "Sexual Harassment" at 480-1.

45   It is not entirely clear what she meant by this, and I neglected to ask her. However, she did not meet the old stereotype of the type of women who are subjected to sexual harassment.

46   Susan Bisom-Rapp, "Scripting Reality in the Legal Workplace: Women Lawyers, Litigation Prevention Measures, and the Limits of Anti-Discrimination Law" (1996) 6(1) *Columbia Journal of Gender and Law* 385.

47   Discussed in Joan Brockman, "The Use of Self-Regulation to Curb Discrimination and Sexual Harassment in the Legal Profession" (1997) 35(2) *Osgoode Hall Law Journal* 209 at 212-13.

48   Ibid., at 232 and 224.

49   Ibid., at 241.

50   See Gail H. Forsythe, "After the First Year: Are Services in Demand? What are the Results?" *Benchers' Bulletin* (January-February 1996) at 7, for a list of benefits to resolving conflicts in an informal manner.

51   Forsythe, "After the First Year" at 7.

52   Bisom-Rapp, "Scripting Reality" at 323.

53   Ibid., at 330.

54   Ibid., at 329. The rules have also been attacked by lawyers in court on a number of legal grounds, such as vagueness. See, for example, Brenda Jones Quick, "Ethical Rules Prohibiting Discrimination by Lawyers: The Legal Profession's Response to Discrimination on the Rise" (1993) 7(1) *Notre Dame Journal of Law, Ethics, and Public Policy* 5.

55   Ibid., at 343, summarizing and quoting Linda H. Krieger, "The Content of Our Categories: A Cognitive Bias Approach to Discrimination and Equal Employment Opportunity" (1995) 47 *Stanford Law Review* 1161 at 1164.

56 Bisom-Rapp, ibid., at 347.
57 Ibid., at 348, quoting Deborah Rhode, "Perspectives on Professional Women" (1988) *Stanford Law Review* at 1193.
58 Ibid., at 351.
59 Ibid., at 385.

Chapter 5: Reluctant Adversaries
1 Raymond A. Belliotti, "Our Adversary System: In search of a Foundation" (1988) 1 *Canadian Journal of Law and Jurisprudence* 19 at 19.
2 Michael Davis and Frederick A. Elliston (eds.), *Ethics and the Legal Profession* (New York: Prometheus Books, 1986), 185-6.
3 Recent, in the sense that it began to emerge around the 1640s and became established in the late 1700s to early 1800s in England and the United States; Stephan Landsman, "A Brief Survey of the Development of the Adversary System" (1983) 44 *Ohio State Law Review* 713; Stephan Landsman, "The Rise of the Contentious Spirit: Adversary Procedure in Eighteenth Century England" (1990) 75 *Cornell Law Review* 497.
4 Stephan Landsman, *The Adversary System: A Description and Defense* (Washington, DC: American Enterprise Institute for Public Policy Research, 1984), Chapter 1.
5 Belliotti, "Our Adversary System" at 19. Also see the discussion by Stephen Coughlan, "The 'Adversary System': Rhetoric or Reality?" (1993) 8(2) *Canadian Journal of Law and Society* 139 at 142-5.
6 Based on Charles Feid, "The Lawyer as Friend: The Moral Foundation of the Lawyer-Client Relation" (1976) 85 *Yale Law Journal* 1060.
7 Belliotti, "Our Adversary System" at 34.
8 Deborah L. Rhode, "Ethical Perspectives on Legal Practice" (1985) 37 *Stanford Law Review* 589 at 576. At 596-7, she observes, "lawyers are concerned with the production of belief, not of knowledge," and she asks why we assume fairness will "emerge from two advocates arguing as unfairly as possible on opposite sides."
9 Landsman, *The Adversary System* at 52. Belliotti, in "Our Adversary System" at 20, writes, "the force of law is conceived as beginning where communal bonds end ... Quakers, Puritans, Mormons, and Jews, among others, believed that adversarial, formal processes of law were antithetical to communal harmony. Such groups contend that once an adversarial framework was in place, it supported competitive aggression to the exclusion of the cornerstones of community: reciprocity and empathy. Courts were perceived as inclined toward sterilizing a dispute by emptying it of its social content and translating it into the bloodless, abstract, impersonal language of the law ... Formal adversarial litigation is thus conceived as fomenting alienation rather than responsibility and trust; social fragmentation rather than solidarity and mutual access ... " Belliotti acknowledged what he refers to as an "unresolvable question": does the adversarial system create or reflect social disharmony?
10 Ibid., at 52.
11 David Luban, "Introduction: A New Canadian Legal Ethics" (1996) 9(1) *Canadian Journal of Law and Jurisprudence* 3 at 4. The response was to the writing of such authors as Fried, "The Lawyer as Friend" and Monroe Freedman, *Lawyers' Ethics in an Adversary System* (New York: Bobbs-Merrill, 1975), who suggested that lawyers were obliged to put forward their client's perspective, regardless of the truth or other moral considerations.
12 See discussion in Alice Woolley, "Integrity in Zealousness: Comparing the Standard Conceptions of the Canadian and the American Lawyer" (1996) 9(1) *Canadian Journal of Law and Jurisprudence* 61.
13 Jerome E. Bickenbach, "The Redemption of the Moral Mandate of the Profession of Law" (1996) 9(1) *Canadian Journal of Law and Jurisprudence* 51; Gavin MacKenzie, "Breaking the Dichotomy Habit: The Adversary System and the Ethics of Professionalism" (1996) 9(1) *Canadian Journal of Law and Jurisprudence* 33; Gavin MacKenzie, *Lawyers and Ethics: Professional Responsibility and Discipline*, 2nd ed. (Toronto: Carswell, 1999); Alvin Esau, "Teaching Professional Responsibility in Law School" (1988) 11 *Dalhousie Law Journal* 403.
14 See, for example, David Luban, *Lawyers and Justice: An Ethical Study* (New Jersey: Princeton University Press, 1988); Stephen Ellman, "Lawyering for Justice in a Flawed Democracy:

Review of Luban, Lawyers and Justice (1988)" (1990) 90 *Columbia Law Review* 116; Stephen Ellman, "The Ethics of Care as an Ethic for Lawyers" (1993) 81 *Georgetown Law Journal* 2665; Craig Down, "Crying Woolf? Reform of the Adversarial System in Australia" (1998) 7 *Journal of Judicial Administration* 213-28.

15   See for example, Stanley Anderson, "The Transition From Inquisitorial to Adversarial Criminal Procedure in Denmark" (1992) 64 *Scandinavian Studies* 1; William T. Pizzi and Luca Marafioti, "The New Italian Code of Criminal Procedure: The Difficulties of Building an Adversarial Trial on a Civil Law Foundation" (1992) 17 *Yale Journal of International Law* 1; Michael Zander, "From Inquisitorial to Adversarial – The Italian Experiment" (1991) 141 *New Law Journal* 678; Louis F. DelDuca, "An Historic Convergence of Civil and Common Law Systems: Italy's New Adversarial Criminal Procedure System" (1991) 10 *Dickinson Journal of International Law* 73. For a more cautionary approach to such changes see Johannes R. Nijboer, "The American Adversarial System in Criminal Cases: Between Ideology and Reality" (1997) 5 *Cardozo Journal of International and Comparative Law* 79.

16   For a more in-depth examination of this critique see Carrie Menkel-Meadow, "The Trouble with the Adversary System in a Postmodern, Multicultural World" (1996) 38(1) *William and Mary Law Review* 5.

17   Eve Hill, "Alternative Dispute Resolution in a Feminist Voice" (1990) 5(2) *Journal on Dispute Resolution* 337 at 341-3.

18   Ibid., at 344. See also Menkel-Meadow, "The Trouble with the Adversary System" who, at 37, writes that many of the alternative dispute resolution forms are "becoming corrupted by the persistence of adversarial values."

19   Hill, "Alternative Dispute Resolution" at 353.

20   Ibid., at 354.

21   John S. Dzienkowski, "Lawyering in a Hybrid Adversary System" (1996) 38(1) *William and Mary Law Review* 45 at 53, note 46.

22   James Foster, "Antigones in the Bar: Women Lawyers as Reluctant Adversaries" (1986) 10 *Legal Studies Forum* 289; Carla Hotel and Joan Brockman, "The Conciliatory-Adversarial Continuum in Family Law Practice" (1994) 12(1) *Canadian Journal of Family Law* 11; Carla Hotel and Joan Brockman, "Legal Ethics in the Practice of Law: Playing Chess While Mountain Climbing" (1997) 16 *Journal of Business Ethics* 809; Rand Jack and Dana Crowley Jack, *Moral Vision and Professional Decisions: The Changing Values of Women and Men Lawyers* (Cambridge: Cambridge University Press, 1989); Carolyn Jin-Myung Oh, "Questioning the Cultural and Gender-Biased Assumptions of the Adversary System: Voices of Asian-American Law Students" (1992) 7 *Berkeley Women's Law Journal* 125.

23   Madame Justice Wilson suggested that women might "succeed in infusing the law with an understanding of what it means to be fully human"; Madame Justice Bertha Wilson, "Will Women Judges Really Make a Difference?" (1990) 28 *Osgoode Hall Law Journal* 507 at 522. See also Carrie Menkel-Meadow, "The Comparative Sociology of Women Lawyers: The 'Feminization' of the Legal Profession" (1987) 24 *Osgoode Hall Law Journal* 897; Carrie Menkel-Meadow, "Portia in a Different Voice: Speculations on a Woman's Lawyering Process" (1985) 1 *Berkeley Women's Law Journal* 39; Mary Jane Mossman, "'Invisible' Constraints on Lawyering and Leadership: The Case of Women Lawyers" (1988) 20(3) *Ottawa Law Review* 567; Mary Jane Mossman, "Portia's Progress: Women as Lawyers – Reflections on Past and Future" (1988) 8 *Windsor Yearbook Access to Justice* 252.

24   Foster, "Antigones in the Bar" at 288.

25   Ibid., at 290.

26   Joan Brockman, "Leaving the Practice of Law: The Wherefores and the Whys" (1994) 32(1) *Alberta Law Review* 116 at 129.

27   Carla Hotel and Joan Brockman, "The Conciliatory-Adversarial Continuum in Family Law Practice" (1994) 12(1) *Canadian Journal of Family Law* 11 at 30. A snowball sample (as opposed to a representative sample) was used in this study, and Hotel interviewed eighteen women and eighteen men.

28   These categories are borrowed from Jack and Jack, *Moral Vision and Professional Decisions*. Maximum role identification means that the lawyer identifies with the professional role to the point at which there is no obligation to anyone other than the client – the hired-gun

approach. Minimum role identification means that the lawyer's personal standards are maintained, despite the fact that it conflicts with professional standards. Jack and Jack suggest that the best approach to the practice of law is somewhere in between to achieve a "more ethically reflective form of practice." Discussed in Hotel and Brockman, "Legal Ethics in the Practice of Family Law" at 810.

29 Hotel and Brockman, "Legal Ethics in the Practice of Family Law" at 812-13.

30 The question asked was, "There are studies which theorize that there is a continuum in the way law is practised – from a very conciliatory approach to a very adversarial approach. How would you describe the approach you generally take to your practice, on a scale of one (a very conciliatory approach) to seven (a very adversarial approach)?" The respondents were given a scale to look at, and then were asked why they described themselves as they did. Those who rated themselves one to three were considered to be conciliatory, and those who rated themselves five to seven were considered to be adversarial in their approach.

31 The questions asked were, "In your experience, how would you describe most of the lawyers you encounter in your work, on a scale of one (very conciliatory approach) to seven (very adversarial approach)? Why do you describe them as a [number]?" "Would you describe the women and men lawyers you encounter in your work differently, on the scale of one (very conciliatory approach) to seven (very adversarial approach)? Why do you describe them as ... ?"

32 The respondents who rated themselves one to three on the scale (indicating an approach ranging from very conciliatory to conciliatory), who said they worked in the range from one to four (very conciliatory to conciliatory), or who said they started out as conciliatory were categorized as conciliatory.

33 The fact that many results in the criminal justice system are negotiated is nothing new. See for example, Richard V. Ericson and Patricia M. Baranek, *The Ordering of Justice: A Study of Accused Persons as Dependants in the Criminal Process* (Toronto: University of Toronto Press, 1983); Oonagh E. Fitzgerald, *The Guilty Plea and Summary Justice: A Guide for Practitioners* (Toronto: Carswell, 1990); and John F. Klein, *Let's Make a Deal: Negotiating Justice* (Lexington, MA: Lexington Books, 1976).

34 Hotel and Brockman, "The Conciliatory-Adversarial Continuum" at 30.

35 The numbers here are too small to suggest that women do not take the adversarial approach and that men do not take the conciliatory approach. It is much more likely that, as Hotel and Brockman found, women are more likely than men to use the conciliatory approach in family law, and that men are more likely than women to use the adversarial approach, but that women and men can be found at both extremes.

36 It is important to note that they were not asked this question, and it is therefore impossible to know how many would have used their clients' wishes to explain their approach had they been asked.

37 I am grateful to one of the reviewers of this manuscript for pointing this out.

38 The question asked was, "Do you think that the adversarial system is effective in resolving differences or disputes? [Why or why not?]."

39 This question was added to the interview schedule after the first two interviews, so two women were not asked this question.

40 This phrase is used by Herbert Hacob, "The Elusive Shadow of the Law" (1992) 26(3) *Law and Society Review* 565, and Austin Sarat and William L.F. Felstiner, *Divorce Lawyers and Their Clients: Power Meaning and the Legal Process* (New York: Oxford University Press, 1995) at 121.

41 For the most part, the respondents seemed to think of negotiations and mediation in the context of our adversarial system. They were not probed on this aspect of their responses.

42 While there is a growing literature on judicial bias, it was only a minor factor in this study. See Boyd et al., *Canadian Feminist Perspectives on Law,* and Jewel Amoah, *Critical Race Theory Bibliography* (Ottawa: Canadian Bar Association, 1999).

43 Duncan Kennedy, "Ideas: The Legal Mind" (Canadian Broadcasting Corporation Radio Broadcast, 29 October 1990) as quoted in Margaret Ann Wilkinson, Peter Mercer, and Terra Strong, "Mentor, Mercenary or Melding: An Empirical Inquiry into the Role of the Lawyer" (1996) 28(2) *Loyola University Chicago Law Journal* 373 at 375.

44 See, for example, Ericson and Baranek, *The Ordering of Justice;* Fitzgerald, *The Guilty Plea;* John F. Klein, *Let's Make a Deal: Negotiating Justice* (Lexington, MA: Lexington Books, 1976); Naffine, *Law and the Sexes.*
45 Wilkinson et al., "Mentor" at 409.

Chapter 6: The Balancing Act

1 Chris Kynaston, "The Everyday Exploitation of Women: Housework and the Patriarchal Mode of Production" (1996) 19(3) *Women's Studies International Forum* 221 at 221. See also Stevi Jackson, "Towards a Historical Sociology of Housework: A Materialist Feminist Analysis" (1992) 15(2) *Women's Studies International Forum* 153.
2 Kynaston, "The Everyday Exploitation of Women" at 222.
3 Ibid., at 228. See also Julie Seymour, "'No Time to Call my Own:' Women's Time as a Household Resource" (1992) 15(2) *Women's Studies International Forum* 187 who at 188 writes, "While some women may take on the responsibilities of being the household's main wage-earner they do not concomitantly adopt the ideology of the breadwinner and shed their domestic responsibilities."
4 Margrit Eichler, *Family Shifts: Families, Policies, and Gender Equality* (Toronto: Oxford University Press, 1997), Chapter 1.
5 Ibid., at 60, where she provides references to numerous studies.
6 Ibid., at 60, quoting K. Dempsey, "Exploitation in the Domestic Division of Labour: An Australian Case Study" (1988) 24(3) *Australian and New Zealand Journal of Sociology* 420 at 434.
7 Eichler, *Family Shifts*, at 61.
8 Ibid., at 75.
9 See Susan B. Boyd, "Challenging the Public/Private Divide: An Overview" in Susan B. Boyd, ed., *Challenging the Public/Private Divide: Feminism, Law and Public Policy* (Toronto: University of Toronto Press, 1997), and the numerous citations contained therein; Margaret Thornton, ed., *Public and Private: Feminists Legal Debates* (Melbourne: Oxford University Press, 1995).
10 Boyd, "Challenging the Public/Private Divide" at 6-7.
11 See Susan B. Boyd, "Can Law Challenge The Public/Private Divide? Women, Work and Family" (1996) 15 *Windsor Yearbook Access to Justice* 161; Kay, "Balancing Acts"; and Wilson, *Touchstones for Change.*
12 Joan Williams, *Unbending Gender: Why Family and Work Conflict and What to Do About It* (New York: Oxford University Press, 2000). Hilary Sommerlad and Peter Sanderson, *Gender, Choice, and Commitment: Women Solicitors in England and Wales and the Struggle for Equal Status* (Aldershot: Dartmouth Publishing, 1998), use Pierre Bourdieu's concept of juridical fields to examine how the ethos of the culture of law and the gendered expectations in the social field of domestic responsibilities affect women solicitors in England.
13 Kathleen Gerson, *Hard Choices: How Women Decide About Work, Career and Motherhood* (Berkeley: University of California Press, 1985) at 99.
14 My intention was to provide an inclusive category which would include gay and lesbian relationships, although I was aware of all of the difficulties of referring to gay and lesbian relationships, and some heterosexual relationships, as "similar" to marriage. All three self-identified lesbians said they were living in such a relationship and are included in my analysis as living in a "married or similar" relationship, and the one self-identified gay respondent said he was not in such a relationship. There were probably other lesbian and gay lawyers among my respondents and it is not possible to determine how they responded, as I did not ask my respondents their sexual orientation. Eichler, *Family Shifts* at 2, notes that twenty years ago the definition of spouse was not defined in the income tax guide, whereas in 1994 it took up "a good portion of a page"! She discusses the blurring of spousal relationships and definitions in Chapter 3.
15 The change in women's role during this period is discussed in Alison Prentice, Paula Bourne, Gail Cuthbert Brandt, Beth Light, Wendy Mitchinson, and Naomi Black, *Canadian Women: A History* (Toronto: Harcourt Brace Jovanovich, 1988), chapters 12 to 16. For example, married women were not allowed to work in the federal civil service following

the war until 1955 (at 306). In the 1950s and 1960s, wives of RCMP officers were expected to stay at home and play a supportive role (answering the phone, dealing with female prisoners, and so on). Working outside the home was frowned upon; personal communication with the spouse of a retired RCMP officer.

16 As a faculty member, I had to endure a Director's opinion that my male colleague should be paid more than I because he had an ex-wife and child to support, whereas I had a spouse who supposedly supported me. However, he did not rush to support a salary increase for me when my spouse left the paid workforce. Prentice et al. also talk about this attitude historically, but my experience was in the early 1990s.

17 Joan Williams, *Unbending Gender* at 2, cites a study in 1998 that found that two-thirds of people in the United States believe that it would be best for women to stay at home and take care of children and the family.

18 A study of managerial women found that 65% were childless at the age of forty. Another study showed that while 95% of male corporate leaders had children, only 39% of women at equivalent levels had children; Joan Williams, "Gender Wars: Selfless Women in the Republic of Choice" (1991) 66 *New York University Law Review* 1559 at 1597.

19 This is especially true if their spouses limit the hours they work in the paid workforce. A study in the United Kingdom found that a wife working forty hours per week resulted in a 15% reduction in the husband's income; D.H. Blackaby, P.S. Carlin, and P.D. Murphy. "What a Difference a Wife Makes: The Effect of Women's Hours of Work on Husbands' Hourly Earnings" (1998) 50(1) *Bulletin of Economic Research* 1. The study did not determine why this was so, but (at 2-3) they summarize other studies that suggest a number of possibilities:

1 Dual-earner husbands are less mobile and are therefore easier to exploit.
2 Employers may favour single-earner husbands because they conform to social expectations or they are perceived to be in greater need of more pay.
3 Dual-earner husbands are less productive because they spend more time on household production or single-earner husbands are more productive because of the contributions their wives make to their paid work.
4 Wives with higher-income husbands may choose to work fewer hours in the paid workforce.

20 Williams, "Gender Wars" at 1597-8. For some men (whether they be gay or otherwise uninterested in a heterosexual marriage), the pressure to marry may be as unpleasant as the pressure experienced by some women not to marry in order to have a successful career.

21 Joan Brockman, *Identifying the Barriers: A Survey of Members of the Law Society of British Columbia*. A Report Prepared for the Law Society of British Columbia's Subcommittee on Women in the Legal Profession; Appendix 2 in Kate Young (chair), *Women in the Legal Profession* (Vancouver: Law Society of British Columbia, 1991) at 13.

22 Brockman, "Bias in the Legal Profession" at 752.

23 Fiona M. Kay, Nancy Dautovich, and Chantelle Marlor, *Barriers and Opportunities Within Law: Women in a Changing Legal Profession: A Longitudinal Survey of Ontario Lawyers* (Toronto: Law Society of Upper Canada, 1996) at 96.

24 This includes the three self-identified lesbians living in relationships.

25 In retrospect, I realize that my question appears to assume that being in a married or similar relationship would be the preferred marital status of my respondents, when in fact I know that this might not be the case for some people, and it was not the case for some of my respondents.

26 For a discussion of men looking for someone to take care of them, see Arlie Russell Hochschild, *The Second Shift: Working Parents and the Revolution at Home* (New York: Avon, 1989) at 28.

27 Williams, "Gender Wars" at 1599.

28 Brockman, *Identifying the Barriers*, at 14-15.

29 Brockman, "Bias in the Legal Profession" at 754.

30 Kay et al., *Barriers and Opportunities* at 96. Kay studied lawyers called between 1975 and

1990, and included lawyers who were temporarily absent from law and who had departed from the practice of law. This likely explains why the difference is less pronounced in her study.

31 Two of the women said they had stepchildren only, so only 22% or fewer of the women had given birth to children. Respondents were not specifically asked whether their children were stepchildren, so there may have been additional women who had only stepchildren, but who did not volunteer this information. The issue of whether a person has children is becoming much more complex in a society in which divorce and remarriage is becoming more common. Reproductive technologies are making parenthood even more complicated; for a discussion, see Eichler, *Family Shifts,* Chapter 4.

32 According to Ellen Gee, childlessness is difficult to measure, and it can be either voluntary or involuntary. The rate has varied over the years, but is expected to be between 15% and 20% for young women; Ellen Gee, "The Life Course of Canadian Women: An Historical and Demographic Analysis" (1986) 18 *Social Indicators Research* 263.

33 Josephine E. Olson, Irene Hanson Frieze, and Ellen G. Detlefsen, "Having It All: Combining Work and Family in a Male and a Female Profession" (1990) 23(9-10) *Sex Roles* 515 at 531. However, the average age of the librarians was thirty-seven, compared with thirty-two for the MBAs, so the gap between the two groups could reduce over time.

34 In Canada in 1996, 69% of women over the age of fifteen, living in private households with children at home, were in the paid workforce (up from 68% in 1991 and 52% in 1981). For women who were married, living with their spouse and had children at home, the participation rate was 71% in 1996 (up from 70% in 1991 and 52% in 1981). If one limits this latter group to those with children under the age of six, the participation rate was 71% in 1996 (up from 69% in 1991 and 49% in 1981). Statistics Canada, *1996 Census;* Statistics Canada, *Labour Force Activity of Women by Presence of Children,* no. 93-325 (Ottawa: Statistics Canada, 1993) at 8 and 16, and Statistics Canada, *The Daily* (2 March 1993) at 4. Also see Mary Lou Coates, *Working and Family Issues: Beyond "Swapping and Mopping and Sharing and Caring"* (Queen's University: Industrial Relations Centre, 1991), for some of the problems that have arisen out of the changing nature of the workforce and the family structure.

35 Judith L. MacBride-King, *Work and Family: Employment Challenge of the '90s* (Ottawa: Conference Board of Canada, 1990). In addition, women spent an average of 25.3 hours per month, compared with 18.7 hours per month by men, on elder care and other relatives.

36 Wallace Clement and John Myles, *Relations of Ruling: Class and Gender in Postindustrial Societies* (Kingston: McGill-Queen's University Press, 1994) at 164.

37 Statistics Canada, "1996 Census: Labour Force Activity, Occupation and Industry, Place of Work, Mode of Transportation and Unpaid Work" (17 March 1998) *The Daily* at 27. The Report uses the words "wife" and "husband," by which they appear to mean "spouse," including common law spouses, of the opposite sex (at 26). The Report can be found at <www.statcan.ca/Daily>.

38 See Brockman, "Gender Bias in the Legal Profession" at 126-7 (British Columbia), and Brockman, "Bias in the Legal Profession" at 761 (Alberta).

39 Kay et al., *Barriers and Opportunities* at 97-8. One of the reasons the amount of time for women in Ontario is so much higher than that in British Columbia and Alberta is that I used the median number of hours, and Kay used the mean. The mean can be much larger than the median when some respondents provide large outlying numbers – 1.6% of Kay's women respondents reported spending 168 hours per week on child care.

40 Jean McKenzie Leiper, "Women Lawyers and Their Working Arrangements: Time Crunch, Stress and Career Paths" (1998) 13(2) *Canadian Journal of Law and Society* 117 at 131.

41 This was suggested by Mossman, "Gender Bias" at 159.

42 This is a rather abbreviated version of this model.

43 Mary Jane Mossman, "Lawyers and Family Life: New Directions for the 1990s (Part I)" (1994) 11(1) *Feminist Legal Studies* 61 at 73. Also see Mary Jane Mossman, "Lawyers and Family Life: New Directions for the 1990s: Part II, The Search for Solutions" (1994) 11(2) *Feminist Legal Studies* 159.

44 Margaret Thornton, *Dissonance and Distrust: Women in the Legal Profession* (Melbourne: Oxford University Press, 1996), at 237-8.
45 Williams, *Unbending Gender* at 143.
46 Needless to say, this is a difficult concept to measure, and the variation in the results may be because of their different methodologies; see Julie E. Press and Eleanor Townsley, "Wives' and Husbands' Housework Reporting: Gender, Class, and Social Desirability" (1998) 12(2) *Gender and Society* 188. John P. Robinson and Melissa A. Milkie, "Back to the Basics: Trends in and Role Determinants of Women's Attitudes Toward Housework" (1998) 60(1) *Journal of Marriage and the Family* 205 at 206, cite studies that found women who work full time in the paid labour force do more than 60% of the housework. Scott J. South and Glenna Spitze, "Housework in Marital and Nonmarital Households" (1994) 59 *American Sociological Review* 327 at 332 cites studies showing that women do more than 70% of the housework, even when they are in the paid workforce. Chloe E. Bird, "Gender, Household Labor, and Psychological Distress: The Impact of the Amount and Division of Housework" (1999) 40(1) *Journal of Health and Social Behavior* 32 at 41-2, found that married men in the workforce reported doing 36.7% of the housework and married women in the workforce reported doing more than 70%. The authors (at 43) suggest that since men do less of the housework, they might underestimate the amount that needs to be done, and therefore overestimate the amount they do. Press, "Wives" at 212, found that women overreported by 12.8 hours and men overreported by 5.8 hours; however, the relative over-report was only 68% for women, but 149% by men. In addition, "traditional attitudes reduce husbands' reporting gap while they increase wives'" (at 212).
47 Janeen Baxter, "Gender Equality and Participation in Housework: A Cross-National Perspective" (1997) 28(3) *Journal of Comparative Family Studies* 220 at 224, stating that women still do 60% of the work in this situation.
48 Statistics Canada, "1996 Census: Labour Force Activity, Occupation and Industry, Place of Work, Mode of Transportation and Unpaid Work" (17 March 1998) *The Daily* at 26.
49 Rosalind C. Barnett and Yu-Chu Shen, "Gender, High- and Low-Schedule-Control Housework Tasks, and Psychological Distress: A Study of Dual-Earner Couples" (1997) 18(4) *Journal of Family Issues* 403 at 422. The authors suggest that household tasks be divided into high- and low-schedule control, rather than male/female. Although they recognize that there is considerable overlap, women are more likely to be allocated the low-schedule-control tasks. Wallace Clement and John Myles, *Relations of Ruling: Class and Gender in Postindustrial Societies* (Kingston: McGill-Queen's University Press, 1994) at 176, write that women, whose schedules are confined by the external pressures of children, housework and spouses, "experience the labour force differently from men."
50 Baxter, "Gender Equality" at 222.
51 This includes at least three who were in a lesbian relationship, and there is some indication that domestic responsibilities in same-sex relationships may be quite different: Sarah Oerton, "'Queer Housewives?': Some Problems in Theorising the Division of Domestic Labour in Lesbian and Gay Households" (1997) 20(3) *Women's Studies International Forum* 421.
52 Kynaston, "The Everyday Exploitation of Women" at 232.
53 Bird, "Gender, Household Labor"; Catherine E. Ross and Chloe E. Bird, "Sex Stratification and Health Lifestyles: Consequences for Men's and Women's Perceived Health" (1994) 35 *Journal of Health and Social Behavior* 161.
54 Bird, "Gender" at 42.
55 Ibid., 43.
56 Professor Mary Jane Mossman identifies three of these issues: 1) the nature and organization of legal work, 2) the impact of gendered societal expectations for women and men, and 3) the scope of "familial" responsibilities within the legal profession; Mary Jane Mossman, "Women and Men in the Legal Profession: New Directions" in *Gender Equality: A Challenge for the Legal Profession* (Ottawa: Canadian Bar Association, 1992). See also Mary Jane Mossman, "Gender Bias and the Legal Profession: Challenges and Choices" in Joan Brockman and Dorothy E. Chunn, *Investigating Gender Bias: Law, Courts and the Legal Profession* (Toronto: Thompson Educational Publishing, 1993).

57   Mossman, "Lawyers and Family Life (Part I)" at 61.
58   Kay et al., 1996 at 55.
59   Joan Brockman, "Exclusionary Tactics: The History of Women and Minorities in the Legal Profession in British Columbia" in Hamar Foster and John P.S. McLaren, ed., *Essays in the History of Canadian Law, Volume VI, British Columbia and the Yukon.* (Toronto: Osgoode Society, 1995) 508 at 535. For a similar discussion of women lawyers in the United States, see Virginia G. Drachman, *Sisters in Law: Women Lawyers in Modern American History* (Cambridge, MA: Harvard University Press, 1998).
60   Brockman, "Exclusionary Tactics" at 535. Unfortunately, my study did not examine another aspect of women's work, the emotional labour expected of women in the paid workforce. See Jennifer L. Pierce, *Gender Trials: Emotional Lives in Contemporary Law Firms* (Berkeley: University of California Press, 1995). Although she was comparing the working lives of lawyers and paralegals, her ethnographic study illustrates how both social structure and individual agency work to recreate hierarchy and inequality in the paid workforce.

Chapter 7: Breaking the Mould

1   The remaining respondents were in the mid-range, ambivalent, or no longer in practice.
2   The attrition rates, as of April 1993 when the sample was drawn, were as follows:

Year of call	Women	Men
1986	35%	23%
1987	40%	35%
1988	30%	22%
1989	30%	23%
1990	24%	25%

Note: Calculated from information supplied to the author by the Law Society of British Columbia.

3   I am sensitive to Tancred's critique in "Outsiders/Insiders" of definitions which exclude women's experiences, and under her analysis, many of these women and men have not left the profession.
4   For example, see Bryan Mahoney, "Changing Times – Workplace Options" (October-November 1992) *Newsletter* 5; "Career Options: Breaking Away in the 1990's," (July 1992) 27 *Bencher's Advisory* 1, describes a seminar sponsored by the Law Society of Alberta and the Legal Education Society of Alberta. On 17 January 2000, the British Columbia Branch of the Canadian Bar Association hosted a Joint Meeting of Gender Issues and Women Rainmakers Sections, and one of the topics was "Lawyers Who Have Left the Practice to Pursue Alternative Careers" (fax received by author).
5   A survey of lawyers by Joan Brewster for the Addiction Research Foundation of Ontario found that almost one-third were "problem drinkers" (defined as one of the following happening at least once a month: calling in sick, showing up late for work, drinking during work, or facing criticism by family and friends about their drinking), 20% were frequent drinkers (using alcohol at least twenty days each month), 8% had used marijuana in the last year, and 2% were regular users of narcotics. See Kirk LaPointe, "Study Cites Drugs, Liquor use among MDs, Lawyers" (7 June 1993) *Vancouver Sun* A2. Also see Paul McLauglin, "Forensic Accounting: Tales of Greed and Cunning" (April 1993) *National* 20 at 22. Janice Mucalov, "The Stress Epidemic: Succumbing to the Pressures of Practice in the 90s" (May 1993) *Canadian Lawyer* 18; Gerry Bellett, "Stressed for Success: The High-Octane Life of Lawyers" *Vancouver Sun* (10 October 1992) B1.
6   This should not be taken to assume that there is no discrimination in the public sector. See The Honourable Bertha Wilson (chair), *Touchstones for Change: Equality, Diversity, and*

Accountability (Ottawa: Canadian Bar Association, August 1993), Chapter 6. See also The Report of the Task Force on Barriers to Women in the Public Service, *Beneath the Veneer* (Ottawa: Canadian Government Publishing Centre, 1990).

7 Margaret Thornton, *Dissonance and Distrust: Women in the Legal Profession* (Melbourne: Oxford University Press, 1996) at 162, identifies a similar trend in Australia.

8 Ken MacQueen, "Men Are From Mars, Women Are From Typing Pools" (22 March 1996) *Vancouver Sun* A19; *Looking to the Future: Challenging the Culture and Attitudinal Barriers to Women in the Public Service* (Ottawa: Planning and Communications Directorate, Treasury Board of Canada, 1995). The Report can be found at <www.tbs-sct.gc.ca/pubs>.

9 This was a concern expressed by women in the *Looking to the Future* Report. Also see Thornton, *Dissonance and Distrust*, at 162.

10 *Looking to the Future* Report, Introduction.

11 Susan Bisom-Rapp, "Scripting Reality in the Legal Workplace: Women Lawyers, Litigation Prevention Measures, and the Limits of Anti-Discrimination Law" (1996) 6(1) *Columbia Journal of Gender and Law* 323 at 329.

12 Terri Apter, *Professional Progress: Why Women Still Don't Have Wives*, 2nd ed. (Hampshire: MacMillan Press, 1993) at 244.

13 Kay, "Flight from Law" at 327.

14 Thornton, *Dissonance and Distrust* at 271.

15 Ibid., at 3, 47, and 262.

16 Deborah L. Rhode, "Gender and Professional Roles" (1994) 63 *Fordham Law Review* 39 at 64.

17 See Joan Brockman, "The Use of Self-Regulation to Curb Discrimination and Sexual Harassment in the Legal Profession" (1997) 35(2) *Osgoode Hall Law Journal* 209.

18 Wilson, *Touchstones* at 268-71 discusses six points of resistance:

1 The "progress is being made" myth
2 Economics (economic insecurity may deter people from raising discrimination issues and firms may use economics as an excuse not to take action)
3 A misunderstanding of equality and a belief that there is reverse discrimination
4 A denial of bias
5 Perceptions of "women's nature"
6 Backlash.

According to Sheila McIntyre's assessment of the climate in the early 1990s, I conducted my interviews following a heightened backlash against equality across university and colleges campuses in Canada and the United States; Sheila McIntyre, "Backlash Against Equality: The Tyranny of the 'Politically Correct'" (1993) 38(1) *McGill Law Journal* 1. While there did appear to be some reflected in a small minority of the interviews I conducted, it did not appear widespread. For further information on the topic of backlash, see Mary Hawkesworth, "Analyzing Backlash: Feminist Standpoint Theory As Analytical Tool" (1999) 22(2) *Women's Studies International Forum* 135. The issue of backlash is presently being studied under a SSHRC grant "Feminism, Law and Social Change in Canada 1967-1997: Reaction and Resistance." Principal Investigator: Dorothy E. Chunn; Co-Investigators: Susan Boyd, Hester Lessard, Robert Menzies, Claire Young. See Hester Lessard, "Farce or Tragedy? Judicial Backlash and Justice McClung" (1999) 10(3) *Constitutional Forum* 65; Susan B. Boyd, "Can Child Custody Law Move Beyond the Politics of Gender?" (2000) 49 *University of New Brunswick Law Journal* 157.

19 Wilson, *Touchstones* at 271.

20 Mary Jane Mossman, "Gender Equality Education and the Legal Profession" (2000) 12 *Supreme Court Law Review* 187.

21 High income men are more likely to have stay-at-home wives to support their careers, even though these wives are more highly educated than those of lower income males. One study in the United States found that "wives of high-income husbands [were] half as likely to work outside the home than wives of median income men"; Williams, "Gender Wars," at 1602-3.

22   Virginia G. Drachman, "'My Partner' in Law and Life: Marriage in the Lives of Women Lawyers in Late 19th- and Early 20th-Century America" (1989) 14 *Law and Social Inquiry* 221; Virginia G. Drachman, *Women Lawyers and the Origins of Professional Identity in America: The Letters of the Equity Club, 1887-1890* (Ann Arbor: University of Michigan Press, 1993).

23   Joan Brockman, "Exclusionary Tactics: The History of Women and Minorities in the Legal Profession in British Columbia" in Hamar Foster and John P.S. McLaren, ed., *Essays in the History of Canadian Law, Volume VI, British Columbia and the Yukon.* (Toronto: Osgoode Society, 1995) 508 at 530.

24   "Women Gaining Confidence at Work by Retaining Identity" (14 October 1997) *Vancouver Sun* D2, suggests that "women are rejecting the role of the mythical superwoman, who runs ragged shouldering the burdens of home and work."

25   This was also found to be the case in the United States; see Epstein, *Women in Law* at 431.

26   Ruth H. Bloch, "The Gendered Meanings of Virtue in Revolutionary America" (1987) 13 *Signs* 37, as summarized by Joan Williams, "Gender Wars: Selfless Women in the Republic of Choice" (1991) 66 *New York University Law Review* 1559 at 1565.

27   Williams, "Gender Wars" at 1567.

28   Ibid., at 1568.

29   Ibid., at 1598.

30   Ibid., at 1564.

31   Ibid., at 1562.

32   Ibid., at 1607.

33   Ibid., at 1610.

34   Ibid., at 1614-15.

35   Williams, *Unbending Gender* at 244-5.

36   Katharine K. Baker, "Power, Gender and Juggling the Work/Family Conflict." A review of *Unbending Gender: Why Family and Work Conflict and What to Do about It.* By Joan Williams. Oxford University Press. Reviewed March 2000. At *Jurist* <http://jurist.law.pitt.edu/lawbooks/revmar00.htm#Baker>. Also see Williams's response, "Are Men Pigs?" at the same Web site.

37   Dianne E. Looker and Victor Thiessen, "Images of Work: Women's Work, Men's Work, Housework" (1999) 24(2) *Canadian Journal of Sociology* 225. Also see Jane Gaskell, "The Reproduction of Family Life: Perspectives of Male and Female Adolescents" (1983) 4(1) *British Journal of Sociology of Education* 19 for a discussion of how the ideology of domesticity affects both girls and boys. She concludes that the "waning of domestic ideology among the girls is not enough to stop them from planning their lives around it."

38   Jean L. Potuchek set out to examine the role of breadwinning in dual-earner marriages after her college students conducted a survey of 100 of their classmates and reported the results of the question, "Assuming that you earn a sufficient income, would you expect your spouse to work?" Approximately two-thirds of the men thought that the decision of whether their wives would work would be up to their wives, whereas, more than 80% of the women expected their husbands to work, even though they were making sufficient income to support them; Jean L. Potuchek, *Who Supports the Family? Gender and Breadwinning in Dual-Earning Marriages* (Stanford, CA: Stanford University Press, 1997).

39   Arlie Russell Hochschild, *The Second Shift: Working Parents and the Revolution at Home* (New York: Avon, 1989). Also see Susan Boyd, "A Review of *The Second Shift: Working Parents and the Revolution at Home* by Arlie Hochschild, with Anne Machung" (1990) 4 *Canadian Journal of Women and the Law* 325.

40   Arlie Russell Hochschild, *The Time Bind: When Work Becomes Home and Home Becomes Work* (New York: Metropolitan Books, 1997).

41   Williams, "Gender Wars," at 1599.

42   Ibid., at 1600.

43   Hochschild, *The Time Bind,* at 22.

44   Ibid., at 25.

45   Ibid., at 28-31.

46 Ibid., at 38-40.

47 Summarized ibid., at 40.

48 Ibid., at 41, quoting Grace Baruch, Lois Biener, and Rosalind Barnett, "Women and Gender in Research on Work and Family Stress" (1987) 42 *American Psychologist* 130. One of the respondents in their study commented, "A job is to a woman as a wife is to a man."

49 Hochschild, *The Time Bind,* at 45.

50 Ibid., at 45.

51 Ibid., at 51.

52 Ibid. A "Taylorized home" refers to Frederick W. Taylor, who, in the 1890s, applied engineering precision and scientific management to the workplace to increase efficiency. Here Hochschild is extending this approach to the home.

53 Randy Ray, "Quality of Life: A Vancouver Law Firm Reverses the Trend to Longer Hours, More Money and Less Leisure" (May 1990) National 1.

54 Deborah L. Rhode, "Gender and Professional Roles" (1994) 63 *Fordham Law Review* 39 at 63.

55 Barbara A. Gutek, "Asymmetric Changes in Men's and Women's Roles" in Bonita C. Long and Shraon E. Kahn, eds., *Women, Work, and Coping* (Kingston: McGill-Queen's University Press, 1993) at 26.

56 Prentice et al., *Canadian Women* at 139-41 and 203-7 about the influx of Canadian women into the labour force to work on farms and factories in the First World War, and 295 for women's work during the Second World War. In discussing pre-industrial life, Kynaston, "The Everyday Exploitation of Women" at 227, suggests that "women may be called upon to do 'men's' work when necessary, but only women will ever do 'women's' work."

57 Kathryn Abrams, "Gender Discrimination and the Transformation of Workplace Norms" (1989) 42 *Vanderbilt Law Review* 1183 at 1223, quoting A. Kessler-Harris, *Women Have Always Worked* at 141-3.

58 Prentice et al., at 298-9. The nurseries admitted children between the ages of two and six years. Homecare was arranged for younger children and after-school care for school children.

59 Abrams, "Gender Discrimination" at 1223, summarizing the work of D. Hayden, *Redesigning the American Dream: The Future of Housing, Work, and Family Life* (1984).

60 Prentice et al., at 303-4. In 1944, a Gallup poll found that 75% of the women and 68% of the men thought that men should be given priority in employment following the war.

61 Ibid., at 305.

62 Edward Alden, "Women Hardest Hit by Job Losses" (6 March 1997) *Vancouver Sun* at A8, citing a report by the Canadian Labour Congress, *Women's Work: A Report.*

63 Cynthia Fuchs Epstein, "Glass Ceilings and Open Doors: Women's Advancement in the Legal Profession" (1995) 64 *Fordham Law Review* 291.

64 Canadian Mental Health Association, *Work and Well-Being: The Changing Realities of Employment* (Ottawa: Canadian Mental Health Association, 1984) at 17.

65 Robert Jin, Chandrakant Shah, and Tomislav Svoboda, "The Impact of Unemployment on Health: A Review of the Evidence" (1997) 18(3) *Journal of Public Health Policy* 275 at 295, report that "evidence strongly supports an association between unemployment and a greater risk of morbidity (physical or mental illness or use of health care services) care services ... and a greater rate of mortality." Also discussed in Eric Beauchesne, "Unemployment Can Kill, Doctors Discover" (9 September 1995) *Vancouver Sun* 12. Ernie J. Zelinski, *The Joy of Not Working* (Edmonton: Visions International Publishing, 1991) at 54, writes "Workaholism is a serious disease. If not treated in time, workaholism can result in mental and physical health problems." According to Barbara Killinger, author of *Workaholics: The Respectable Addicts,* workaholics are "emotional cripples."

66 Jeremy Rifkin, *The End of Work: The Decline of the Global Labor Market Force and the Dawn of the Post-Market Era* (New York: G.P. Putman's Sons, 1995) at 25-9.

67 "Cut Working Hours BC Legion Urges" (22 August 1933) *Victoria Daily Times* at 2; "Labour Urges Six-Hour Day for BC" (14 February 1934) *Vancouver Sun* at 24; "Six-hour Day Rejected by BC Legislature" (20 March 1935) *Vancouver Sun* at 1; "30-Hr. Week for BC:

Labor Demands Presented at Victoria" (4 November 1936) *Vancouver Sun* at 1; "Labor Asking 30-Hour Week: Canadian Congress Will Seek Schedule of Five Six-Hour Days" (14 September 1937) *Victoria Daily Times* at 1-2.

68 Marc LaPlante, "Leisure in Canada by 1980" in *Leisure in Canada,* The Proceedings of the Montmorency Conference on Leisure, 2-6 September 1969 (Ottawa: Fitness and Amateur Sport Directorate, Department of National Health and Welfare, 1969) at 31.

69 S.M.A. Hameed, "Economic and Institutional Determinants of the Average Work-week in Canada" in S.M.A. Hameed and D. Cullen, eds., *Work and Leisure in Canada* (Edmonton: University of Alberta Faculty of Business Administration and Commerce, 1971) at 18.

70 Juliet Schor, *The Overworked American: The Unexpected Decline of Leisure* (New York: Basic Books, 1991) at 4.

71 Margaret Munro, "Life in 2030" (1 May 1993) *Vancouver Sun* at B1.

72 *betterTIMES* (February 2000) at 9. The article concludes that the longer hours and higher unemployment figures (compared with many European countries that have reduced the workweek), is a "bad deal for working people, an inefficient use of labour, and an extremely destructive force that is eroding the cohesion of families and communities."

73 See the Web sites of 32HOURS: Action for Full Employment <www.web.net/32hours>, Time Work Web – the official Web site of the Shorter Work Time Network of Canada www.vcn.bc.ca/timework, and the Shorter Work-Time Group and the Society for the Reduction of Human Labor (United States) <www.swt.org>. Links to other Web sites show that many countries in Europe have moved or are moving to a thirty-five-hour workweek with a corresponding reduction in the unemployment rate.

74 Bruce O'Hara, *Working Harder Isn't Working: How We Can Save the Environment, the Economy and our Sanity by Working Less and Enjoying Life More* (Vancouver: New Star Books, 1993). See also Bruce O'Hara, *Put Work in its Place: How to Redesign Your Job to Fit Your Life* (Vancouver: New Star Books, 1994).

75 Depending on how you count the unemployed and underemployed, O'Hara is of the view that as many as 30% of Canadians are unemployed or underemployed.

76 Statistics Canada, "General Social Survey: Time Use" (9 November 1999) *The Daily.* About one-third of women and men between the ages of 25 and 44 reported that they were workaholics, and a little more than half felt that they did not have sufficient time for their family or friends.

77 Statistics Canada, "Longer Working Hours and Health" (16 November 1999) *The Daily.* The study examined women and men who had increased their standard workweek from thirty-five to forty hours per week to forty-one hours or more, and controlled for age, education, occupation, and work stress.

78 Leanne Lehmkuhl, "Health Effects of Long Work-weeks." August 1999. At <www.web.ca/ ~freetime/Health%20Effects%20v2.htm>.

79 Jenny Lee, "Dealing With Stress Now an Investment" (5 April 1999) *Vancouver Sun* at C1.

80 O'Hara, *Working Harder* at 1-2.

81 Ibid., at 97, quoting Samuel Gompers from B.K. Hunnicutt, *Work Without End* (Philadelphia: Temple University Press, 1988).

82 Nancy Dehart, "Reality Tramples Life of Leisure Predicted by Past Futurists" (14 April 1997) *Vancouver Sun* at A1, A10.

83 Noah M. Meltz, Frank Reid, and Gerald S. Swartz, *Sharing the Work: An Analysis of the Issues in Worksharing and Jobsharing* (Toronto: University of Toronto Press, 1981) at 67.

84 Ibid., at 72.

85 Nineteenth-century doggerel quoted in Benjamin Kline Hunnicutt, *Working Without End: Abandoning Shorter Hours for the Right to Work* (Philadelphia: Temple University Press, 1988) at 7.

86 Juliet Schor, author of *The Overworked American: The Unexpected Decline of Leisure* (New York: Basic Books, 1991) at 1.

87 Rifkin, *The End of Work,* especially Chapter 15.

88 Jim Beatty, "30-hour Work-week is a Long Way Away, Premier Says" (3 March 1997) *Vancouver Sun* A5.

89 Williams, "Gender Wars" at 1619.

90 Alanna Mitchell, Karen Unland, and Chad Skelton, "Canadians Pay for Busy Lives" (19 July 1997) *Vancouver Sun* A1.

91 Mary Jane Mossman, "Lawyers and Family Life: New Directions for the 1990s: Part II, The Search for Solutions" (1994) 11(2) *Feminist Legal Studies* 159 at 162. Unfortunately, I didn't ask my respondents whether they were working full time or part time.

92 Diana Pitt, "When Lawyers Need Help: A Model Wellness Program Is Being Developed to Help Lawyers Deal with Substance Abuse, Stress and Depression" (16 September 1994) *Lawyers' Weekly* 1, 36 at 36.

93 Ann Macaulay, "Study Finds 1 in 3 Lawyers are Problem Drinkers" (18 June 1993) *Lawyers' Weekly* 4.

94 Rhode, "Gender" at 63.

95 Pitt, "When Lawyers Need Help" at 1.

96 Long working hours create poor health and are associated with poor lifestyles that lead to health problems: smoking, improper diet, and lack of exercise; Sparks, Kate, Cary Cooper, and Arie Shirom. "The Effects of Hours of Work on Health: A Meta-Analytic Review" (1997) 70 *Journal of Occupational and Organizational Psychology* 391 at 391.

97 "New Alternative to Burnout: Get Fired, Find New Challenge" (22 November 1994) *Vancouver Sun* at D9.

98 Carolyn Susman, "Lunch at the Desk Now Common, Survey Says" (12 April 1999) *Vancouver Sun* B12.

99 Monique Conrod, "Unemployment and Under-employment: The Harsh Reality Facing New Lawyers" (16 September 1994) *Lawyers' Weekly* 5, 12.

100 Stephen Bindman, "Study to Look at Rising Crisis Facing Lawyers Seeking Work" (26 August 1996) *Vancouver Sun* B2. This was a report from the Canadian Bar Association convention. Another report from the convention had Justice Minister Allen Rock suggesting that the *Canadian Human Rights Act* might be amended so that the Commission could launch investigations of "systemic discrimination" on its own. There was no connection made between "too many" lawyers and "systemic discrimination." To be fair, most lawyers would be governed by provincial, rather than federal, human rights legislation.

101 See the first note at the beginning of this chapter.

102 Scott J. South and Glenna Spitze, "Housework in Marital and Nonmarital Household" (1994) 59 *American Sociological Review* 327 at 332 referring to the work of Heidi Hartmann, "The Family as the Locus of Gender, Class, and Political Struggle: The Example of Housework" (1981) 6 *Signs* 366.

103 South and Spitze, "Housework" at 329.

104 Ibid., at 328-9.

105 Ibid., at 329.

106 Kynaston, "The Everyday Exploitation of Women" at 229.

107 Ibid., at 228.

108 In the Netherlands, reduced workweek laws which prohibit discrimination in benefits and opportunities between part-time and full-time workers, and campaigns for men to consider part-time work with slogans like, "Good morning, I'm your father," has made it more fashionable for men to spend more time with their children. Unfortunately, they have not found an equally catchy slogan to get men to do their share of the unpaid housework, and women continue to be mainly responsible for it; Anders Hayden, *Sharing the Work, Sparing the Planet: Work Time, Consumption and Ecology* (Between the Lines, 1999). A survey of 500 French workers asked them what they would devote their extra time to in face of new thirty-five-hour legislation – 71% of the men and 66% of the women would spend more time with their children and family; only 29% of the men, but 62% of the women, would spend more time on daily tasks, and 48% of the men and only 29% of the women would spend more time on sports, cultural or artistic activities. Not surprisingly, 48% of the women and 24% of the men would rest more; cited in *betterTIMES* (February 2000) at 5.

109 Oriel Sullivan, "The Division of Housework Among 'Remarried' Couples" (1997) 18(2) *Journal of Family Issues* 205 at 219.

110 Epstein et al., "Glass Ceilings" as cited in Bisom-Rapp, "Scripting Reality" at 336.

111 Ibid., as cited in Bisom-Rapp, "Scripting Reality" at 337.
112 Bruce Feldthusen, "The Gender Wars: Where the Boys Are" (1990) 4 *Canadian Journal of Women and the Law* 66.
113 Rhode, "Gender" at 65.
114 Thornton, *Dissonance and Distrust* at 24.
115 Carole Pateman, *The Sexual Contract* (Oxford: Polity Press, 1988).
116 Williams, *Unbending Gender* at 271.
117 Ibid. For a more detailed analysis of how this applies to lawyers, see Hilary Sommerlad and Peter Sanderson, *Gender, Choice and Comitment: Women Solicitors in England and Wales and the Struggle for Equal Status* (Aldershot: Dartmouth Publishing, 1998).
118 Susan B. Boyd, "Can Law Challenge The Public/Private Divide? Women, Work and Family" (1996) 15 *Windsor Yearbook Access to Justice* 161 at 184. Privatization is "ultimately doomed" because of the "overtaxed women in the private sphere." See Eichler, *Family Shifts* for a social responsibility model of the family.
119 Mona Harrington, *Care and Equality: Inventing a New Family Politics* (New York: Alfred A. Knopf, 1999) at 41 and Chapter 3. For years we have had government paying for child care from grades one, and then kindergarten, to grade twelve. It would be no great leap for early child-care workers to also join the paid public service.

Bibliography

Abell, Jennie. "Women, Violence, and the Criminal Law: 'It's the Fundamentals of Being a Lawyer that Are at Stake Here'" (1992) 17 *Queen's Law Journal* 147.

Abrams, Kathryn. "Gender Discrimination and the Transformation of Workplace Norms" (1989) 42 *Vanderbilt Law Review* 1183.

Adam, Barry D. "Stigma and Employability: Discrimination by Sex and Sexual Orientation in the Ontario Legal Profession" (1981) 18(2) *Canadian Review of Sociology and Anthropology* 216.

–, and Douglas E. Baer. "The Social Mobility of Women and Men in the Ontario Legal Profession" (1984) 21(1) *Canadian Review of Sociology and Anthropology* 21.

–, and Kathleen A. Lahey. "Professional Opportunities: A Survey of the Ontario Legal Profession" (1981) 59 *Canadian Bar Review* 674.

Alden, Edward. "Women Hardest Hit by Job Losses" (6 March 1997) *Vancouver Sun* A8.

Alvi, Tariq, Rose Boyko, Lilian Ma, Wade MacLauchlan, Trish Monture, Yvonne Peters, and Joanne St. Lewis. *Equality in Legal Education: Sharing a Vision, Creating the Pathways* (Special Advisory Committee to the Canadian Association of Law Teachers 1992). Reprinted in (1992) 17 *Queen's Law Journal* 174.

Amoah, Jewel. *Critical Race Theory Bibliography* (Ottawa: Canadian Bar Association, 1999).

Anderson, Stanley. "The Transition From Inquisitorial to Adversarial Criminal Procedure in Denmark" (1992) 64 *Scandinavian Studies* 1.

Apter, Terri. *Professional Progress: Why Women Still Don't Have Wives*, 2nd ed. (Hampshire: MacMillan Press, 1993).

Arron, Deborah. "Running From the Law" (February 1990) *Canadian Lawyer* 19.

Arthurs, Harry A. (chair). *Law and Learning: Report to the Social Sciences and Humanities Research Council of Canada by the Consultative Group on Research and Education in Law* (Ottawa: Social Sciences and Humanities Research Council of Canada, 1983).

Arthurs, H.W., R. Weisman, and F.H. Zemans. "The Canadian Legal Profession" (1987) 3 *American Bar Foundation Research Journal* 447.

Arthurs, H.W., J. Willms, and L. Taman, "The Toronto Legal Profession: An Exploratory Survey" (1971) 21 *University of Toronto Law Journal* 498.

Aylward, Carol. "Adding Colour: A Critique of 'An Essay on Institutional Responsibility: The Indigenous Blacks and Micmac Programme at Dalhousie Law School'" (1995) 8(2) *Canadian Journal of Women and the Law* 470.

Backhouse, Constance. "Clara Brett Martin: Canadian Heroine or Not?" (1992) 5(2) *Canadian Journal of Women and the Law* 263.

–. "Gretta Wong Grant: Canada's First Chinese-Canadian Female Lawyer" (1996) 15 *Windsor Yearbook of Access to Justice* 3.

–. "'To Open the Way for Others of my Sex': Clara Brett Martin's Career as Canada's First Woman Lawyer" (1985) 1(1) *Canadian Journal of Women and the Law* 1.

–. "Racial Segregation in Canadian Legal History: Viola Desmond's Challenge, Nova Scotia, 1946" (1994) 17(2) *Dalhousie Law Journal* 299.

–, and L. Cohen. *The Secret Oppression: Sexual Harassment of Working Women* (Toronto: Macmillan, 1978).

Baines, Beverley. "Women and the Law" in Sandra Burt, Lorraine Code, and Lindsay Dorney, eds., *Changing Patterns: Women in Canada* (Toronto: McClelland and Stewart, 1988) 157.

Baker, Katharine K. "Power, Gender and Juggling the Work/Family Conflict." A review of *Unbending Gender: Why Family and Work Conflict and What to Do about It*. By Joan Williams. Oxford University Press. Reviewed March 2000. At *Jurist* <http:// jurist.law.pitt.edu/lawbooks/revmar00.htm#Baker>.

Bankier, Jennifer K. "Women and the Law School: Problems and Potential" (1974) 22(5) *Chitty's Law Journal* 171.

Barnett, Rosalind C., and Yu-Chu Shen, "Gender, High- and Low-Schedule-Control Housework Tasks, and Psychological Distress: A Study of Dual-Earner Couples" (1997) 18(4) *Journal of Family Issues* 403.

Baxter, Janeen. "Gender Equality and Participation in Housework: A Cross-National Perspective" (1997) 28(3) *Journal of Comparative Family Studies* 220.

Beatty, Jim. "30-hour Work-week is a Long Way Away, Premier Says" (3 March 1997) *Vancouver Sun* A5.

Beauchesne, Eric. "Unemployment Can Kill, Doctors Discover" (9 September 1995) *Vancouver Sun* 12.

Bellett, Gerry. "Stressed for Success: The High-Octane Life of Lawyers" (10 October 1992) *Vancouver Sun* B1.

Belliotti, Raymond A. "Our Adversary System: In Search of a Foundation" (1988) 1 *Canadian Journal of Law and Jurisprudence* 19.

Benson, D.J., and G.E. Thompson. "Sexual Harassment on a University Campus: The Confluence of Authority Relations, Sexual Interest and Gender Stratification" (1982) 29 *Social Problems* 236.

Betcherman, Lita-Rose. "Clara Brett Martin's Anti-Semitism" (1992) 5(2) *Canadian Journal of Women and the Law* 280.

Bickenbach, Jerome E. "The Redemption of the Moral Mandate of the Profession of Law" (1996) 9(1) *Canadian Journal of Law and Jurisprudence* 51.

Bindman, Stephen. "Study to Look at Rising Crisis Facing Lawyers Seeking Work" (26 August 1996) *Vancouver Sun* B2.

Bird, Chloe E. "Gender, Household Labor, and Psychological Distress: The Impact of the Amount and Division of Housework." (1999) 40(1) *Journal of Health and Social Behavior* 32.

Bisom-Rapp, Susan. "Scripting Reality in the Legal Workplace: Women Lawyers, Litigation Prevention Measures, and the Limits of Ant-Discrimination Law" (1996) 6(1) *Columbia Journal of Gender and Law* 323.

Blackaby, D.H., P.S. Carlin, and P.D. Murphy. "What a Difference a Wife Makes: The Effect of Women's Hours of Work on Husbands' Hourly Earnings" (1998) 50(1) *Bulletin of Economic Research* 1.

Boyd, Susan B. "Can Child Custody Law Move Beyond the Politics of Gender?" (2000) 49 *University of New Brunswick Law Journal* 157.

–. "Can Law Challenge The Public/Private Divide? Women, Work and Family" (1996) 15 *Windsor Yearbook Access to Justice* 161.

–. "Challenging the Public/Private Divide: An Overview" in Susan B. Boyd, ed., *Challenging the Public/Private Divide: Feminism, Law and Public Policy* (Toronto: University of Toronto Press, 1997).

–. "A Review of *The Second Shift: Working Parents and the Revolution at Home* by Arlie Hochschild, with Anne Machung" (1990) 4 *Canadian Journal of Women and the Law* 325.

–, Elizabeth Sheehy, and Josée Bouchard. *Canadian Feminist Perspectives on Law: An Annotated Bibliography of Interdisciplinary Writings (1989-99)* (1999) 11(1&2) *Canadian Journal of Women and the Law* (entire volume).

Boyle, Christine. "Criminal Law and Procedure: Who Needs Tenure?" (1985) 23 *Osgoode Hall Law Journal* 427.

–. "Teaching Law as if Women Really Mattered, or What about the Washrooms?" (1986) 2(1) *Canadian Journal of Women and the Law* 96.

Bright, David. "The Other Woman: Lizzie Cyr and the Origins of the 'Persons Case'" (1998) 13(2) *Canadian Journal of Law and Society* 99.

Brockman, Joan. "'Better to Enlist their Support than to Suffer their Antagonism': The Game of Monopoly between Lawyers and Notaries in British Columbia, 1930-81" (1997) 4(3) *International Journal of the Legal Profession* 197.

–. "Bias in the Legal Profession: Perceptions and Experiences" (1992) 3(3) *Alberta Law Review* 747.

–. "A Cold-Blooded Effort to Bolster Up the Legal Profession: The Battle Between Lawyers and Notaries in British Columbia, 1871-1930" (1999) 32(64) *Social History* 209.

–. "Exclusionary Tactics: The History of Women and Minorities in the Legal Profession in British Columbia" in Hamar Foster and John P.S. McLaren, eds., *Essays in the History of Canadian Law, Volume VI, British Columbia and the Yukon* (Toronto: Osgoode Society, 1995) 508.

–. "'Fortunate Enough to Obtain and Keep the Title of Profession': Self-Regulating Organizations and the Enforcement of Professional Monopolies" (1998) 41(4) *Canadian Public Administration* 587.

–. "Gender Bias in the Legal Profession: A Survey of Members of the Law Society of British Columbia" (1992) 17 *Queen's Law Journal* 91.

–. *Identifying the Barriers: A Survey of Members of the Law Society of British Columbia.* A Report Prepared for the Law Society of British Columbia's Subcommittee on Women in the Legal Profession; Appendix 2 in Kate Young (chair), *Women in the Legal Profession* (Vancouver: Law Society of British Columbia, 1991).

–. "Leaving the Practice of Law: The Wherefores and the Whys" (1994) 32(1) *Alberta Law Review* 116.

–. "'Resistance by the Club' to the Feminization of the Legal Profession" (1992) 7(2) *Canadian Journal of Law and Society* 47.

–. "Social Authority, Legal Discourse and Women's Voices" (1992) 21(2) *Manitoba Law Journal* 213.

–. "The Use of Self-Regulation to Curb Discrimination and Sexual Harassment in the Legal Profession" (1997) 35(2) *Osgoode Hall Law Journal* 209.

–. "'A Wild Feminist at Her Raving Best': Reflections on Studying Gender Bias in the Legal Profession" (2000) 28(1&2) *Resources for Feminist Research* 61.

Brockman, Joan, Denise Evans, and Kerri Reid. "Feminist Perspectives for the Study of Gender Bias in the Legal Profession" (1992) 5 *Canadian Journal of Women and the Law* 37.

Brockman, Joan, and Dale Phillippe. "The Task Force Approach to Studying Gender Bias in the Courts: A Consideration of Feminist Methods and Perspectives" (1991) 16(2) *Atlantis: A Women's Studies Journal* 32.

Brockman, Joan, and Dorothy Chunn, eds. *Investigating Gender Bias: Law, Courts and the Legal Profession* (Toronto: Thompson Educational Publishing, 1993).

–. "Gender Bias in Law and the Social Sciences" in Joan Brockman and Dorothy E. Chunn, eds., *Investigating Gender Bias: Law, Courts and the Legal Profession* (Toronto: Thompson Educational Publishing, 1993) 3.

Buckley, Melina. *Synthesis of Provincial Law Society Reports* (Appendix 4 to Madame Justice Bertha Wilson (chair), *Touchstones for Change: Equality, Diversity and Accountability* (Ottawa: Canadian Bar Association, 1993).

–. "Touchstones for Change: A Response" (1993) 51(6) *The Advocate* 853.

Burt, Sandra. "Legislators, Women and Public Policy" in Sandra Burt, Lorraine Code, and Lindsay Dorney, eds., *Changing Patterns: Women in Canada* (Toronto: McClelland and Stewart, 1988) at 129.

Canadian Bar Association. *The Challenge of Racial Equality: Putting Principles into Practice.* Co-chairs, Joanne St. Lewis and Benjamin Trevino (Ottawa: Canadian Bar Association, 1999).

–. *Virtual Justice: Systemic Racism and the Canadian Legal Profession.* An Independent Report by Joanne St. Lewis, co-chair of the Working Group on Racial Equality in the Legal Profession (Ottawa: Canadian Bar Association, 1999).

–. *The Legal Duty to Accommodate Lawyers with Family Responsibilities*. A report of the Working Group on the Legal Duty to Accommodate Lawyers with Family Responsibilities (Sheilah Martin, chair) (Ottawa: Canadian Bar Association, 1995).

–. *Touchstones for Change: Equality, Diversity, and Accountability*. A Report on Gender Equality in the Legal Profession. Madame Justice Bertha Wilson (chair) (Ottawa: Canadian Bar Association, 1993).

Canadian Mental Health Association. *Work and Well-Being: The Changing Realities of Employment* (Ottawa: Canadian Mental Health Association, 1984).

Carasco, Emily. "A Case of Double Jeopardy: Race and Gender" (1993) 6(1) *Canadian Journal of Women and the Law* 142.

Cassels, Jamie, and Maureen Maloney. "Critical Legal Education: Paralysis With a Purpose" (1989) 4 *Canadian Journal of Law and Society* 99-138.

Clement, Wallace, and John Myles. *Relations of Ruling: Class and Gender in Postindustrial Societies* (Kingston: McGill-Queen's University Press, 1994).

Coates, Mary Lou. *Working and Family Issues: Beyond "Swapping and Mopping and Sharing and Caring"* (Queen's University: Industrial Relations Centre, 1991).

Conrod, Monique. "Unemployment and Under-employment: The Harsh Reality Facing New Lawyers" (16 September 1994) *Lawyers' Weekly* 5, 12.

Coontz, Phyllis D. "Gender in the Legal Profession: Women 'See' It, Men Don't" (1995) 15(2) *Women and Politics* 1.

Cossman, Brenda, and Marlee Kline. "'And If Not Now, When?': Feminism and Anti-Semitism Beyond Clara Brett Martin" (1992) 5(2) *Canadian Journal of Women and the Law* 298.

Coughlan, Stephen. "The 'Adversary System': Rhetoric or Reality?" (1993) 8(2) *Canadian Journal of Law and Society* 139.

Cowper, Mr. Justice Sedgwick. "Confidences of a Woman Lawyer" (1912) 39(2) *Canadian Magazine* 141.

Crocker, Diane, and Valery Kalemba. "The Incidence and Impact of Women's Experiences of Sexual Harassment in Canadian Workplaces." (1999) 36(4) *Canadian Review of Sociology and Anthropology* 541.

Davies, Lorraine, and Patricia Jane Carrier. "The Importance of Power Relations for the Division of Household Labour" (1999) 24(1) *Canadian Journal of Sociology* 35.

Davis, Michael, and Frederick A. Elliston, eds. *Ethics and the Legal Profession* (New York: Prometheus Books, 1986).

Dehart, Nancy. "Reality Tramples Life of Leisure Predicted by Past Futurists" (14 April 1997) *Vancouver Sun* at A1, A10.

DeKeserdy, Walter S., Shahid Alvi, and Barbara Perry. "Violence against and the Harassment of Women in Canadian Public Housing: An Exploratory Study" (1999) 36(4) *Canadian Review of Sociology and Anthropology* 499.

DelDuca, Louis F. "An Historic Convergence of Civil and Common Law Systems: Italy's New Adversarial Criminal Procedure System" (1991) 10 *Dickinson Journal of International Law* 73.

Down, Craig. "Crying Woolf? Reform of the Adversarial System in Australia" (1998) 7 *Journal of Judicial Administration* 213-28.

Drachman, Virginia G. "'My Partner' in Law and Life: Marriage in the Lives of Women Lawyers in Late 19th- and Early 20th-Century America" (1989) 14 *Law and Social Inquiry* 221.

–. *Sisters in Law: Women Lawyers in Modern American History* (Cambridge, MA: Harvard University Press, 1998).

–. *Women Lawyers and the Origins of Professional Identity in America: The Letters of the Equity Club, 1887-1890* (Ann Arbor: University of Michigan Press, 1993).

Dranoff, Linda Silver. "Women in Law in Toronto" (1972) 10(1) *Osgoode Hall Law Journal* 177.

Dziech, B., and L. Weiner. *The Lecherous Professor* (Boston: Beacon Press, 1984).

Dzienkowski, John S. "Lawyering in a Hybrid Adversary System" (1996) 38(1) *William and Mary Law Review* 45.

Eichler, Margrit. *Family Shifts: Families, Policies, and Gender Equality* (Toronto: Oxford University Press, 1997).

Ellman, Stephen. "The Ethics of Care as an Ethic for Lawyers" (1993) 81 *Georgetown Law Journal* 2665.

–. "Lawyering for Justice in a Flawed Democracy: Review of Luban, Lawyers and Justice (1988)" (1990) 90 *Columbia Law Review* 116.

Epstein, Cynthia Fuchs. "Glass Ceilings and Open Doors: Women's Advancement in the Legal Profession" (1995) 64 *Fordham Law Review* 291.

–. *Women in Law*, 2nd ed. (Chicago: University of Illinois Press, 1993).

Ericson, Richard V., and Patricia M. Baranek. *The Ordering of Justice: A Study of Accused Persons as Dependants in the Criminal Process* (Toronto: University of Toronto Press, 1983).

Esau, Alvin. "Teaching Professional Responsibility in Law School" (1988) 11 *Dalhousie Law Journal* 403.

Farley, L. *Sexual Shakedown: The Sexual Harassment of Women on the Job* (New York: Warner, 1978).

Feid, Charles. "The Lawyer as Friend: The Moral Foundation of the Lawyer-Client Relation" (1976) 85 *Yale Law Journal* 1060.

Feldthusen, Bruce. "The Gender Wars: 'Where the Boys Are'" (1990) 4(1) *Canadian Journal of Women and the Law* 66.

Ferguson, Gerry. "Ethnic and Linguistic Diversity of BC Lawyers" (1997) 55(6) *Advocate* 873.

Fitzgerald, Oonagh E. *The Guilty Plea and Summary Justice: A Guide for Practitioners* (Toronto: Carswell, 1990).

Forsythe, Gail H. "After the First Year: Are Services in Demand? What are the Results?" (January-February 1996) *Benchers' Bulletin* 7.

Foster, James. "Antigones in the Bar: Women Lawyers as Reluctant Adversaries" (1986) 10 *Legal Studies Forum* 289.

Freedman, Monroe. *Lawyers' Ethics in an Adversary System* (New York: Bobbs-Merrill, 1975).

Fromm, Delee, and Marjorie Webb. "The Work Experience of University of Alberta Law Graduates" (1985) 23 *Alberta Law Review* 366.

Gardner, C.B., ed. *Passing By: Gender and Public Harassment* (Berkeley: University of California Press, 1995).

Gaskell, Jane. "The Reproduction of Family Life: Perspectives of Male and Female Adolescents" (1983) 4(1) *British Journal of Sociology of Education* 19.

Gee, Ellen. "The Life Course of Canadian Women: An Historical and Demographic Analysis" (1986) 18 *Social Indicators Research* 263.

Gerson, Kathleen. *Hard Choices: How Women Decide About Work, Career and Motherhood* (Berkeley: University of California Press, 1985).

Gillett, Margaret. *We Walked Very Warily: A History of Women at McGill* (Montreal: Eden Press Women's Publications, 1981).

Gochnauer, Myron. *Survey 1991*. Report by the Ad Hoc Committee on Gender Related Policy (Fredericton, New Brunswick: Faculty of Law, University of New Brunswick, October 1991).

Gutek, Barbara A. "Asymmetric Changes in Men's and Women's Roles" in Bonita C. Long and Sharon E. Kahn, eds., *Women, Work, and Coping* (Kingston: McGill-Queen's University Press, 1993).

–. *Sex and the Workplace: The Impact of Sexual Behavior and Harassment on Women, Men, and Organization* (San Francisco: Jossey-Bass, 1985).

Hacob, Herbert. "The Elusive Shadow of the Law" (1992) 26(3) *Law and Society Review* 565.

Hagan, John, and Fiona Kay. *Gender in Practice: A Study of Lawyers' Lives* (Oxford: Oxford University Press, 1995).

–. "Hierarchy in Practice: The Significance of Gender in Ontario Law Firms" in Carol Wilton, ed., *Inside the Law: Canadian Law Firms in Historical Perspective* (Toronto: University of Toronto Press, 1996).

Hagan, John, Marie Huxter, and Patricia Parker. "Class Structure and Legal Practice:

Inequality and Mobility Among Toronto Lawyers" (1988) 22(1) *Law And Society Review* 501.

Hagan, John, Marjorie Zatz, Bruce Arnold, and Fiona Kay. "Cultural Capital, Gender, and the Structural Transformation of Legal Practice" (1991) 25(2) *Law and Society Review* 239.

Hameed, S.M.A. "Economic and Institutional Determinants of the Average Work Week in Canada" in S.M.A. Hameed and D. Cullen, eds., *Work and Leisure in Canada* (Edmonton: University of Alberta Faculty of Business Administration and Commerce, 1971).

Harding, Sandra, ed. *Feminism and Methodology* (Bloomington: Indiana University Press, 1987).

–. *The Science Question in Feminism* (Ithaca, NY: Cornell University Press, 1986).

–. *Whose Science? Whose Knowledge? Thinking From Women's Lives* (Ithaca, NY: Cornell University Press, 1991).

Harrington, Mona. *Care and Equality: Inventing a New Family Politics* (New York: Alfred A. Knopf, 1999).

–. *Women Lawyers: Rewriting the Rules* (New York: Alfred A. Knopf, 1994).

Harvey, Cameron. "Women in Law in Canada" (1970) 4 *Manitoba Law Journal* 9.

Hawkesworth, Mary. "Analyzing Backlash: Feminist Standpoint Theory as Analytical Tool" (1999) 22(2) *Women's Studies International Forum* 135.

Hill, Eve. "Alternative Dispute Resolution in a Feminist Voice" (1990) 5(2) *Journal on Dispute Resolution* 337.

Hochschild, Arlie Russell. *The Time Bind: When Work Becomes Home and Home Becomes Work* (New York: Metropolitan Books, 1997).

–. *The Second Shift: Working Parents and the Revolution at Home* (New York: Avon, 1989).

Hotel, Carla, and Joan Brockman. "Legal Ethics in the Practice of Law: Playing Chess While Mountain Climbing" (1997) 16 *Journal of Business Ethics* 809.

–. "The Conciliatory-Adversarial Continuum in Family Law Practice" (1994) 12 *Canadian Journal of Family Law* 11.

Howay, F.W. *British Columbia: From the Earliest Times to the Present, Volume II* (Vancouver: S.J. Clarke Publishing, 1914).

Hughes, E.N. (Ted) (chair), Alison MacLennan, John McAlpine, Stephen F.D. Kelleher, Marguerite Jackson, and Wendy Baker. *Gender Equality in the Justice System* (Vancouver: Law Society of British Columbia, 1992).

Hunnicutt, Benjamin Kline. *Working Without End: Abandoning Shorter Hours for the Right to Work* (Philadelphia: Temple University Press, 1988).

Jack, Rand, and Dana Crowley Jack. *Moral Vision and Professional Decisions: The Changing Values of Women and Men Lawyers* (Cambridge: Cambridge University Press, 1989).

Jackson, Stevi. "Towards a Historical Sociology of Housework: A Materialist Feminist Analysis" (1992) 15(2) *Women's Studies International Forum* 153.

Jin, Robert, Chandrakant Shah, and Tomislav Svoboda. "The Impact of Unemployment on Health: A Review of the Evidence" (1997) 18(3) *Journal of Public Health Policy* 275.

Job, Dean. "'Delicious Irony': Trailblazer Wilson Overcame Extreme Scepticism When She Embarked on her Distinguished Legal Career" (October 1991) *National* 22.

Kanter, Rosabeth Moss. *Men and Women of the Corporation* (New York: Basic Books, 1977).

Kay, Fiona M. "Balancing Acts: Career and Family Among Lawyers" in Susan Boyd, ed., *Challenging the Public/Private Divide: Feminism and Socio-Legal Policy* (Toronto: University of Toronto Press, 1997) 184.

–. "Flight From Law: A Competing Risks Model of Departures from Law Firms" (1997) 31(2) *Law and Society Review* 301.

–. *Transition in the Ontario Legal Profession: A Survey of Lawyers Called to the Bar Between 1975-1990*. A Report to the Law Society of Upper Canada. (Toronto: Osgoode Hall, 1991).

–. *Women in the Legal Profession*. A Report to the Law Society of Upper Canada (Toronto: Osgoode Hall, 1989).

–. "Women in the Legal Profession" (1990) 24(1) *Law Society Gazette* 55.

–, and Joan Brockman. "Barriers to Gender Equality in the Canadian Legal Establishment." (2000) 8 *Feminist Legal Studies* 169.

Kay, Fiona M., and John Hagan. "Changing Opportunities for Partnership for Men and Women Lawyers During the Transformation of the Modern Law Firm" (1994) 32(3) *Osgoode Hall Law Journal* 413.

–. "Cultivating Clients in the Competition for Partnership: Gender and the Organizational Restructuring of Law Firms in the 1990s" (1999) 33(3) *Law and Society Review* 517.

–. "The Persistent Glass Ceiling: Gendered Inequalities in the Earnings of Lawyers" (1995) 46(2) *British Journal of Sociology* 279.

–. "Raising the Bar: The Gender Stratification of Law Firm Capitalization" (1998) 63(5) *American Sociological Review* 728.

Kay, Fiona M., Nancy Dautovich, and Chantelle Marlor. *Barriers and Opportunities within Law: Women in a Changing Legal Profession* (Toronto: Law Society of Upper Canada, 1996).

Kee, Janet. 1986. "Portrait of a Young Woman as Lawyer" (June 1986) *Canadian Lawyer* 32-4.

Kinnear, Mary. "That There Woman Lawyer: Women Lawyers in Manitoba 1915-1970" (1992) 5(2) *Canadian Journal of Women and the Law* 411.

Klein, John F. *Let's Make a Deal: Negotiating Justice* (Lexington, MA: Lexington Books, 1976).

Krauchek, Vivian, and Gillian Ranson. "Playing by the Rules of the Game: Women's Experiences and Perceptions of Sexual Harassment in Sport" (1999) 36(4) *Canadian Review of Sociology and Anthropology* 585.

Krieger, Linda H. "The Content of Our Categories: A Cognitive Bias Approach to Discrimination and Equal Employment Opportunity" (1995) 47 *Stanford Law Review* 1161.

Kynaston, Chris. "The Everyday Exploitation of Women: Housework and the Patriarchal Mode of Production" (1996) 19(3) *Women's Studies International Forum* 221.

Lahey, Kathleen A. "Introduction" (1991) 16(2) *Queen's Law Journal* 231.

Landsman, Stephan. *The Adversary System: A Description and Defense* (Washington: American Enterprise Institute for Public Policy Research, 1984).

–. "A Brief Survey of the Development of the Adversary System" (1983) 44 *Ohio State Law Review* 713.

–. "The Rise of the Contentious Spirit: Adversary Procedure in Eighteenth Century England" (1990) 75 *Cornell Law Review* 497.

LaPlante, Marc. "Leisure in Canada by 1980" in *Leisure in Canada*, The Proceedings of the Montmorency Conference on Leisure, 2-6 September 1969 (Ottawa: Fitness and Amateur Sport Directorate, Department of National Health and Welfare, 1969).

LaPointe, Kirk. "Study Cites Drugs, Liquor Use among MDs, Lawyers" (7 June 1993) *Vancouver Sun* A2.

Larson, Magali Sarfatti. *The Rise of Professionalism: A Sociological Analysis* (Berkeley: University of California Press, 1977).

Law Society of British Columbia. *Aboriginal Law Graduates in British Columbia* (Vancouver: Law Society of British Columbia, 1996).

–. *Addressing Discriminatory Barriers Facing Aboriginal Law Students and Lawyers*. Gerry Ferguson, chair (Vancouver: Law Society of British Columbia, 2000).

–. *Report on the Survey of Aboriginal Law Graduates in British Columbia* (Vancouver: Law Society of British Columbia, 1996).

–. *Summary and Discussion of the Aboriginal Law Graduates Focus Groups* (Vancouver: Law Society of British Columbia, 1998).

–. *Women in the Legal Profession*. Kate Young, chair. A Report of the Women in the Legal Profession Subcommittee (Vancouver: Law Society of British Columbia, 1991).

Lee, Carol F. "The Road to Enfranchisement: Chinese and Japanese in British Columbia" (1976) 30 *BC Studies* 44.

Lee, Jenny. "Dealing With Stress Now an Investment" (5 April 1999) *Vancouver Sun* at C1.

Lehmkuhl, Leanne. "Health Effects of Long Work-weeks" (August 1999). At <www.web.ca/~freetime/Health%20Effects%20v2.htm>.

Leiper, Jean McKenzie. "It was like Wow! The Experience of Women Lawyers in a

Profession Marked by Linear Careers" (1997) 9(1) *Canadian Journal of Women and the Law* 115.

–. "Women Lawyers and Their Working Arrangements: Time Crunch, Stress and Career Paths" (1998) 13(2) *Canadian Journal of Law and Society* 117.

Lenton, Rhonda, Michael D. Smith, and Norman Morra. "Sexual Harassment in Public Places: Experiences of Canadian Women" (1999) 36(4) *Canadian Review of Sociology and Anthropology* 517.

Lentz, Bernard F., and David N. Laband. *Sex Discrimination in the Legal Profession* (Westport, CT: Quorum Books, 1995).

Lepofsky, David M. "Disabled Persons and Canadian Law Schools: The Right to Equal Benefit of the Law School" (1991) 36 *McGill Law Journal* 636.

Lessard, Hester. "Farce or Tragedy? Judicial Backlash and Justice McClung" (1999) 10(3) *Constitutional Forum* 65.

Looker, Dianne E., and Victor Thiessen, "Images of Work: Women's Work, Men's Work, Housework" (1999) 24(2) *Canadian Journal of Sociology* 225.

Luban, David. *Lawyers and Justice: An Ethical Study* (New Jersey: Princeton University Press, 1988).

–. "Introduction: A New Canadian Legal Ethics" (1996) 9(1) *Canadian Journal of Law and Jurisprudence* 3.

Macaulay, Ann. "Study Finds 1 in 3 Lawyers are Problem Drinkers" (18 June 1993) *Lawyers' Weekly* 4.

MacBride-King, Judith L. *Work and Family: Employment Challenge of the '90s* (Ottawa: Conference Board of Canada, 1990).

MacBride-King, Judith L., and Hélène Paris. *Balancing Professional and Family Responsibilities: A Survey of Lawyers and Law Firms* (A Report Prepared for l'Association du Jeune Barreau de Montréal. Ottawa: Conference Board of Canada, 1989).

–. "Balancing Work and Family Responsibilities" (1989) 16(3) *Canadian Business Review* 1.

Macdonald, Keith M. *The Sociology of the Professions* (London: Sage Publications, 1995).

McEachern, Angela, and Joan Brockman. "The Exodus from Law: Attractions and Distractions"; presented at the Learned Societies Conference, Calgary, Alberta, 13 June 1994.

Macfarlane, Julie. "A Feminist Perspective on Experienced-Based Learning and Curriculum Change" (1994) 26(2) *Ottawa Law Review* 357.

–. "Teacher Power in the Law School Curriculum" (1996) 19(1) *Dalhousie Law Journal* 71.

MacFarlane, P. Dianne. "The Legal Profession in Canada: A Research Perspective and Prospectus" (1980) 28 *Chitty's Law Journal* 50.

McGlynn, Clare. *The Woman Lawyer: Making the Difference* (UK: Butterworths, 1998).

McIntyre, Sheila. "Backlash Against Equality: The Tyranny of the 'Politically Correct'" (1993) 38(1) *McGill Law Journal* 1.

–. "Gender Bias Within the Law Schools: 'The Memo' and Its Impact" (1987) 2 *Canadian Journal of Women and the Law* 362.

–. "Promethea Unbound: A Feminist Perspective on Law in the University" (1989) 38 *University of New Brunswick Law Journal* 157.

McIvor, Sharon, and Teressa Nahanee. *Aboriginal Women in the Legal Profession* (Appendix 11 to Madame Justice Bertha Wilson (chair), *Touchstones for Change: Equality, Diversity, and Accountability* (Ottawa: Canadian Bar Association, 1993).

MacKenzie, Gavin. "Breaking the Dichotomy Habit: The Adversary System and the Ethics of Professionalism" (1996) 9(1) *Canadian Journal of Law and Jurisprudence* 33.

–. *Lawyers and Ethics: Professional Responsibility and Discipline,* 2nd ed. (Toronto: Carswell, 1999).

MacKinnon, C.A. *Sexual Harassment of Working Women: A Case of Sex Discrimination* (New Haven, CT: Yale University Press, 1979).

MacKinnon, P., and P. Rhodes. "The First Canadian Program of Legal Studies for Native People" (1974) 38 *Saskatchewan Law Review* 40.

McLauglin, Paul. "Forensic Accounting: Tales of Greed and Cunning" (April 1993) *National* 20.

McQuaig, Linda. *Shooting the Hippo: Death by Deficit and Other Canadian Myths* (Toronto: Penguin Books, 1995).

MacQueen, Ken. "Men are From Mars, Women are From Typing Pools" (22 March 1996) *Vancouver Sun* A19.

Mahoney, Bryan. "Changing Times – Workplace Options" (October-November 1992) *Newsletter* 5.

Majury, Diana. "Collective Action on a Systemic Problem" in Carmen Lambert, ed., *Towards a New Equality: The Status of Women in Canadian Universities* (Ottawa: Social Science Federation of Canada, 1991).

Marshall, Katherine. "Women in Male Dominated Professions" in *Canadian Social Trends* (Ottawa: Statistics Canada, 1987).

–. "Women in Professional Occupations: Progress in the 1980s" in *Canadian Social Trends* (Ottawa: Statistics Canada, 1989).

Martin, Sheilah L. "Proving Gender Bias in the Law and the Legal System" in Joan Brockman and Dorothy E. Chunn, eds., *Investigating Gender Bias: Law, Courts and the Legal Profession* (Toronto: Thompson Educational Publishing, 1993).

–, and Gaylene Schellenberg. *Equality of Women in the Legal Profession: A Facilitator's Manual* (Ottawa: Canadian Bar Association, 1995).

Mazer, Brian M. "An Analysis of Gender in the Admission to the Canadian Common Law Schools From 1985-86 to 1994-95" (1997) 20(1) *Dalhousie Law Journal* 135.

Meltz, Noah M., Frank Reid, and Gerald S. Swartz. *Sharing the Work: An Analysis of the Issues in Worksharing and Jobsharing* (Toronto: University of Toronto Press, 1981).

Menkel-Meadow, Carrie. "The Trouble with the Adversary System in a Postmodern, Multicultural World" (1996) 38(1) *William and Mary Law Review* 5.

–. "The Comparative Sociology of Women Lawyers: The 'Feminization' of the Legal Profession" (1987) 24 *Osgoode Hall Law Journal* 897.

–. "Portia in a Different Voice: Speculations on a Woman's Lawyering Process" (1985) 1 *Berkeley Women's Law Journal* 39.

Mitchell, Alanna, Karen Unland, and Chad Skelton. "Canadians Pay for Busy Lives" (19 July 1997) *Vancouver Sun* A1.

Monture, Patricia A. "Now That the Door Is Open: First Nations and the Law School Experience" (1990) 15(2) *Queen's Law Journal* 179.

–. "Reflecting on Flint Woman" in Richard F. Devlin, ed., *Canadian Perspectives on Legal Theory* (Toronto: Edmond Montgomery Publications, 1991).

Mossman, Mary Jane. "Challenging 'Hidden' Assumptions: (Women) Lawyers and Family Life" in Martha Albertson Fineman and Isabel Karpin, eds., *Mothers in Law: Feminist Theory and the Legal Regulation of Motherhood* (New York: Columbia University Press, 1995).

–. "Educating Men and Women for Service Through Law: Osgoode Hall Law School 1963-1988" (1988) 11(3) *Dalhousie Law Journal* 885.

–. "Gender Bias and the Legal Profession: Challenges and Choices" in Joan Brockman and Dorothy E. Chunn, eds., *Investigating Gender Bias in the Law* (Toronto: Thompson Educational Publishing, 1993) 147.

–. "Gender Equality Education and the Legal Profession" (2000) 12 *Supreme Court Law Review* 187.

–. "'Invisible' Constraints on Lawyering and Leadership: The Case of Women Lawyers" (1988) 20(3) *Ottawa Law Review* 567.

–. "Lawyers and Family Life: New Directions for the 1990's (Part One)" (1994) 2(1) *Feminist Legal Studies* 61.

–. "Lawyers and Family Life: New Directions for the 1990's (Part Two)" (1994) 2(2) *Feminist Legal Studies* 159.

–. "Lawyers and Family Life? A Review of the CBA Task Force on Gender Equality" (1994) 7(1) *Canadian Journal of Women and the Law* 238.

–. "On Sleepwalking, Surveys and the Law Schools" (1992) 99(1) *Queen's Quarterly* 240.

–. "'Otherness' and the Law School: A Comment on Teaching Gender Equality" (1985) 1(1) *Canadian Journal of Women and the Law* 213.

–. "The Past As Prologue: Women and the Law" in *Lawyering and Legal Education into the 21st Century: Seminars in Honour of the 75th Anniversary of Manitoba Law School* (Legal Research Institute of the University of Manitoba, 1990) 27.

–. "Shoulder to Shoulder: Gender and Access to Justice" (1990) 10 *Windsor Yearbook of Access to Justice* 351.

Mucalov, Janice. "The Stress Epidemic: Succumbing to the Pressures of Practice in the 90s" (May 1993) *Canadian Lawyer* 18.

Munro, Margaret. "Life in 2030" (1 May 1993) *Vancouver Sun* at B1.

Naffine, Ngaire. *Law and the Sexes: Explorations in Feminist Jurisprudence* (Sydney: Allen and Unwin, 1990).

Neallani, Shelina. "Women of Colour in the Legal Profession: Facing the Familiar Barriers of Race and Sex" (1992) 5 *Canadian Journal of Women and the Law* 148.

Nijboer, Johannes R. "The American Adversarial System in Criminal Cases: Between Ideology and Reality" (1997) 5 *Cardozo Journal of International and Comparative Law* 79.

Oerton, Sarah. "'Queer Housewives?': Some Problems in Theorising the Division of Domestic Labour in Lesbian and Gay Households." (1997) 20(3) *Women's Studies International Forum* 421.

Office des professions du Québec. *The Evolution of Professionalism in Québec* (1976).

Oh, Carolyn Jin-Myung. "Questioning the Cultural and Gender-Biased Assumptions of the Adversary System: Voices of Asian-American Law Students" (1992) 7 *Berkeley Women's Law Journal* 125.

O'Hara, Bruce. *Put Work in its Place: How to Redesign Your Job to Fit Your Life* (Vancouver: New Star Books, 1994).

–. *Working Harder Isn't Working: How We Can Save the Environment, the Economy and our Sanity by Working Less and Enjoying Life More* (Vancouver: New Star Books, 1993).

Olson, Josephine E., Irene Hanson Frieze, and Ellen G. Detlefsen. "Having it All: Combining Work and Family in a Male and a Female Profession" (1990) 23(9-10) *Sex Roles* 515.

Otvos, Mary. "Why I'm Leaving Law" *Canadian Lawyer* (February 1992) 12.

Paludi, Michele A., ed. *Sexual Harassment on College Campuses: Abusing the Ivory Power* (Albany: State University of New York Press, 1996; a revised and expanded edition of *Ivory Power: Sexual Harassment on Campus* (1990).

Pateman, Carole. *The Sexual Contract* (Oxford: Polity Press, 1988).

Paul, Daniel M. *We Are Not Savages: A Micmac Perspective on the Collision of European and Aboriginal Civilizations* (Halifax: Nimbus Publishing, 1993).

Pearlman, Lynne. "Rethinking Clara Brett Martin: A Jewish Lesbian Perspective" Originally published as "Through Jewish Lesbian Eyes: Rethinking Clara Brett Martin" (1992) 5(2) *Canadian Journal of Women and the Law* 317.

Pemberton, Kim. "First Indian Judge Back to Practising Law" (10 February 1995) *Vancouver Sun* B8.

Petersen, Cynthia. "Living Dangerously: Speaking Lesbian, Teaching Law" (1994) 7(2) *Canadian Journal of Women and the Law* 318.

Petersson, Sandra. "Ruby Clements and Early Women of the Alberta Bar" (1997) 9(2) *Canadian Journal of Women and the Law* 365.

Pierce, Jennifer L. *Gender Trials: Emotional Lives in Contemporary Law Firms* (Berkeley: University of California Press, 1995).

Pitt, Diana. "When Lawyers Need Help: A Model Wellness Program Is Being Developed to Help Lawyers Deal with Substance Abuse, Stress and Depression" (16 September 1994) 1 *Lawyers' Weekly* 36.

Pizzi, William T., and Luca Marafioti. "The New Italian Code of Criminal Procedure: The Difficulties of Building an Adversarial Trial on a Civil Law Foundation" (1992) 17 *Yale Journal of International Law* 1.

Pothier, Dianne. "A Comment on the Canadian Bar Association's Gender Equality Task Force Report" (1993) 16(2) *Dalhousie Law Journal* 484.

Potuchek, Jean L. *Who Supports the Family? Gender and Breadwinning in Dual-Earning Marriages* (Stanford, CA: Stanford University Press, 1997).

Prentice, Alison, Paula Bourne, Gail Cuthbert Brandt, Beth Light, Wendy Mitchinson, and Naomi Black. *Canadian Women: A History* (Toronto: Harcourt Brace Jovanovich, 1988).

Press, Julie E., and Eleanor Townsley. "Wives' and Husbands' Housework Reporting: Gender, Class, and Social Desirability" (1998) 12(2) *Gender and Society* 188.

Pue, W. Wesley. *Law School: The Story of Legal Education in British Columbia* (Vancouver: University of British Columbia Faculty of Law, 1995).

Quick, Brenda Jones. "Ethical Rules Prohibiting Discrimination by Lawyers: The Legal Profession's Response to Discrimination on the Rise" (1993) 7(1) *Notre Dame Journal of Law, Ethics, and Public Policy* 5.

Ray, Randy. "Quality of Life: A Vancouver Law Firm Reverses the Trend to Longer Hours, More Money and Less Leisure" (May 1990) *National* 1.

Rhode, Deborah L. "Ethical Perspectives on Legal Practice" (1985) 37 *Stanford Law Review* 589.

–. "Gender and Professional Roles" (1994) 63 *Fordham Law Review* 39.

Rifkin, Jeremy. *The End of Work: The Decline of the Global Labor Force and the Dawn of the Post-Market Era* (New York: G.P. Putnam's Sons, 1995).

Robertson, Susan. *A Study of Gender and the Legal Profession in Saskatchewan, 1990-91* (Regina: Law Society of Saskatchewan and Canadian Bar Association, 1992).

Robinson, John P., and Melissa A. Milkie. "Back to the Basics: Trends in and Role Determinants of Women's Attitudes Toward Housework." (1998) 60(1) *Journal of Marriage and the Family* 205.

Rose, V. Gordon. "OUCH! Banging Heads on the Glass Ceiling: An Examination of Gender Inequality in the Income of BC Lawyers" (Unpublished paper written for a Course at Simon Fraser University: Statistics 402, 28 November 1994).

Ross, Catherine E., and Chloe E. Bird. "Sex Stratification and Health Lifestyles: Consequences for Men's and Women's Perceived Health" (1994) 35 *Journal of Health and Social Behavior* 161.

Rossides, Daniel W. *Professions and Disciplines: Functional and Conflict Perspectives* (New Jersey: Prentice-Hall, 1998).

Roy, Patricia E. "British Columbia's Fear of Asians: 1900-1950" in Patricia E. Roy, *A History of British Columbia: Selected Readings* (Toronto: Copp Clark Pitman, 1989).

–. *A White Man's Province: British Columbia Politicians and Chinese and Japanese Immigrants, 1858-1914* (Vancouver: University of British Columbia Press, 1989).

St. Lewis, Joanne (co-chair). *Virtual Justice: Systemic Racism and the Canadian Legal Profession.* An independent report of the Working Group on Racial Equality in the Legal Profession (Ottawa: Canadian Bar Association, 1999).

St. Lewis, Joanne, and Benjamin Trevino (co-chairs). *The Challenge of Racial Equality: Putting Principles into Practice* (Ottawa: Canadian Bar Association, 1999).

Sarat, Austin, and William L.F. Felstiner. *Divorce Lawyers and Their Clients: Power Meaning and the Legal Process* (New York: Oxford University Press, 1995).

Savarese, J., M. Keet, and K. Sutherland. *Survey of Women Graduates From the College of Law* (Saskatoon: Women and the Law, 1988).

Schellenberg, Gaylene, Melina Buckley, Tshepo Mofitksana, and Susan Zimmerman. *Annotated Bibliography on Gender Equality in the Legal Profession* (Ottawa: Canadian Bar Association, 1993).

Schmitz, Cristin. "Fewer Lawyers Applying and Accepted to Bench" (12 June 1998) *Lawyers' Weekly* 10.

Schor, Juliet. *The Overworked American: The Unexpected Decline of Leisure* (New York: Basic Books, 1991).

Sev'er, Aysan. "Sexual Harassment: Where We Were, Where We Are, and Prospects for the New Millennium, Introduction to the Special Issue" (1999) 36(4) *Canadian Review of Sociology and Anthropology* 469.

Seymour, Julie. "'No Time to Call my Own:' Women's Time as a Household Resource" (1992) 15(2) *Women's Studies International Forum* 187.

Smith, Lynn, Marylee Stephenson, and Gina Quijano. "The Legal Profession and Women: Finding Articles in British Columbia" (1973) 8(1) *University of British Columbia Law Review* 137.

Sommerlad, Hilary, and Peter Sanderson. *Gender, Choice, and Commitment: Women Solicitors in England and Wales and the Struggle for Equal Status* (Aldershot: Dartmouth Publishing, 1998).

South, Scott J., and Glenna Spitze. "Housework in Marital and Nonmarital Households" (1994) 59 *American Sociological Review* 327.

Sparks, Corrine. "Women of Colour in the Legal Profession: A Panoply of Multiple Discrimination." Appendix 10 to Madame Justice Bertha Wilson (chair), *Touchstones for Change: Equality, Diversity, and Accountability* (Ottawa: Canadian Bar Association, 1993).

Sparks, Kate, Cary Cooper, and Arie Shirom. "The Effects of Hours of Work on Health: A Meta-Analytic Review" (1997) 70 *Journal of Occupational and Organizational Psychology* 391.

Stager, David A.A., and Harry W. Arthurs. *Lawyers in Canada* (Toronto: University of Toronto Press, 1991).

Statistics Canada. "General Social Survey: Time Use" (9 November 1999) *The Daily.*

–. *Labour Force Activity of Women by Presence of Children*, no. 93-325 (Ottawa: Statistics Canada, 1993) at 16, and Statistics Canada, *The Daily* (2 March 1993).

–. "Longer Working Hours and Health" (16 November 1999) *The Daily.*

Stockdale, M., ed. *Women and Work: Sexual Harassment in the Workplace* (Thousand Oaks, CA: Sage, 1996).

Stoddart, Jennifer. "The Woman Suffrage Bill in Quebec" in Marylee Stephenson, *Women in Canada* (Toronto: New Press, 1973).

Sullivan, Oriel. "The Division of Housework Among 'Remarried' Couples" (1997) 18(2) *Journal of Family Issues* 205.

Susman, Carolyn. "Lunch at the Desk Now Common, Survey Says" (12 April 1999) *Vancouver Sun* B12.

Tancred, Peta. "Outsiders/Insiders: Women and Professional Norms" (1999) 14(1) *Canadian Journal of Law and Society* 31.

Thompson, Ruth. "The University of Saskatchewan Native Law Centre" (1988) 11 *Dalhousie Law Journal* 712.

Thornton, Margaret. *Dissonance and Distrust: Women in the Legal Profession* (Melbourne: Oxford University Press, 1996).

–, ed. *Public and Private: Feminists Legal Debates* (Melbourne: Oxford University Press, 1995).

Tong, Dawna. *Gatekeeping in Canadian Law Schools: A History of Exclusion, The Rule of 'Merit,' and a Challenge to Contemporary Practices* (Master of Laws Thesis, University of British Columbia 1996).

–. "A History of Exclusion: The Treatment of Racial and Ethnic Minorities by the Law Society of British Columbia in Admissions to the Legal Profession" (1998) 56(2) *Advocate* 197.

Treasury Board of Canada. *Looking to the Future: Challenging the Culture and Attitudinal Barriers to Women in the Public Service* (Ottawa: Planning and Communications Directorate, Treasury Board of Canada, 1995).

–. The Report of the Task Force on Barriers to Women in the Public Service, *Beneath the Veneer* (Ottawa: Canadian Government Publishing Centre, 1990).

Wallace, Jean E. *Why Lawyers Decide to Quit Their Jobs: A Study of Job Satisfaction and Organizational Commitment Among Calgary Lawyers.* A report submitted to the Alberta Law Foundation (1991).

Ward, W. Peter. *White Canada Forever: Popular Attitudes and Public Policy Toward Orientals in British Columbia*, 2nd ed. (Montreal and Kingston: McGill-Queen's University Press, 1991).

Watts, Alfred. *History of the Legal Profession in British Columbia* (Vancouver: Law Society of British Columbia, 1984).

Weeks, E.L., J.M. Boles, A.P. Garbin, and J. Bount. "The Transformation of Sexual Harassment from a Private Trouble to a Public Issue" (1986) 54(2) *Sociological Inquiry* 432.

Weinrib, Lorraine E. "Women in the Legal Profession: Old Issues, Current Problems" (1990) 24(1) *Law Society Gazette* 71.

Welsh, Sandy, and A. Nierobisz. "How Prevalent is Sexual Harassment: A Research Note on Measuring Sexual Harassment in Canada" (1997) 22(4) *Canadian Journal of Sociology* 505.

–, and James E. Gruber. "Not Taking It Any More: Women Who Report or File Complaints of Sexual Harassment" (1999) 36(4) *Canadian Review of Sociology and Anthropology* 559.

White, James J. "Women in the Law" (1967) 65 *Michigan Law Review* 1051.

Wilkinson, Margaret Ann, Peter Mercer, and Terra Strong. "Mentor, Mercenary or Melding: An Empirical Inquiry into the Role of the Lawyer" (1996) 28(2) *Loyola University Chicago Law Journal* 373.

Williams, Joan. "Gender Wars: Selfless Women in the Republic of Choice" (1991) 66 *New York University Law Review* 1559.

–. *Unbending Gender: Why Family and Work Conflict and What to Do About It* (New York: Oxford University Press, 2000).

Wilson, The Honourable Bertha (chair). *Touchstones for Change: Equality, Diversity and Accountability* (Ottawa: Canadian Bar Association, 1993).

–. "Will Women Judges Really Make a Difference?" (1990) 28 *Osgoode Hall Law Journal* 507.

Witz, Anne. *Professions and Patriarchy* (London: Routledge, 1992).

Wise, S., and S. Stanley. *Georgie Porgie: Sexual Harassment in Everyday Life* (London: Pandora, 1987).

Wood, Robert G., Mary E. Corcoran, and Paul N. Courant. "Pay Differences among the Highly Paid: The Male-Female Earnings Gap in Lawyers' Salaries" (1993) 11(3) *Journal of Labor Economics* 417.

Woolley, Alice. "Integrity in Zealousness: Comparing the Standard Conceptions of the Canadian and the American Lawyer" (1996) 9(1) *Canadian Journal of Law and Jurisprudence* 61.

Yorke, Lois K. "Mabel Penery French (1881-1955): A Life Re-Created" (1993) 42 *University of New Brunswick Law Journal* 3.

Zander, Michael. "From Inquisitorial to Adversarial: The Italian Experiment" (1991) 141 *New Law Journal* 678.

Zelinski, Ernie J. *The Joy of Not Working* (Edmonton: Visions International Publishing, 1991).

Zuker, M., and J. Callwood. *Canadian Women and the Law* (Toronto: The Copp Clark Publishing, 1971).

Index